MANAGEMENT
AND
IDEOLOGY

MANAGEMENT AND IDEOLOGY

The Legacy of the International
Scientific Management Movement

JUDITH A. MERKLE

UNIVERSITY OF CALIFORNIA PRESS
Berkeley • Los Angeles • London

University of California Press
Berkeley and Los Angeles, California
University of California Press, Ltd.
London, England
© 1980 by
The Regents of the University of California
Printed in the United States of America

1 2 3 4 5 6 7 8 9

Library of Congress Cataloging in Publication Data

Merkle, Judith A
    Management and ideology: The legacy of the international scientific management movement
    Bibliography: p.
    Includes index.
    1. Industrial management—History. 2. Comparative management—History. I. Title.
II. Title: Scientific management movement.
HD30.5.M47   658'.009   78-59447
ISBN 0-520-03737-5

For my father —
he would have known why

Contents

Acknowledgements

During the time spent in the preparation of this book, I have been fortunate to possess friends, critics, and family who have been consistently insightful, enthusiastic, and kind. While they should not be blamed for the flaws in the manuscript, they certainly deserve credit for its existence. I am especially indebted to Dwight Waldo for his extensive and critical review of the manuscript and his generous concern for the project, and to Thomas Blaisdell, Jr., for his detailed reading of the manuscript and thoughtful advice. I also owe special thanks to Martin Landau, whose encouragement and assistance meant so much.

I am very grateful to Val Lorwin, the Council for European Studies, and the Deutscher Akademischer Austauschdienst for giving me an opportunity to complete necessary research in the Federal Republic of Germany. I must also thank Vicki Van Nortwick for the careful effort she spent in typing the draft.

I owe more than I can say to the intellectual companionship and loving support of my husband, Parkes Riley.

Introduction

It is a commonplace assumption of our times that modern technology and highly developed industrialism have created a sort of universal culture marked by both the benefits of mass production and the burden of alienation, depersonalization, excessive specialization, and bureaucratization. This technocratic, materialist, time-pressed, and fragmented society is seen as the inevitable by-product of the "machine" in modern life; it is international in scope and its negative characteristics are the unavoidable price paid for the abundant life.

As the effects of the negative side of "modernization" on the entire edifice of industrialism become more apparent, a host of critics have come forward to offer a wide range of solutions. These cures for low productivity, low morale, high error rates, and high wastage of human and material resources range from the redivision of labor to the advocacy of pure democracy in the place of work, from the rebuilding of "community" in society to the attempt to re-create a romanticized pre-industrial past.

Yet many of these proposals for change run headlong into the inescapable fact that their suggested plans for the amelioration of industrial malaise require the dismantling of the massive administrative and organizational structures that surround and control machine technology. These structures, it is often assumed, are the natural result of machine rationality in society. This idea of the spontaneous generation of the social order by the machine lends an often spurious aura of inevitability and permanence to many of the organizational traits of advanced industrialism. It is the theme of this work that these organizational structures are not, in fact, simply natural by-products of machine rationality in society, but are in large part the legacy of a systematic and massive industrial engineering crusade, the international Scientific Management movement, carried out in the first two decades of the twentieth century.

Scientific Management was a name invented in 1911 to describe a

1

new movement in factory organization which had previously been known by the name of its originator, Frederick W. Taylor, as the "Taylor system." Although "discovered" in the 1880s, the system was not a single invention, but a series of tools, methods, and organizational arrangements designed by Taylor and his associates to increase the efficiency and speed of machine shop production. It began with a system of timing work that was to eliminate once and for all the struggle between workers and owners over the appropriate returns to capital and labor by establishing a scientific measure of "what constitutes a fair day's work."[1] It included various bookkeeping and accounting techniques, an array of techniques for measuring work input, and various methods of organizing storerooms, tool repair, and other potentially time-wasting elements of the work process. It also included a method of charting work and waste and a managerial bonus plan devised by Henry Laurence Gantt, a slide rule for the calculation of machine speeds by Carl G. Barth, and the "science" of motion study and all its branches developed by Frank and Lillian Gilbreth.

The system was unified not by the uniqueness of its managerial devices, but by the manner in which they were organized, by the way it fragmented work and invested control or the organization of a planning process in the hands of a technical elite, and by the obsessive and puritanical style of F.W. Taylor himself. Taylor's system was an entrepreneurial scheme for selling organizational methods as science, and it contained a powerful social message. He promised to use "science" to increase profits, get rid of unions, increase the thrift and virtue of the working classes, and raise productivity to the point where society could enter a new era of harmony based on the high consumption of mass-produced goods by the previously deprived laboring classes.[2] The movement that he started was a new kind of efficiency evangelism that swept through the world from Petrograd to Tokyo. Taylor himself called his system a "mental revolution," and it is the contention of this book that this description was not altogether inaccurate.

1. Frederick W. Taylor, *The Principles of Scientific Management* (1st ed., 1911; New York: W. W. Norton & Co., 1967), p. 143. Taylor clearly relates the increase in productivity and wages to an expansion of the market for manufactured goods, the "necessities and luxuries of life," and continued employment "even in dull times."

2. Ibid., pp. 27, 138.

The continuity and extent of the Scientific Management movement have often been underestimated by all but its practitioners. Because Scientific Management presented itself as a management technique, its content and influence have rarely been considered fit subjects for intellectual journals or the interest of professional social scientists and historians. Because its most visible manifestations date from the first part of the century, it was easy to dismiss it as a dead administrative fad. Because, for various political and tactical reasons, its techniques were often renamed, it was extraordinarily difficult to make a full accounting of their influence on industry, government, and general administration.

The underestimation of the international Scientific Management movement has led to a misestimation of the unity, direction, and harmony of industrial culture. The accurate estimation of the balance of social forces built into many of the central processes of modern industrial society requires the understanding of the profound effects that Scientific Management had on both the management and the ideology of the modern state and its industrial and business enterprises. While the development of Scientific Management was not the only or the most influential event in the evolution of the twentieth century state, it is distinguished by being one of the most pervasive and invisible of the forces that have shaped modern society. Through the media of technical exchanges, machinery purchases, and engineering journals it spread both at home and abroad not just a management technology, but an ideology about management and for managers. Indeed, the influence of Scientific Management has been such that any major attempt to change the nature of industrial organization must deal with it not just as a series of techniques, but as a way of thinking about the organization and goals of technology.

It is, perhaps, curious to discuss an "objective" management technology as ideology, but then, Scientific Management is a curious ideology. Taking ideology in its most common sense, as the shared beliefs of a group about the proper goals of a society and the appropriate distribution of power and benefits within that society, it is apparent that most ideologies are transmitted with a large proportion of words and a small proportion of objects. Many of these objects, such as banners, pamphlets, and mimeograph machines, themselves have to do with words. Scientific Management, on the other hand, was transmitted with a large proportion of objects and a relatively small proportion of words. The relations between objects—machine tools, materials, and work stations—and the paper analogues of these relations—flow charts, planning documents, and work blanks—were used to symbolize idealized social relations, that is, the appropriate relations of the individual to hierarchies of specialization, to authority, and to other people, as well as the correct attitude toward work and the reward for work.

This is not to say that successful ideologies do not often possess a large number of impressive physical objects with which to transmit their message, as witness the great cathedrals of Europe. But the binding of an incipient or new ideology to the systematic use of extensive material rituals had not been accomplished before. The technical rituals of interdependence devised by Père Enfantin for the Saint-Simonian cult are but the frailest predecessors of the powerful symbolism of the modern mass-production process, timed and attended by its white-robed adepts. Scientific Management's message, tied to the rituals of time-and-motion study, Gantt charting, differential piecework, and high-speed steel, was not presented as social philosophy, but as Truth. Its proof was presented in material objects. Its social goals were modeled in the realities of factory organization. It was indeed an odd ideology, for it tended to export objects first, and to follow them with its message, rather than the reverse. It was a faith designed for pragmatists.

The chapters that follow will describe the Scientific Management movement as it took form in the United States and as it spread, with varying degrees of success, through France, England, Germany, and the Soviet Union. Scientific Management was by no means limited to these nations, but the wide variety of regimes, social structures, and pre-existing political ideologies in this small sample will show clearly the kinds of social, economic, and intellectual factors that advanced Scientific Management or retarded its influence; it will also demonstrate the extraordinary ability of the scientific managers to cross political barriers as they affected national planning, work organization, and social control. The portrait that emerges of Taylor's "mental revolution" at work shows how Scientific Management's solution to the technical and social problems of turn-of-the-century mass production became the common cultural legacy of modern industrial nations. If it is sometimes difficult to avoid the conclusion that yesterday's solution may have become today's problem, it is also impossible to fault the brilliance with which Scientific Management created a lasting technocratic formula to resolve the social problems of industrial organization.

PART I

FROM TAYLORISM TO SCIENTIFIC MANAGEMENT

Throughout my apprenticeship, I had my eye on the bad industrial conditions which prevailed at the time, and gave a good deal of time and thought to some possible remedy for them.

FREDERICK WINSLOW TAYLOR

CHAPTER 1

The Origins of the Taylor System

Scientific management will mean, for the employers and the workmen who adopt it . . . the elimination of almost all causes for dispute and disagreement between them.

FREDERICK W. TAYLOR[1]

In 1895, an engineer named Frederick Winslow Taylor presented a paper to the American Society of Mechanical Engineers, titled "A Piece-Rate System: A Step Toward Partial Solution of the Labor Problem."[2] This was the first formal presentation of a system of management which he had devised and applied in several factories in the course of his engineering work. It was not the first paper dealing with new systems of incentive payments that had been presented to the society, but it was the first of its type: unique in a number of ways, the paper was the first of a series of statements which would later be called "Taylorism," "The Taylor System of Scientific Management," or, simply, "Scientific Management," and whose practice and theory would spread throughout the industrial establishments of the world.

Taylor's paper followed a series of papers based on collective benefit plans: Kent's "A Problem in Profit Sharing" (1887), Towne's "Gain-Sharing" (1889), and Halsey's "The Premium Plan of Paying for Labor" (1891).[3] Taylor's "A Piece-Rate System" took to task all the schemes previously presented, although Towne was, in many ways, Taylor's benefactor. For Taylor's was the first plan to stress individualism, to discard utopian ideas such as profit-sharing, to appeal directly to individual desire for higher wages in a way expressly designed to break up "groups, combinations, and classifi-

1. Taylor, *Principles of Scientific Management*, p. 142.
2. Frank B. Copley, *Frederick W. Taylor: Father of Scientific Management*, 2 vols. (New York: Harper & Co., 1923), 2:407.
3. Ibid.

cations" of workers leading to "soldiering" and trade unionism, and to do this by a process which was "scientifically" based on records of labor productivity, thus eliminating the "guesswork" in rate-setting on the part of the management.

The system set out in this first paper was a finished plan, whose details had been worked out in the years prior to its formal presentation, when its author changed from the practice of engineering to what might be called engineering management. In essence, the system was the outcome of twelve years of work at the Midvale Steel Company, was based on direct observation and practice, as had been Taylor's engineering education, and was a curious combination of technology and organization which could only have resulted from Taylor's peculiar background and training. As the system evolved through its application in other plants, it first multiplied technical applications and then gradually divested itself of its technical origins, for it was, as its author claimed it to be, a state of mind rather than a series of specific techniques. The system gained mathematical sophistication when Taylor gained college-trained assistants; Taylor himself, in spite of his night-school engineering training, admitted that he lacked the background in mathematics to do more than the logical outlines of the system and to apply them by force (both figuratively and literally—he received death threats in the course of his reorganization work) to practical organizational situations based on technological problems.

After Taylor's death, Scientific Management became somewhat softened in the hands of his followers: the harshest penalties of the piecework system were eliminated in the face of heavy union opposition, for his followers knew how to compromise when Taylor had not. In a like fashion, the different influences of his various successors became evident in the directions that Scientific Management took after 1915: Henry Laurence Gantt's work developed further many of the political implications of the system; the hand of Lillian Gilbreth, humanistically trained, could be seen in a shifting emphasis from "work" studies to "fatigue" studies, and in the branching out of Scientific Management to deal with "efficiency in personal affairs" and "efficiency in the home."

In spite of the fact that Scientific Management became, after its sensational public debut in the Eastern Rates case of 1911, the most widely known and influential system of factory management in the industrial world, it is difficult to define Taylorism in terms of content alone. Even before the name "Scientific Management" was chosen for the Taylor system, the precise content of the management formula had begun to change, and, as indicated above, its evolution did not cease with the death of its inventor. We must ask, then, what exactly did Scientific Management mean?

In 1912, the Senate Committee on Education and Labor arrived at a definition of Scientific Management in relation to the passage of regulatory legislation. It was, said the committee, a generic term for "several systems of shop management now upon the market which have been invented by efficiency engineers. They are severally known as the Taylor system, the Stimpson system, the Emerson system, the Gantt system, etc., all of which have practically the same basic principles of operation but which differ somewhat as to details."[4]

> Many of those systems have much in them that is commendable and proper, since a large portion of their details consists of a compilation of business methods and shop practice which have proven successful and not harmful to the workman; such as the proper grouping of machines, standardizing tools and equipment and methods of doing work, elimination of waste, modern methods of issuing materials and cost keeping, etc. On the other hand, in the effort to get the utmost amount of work out of the employees, excesses are committed which should be curbed.[5]

Clearly, then, Scientific Management was not simply a set of rapidly outmoded ideas on factory belting and typed orders. Nor was it only a popular phrase justifying any and all management "efficiency" reorganization. And, although used as such, it was not just a vaguely defined commodity readily marketable by private consultants to manufacturers eager for a definitive solution to problems of competitive production and sales.

The historical record has been obscured when it comes to a more precise definition of Scientific Management and its influence. In part, this represents the legacy of the violent internecine quarrels of the first little band of Taylorites. In addition, the vast extent of the movement and the ephemeral quality of many of its documents render the record unclear. And, finally, this obscurity is to some extent the product of political motives in the organizations and nations that used Taylorism

---

4. U.S., Congress, Senate, Committee on Education and Labor, *Systems of Shop Management*, Report no. 930 17 July (Washington, D.C.: Government Printing Office, 1912), p. 1. Cited hereafter as Senate Hearings (1912).
5. Ibid., p. 2.

not only as a technique of speeding work but as a method of social pacification.

For many practical reasons, then, the users of Scientific Management have found it advantageous to define it as a series of its own component parts. The general result is to dispel the reputation of Taylorism and its inventor as a myth produced by the nineteenth-century enthusiasm for great men, or as a quaint turn-of-the-century fad in management which has happily long disappeared. Yet it may be argued that the very elements which obscure the origins of Scientific Management constitute evidence of the importance and extent of this system of industrial control.

The claim that Taylorism was simply a series of common-sense techniques was motivated by everything from the fear of patent infringements to professed adherence to Marxist principles of workers' control. For example, because Taylorism began its life as the arch-enemy of unionization, a professed concern for organized labor was felt to be incompatible with the formal acknowledgment of the influence of Scientific Management on industrial and political organization. In addition, because Scientific Management was a commodity sold by "efficiency engineers," a great deal of rivalry was generated by competing claims to the invention of specific Scientific Management techniques. When rivals downgraded each other's originality, they added to the general impression that there was in fact nothing new in the system. So, while the internecine wars among various kinds of efficiency experts have died, the legacy of anonymity and of multiple names for single ideas has persisted.

What gave Taylor the title of "Father of Scientific Management" in the estimation of his contemporaries was not his invention of all of the techniques of Scientific Management. Taylor's works introduced a complex of technical, organizational, and ideological elements which can be traced to specific currents of thought in his time, and which proved to have differential decay rates during the years that followed his death. The synthesis of ideas that he put forward was the original development. It is this synthesis rather than the ideas alone that has been acknowledged as the identifiable body of Taylorism. This new type of linkage between pre-existing ideas accounts for the unique social reaction to Taylorism, not aroused by its neglected and forgotten predecessors. Other innovators had offered partial answers, but only Taylor's synthesis answered simultaneously problems of production and organization, at the same time that it responded with solutions to the industrial disruption of American society. Taylor's idea seemed to many the perfect solution; projected by the force of his personality, it set off a genuine social movement with broad political ramifications. This movement affected factory owners, workmen, and government employees alike, gathered serious disciples, and set the American image of "efficiency engineer" permanently in the national consciousness.

Scientific Management, then, must be defined principally in terms of a specific relationship between ideas. It was not a single invention or series of inventions, but a complex system devised of elements in large part pre-existing and well known. In tracing the history of industrial organization technologies, we find Scientific Management, regardless of nomenclature, a clearly marked complex that ties together patterns of technological innovation with techniques of organization and larger designs for social change, unifying its entire structure with an ideology of science as a form of puritanism, or impersonal asceticism. The details of this overarching pattern of relationships grow out of its personal and historical origins. Its longevity has been the result of great social forces pressing toward the total control of industrial society.

THE ELEMENTS OF THE TAYLOR SYSTEM

Taylor himself dated the formal origins of his system from that period in the early 1880s when, as a young engineer at the Midvale Steel Company, he began a series of time studies designed to increase the productivity of the machine shop.[6] The "Taylor System of Scientific Management" that grew out of these experiments appeared, at first glance, to be a collection of new and made-over techniques both in production engineering and organization which had the direct outcome of raising the tempo of production and thus lowering the costs per unit. The first link in the chain of developments that unfolded into an entire management "system" was the investigation of machine speeds for metal cutting.[7] These investigations led to the discovery of high-speed steel, which could hold its cutting edge while red hot, permitting a vast increase in machine speeds.

The utilization of the benefits of these increased machine speeds

6. Copley, 1:222-26.
7. This summary is drawn from Taylor's basic writings: *Shop Management* (New York: Harper Bros., 1919); *Principles of Scientific Management*; and "A Piece-Rate System," and "Notes on Belting," in *Two Papers on Scientific Management* (London: Routledge & Kegan Paul, 1919).

required a speeding of the work process to and from the machine, and this necessitated a further division of labor. One of the first tasks of Scientific Management was, therefore, the analysis of the work process around the machines with the aim of subdividing tasks into their component parts, and then timing the components to discover in what manner the whole job could be speeded up. For example, machinists performed many subsidiary duties which took them from their primary task and varied what might otherwise be monotonous labor; they sharpened their own tools (more or less according to their own judgments about maintenance), and frequently went hunting about in disorganized stockpiles and storerooms to find the materials needed to complete a job. Taylorism subdivided these tasks, giving the greater part of them to unskilled or semiskilled laborers, in order to keep the higher-priced or skilled workers directly at their most productive tasks.

The coordination of this subdivided work pattern was more difficult: breakdowns at any one point jeopardized the operations of the whole system. For this reason, Taylor had written work orders prepared for each job, and all the elements tending to interrupt the process were reorganized. Machines were run from a central power source by means of overhead belting. A break in the belting due to incorrect maintenance stopped the work process. In response to this problem, Taylor wrote his "Notes on Belting." The disorganization of stockrooms and toolrooms made it difficult to know what was on hand, or to find it in case of emergency. Hence the reorganization of stocks and tools, and the derivation of the Taylor mnemonic system to designate machine parts. The use of tools of different sizes (frequently because they were owned by the workers who used them) made it difficult to standardize the time for the accomplishment of tasks which coordination of a speeded-up work system required. Therefore, Taylor and his associates experimented to find the best tools for each job; then they required the factory to supply and the worker to use them.

Maintaining the degree of speed required in each subdivided task made necessary further control of the incentive system and, to prevent the gradual exhaustion of the workers, closely timed rest periods at regular intervals were established.[8] Continual time-and-motion stud-

8. See Charles D. Wrege and Amedeo G. Perroni, "Taylor's Pig Tale: A Historical Analysis of Frederick W. Taylor's Pig Iron Experiments," *Acad-*

ies broke down jobs into their component parts with a view toward selecting the fastest methods for the completion of whole jobs. They also determined the most efficient spacing of rest periods. Not only were the workers thus to be "tuned up" to machine speeds, as the physical analogue of the machines in the system, but their will power and zest were to be enlisted by a differential piecework rate that would clearly demonstrate the connection between increased output and increased financial return, as well as by the excitement that would be generated by the chance to participate in a scientific endeavor. Of course, there had to be sanctions in the system as well. The piecework rate was also punitive in the case of below-speed work. Taylor tolerated only "first-class men" in his system. Likewise, the true differential in the value of inceased output was not reflected in the bonus plan. Taylor believed that anything over a 30 to 60 percent increase in a worker's pay would be spent on drink, which would indirectly break down the productive process.

The importance of keeping accurate records for a complex incentive plan, and of measuring the benefits of much of the work of reorganization required an improvement in the accounting system. (After all, if management did not know what supplies were in storage, how could it know that money had been *saved* by the expensive process of organizing such supplies?) In spite of his longstanding hatred of accounting,[9] Taylor was forced to devise new financial measures of efficiency. This specialized accounting system makes it clear that the power to define categories of classification in terms of the prevailing standard of worth (money, in this case) is the power to convince. In this way, accounting itself can become a form of ideology, in that it depicts systems, which may in fact be partisan, in terms apparently impartial. One might even propose that no reorganization or reform can long exist in terms of an old accounting system, but must be accompanied by the kind of redefinition of the "rules of the game" that only an accounting reform can bring.

The Taylor system of speeding work by subdividing it effectively removed the element of personal judgment from factory tasks and, in doing so, removed the forms of built-in work coordination which such judgment provided. Thus, a substitute coordinative process had

---

emy of Management Journal 17, no. 1:6-27, for a re-examination of Taylor's original data proving that his famous "rest breaks" were falsified.

9. As revealed by Copley, 1:363. This is not the impression that one would gain from Taylor's stress on quantification; cf. *Shop Management.*

to take the place of individual judgment. This coordinative element was supplied by "science," in the form of an elaborate system of records, mathematical formulae and slide rules for determining machine speeds, and systematic production planning, both short and long range. Many of the specific planning techniques were worked out by Taylor's assistants, who had more formal engineering training than he. The Taylor contribution was the overall conception of the planning system, and its integration with the continual technical and organizational experimentation that time-and-motion studies represented; he also symbolically separated this "mental" function from the rest of production by insisting that Scientific Management specialists have a separate "planning room" within the plant itself.

Yet Scientific Management comprised considerably more than the techniques of industrial engineering, or the systematic planning of work; in many ways its most characteristic elements resembled a consciously propagated evangelical faith. Or, to use the words of Taylor and his followers, the essence of Scientific Management was a "mental revolution." As Taylor himself said:

> Scientific Management is not an efficiency device, nor is it any bunch or group of efficiency devices. It is not a new system of figuring costs; it is not a new scheme of paying men; it is not holding a stop watch on a man and writing things down about him; it is not time study; it is not motion study nor an analysis of the movements of men; it is not the printing and ruling and unloading of a ton or two of blanks on a set of men and saying, "there's your system; go to it." It is not divided foremanship or functional foremanship; it is not any of the devices which the average man calls to mind when Scientific Management is spoken of . . .
>
> Now, in its essence, Scientific Management involves a complete mental revolution on the part of the workingman engaged in any particular establishment or industry—a complete mental revolution on the part of these men as to their duties toward their work, toward their fellow man, and toward their employers. And it involves the equally complete mental revolution on the part of those on the management's side—the foreman, the superintendent, the owner of the business, the board of directors—a complete mental revolution on their part as to their duties toward their fellow workers in the management, toward their workmen, and toward all of their daily problems. And without this complete mental revolution on both sides, Scientific Management does not exist.
>
> The great revolution that takes place in the mental attitude of the two parties under Scientific Management is that both sides take their eyes off of

the division of the surplus as the important matter, and together turn their attention toward increasing the size of the surplus. . . .[10]

The core of Taylorism was clearly an explicit call for reconciliation between capital and labor, on the neutral ground of science and rationality. The bribe was higher productivity, by as yet to be discovered means. Science would replace the old relations of tyranny and resistance in industrial society—but the reconciliation, quite obviously, was to be made on the terms of neither party, but in terms of "rationality" *as interpreted by Taylor himself.* That is, power in the production process was to be transferred to the hands of those custodians who knew more about the system, and what was really good for it, through the aid of their scientific insight. In short, power would be in the hands of Taylor, the scientific managers, and the category of well-intentioned, rational, public-spirited, virtuous, middle-class technicians that they represented. This power was the essential condition for the imposition of their world-view upon the production situation. The violent nineteenth century world of conflict between the upper and lower classes could become peaceful and productive only if it conformed to the middle-class image of reality. Only power could create such conformity, and, once created, it would continue to reinforce and enlarge that power. Taylorism, devised in an era of industrial unrest, demanded middle-class ascendancy in the form of management control over both owners and workers as the "payment of the piper" for ridding the industrial system of its growing social and productive dysfunctions.

Examination of the historical conditions under which Taylorism was devised makes it apparent that the Taylor System of Scientific Management, which was to become the foundation of modern industrial management practice, was far more than a technique of organization. In an industrial society whose members were increasingly subscribing to theories of inevitable class conflict, Taylorism represented a technically based ideology. It painted a picture of a conflict-free, high-consumption utopia based on mass production; it presented techniques for the suppression of class conflict and advocated a new unity of social interest; it provided an avenue for

10. Copley, 2:404.

middle-class mobility and the growth of a new professionalism. While the competition between industrial organizations and industrial nations explains the immediate popularity of Taylor's "efficiency engineering," the long-lasting and profound influence of Taylorism as a social philosophy can be shown to be a product of general historical and social conditions growing out of the industrial revolution itself. Taylorism's strength lay not in its patented mechanisms, its mnemonic and accounting systems, but in its applications as a device for social control and a strategy of social action in times of unrest. The proposals of the scientific managers became basic tenets of modern American organizational life: the destruction of ideologies of class warfare by the establishment of control according to neutral expertise in the hands of a nonowning, nonlaboring, professional, middle class. This was to become the American "One Best Way."

LABOR, CAPITAL, AND POLITICS: THE SENATE INVESTIGATION OF 1885

> *Q. What do they apprehend?—A. They apprehend a revolution.*
> *Q. From what source do they apprehend this revolution? —A. From economic causes.*
>
> SENATOR HENRY W. BLAIR, questioning CHARLES LENZ, editor of a labor newspaper, August 1883.[11]

Taylorism did not come unbidden into the industrial world of the 1880s. From the time of the Paris Commune of 1870, the fear of labor unrest and the agitation of foreign "anarchists" had occupied many members of the government and of the merchant and manufacturing classes. Only the most knowledgeable distinguished between trade unionism, socialism, "anarchical socialists," and communists. The threat to property, to the state, and to the "free market for labor" were equally dangerous products of the new industrial economy of the Gilded Age; for this reason, the authorities sought new methods that

11. U.S., Congress, Senate, Committee on Education and Labor, *Report of the Committee of the Senate upon the Relations between Labor and Capital, and Testimony Taken by the Committee*, 5 vols. (Washington, D.C.: Government Printing Office, 1885), 1:243.

would control labor and reduce the attraction of agitators and the theorists of revolution.

In 1878, the House Committee on Education and Labor, apparently worried by the political threat posed by labor radicalism, investigated the condition of European labor in order to ascertain the causes of European socialism, and to contrast unfavorable conditions abroad with the wealth of American labor, for purposes of propaganda. States one of the authors of the report,

> We are not a nation of capitalists and laborers; we are a nation of republican citizens. Let us, then, ignore these dividing lines, and, each accepting that position for which his capacity best fits him, work upward and onward in the scale of respectable citizenship, doing that which is best for all.[12]

The study of wages and working conditions in Europe marked the beginning of a fear that major social changes had taken place since the Civil War, changes with profound political implications. Industrial society had gained predominance over agrarian society; America had become a nation of immigrants, not Anglo-Saxon colonists; the cities were growing, the frontier vanishing. European workers had brought European philosophies with them; with the rise of trade unionism and the introduction of Marxism, class conflict seemed to be increasing.

> Under no consideration must we have strikes; under no consideration must our factories lie idle. If our manufacturers cannot run their establishments profitably—and capital will no more remain permanently invested unprofitably than will labor work for nothing—and pay the prevailing wages, our working people must help them to make profit by consenting to a reduction of wages.
>
> If our workingmen, native and naturalized, will only read these reports in that national spirit with which I have endeavored to point out some of the principal features therein, and drive from their midst communism, strikes, and drink—evil spirits born of oppression, and foreign to our country and our institutions, fatal to them should these vicious principles ever attain national proportions—labor faithfully and intelligently, like free men; live within their means, like frugal and sensible men; and choke down all demogogical attempts to divide the American people into hostile ranks as capitalists and laborers, there can be no reasonable limit set to the development of our manufactures and commerce . . .[13]

12. U.S., Congress, House, *State of Labor in Europe: 1878* (Washington, D.C.: Government Printing Office, 1879), p. 39.

13. Ibid., p. 38.

Four years prior to the Haymarket bombing of 1886, the Senate Committee on Education and Labor, seeking to uncover the causes and devise legislative remedies for the state of social unrest in the United States, began an investigation into the relations between labor and capital. From 1882 until 1885 the committee heard testimony on wages and hours, and on the conditions of factory labor, on the decline of crafts, the organization of trade unions, and the hardening of class lines between the rich and poor. They heard the opinions both of celebrated capitalists and of witnesses who risked serious employer reprisals testifying on the fair return to labor of the profits from productive enterprise. They personally inspected manufacturing establishments and workers' homes, and requested the testimony of the elderly on working-class living conditions in the early part of the century. The published record of the investigation not only indicates the level of popular and governmental concern about urban decay and labor agitation, but provides an important and detailed account of working conditions and management ideology at the time that Scientific Management was being developed.

Perhaps the most recurrent theme of the testimony was that the "myth of rags to riches" was already moribund at the time that Horatio Alger, Jr., was enshrining it in his series of uplifting tales for boys. Alger himself always emphasized the indispensability of a wealthy patron, and while witness after witness from the working class described the closing of opportunity in the factory system, it was the millionaires who appeared to believe in the Alger theme. One, indeed, in order to illustrate the boundless opportunities that await a clean-living youth, described how he made a point of giving his patronage and a large tip to bootblacks who did not smoke.[14]

The effect of capital accumulation was to create a new gulf between owners and workers, as it became apparent that it was increasingly difficult for a man of little capital to go into business for himself. Wages were frequently at the subsistence level, or, in some cases such as that of women skirt-makers, below subsistence level. On the other hand, a new class of plutocrats was in evidence. As an agrarian society was transformed into an urban manufacturing one, material goods became more abundant and money was in greater supply. Old men testified that in the 1820s, a man who owned a farm worth four or five thousand dollars was a very substantial citizen in a New England

14. Senate Report on Labor and Capital (1885), 2:119.

village, while one hundred thousand dollars marked a "man of great wealth" in New York City.[15] Shoes, machine-woven cloth, and a multitude of mechanical conveniences made life more abundant and in some ways less laborious, but the wages of "mechanics" had slipped to the point where they no longer considered themselves middle class.

Observation and popular myth blend in the description of the evils of cities. Long before Thorstein Veblen coined the phrase "conspicuous consumption," it was felt that the vulgar ostentation of the new rich was inciting the poor to emulate them to the extent that their morality had declined irreparably. Emulation had caused the decline in church attendance, the loss of thrifty habits, and the "get rich quick" spirit that undermined the desire to do honest labor. Temperance leaders discoursed on the relation between drink and poverty. Suffragists felt that the vote would improve women's wages.[16]

The problem was not, however, the determination that there was indeed a rift between labor and capital, but how to effect the reconciliation between them—to stop the relative decline of the middle class, to increase the production of inexpensive manufactured goods, to prevent urban violence, and to break up trade unions and radical movements. Conservative opinion held that the reconciliation of labor and capital should be on the terms of capital alone. Manufacturers referred to trade union organization as "cornering the labor market"; they damned it for opposing the spirit of free enterprise, and blamed it for higher consumer prices. Jay Gould declared that labor was getting a fair share of the increased wealth originating from the use of capital; he maintained that the returns to capital were becoming progressively lower. There was no basic conflict between labor and capital, for without capital, labor could produce nothing. Trade unionism was a disease of European tyrannies and unnecessary in a democratic state.[17]

The interests of the middle class were not wholly identified with those of the plutocrats, however, for while the middle class wanted the virtues of social stability and the higher output of the industrial system, they did not want the side effects of increased class distinction, decreased political and social power, and class-based violence. Their conclusion, then, was that the real quarrel was not between capital and labor, but between *monopoly* capital and labor. Whatever poverty and social unrest had been created by the new industrial

15. Ibid., 1:830.   16. Ibid., 1:616.   17. Ibid., 1:1090-91.

system was not the fault of the system itself, but of the monopolists who perverted it, driving wages down and prices up. The restoration of a completely free market for both labor and capital was the solution they proposed, for then there would be as much competition for the employment of capital as for labor, eliminating the conflict between labor and "aggregrated capital."[18]

The focus of the capital and labor problem that had originated in the factories was the question of who owned the state. While the Senate committee was horrified to verify that the capture of the state was indeed the goal of the socialist movements among the working class, it was the contention of the middle-class based Progressive movement that the state was already in the possession of the big capitalists, who conspired with urban bosses to buy the votes of the poor and immigrant classes which they themselves had created.

> Two enemies, unknown before, have risen like spirits of darkness on our social and political horizon—an ignorant proletariat and a half-taught plutocracy.[19]

A powerful political movement deriving from middle-class views that culminated in Progressivism had as its program three interlocking elements: the elimination of monopoly capital by anti-trust legislation, the uplifting of the poor, and the breaking of the power of the plutocrats and bosses in government by the establishment of a merit civil service that would recruit the "college-bred."

The crown of such reforms was Woodrow Wilson's proposal for a "merit presidency."[20] By arguing for the substitution of electoral methods by the application of criteria of merit, the struggle between groups for the possession of office would be removed from the political realm and transformed into a question of technique—that of the proper definition and assessment of merit. Needless to say, this transformation would give the educated middle class a considerable advantage in defining the rules of the game to suit themselves, an advantage not unnoticed at the time.

18. Ibid.
19. Samuel Haber, *Efficiency and Uplift: Scientific Management in the Progressive Era, 1890-1920* (Chicago: University of Chicago Press, 1964), p. 95.
20. Ibid., p. 99.

TRADITIONAL MANAGEMENT
AND THE FAILURE OF AUTHORITY

There was the chasm—labor and capital at war, neither
producing anything. . . . The issue was not wages; it was
who had a right to rule; whether these men were to work
for me ten hours or whether they were to work eight.

JOHN ROACH, shipbuilder, 1883[21]

Traditional patterns of factory management in the United States mirrored the problems of society outside of the factory; the social displacement that accompanies nascent industrialism, the decay of agrarian values, and the breakdown of traditional patterns of authority. Both Taylor and his followers clearly understood that the problems of disorder, production, and distribution that Taylor set himself to correct in the machine shop had broad social implications.

The formal goal of the Taylor system was not less than the reconciliation of capital and labor through the distribution of higher benefits to both, based on the general increase in industrial productivity made possible by better management. The crux of the problem, as Taylor saw it, was the question of appropriate wage payments in a production system over which ownership exercised little effective control. The villain of the piece was the day wage, which "herded men into classes" and encouraged them to "soldier," or organize to avoid work. The hero was an entirely new figure on the industrial scene: the "objective scientist" who bowed to the interests of neither labor nor capital, but instead acted as arbitrator between them, calculating, on the basis of specialized measurements, the appropriate return to labor. He was, then, the industrial equivalent of the middle-class "merit" administrator in the newly reformed civil service.

The growth in scale of industrial enterprises in the course of the nineteenth century had undermined the informal and frequently familial bases of authority in manufacturing. The new owner was not a Master, in the traditional sense of the word; he had little direct experience with the production process and fewer moral and personal ties to his numerous workers; he had little of the traditional obligation to provide them with training and sustenance. With the new specialization that went with size, the owner was largely an investor of capital. When a man with two or three assistants had worked out of

21. Senate Report on Labor and Capital (1885), 2:100.

his house, no matter what the opportunities for personal despotism inherent in such a situation, all parties had a clear idea of the relationship between work, profit, and continued employment. The owners of such small manufacturing establishments handled procurement of raw materials, storage, and marketing of their own product. They knew where things were, what people were doing, and how much they were making.

This was no longer true in the factory, which brought together men in groups, but did not yet organize them as a unit. Vast areas of near-total confusion existed in which traditional, instinctive methods of organization were not sufficient to keep the whole enterprise operating to the profit of all those concerned. In a situation of increasing competition between ever larger organizations, these old internal structures were simply reinforced with greater hierarchy and added methods of coercion. Bad wages and punitive working conditions were not simply indications of competitive cost-cutting practices, but symptoms of the failure of authority due to the increased size and complexity of organization and the concomitant loss of control over employees.

In particular, the payment system in the factories was left over from the days of the four-man shop: wages were set at various rates depending on skill, and paid by the day. An alternative, the piece-rate system, had advantages of economy which were offset by its requirement for greater skill in accounting and for work amenable to piece counting. A more important disadvantage, however, was the long-standing opposition of labor, which had been noted as early as the sixteenth century when journeymen attempted to preserve hiring by the year in an effort to control the "piecemasters" who undercut prices by farming out piecework to individual craftsmen's homes.[22] In some industries in the United States, such as the home sewing of petticoats or the manufacture of artificial flowers and other small commodities, the piece-rate system was longstanding practice. But for most types of labor, the day wage was the simplest and most practical method of payment, although growth in the scale of enterprises had increased the problems of supervision.

The day wage had certain advantages: by putting a fence around the plant and a timekeeper at the gate, it was a simple matter to account for each man's presence during the working day. When high costs or

22. George Unwin, *Industrial Organization in the Sixteenth and Seventeenth Centuries* (1st ed., 1904; London: Frank Cass & Co., 1963).

dispersed work prevented the building of a fence, it was possible to have the timekeeper make spot checks on the work crews. The day wage, set by management considering little but the company's financial needs, set a premium on the evasion of work by the laborers and led to an escalation of force on the part of management. By the turn of the century, abuses had multiplied. Timekeepers discovered that of the men checked in, fully twenty percent could never be located; in one shipyard work crews would delegate one man to make loud hammering noises on the hull of a ship under construction, while the rest played cards.[23]

The response of management tended toward the increased use of arbitrary force, such as random "on-the-spot" firings, delegated to the foremen, who were given total power over hiring and overseeing the workers in their jurisdictions. Since the owners frequently had grown out of touch with the employees and technical processes of their plants, they simply set the wage and gave orders that the foreman should exact as much work as possible in return. The result of this delegation of authority was to "feudalize" the factory under the authority of the foreman. In a miniature replica of urban bossism, foremen dealt with crafts and ethnic groups, fired, hired, collected kickbacks, and in many other ways acted as intermediaries between the employees and the directors of the plant.

Intensifying further the problem of control was the general decrease in the ability of the foremen as a group that observers felt was a product of the general American pressure for social mobility. A "brain drain" from the factory floor into sales reflected the difference between inferior jobs involving manual labor and the comfortable office, large wages, and travel in "first-class parlour cars" that were the lot of the salesman. "Inferior men"—those either too unskilled to get machinists' wages and incompetent at sales—were left on the factory 'or:

ong hours, unpleasant working conditions, poor pay and loss of caste
'ially have conspired to drive men of brains and ambition out of the
\ry.[24]

ame of evasion of work took a new turn when the technical
\' of the foreman was exceeded by that of his workers.

T. Farnham, *America versus Europe in Industry: A Compari-
\l Policies and Methods of Management* (New York: Ronald
271.
\.

Accounts of factory life of the period depict foremen resorting to public shows of ferocity to preserve their control; observers commented knowingly that authority combined with ignorance could hardly be expected to raise productivity. Taylor and his followers saw that the power of the traditional foremen as a class stood in the way of innovation.

For industries engaged in intense competition, there were only a few ways of lowering costs. Elimination of competition by the formation of monopolies was regulated by the Sherman Anti-Trust Act of 1890 and by subsequent legislation. The attempt to lower the costs of materials through exploration, colonial expansion, and research was in progress. The search for cheaper labor had led to the exploitation of the family by the employment of women and children at less than subsistence wages—a process that was reaching the end of its usefulness and meeting with increasing labor resistance. The last avenue of cost reduction still open was to combine labor and materials more efficiently, and this was limited by the difficulties in supervising labor under the current organization and incentive systems. Supervision must somehow be improved by internalizing labor discipline in order to stop soldiering—the game of avoiding work:

> When one man supervises ten work crews, the chances are ten to one that they can evade supervision.[25]

The obvious answer was to gear wages more directly to actual performance, but this required a better work-accounting system. But the use of such a system to break up soldiering broke up the established power relations in the factory, and set limits to the arbitrary authority of management itself. Recordkeeping and the installation of a time clock may force more effort out of labor, but the current battle of waitresses and other "casual" laborers to have such systems installed reminds us that such devices are also a check on the rapacity of employers. More accurate work accounting at this phase of industrial development was frequently construed as a direct attack on the prerogatives of management.

Another direct way to increase labor productivity required the restructuring of incentives to increase labor cooperation by tying the fortunes of the workers more directly to the success of the business. This, however, appeared even more dangerous to the vested interest

25. Ibid., p. 276.

of the owners. Profit-sharing and similar plans were anathema, denounced by manufacturers as "unrealistic," since workers were considered too simple-minded to connect daily effort with an annual or even a monthly bonus. Not only would such reorganization of incentives break the power of the foremen, it would increase the ability of labor to withhold effort in order to obtain higher wages. The problem was then to increase labor productivity without giving a greater proportion of control over wages and policy to the workers. The answer to the problem required an increase in knowledge of the production process on the part of management, a scheme for breaking up worker combinations, the replacement of direct coercion by the socialization of individual workmen into company goals, and a return to the piecework rate.

Throughout the latter part of the nineteenth century, many people had tinkered with new schemes of organization designed to cure the ills of the factory system. The common point of most of these schemes was the development of various kinds of piecework rates to replace the day wage. The problems of piecework rates were no less complex than those of the day wage, however. It was difficult to set a piecework rate that reflected at the same time the needs of competition, the needs of workers for a daily take-home pay that they could live on, and the appropriate use of differentiated wages as a financial incentive.

An additional problem with piecework was the competition it engendered between workers of varying skills; this competition produced, over time, a number of unintended social consequences. For example, setting wage rates according to craft skill, as was done during this period, favored age and experience, whereas piece rates favored energy alone. When machine-controlled processes came to dominate the industrial environment, skilled crafts were put in the position of demanding wages equivalent to those of highly paid nonskilled assembly line workers. Likewise, the predominance of the piece rate set the peak earning power of unskilled labor comparatively early in life, with earnings declining with age. These pressures produced strong incentives to restore culturally approved norms through labor organization.[26]

Historically, the "speed-up" had always followed in the wake of the piecework system. That is, when the system of paying workers by the

26. The problem of varying competencies and its latter-day complications were suggested by Thomas C. Blaisdell, Jr.

number of pieces induced them to produce more, the rate per piece was cut so that workers would do more work for less money. The speed-up created the same supervision problems that had existed under the day wage. It came into being because of management ignorance of exactly how much labor it took to produce goods, and their fear that workers were hiding their abilities in order to make higher wages. Behind this attitude lay class arrogance; even if it were economically sound to pay individuals more in order to raise productivity and lower prices, for a number of extraneous social reasons, it was felt that workers should not make too much.

Workers, knowing that under the speed-up they could not expect to take home a living wage for anything less than superhuman effort, did in fact arrange to limit their productivity. By combining informally without the knowledge of management, they set production rates judged suitable for a "fair" wage, and threatened potential rate breakers with severe sanctions. Bizarre distortions of production rationality under the piecework system occurred when labor organized slowdowns, as well as when finished assemblies were hidden under work benches and sold to successors on the job. In spite of the introduction of time-and-motion studies, these practices may be observed today, where they serve the function of providing organizational slack for the workers, and, in the case of the practice of selling finished work, they allow a new man on the job time to learn his task without suffering wage cutbacks.[27]

Because of labor's long-standing hatred of the speed-up, there was a series of attempts by organizational innovators to build protection for both management and "honest" laborers into the piece-rate system. Elaborations on the system proliferated: base pay plus piecework bonus, profit-sharing based on productivity, and so forth. The core of the problem was how to get management and labor to agree on how to determine to the satisfaction of both parties just what "a fair day's work for a fair day's pay" actually was. Taylor's contribution to the solution of this problem was a differential piecework wage embedded in a new system of subdivided labor. Coordinating this system was a structure of formal records that increased the control of ownership over manufacturing through the intervention of a new class: the white-

---

27. See Farnham, p. 275. One of my students tells the story of an ambidextrous man who set up his lathe for the left hand when the time-study man was setting the rates, and reversed it again for the right after the rates had been set at this artificially low speed.

collar production manager. The social implications of this system were enormous.

SOURCES OF OPPOSITION TO AND ADVOCACY OF THE TAYLOR SYSTEM

The social significance of Taylorism is perhaps clearer if, instead of simply taking at face value its stated goal of universal industrial welfare, one asks in addition the traditional question *cui bono*? The Taylor system claimed to improve the condition of labor; to raise wages, to decrease hours and fatigue by establishing "rest breaks," to provide avenues of advancement into white-collar planning work for ambitious workers, to establish a new technical basis for "functional foremanship," and to train the unskilled in scientifically determined "trades."

Neither workers nor management were pleased with the Taylor system. The opposition of labor was, perhaps, the most active. If the first task of Taylorism in the shop was "to break the power of the foremen," the immediate response of the foremen was mass resignation, violence, and threats of violence. Taylor met threats of death with bravado and refused to go armed, advancing the cause of his science with persuasive arguments that included artistic, multilingual swearing. Taylor's war against soldiering, however, evidently had an emotional basis and began long before his system was fully elaborated. According to his biographer, he began experimenting with the speed-up in practice before he ever began a formal study of the "science" of the speed-up.[28] At every stage of the system's development, it met with bitter opposition, as Taylor insisted on his own definition of "a fair day's work" over that of the old craftsmen machinists. Although his writings stress the element of persuasion, he did not hesitate to fire refractory, skilled machinists on the spot, in order to replace them with more docile, untrained laborers. Testifying before Congress, workers complained that the basis of Taylor's "science" was discipline, and that

> The system of discipline advocated by Mr. Taylor consists of—
> 1. Lowering the man's wages.
> 2. Laying him off for a period of time.
> 3. Fining him all the way from 1 cent to $60.
> 4. Discharging him.

28. Copley, 1:228.

It is also regarded as a good plan to continually keep enough men on hand so as to be able to discharge a workman every now and then for failing to continue at the pace required, because of its moral effect on the rest of the workmen.[29]

Perhaps the most frequently quoted episode, used by Taylor to advocate his system and by his detractors to illustrate his callousness, is the dialogue with Schmidt, the pig-iron handler, which is found in *The Principles of Scientific Management*.[30] Schmidt, an "ox-brained" moron of German extraction (Taylor disliked Germans) is harangued by Taylor until he announces in rich Milwaukee Deutsch accents that he is a "high-priced man" and, for an increase in wages, he will work exactly according to system. And thanks to the system, which involves the scientific handling of pig iron and the use of judiciously spaced rest breaks, Schmidt becomes capable of loading forty-seven half-tons of pig iron a day, in place of the daily average of twelve half-tons per man at the time Taylor began reorganizing Bethlehem Steel.

Although the Schmidt illustration became a focal point of international union opposition, and it was frequently proclaimed that its subject had died young from overwork, its use as an example of Taylor's science at work has continued without examination until recently. In 1974, Taylor's account of his harsh, but effective, measures was subjected to close scrutiny, and his private papers yielded up a portrait of his operations far closer to that of his opponents than his followers may have ever suspected. The original model for Schmidt, named Henry Noll, was not "scientifically selected," nor did the dramatic dialogue between Taylor and Schmidt, in all probability, ever take place. Quite simply, when the attempt to introduce piecework at Bethlehem Steel resulted in the opposition of a largely Hungarian work force, Noll was the only member of a specially organized German-Irish piecework loading team who did not quit in exhaustion after the first few days. Having discovered a few workers of unusual physical capacity, Taylor used them in classic "rate-

29. Senate Hearings (1912), p. 4.
30. This dialogue is often quoted in its entirety in management textbooks: See, for example, P. Blau and M. Meyer, *Bureaucracy in Modern Society* (New York: Random House, 1971); Wrege and Perroni also cite M. Blum, *Industrial Psychology and Its Social Foundations* (New York: Harper & Row, 1956); H. Burtt, *Applied Psychology* (New York: Prentice-Hall, 1952); E. Dale, *Management Theory and Practice* (New York: McGraw-Hill, 1965); and numerous other texts.

breaking" fashion, elaborating a "science" of pig-iron handling. The records show that his "pioneer" use of rest breaks was fiction; such "rest" as existed consisted of "walking back empty-handed after loading a pig on a car," rather than the sitting rest breaks that Taylor described. The investigators reached the conclusion that the Schmidt episode was largely a hoax, for "the fact is that Taylor seems to have believed that the end justified the means."[31]

The proof that Taylor's "pig-iron experiments" were falsified does not, however, detract from the value of the Schmidt episode as management history, but enhances it. The fact that the data have remained unexamined for so many decades, particularly in the light of the world wide interest in Scientific Management, appears to be not so much a problem of scholarly oversight, as the investigators of the Schmidt episode charitably suggest, but a product of the extraordinarily powerful ideological thrust of Scientific Management doctrine. So important was Taylor's message that neither he, nor his followers, nor those large segments of industrial society that adhered to his doctrine felt it essential to allow actual scientific findings to interfere with the new technology of labor control. There could be no better proof that Taylorism, from its very inception, was a crusade rather than a technique. And no better example exists of the use of false claims of scientific objectivity for the promotion of ideologically determined goals.

The fact that the struggle over Taylorism was a political rather than a technical battle was recognized early by the labor unions that opposed the Taylor System of Scientific Management. Union representatives claimed that the system would throw men out of work, depriving them of "the only weapons they had for fighting their employers."[32] Organized labor began political agitation against the Taylor system and succeeded in getting Congress to investigate their complaints in 1912, shortly after the Watertown Arsenal strike. As a result, a rider was added to all appropriations bills banning the use of the stopwatch in government installations, as well as certain of the overt features of Taylor's wage payment system. Yet congressional intervention did not eliminate the implementation of Taylor's ideas, even in the Watertown Arsenal itself. Rather, it forced them underground. The banning of the stopwatch failed to banish Taylorism.

31. Wrege and Perroni, p. 26.
32. Copley, 2:273.

Many years later, when Scientific Management had penetrated the fabric of government itself, the anachronistic rider, its significance forgotten, was dropped.[33]

Taylor scorned the political "demagogues" who made ignorant public statements denouncing the stopwatch as the chief tool in a system of forced labor. But it is apparent from his published statements that he did indeed conceive of his system of work timing as one part of an improved method of labor control. In a letter to Bethlehem Steel he stated his management goals in the following fashion:

> The chief objects which I have in view in systematizing the shop are:
>
> First:—To render the management of the shop entirely independent of any one man or any set of men so that the shop will be in a position to run practically as economically if you were to lose your foremen, or if, in fact, a considerable body of your workmen were to leave at any one time.
>
> Second:—To introduce such system and discipline into the shop that any policy which may be decided upon by the management can be properly carried out.
>
> Third:—To introduce the best kind of Piece Work in place of Day Work and also to very materially increase the rate of speed and accuracy of each man in the shop.[34]

He goes on to point out that without job control such as he provides, the introduction of piecework will be a failure, because of the individual resistance of the workers, who tend to hide their best tools and grind those in use so that they are unable to do the required work. He demands loyal assistants and the complete cooperation of management in the installation of the new control system.

In short, Taylorism set about to break skilled labor's "monopoly" on expertise, which had been the basis for allowing the worker discretion in the matter of rate-setting, or control over his own productivity. Skills which were once trade secrets were put in written record form available to management, which could then control output rates more completely, and with those rates, the rate of payment to labor. This change tended to be accomplished not so much by retraining craftsmen as by replacing them, and training cheaper,

    33. See Senate Hearings (1912), and A. G. H. Aitken, *Taylorism at the Watertown Arsenal: Scientific Management in Action, 1908-1915* (Cambridge: Mass.: Harvard University Press, 1960).
    34. Copley, 2:11.

unskilled labor in the mindless repetition of single actions, or even motions, in the giant productive mechanism blueprinted in the Taylor "planning room." The rebellion of skilled labor, under these circumstances, is not to be marvelled at.

The resistance of management is, on the surface, more difficult to understand. Taylorism was, after all, a system designed for the benefit of management. It had opened to the control of employers the formerly "closed box" that the production process represented. This control, by increasing output while cheapening labor (and yet paying individuals wages that tended to be somewhat increased), opened up the possibility for new profits and a profound competitive advantage.

Perhaps the most obvious reason for management opposition was that Taylor and his associates did not count the costs of the transition into the costs of their system. In particular, they disclaimed all losses, due to labor resistance and strikes, as a product of the misuse of their system, not the system itself. Taylor, for example, claimed that unlike his fly-by-night competitors in the efficiency business, there had never been a strike during the introduction of the Taylor System of Scientific Management. He achieved this record by blaming such contretemps as did occur on external agitators and "opposition forces." According to this reasoning, the famous Watertown Arsenal strike can be dismissed as a problem that occurred under the supervision not of Taylor himself, but of his associate, Henry Lawrence Gantt.[35]

The transition period itself appeared to stretch to unseemly lengths in the eyes of some employers, as the Senate Report of 1912 indicates:

Colloquy between Mr. Taylor and Dissatisfied Customer

Mr. Taylor: I think that Mr. Hawkins has also overlooked another important factor, and that is the question of time. If Mr. Hawkins expects large results in six months or a year in a very large works, he is looking for the impossible. If he expects to convert union men to a higher rate of production, coupled with high wages, in six months or a year, he is expecting next to an impossibility. But if he is patient enough to wait for two or three years he can go among almost any set of workmen in this country and not find the trouble which he did in Massachusetts.

Mr. Hawkins: I have waited six years now.

Mr. Taylor: Have you tried the incisive plan of centering on one man instead of going at the whole shooting match at once? I think failure is due to a lack of patient persistence on the part of the employers and then to a

35. For a detailed account of the strike and its aftermath, see Aitken.

lack of centering right onto a single man. No workman can long resist the help and persuasion of five foremen over him. He will either do the work as he is told to or leave.[36]

Although Taylor and his supporters characterized management resisters as narrow-minded local capitalists, the truth was that Taylorism took control from old-style management just as surely as it had from labor. The manager had left labor as master in its own sphere, but he was master in his. With Taylorism, all this was changed. The "old school" bosses complained that they had been robbed of their authority.[37] The Taylor system defined their authority as mere arbitrary force and, indeed, did take it away. For Taylor said that traditional management authority was the power to command, devoid of knowledge about how the command would be carried out. His system proposed to "give" management "more real authority than they ever had before,"[38] according to this new definition of authority.

But the new system, which forced specialization and made the knowledge of the actual workings of the productive process available to management, actually gave the old-style employers very little. Rather, Taylor was giving the Scientific Management specialists in the planning bureau the knowledge which he could then claim belonged to "management"—because he categorized the "new men" as management, too. The old managers now had neither knowledge nor control, for under the new system this passed to the new management specialists, who had the information necessary to make the decisions. Thus, it was the men in the "planning room" who actually took power, not the old bosses. The displeasure of the latter was expressed in their fears of being overrun by clerks, and their complaints about the expense of the great number of "supernumeraries" advocated by the efficiency engineers:

> The clerical force necessary for the maintenance of these elaborate systems makes the overhead charges exceedingly great, and it is a question whether the increased productivity of the workmen in the shop, upon whom the heavy burden falls, is sufficient to pay for all this nonproductive labor which had been added.[39]

Those who benefited most from Taylorism were the members of the new white-collar professional class upon whose work the system

36. Senate Hearings (1912), p. 9.
37. Copley, 2:420.
38. Ibid.
39. Senate Hearings (1912), p. 12.

depended. Thus, the central cause for the success of Taylorism was its creation and promotion of a new element in society: a broadly based *industrial middle class.* For Taylor's system had essentially added a new category to the upper half of the labor-management formula: the new group of managers whose position was justified by the increased output of the entire concern. The following statement by Taylor opened the way for the white-collar revolution:

> As a general rule I can say that the more men you have working efficiently in the management, that is, on the management side, the greater will be your economy.[40]

By definition, however, the "new class" that formed Taylor's principal audience was not located within the factory itself. Taylorism attracted not the shop foreman, but the young college graduate searching for white-collar openings in an era that many felt marked the decline of the middle class.[41] The question is, then, how did Taylorism gain access to the factory, especially in the face of labor and management opposition? To a certain extent, the great influence of Taylorism in government, education, and other organizations depends on the great political movement fostered by precisely these middle-class groups. But a great deal of the initial success of the movement in gaining its foothold in industry depended on the tactical maneuvers of Taylor himself, on his personal gifts, and on the way in which he built up a hard core of disciples.

Taylor's basic tactic was the separation of the individual from the group. By separating the "first-class man" from the slow worker, he increased production. By playing on the ambition, the desire for education, or the eccentric passion for science or order in an individual executive, he could break down the unity of management opposition and gain entry into a plant. Taylor had become independently wealthy from patenting (over the protests of his employer, Bethlehem Steel) the rights to high-speed steel. Retiring at the age of forty-five, he stated that he could "no longer afford to work for

40. Copley, 1:422.
41. While numerous sources deal with the problem of decreasing social opportunity, particularly for the educated middle class (see Anonymous, "Living on the Ragged Edge," *Harper's Magazine*, December 1925, and K. F. Gerould, "The Plight of the Genteel," *Harper's Magazine*, February 1926), a current discussion of the relation of the growth of the myth of opportunity to the decline of actual social mobility can be found in Irvin Wyllie, *The Self-Made Man in America: The Myth of Rags to Riches* (New York: Free Press, 1954).

money," and devoted himself to propagating his system. He could afford to offer key executives, including military officers, a year's salary to attend the management seminars he ran at his house on the outskirts of Philadelphia.[42] And just as important, he made it essential for any company that bought the patent rights for high-speed steel to adopt the Taylor system for speeding up work. Patent rights in the United States were purchased immediately by Bethlehem Steel, William Sellers and Company, and the Link-Belt Engineering Company. The English rights were bought by Vickers. Patent rights were also applied for in Canada, France, Belgium, and Austria. Until a group of British and American manufacturers managed to break the patent, the national and international diffusion of the Taylor System of Scientific Management could be measured by the spread of Taylor-White, high-speed steel.[43]

But Taylor did not rely only on money to convert individuals to his system. By far his most important conversions were accomplished by the strength of his personality. By all accounts, Taylor was a genuine charismatic. His active manner, down-to-earth language, and "mesmeric" blue eyes, while they offended some, swayed many to cast aside their natural doubts and embrace his system of management. His contemporaries called him prophet, genius, revolutionist, fanatic, and madman. Without a doubt, Taylor's character is a central part of his system.

THE ROLE OF TAYLOR'S PERSONALITY

In the early days of Scientific Management, before Louis Brandeis and the Eastern Rates case had made it a household word, but after management and the unions had declared war on the system, a number of influential people wanted to discredit Taylor's theories by proving that he was insane. For this purpose, they hired private detectives to follow him and to question his servants.[44] They were forced to give up the effort when they could prove no such thing. Despite many unusual personal habits, in the context of his times Fred Taylor was as sane as anyone else.

Perhaps because his neuroses were the neuroses of an era, or rather, of a class within that era, Taylor's personal solutions to the problems

---

42. Copley, 2:312-13, describes Taylor's negotiations with an officer of the U.S. Navy for this purpose.

43. Ibid., 2:113-16.   44. Ibid., 2:365.

of order and control were successfully writ large on American society itself. Taylor's "psychobiographer," Sudhir Kakar, postulates a direct connection between Taylor's personal crises and the growth of his new social invention, relating Taylor's psychological growth to social change in the tradition of Erik Erikson.[45] Even the old-fashioned and genial Frank B. Copley, whose usual "no nonsense" approach breaks down into dark references to Sigmund Freud when he confronts Taylor's personal quirks, finds indisputable connections between Taylor's personal history and his system of management.

It is Copley who notes that Taylor's childhood behavior was marked by passionate attachment to rule structures as a means of social control. He was not a boy who took his ball home when he did not win the game. Instead, he made a practice of devising elaborate rules for the game so that, win or lose, his friends were playing on *his* terms. Once he had harassed his companions into playing according to his rules, insisting on the rightness of his decisions, he was then "generous" about conceding them the rest of the game. As one childhood friend, who later became an artist, remarked:

> Fred was a bit of a crank in the opinion of our boyhood band, and we were inclined to rebel sometimes from the strict rules and exact formulas to which he insisted all our games must be subjected.[46]

This excessive zeal for rule-making was just one of a series of exotic manifestations of character that may be attributed to what Copley calls "a *whale* of a New England conscience" inherited from the oldest New England "racial and spiritual stocks."[47] Although somewhat dated, the concept of the New England conscience does indeed sum up a classic American personality type: righteous, rigorously self-disciplined, sexually puritanical, thrifty, individualistic, plagued by black moods (particularly on Sunday), and tortured by dreams of transgression and hell-fire. Taylor coupled this with Yankee ingenuity: the mechanical inventiveness important to settlers in the New World because it compensated for the scarcity of human labor.

Taylor's self-control took the form of Spartan personal habits: abstention from tobacco, coffee (a narcotic beverage), tea, and alcohol, as well as a penchant for saccharin, mineral water, and a regular midnight run in the snow. He was morbidly fearful of illness

---

45. Sudhir Kakar, *Frederick Taylor: A Study in Personality and Innovation* (Cambridge, Mass.: MIT Press, 1970).
46. Copley, 1:56.   47. Ibid., 1:43–45.

and death, and could not bear to have those topics discussed in his presence. As an adolescent, his female impersonations deceived unwary spectators both at the theater and on the street. His insomnia, caused by the nightmares that had plagued him since childhood, caused him to make a habit in adulthood of sleeping bolt upright in a chair, propped up by pillows. This habit frequently wrought havoc in the hotels he stayed at, as the staff searched high and low for the requisite number of pillows. Sometimes he was even forced to rig a substitute by pulling out bureau drawers.[48]

One of the most curious manifestations of Taylor's inventiveness as a boy was a series of increasingly complex and painful machines he designed to combat his nightmares. Beginning with bizarre designs for pillows and corn-husk mattresses, the "nightmare machines" culminated in the creation of "a sort of harness of straps and wooden points, designed to wake him if he turned on his back." He perfected this device at the age of twelve, and from then on continued to use a modified version of it at Phillips Exeter when he was preparing for college.[49] It is clear that with Taylor, the use of the Machine against Nature began early. Until the night when he died (while winding his watch) the central theme of Fred Taylor's life was the use of the machine to combat man's natural potential for evil, and to force him to attain virtue and ultimate redemption. That the Machine would, in the end, destroy Nature was not a by-product of his system, but the core of his teaching.

That Taylor's psychology meshed with the dominant Protestant ethic of his contemporaries may explain his evangelical fervor and his charismatic effect on some of his converts. But to discover the major sources of the doctrine's appeal, especially beyond the borders of the United States, we must look to the broader social currents mirrored by Taylor's life. His early life was a version of the fairly common predicament of the growing American middle class of free professionals, pressured on the one side by large capital and on the other by labor's demand for better wages to give up their share of the pie. By finding a way out for himself through the invention of a new kind of industrial professionalism, he found a way out for the embattled middle class of industrial society in general.

Frederick Winslow Taylor was born on 20 March 1856 on the outskirts of Philadelphia. His mother was one of the early suffragists,

48. Ibid., 1:39 and passim.   49. Ibid., 1:58-59.

who at the age of twenty had accompanied Lucretia Mott to London as a delegate to the International Anti-Slavery Convention of 1842. His father was an upper middle-class lawyer, described by his son as mild-mannered and with a "gentleness which was almost that of a woman."[50] Fred was destined for Harvard and a law career similar to his father's, when his plans changed drastically.

At sixteen, Fred and his nightmare machine went to Exeter, where within two years, because of the strain of excessive studying, he developed a mysterious affliction of the eyes. This ailment, which some authors infer was psychosomatic, prevented him from attending college, although he did pass the entrance examination for Harvard.[51] Without a profession and without capital, he had no choice but to languish at home or to venture forth into the world of salaried employment. And that world was more simply constituted in those days. The gulf between the petty clerkship and the free professional was considerably wider than that between the clerk and the laborer. That last resort of the young and inexperienced middle-class job seeker, the civil service examination, did not yet exist. To escape the boredom of inactivity at home, Fred Taylor began an apprenticeship as a factory worker. At the Enterprise Hydraulic Works he undertook to learn the skilled trades of patternmaker and machinist.

The plunge into the working class of a respectable hero and/or gentleman was an event depicted often in novels in those days; the typical story-line showed the hero's intrinsic merit in even sharper contrast against the background of the depraved lower classes, thereby justifying his inevitable rise to wealth and happiness in the last pages of the story. Taylor was well within the popular tradition of the self-flagellating, ragged rich when he entered the factory. In spite of the fact that he hated manual labor, he refused all clerking and accounting work in order to successfully learn a manual trade.[52] Since a friend of his father owned the factory, and because he could afford to work for minimal wages due to partial parental support, he completed his apprenticeship and advanced rapidly. Early in his success at his self-appointed task, his eyesight was miraculously restored, in spite of his heavy use of his eyes in the reading of detailed blueprints.

Unfortunately, it soon became apparent that the reality of factory life for a declassed bourgeois did not resemble at all the picture presented in fiction. No wealthy friends offered partnerships; no crusty old gentlemen offered capital and presidencies. Without professional training, Taylor had to search for a way that was not commonly available:

> I remember very distinctly the perfectly astonishing awakening at the end of six months of my apprenticeship, when I discovered that the three other young men who were with me in the pattern shop were all smarter than I was. Now when a young man gets it clearly into his head that he is made of the same kind of clay, physically as well as mentally, as these other men, then he sees that his only hope not to be outstripped in the race lies in a better education.[53]

But college education seemed farther than ever out of reach from the perspective of the factory floor. Taylor vacillated between his craving to distinguish himself, and the cultivation of an aggressively plebeian front which only partly disguised his hatred and envy of the "snobs" who occasionally found themselves in the factory. The situation was made all the worse by a depression in the early 1870s which forced him to take work as an ordinary laborer after his apprenticeship.

> Shortly after serving my apprenticeship, I worked in a shop under the superintendence of a college graduate. His natural carriage led him to hold his head rather high in the air, and he had an imperturbable face. Every day he would walk through the shop, hardly saying anything to any of the workmen. In addition to this, he had the habit of using a silk handkerchief with perfume on it. This was not only disliked, but cordially hated by all the men. They could stand the silk handkerchief with perfume, but the corner of the handkerchief which he always left sticking out of the breast pocket of his coat was too much for them, and I must say that I personally cordially shared that feeling. In later years I discovered that he was a very kindly man.[54]

There was a career path midway between manual labor and the gentility that Taylor craved, and this was the "profession" of engineering, then in the throes of becoming a systematized "science" with a recognized status. Much of engineering was still to be learned on the factory floor, although the best new engineers were college trained. In the 1870s, however, even college engineers lacked the status of other college graduates—but the field was not yet closed to ambitious and intelligent young men who lacked formal training, as were the other

53. Ibid., 2:273.   54. Ibid., 1:130.

professions. Taylor's experiences at work let him see clearly that this was the only recognized path out of the working class, and he resolved to become an engineer, to use every available chance to design machinery as his own mechanical bent directed him, and to take night-school engineering courses at the Stevens Institute.

One of the experiences that ranked most important in Taylor's mind at this time was his association with one of the last and the greatest of the old empirical engineers, John Fritz. He was fascinated by the process of trial and error that this pioneer of the Bessemer process used to design machinery. Drawing on the floor with a piece of chalk, or on the floor of the blacksmith shop itself with a stick, Mr. Fritz showed the workmen the design of the machine he wished built. The first model was not expected to work, but after he had studied it, Mr. Fritz could remedy the defects in the second machine. Taylor was amazed at the process; he took it as a prototype of the development of a science from intuition and craft skills which served him as a model the rest of his life. His judgment of the process reveals much about his own attitudes:

> The Science of Engineering started only when a few experts (who were invariably despised and sneered at by the engineers of their day) made the assertion that engineering practice should be founded upon exact knowledge of facts rather than upon general experience and observation.[55]

Taylor did not stop at machine design; engineering could only be a disappointment in the long run, for it became more and more evident that it was a closing field. Taylor also had his problems as an engineer. His machines were ingenious, but tended to be overly elaborate and costly for the job. Frequently, they duplicated the operations of previously existing or simpler machines. His love of invention would run away with him, and he was not "up" on the field. The results added to his fast-growing reputation as a "nut" with a "monkey mind." The views of his employers may be summarized in a conversation Taylor had several years after this period of manic engineering, when he happened to run into one of his old bosses in a hotel lobby:

> "Hello, Taylor, what are you doing now?" inquired his former employer.

Taylor replied that he was systematizing the Cramp shipyards, and inquired how things were for his former chief.

---

55. Ibid., 1:101-2, quotes lengthy excerpts from one of Taylor's speeches, in which he describes traditional engineering.

"Oh, . . . I am doing fine. I am making a lot of money. And do you know what I am going to do when I have made a few more millions? I am going to build the finest insane asylum this world has ever known, and you, Taylor, are going to have there an entire floor."[56]

Very early in his working life, Taylor had become aware of the great problem of the era, industrial productivity and the control of labor. He saw clearly, too, that whoever developed a solution to this problem might rise to great prominence. From Taylor's vantage point and with Taylor's conscience, it was clear that having once seen the need, he would not rest until he could devise some sort of answer. The great contrast of his new life in industry with his former existence gave him fresh insights, as did his divided loyalties to his father's friends who owned the plants, and to the laborers of his own age who combined illegally to slow down work in order to earn a living wage. But most of all, he saw the industrial situation as one of chaos, corruption, and vice run rampant, which must inevitably bring it to ruin in the absence of new plans to restore it to virtue.

> Throughout my apprenticeship, I had my eye on the bad industrial conditions which prevailed at the time, and gave a good deal of time and thought to some possible remedy for them.[57]

Knowing Taylor's background, what else would he use to curb "disorder" (that is, informal organization and soldiering) in the factory but the devices he had used to control his own secret impulses? In place of Fred Taylor, the rule-maker in children's games, was Fred Taylor, the interpreter of science, who told workers and management how to behave, gaining power from his knowledge of the elaborate rules of his own system.

Much as Saint-Simon before him, Taylor saw science as a moral system taking the place of a dying Christianity in the new industrial order. The machine, with its universally imposed discipline, was the visible symbol of that new moral order. The machine that had once controlled the chaos of his adolescent dream life would now bring habits of order to the sinfully self-indulgent lower classes, and thus bring peace to industrial society. Borrowing a technique from an old prep school teacher who timed students with a stopwatch, Taylor installed "scientific" time study of jobs as the missing key to the piece-rate puzzle. Now there could be one impartial measure of a day's

56. Ibid., 1:120.   57. Ibid., 1:130.

work. Industry could now make higher profits while paying higher wages to the "virtuous" worker and punishing only the lazy. Industrial peace would bring social peace. Hand in hand with peace would come the reign of virtue, when vice would be cast down from its place of power by the science of factory management!

The pattern by which the solution to industrial problems would be imposed, however, is an interesting one. It was clearly modeled on the gradual professionalization of engineering; the bearers of the "scientific" solution to the problems of social organization would not only be blessed by virtue of the message they carried; they would become respected, wealthy, and independent men (the Protestant "riches reward virtue" concept). And Frederick Winslow Taylor would be first among them! This idea is so clear in Taylor's writings that there is no doubt as to why one commentator refers to Taylor's final quarrels with Gantt and Gilbreth as "expulsions from the church."[58] Taylorism had from its beginnings a driving moralism that, without a doubt, could be somewhat unpleasant to those not in control of the movement.

Symbolic of the Taylor system's inherent bid for middle-class social mobility is the continual plaintive demand that Taylor makes for a "special room" for the scientific manager, where all of the special records, handbooks, charts, and slide rules might be kept. The room would not be in the executive offices, but near the actual working areas. And yet while near the factory floor, it clearly was to be separate from it—midway between labor and management spacially, symbolically, and organizationally. The separate room represented the "space" of the new job—not just literally, but in terms of an accepted degree of status, a separate life and work pattern.

Frequently, Taylor's battles to install Scientific Management in a plant are described in terms of the acceptance of the "planning room." Were the slide rules and records burned by Taylorism's opponents? Did the planners have to work, like foremen, on the factory floor? As a laborer, Taylor worked shoulder-to-shoulder with other laborers, fought with them, exchanged curses with them, and amazed his middle-class friends by inviting them home to dinner. His parting of the ways with the laboring class, and his craving to return to "his own" status lay behind his demand for a separate room, which began at the same time as Scientific Management itself.

In the end, Taylor had his "special room"—and in it were all of the

58. Haber, p. 34.

time-study experts, planners, management engineers, and clerks that his system called for. A whole new rank of middle-class, white-collar jobs was now available in the production process. They offered new goals for the would-be members of the middle class, who had been formerly frozen out of the new production organizations that had been expanding and taking over the economy. That these comfortable professional positions, including the freedom of the best of them from responsibility to the organization itself, had been purchased at the price of binding the levels beneath them even more tightly into the organization, was not a thought that troubled the new middle class as it rushed to fill them. The true value of the price paid for a successfully operating system under these terms was not to become apparent for many decades, when it was far, far too late to change, or even regret, the bargain.

> Fred Taylor
> inventor of efficiency
> who had doubled the production of the stamping mill
> by speeding up the main lines of shafting from ninetysix
> to twohundred and twentyfive revolutions a minute
>
> . . . .
>
> more steel rails more bicycles more spools of thread
> more armorplate for battleships more bedpans more barbedwire
> more needles more lightningrods more ballbearings more
> dollarbills;
>
> . . . .
>
> the American plan.
> But Fred Taylor never saw the working of the American
> plan;
> in 1915 he went to the hospital in Philadelphia
> suffering from a breakdown
> All his life he'd had the habit of winding his watch
> every afternoon at fourthirty;
> on the afternoon of his fiftyninth birthday, when the
> nurse went into his room to look at him at fourthirty,
> he was dead with his watch in his hand.
>
> from "The American Plan"
> *The Big Money*, John Dos Passos

CHAPTER 2

The National Crusade for Scientific Management

My dream is that the time will come when every drill press will be speeded just so, and every planer, every lathe the world over will be harmonized just like musical pitches are the same all over the world. . . . That dream will come true, some time.

CARL G. BARTH[1]

Scientific Management was not an immediate popular success. Following Taylor's first publications, it became an esoteric skill confined to a few devoted followers and a handful of experimenting companies. And although Taylorism had universal aspirations from the start, its transformation from a minor cult into a national trademark was as much the result of an accident of publicity, as the continued efforts of the small band of hardy practitioners who first translated Scientific Management from a personal vision into a working technique. Unlike these first efforts, the "efficiency craze" that followed government investigation of railroad operations in 1911 was centered more on the ideological than on the technical elements of Taylorism. This craze invaded every phase of national life, finding a broad base of support in the reform-oriented middle class. By the second decade of the twentieth century the concepts of efficiency engineering had in some form invaded every trade journal, newspaper, and household manual in the country. And by the time the fad had run its course, it had left indelible traces on American organizational thinking. Taylorism, the property of specialists, had become Scientific Management, the major technique of modern organization.

TAYLOR'S DISCIPLES

The transformation of Taylorism into Scientific Management was above all due to the ability of Frederick Taylor himself to attract a

1. Carl G. Barth, in testimony to the U.S. Commission on Industrial Relations, as cited by Haber, p. 36.

43

group of fervent, disciplined followers. These disciples of Taylor's, who developed and protected the Taylor system as a specific body of knowledge, had many personal characteristics in common; as individuals, they reflected the social traumas of industrialism in life patterns curiously like Taylor's own. These characteristics were such as to predispose them to Taylor and to what he represented: rigid logic in place of custom and superstition, and the triumph of aggressive rationality over chaos.

Descriptions of Taylor leave no doubt as to his charismatic qualities: his violence in pursuit of Right, his willingness to face overwhelming odds, the strength of the repressed, quarrelsome brand of friendship that he offered, and his "mesmeric intensity."[2] Of the many that were attracted, Taylor weeded out all but those who most closely resembled himself. The patronizing ladies, ambitious but undisciplined college men, and opportunists of various types were discarded. They were to return at the time of the efficiency craze, but they were not among the first promoters of Scientific Management. Those who remained in Taylor's group were selected for qualities which both resembled Taylor and were at the same time well adapted to the spreading of Taylorism as a system of organization. This similarity in personality patterns is apparent even though the biographical data on Taylor's immediate disciples is often not as complete as that on Taylor himself.[3]

Taylor's earliest and closest followers appear to have been what might be called self-made technocrats, who, like Horatio Alger's heroes, overcame great difficulties to pursue successful engineering careers. When one looks closely at their lives, it is clear that, like Taylor, each of them was "declassed" and then restored to the middle class. Energy, self-discipline, and like-mindedness characterize these early apostles of efficiency; the blunt realism and often profane language that their biographers considered typical of the group are a strange contrast to their lofty ideals of universal harmony through social engineering. A strain of quirky asceticism runs through the little

2. Copley, 2:122, 167, 185, repeats the testimony of witnesses as to Taylor's "magnetism," and so forth.
3. Although several outstanding biographies exist for the leading figures in the movement, notably Taylor, Gantt, and the Gilbreths, material on other figures is sketchy; the best collective biographies are those compiled by Lyndall Urwick in vol. 1 of *The Making of Scientific Management*, 3 vols. (London: Management Publications Trust, 1949) and in *The Golden Book of Management* (London: Newman Neame, 1956).

group, although none appear to reach the depths of masochism represented by Taylor's nightmare machine. And it is perhaps an odd, if not significant, coincidence that they appear to be products of homes run by women, where the father was either absent altogether or relatively passive. All appear to have married strong-minded women, and one of the wives, Lillian Moller Gilbreth, became a pioneer of efficiency engineering in her own right, carrying on her husband's business after his premature death from heart failure.

One of Taylor's earliest associates, for example, was Henry Laurence Gantt, inventor of the Gantt chart for planning work output, and of a supervisory bonus system for raising productivity, and an early advocate of "democracy in industry." Gantt's father, a plantation owner, died after being financially ruined by the Civil War. Gantt himself left home at the age of twelve to enter a military farm school for poor boys, and eventually put himself through Johns Hopkins. Known to be blustery in disposition, a migraine sufferer, he loathed both religion and preachers, and when his wife dragged him to church on Sunday shortly after their marriage, he so insulted the minister that he was never asked back. Unlike Taylor, whose wife arranged to adopt children, Gantt had one child; his wife opposed his plans to adopt Belgian war orphans. In his later years, Gantt did government as well as private consulting work, and came to oppose what he called the debating society theory of democracy in favor of running government according to the laws of physics. Before his death in 1919, he produced a number of works on industrial organization and leadership. Through his analysis of industrial productivity, he predicted that a major economic depression would come in the next decade.[4]

Little is known of Carl G. Barth's formative years before his immigration to the United States at the age of twenty-one. His father was a scientist. The best mathematician of the group, Barth invented the Barth slide rule for translating the results of the Taylor lathe-speed experiments into a systematic formula readily available to the individual workman. Among Taylor's close associates, he was considered the most orthodox practitioner of the Taylor system; he, too, dreamed of a universal harmony of industrial culture that would result from systematic rationalization and standardization. Described as a blunt,

4. See L. P. Alford, *Henry Laurence Gantt: Leader in Industry* (New York: Harper & Bros., 1932), Urwick, *Golden Book of Management*, pp. 89-93, Wallace Clark, *The Gantt Chart: A Working Tool of Management* (New York: Pitman Publishing Co., 1925).

fiery-tempered Norwegian, Barth was even accused by Taylor of lacking tact, a circumstance that Taylor's biographer referred to as the pot calling the kettle black. It was Barth who, in 1908, convinced the dean of the newly opened Harvard Business School to accept the Taylor system as the standard of modern management. Before his retirement, Barth held lectureships at both Harvard and the University of Chicago.[5]

Of this group, perhaps it was Frank Bunker Gilbreth, inventor of motion study, and his wife, Lillian Moller Gilbreth, codevelopers of many specialized branches of work and fatigue study, that achieved the most lasting popular reputation. Their attachment to the principles of efficient mass production in all aspects of life was transformed into permanent Americana in the sentimental memoir *Cheaper by the Dozen*, written by two of their twelve children. Gilbreth was the schismatic among Taylor's followers. Forced by financial hardship after his father's death to abandon his plans to attend Massachusetts Institute of Technology, he took an apprenticeship as a bricklayer. On the job he developed his own method of the scientific study of labor (motion study) which differed radically in spirit from Taylor's basically antilabor stance. For Frank Gilbreth liked and was good at manual labor; a union man, he was used to working with the elite of American labor, the independent craftsmen of New England. From this beginning, he built a highly successful, international contracting business. His first book, *Field System*, was a secret organization manual for his company; numbered copies were kept locked up, and Gilbreth employees were approached with bribes by business rivals eager to learn the secrets of his success.[6] Gilbreth's work on bricklaying was "discovered" by Taylor, who cited him in his writings, and

5. See *National Cyclopaedia of American Biography*, s.v. "Barth, Carl G." (New York: J.T. White and Co., 1927), Urwick, *Golden Book of Management*, pp. 80-82, Florence M. Manning, "Carl G. Barth, 1860-1939: A Sketch," in *Norwegian-American Studies and Records*, vol. 13 (Northfield, Minn.: Norwegian-American Historical Association, 1943).

6. Among the methods of *Field System* thus to be enshrined in American management practice and then transferred to government contracting (to the grief of the government) was the CPFF system, called by Gilbreth the "cost-plus-a-fixed-sum" contract. It originally worked to the benefit of both contractor and buyer when it was used to construct buildings for MIT. It involved, however, a simple technology and completely open accounting, with the books always available to the purchaser. See William R. Spriegel, *The Writings of the Gilbreths* (Homewood, Ill.: R.D. Irwin, 1953).

Gilbreth, in a moment of ideological fervor, joined Taylor and abandoned his business, going on to develop an even more successful second business in management consulting.

Gilbreth had planned from the first to train his wife to be his partner, and the intellectual abilities of Lillian Moller, one of the few women who held a master's degree at that time, attracted him. Their partnership was highly productive; he encouraged her to complete her Ph.D. in psychology, the first doctorate in the group that was not *honoris causa*. Her humanistic and social-science training considerably broadened the approach of Scientific Management. Coauthoring and writing alone, she worked in the application of motion study to nearly everything, from the factory and office to the home. Although she had difficulty when she sought admission to the meetings of the Society for the Advancement of Management, and was on one occasion refused a seat on the grounds that she was a woman, she persisted in her writing and consulting work after her husband's death, and eventually developed a distinguished reputation of her own.[7]

Although the quarrels in the Taylor group were, in general, epic, the most passionate and longstanding quarrel was between Gilbreth and Taylor. Taylor laid claim to Gilbreth's independently invented "motion study," stating that it was an implicit factor in his own "time study," and that he had, in fact, invented "time-and-motion study"; he implied that Gilbreth had been commissioned merely to work out the details. Gantt also differed with Taylor, finally breaking with him over the punitive emphasis in the piece-rate system; he advocated in its place a "task-and-bonus" system, and emphasized managerial responsibility for teaching the work force to a degree Taylor disapproved of. But these quarrels, although glossed over in the official histories, were a part of a larger *odi et amo* relationship that had begun with a genuine and passionate devotion of the Chosen to Taylor and his principles. It is even tempting, noting the strength and storminess of these relationships, to speculate that they were somehow bound up with the substitution of the autocratic, domineering, and beneficent F. W. Taylor for the missing father figure in the lives of his

7. See Lillian Gilbreth, *The Quest of the One Best Way; A Sketch of the Life of Frank Bunker Gilbreth* [n. p., 1925]; Frank B. Gilbreth, Jr., and Ernestine Gilbreth Carey, *Cheaper by the Dozen* (New York: T. Y. Crowell Co., 1948); Edna Yost, *Frank and Lillian Gilbreth: Partners for Life* (New Brunswick, N.J.: Rutgers University Press, 1948); Urwick, *Golden Book of Management*, pp. 138-43.

associates. And it is interesting to note that the sanctification of Taylor by the creation of the Taylor Society (renamed for Taylor after his death and against his wishes) was carried out by the greatest of the rebels, among them Frank Gilbreth.[8]

Technical training and common experience unified the thought and activities of these first followers of Taylor. Like him, they were products of an era that had given them the conviction that the world required salvation through technology. And Taylor, in spite of his blustering, did not impose organization on his followers. True to the Protestant model of the inner-directed man, they moved together in the same direction, motivated more by internal ideology than by external organization, even though their principal concern was the construction of such organizations for the motivation of others. Their ideology was to a large extent pre-existing, and needed only to be systematized by people whose characters reflected near-identical, internal order. Taylor's organizational model was grasped intrinsically from the first by these people, and the intense partisan attachment which it evoked merely prepared the way for the more detailed teachings (experimental findings) of the Master.

As the Taylorites developed practices of their own, this pattern of "running together" tended to break up, as their own experimental findings differed. Too late did Taylor try to impose his own findings as "received truth" upon the heretics. By basing his teachings on a system of rational experimentation, he made them open to question by those very laws of science that he claimed justified his supreme authority over the movement. But his followers, moved by their own inner voices, set up experiments which proved their points, not Taylor's; by so doing, they broke down his authority, which he had tied to the truth of *his* system. And so they quarreled over the universal necessity for the piece rate, for antiunionism, for time study. Yet through this quarreling, as we shall see, they broadened the armory of techniques

8. Yost, pp. 186-89, not only describes Gilbreth's important role in the founding and operations of the society, but the obscuring of this role in the official Taylorite histories.

The activities of the Gilbreths and others resulted in the establishment of the Management Division of the ASME in 1920, the American Management Association being founded shortly afterward. In 1910, Gilbreth had organized the Society to Promote the Science of Management, which was renamed the Taylor Society after Taylor's death in 1915. Later, the Taylor Society merged with the Society of Industrial Engineers, forming the Society for the Advancement of Management.

available to Scientific Management without changing the central elements in its philosophy. Scientific Management thus became more flexible, and better able to survive when the anti-Taylor reaction set in; in the end, it was this flexibility that, in large part, helped it gain universality.

THE FIRST TAYLORIZED INDUSTRIES

The first enterprises to adopt Taylorism were perhaps more unusual than the Taylorites themselves, for they represented a paradox: they were large and successful on their own terms, and yet were willing to change over to a little-known management system. As Babcock of the Franklin Company remarked, before the great publicity boom, Taylorism was largely unknown, and "practically untried except by Dr. F. W. Taylor and a few close friends in sympathy with him."[9]

Under these conditions, the adoption of Taylorism was a daring step, especially since the methods already in use were considered to be completely modern and successful. For example, it required the impetus of a business slump (in 1907) and more than four years of studies under the tutelage of Carl Barth before the decision was finally made to operate the Franklin automobile plant according to the principles of Scientific Management.[10] The struggle to install Taylorism in other plants was no less difficult. Yet it was upon this handful of companies, the showplaces of Scientific Management, that the publicity boom and subsequent managerial fad for Taylorism depended.

There has been considerable controversy over the precise number of these pioneer Taylorizing firms since the early days of the efficiency fad, when the process of accounting for their number was hindered by the refusal of some scientific managers to disclose the names of their clients; in the wake of highly publicized, national-labor opposition, companies also refused to reveal Scientific Management consulting contracts. In a recent work, Daniel Nelson has developed a list of firms Taylorized between 1901 and 1917; he indicates that, in eighteen of them, work was begun before 1911, the year that efficiency fever overtook the United States in the wake of the Eastern Rates case.[11]

9. George D. Babcock, *The Taylor System in Franklin Management* (New York: Engineering Magazine Co., 1917), intro.
10. Ibid.
11. Daniel Nelson, *Managers and Workers: Origins of the New Factory*

Accounting after that date is considerably complicated by the numerous organizations that developed partial applications of Taylorism without consulting Taylor and his associates, as well as by the fact that, as Alfred D. Chandler puts it, "no factory owner, even those who consulted Taylor or his disciples, adopted the Taylor system without modifying it."[12]

System in the United States, 1880-1920 (Madison: University of Wisconsin Press, 1975), pp. 68-78. His list is as follows:

FIRMS INTRODUCING SCIENTIFIC MANAGEMENT, 1901-17

Firm	Principal Taylor Expert	Time
Tabor Mfg., Philadelphia	Barth, Hathaway	1903-
Stokes and Smith, Philadelphia	Gantt	1902-3?
Link-Belt Engr., Philadelphia	Barth	1903-7
Sayles Bleachery, Saylesville, R.I.	Gantt	1904-8
Yale & Towne, Stamford, Conn.	Barth	1905-7
Santa Fe Railraod, Topeka, Kan.	Emerson	1904-7
Brighton Mills, Passaic, N.J.	Gantt	1905-8
Ferracute Machine, Bridgeton, N.J.	Parkhurst	1907-10
H. H. Franklin, Syracuse, N.Y.	Barth	1908-9, 1911
Canadian Pacific Railroad, Montreal	Gantt	1908-11
Smith & Furbush Machine, Philadelphia	Barth	1908-10
Joseph Bancroft & Sons, Wilmington, Del.	Gantt	1908-9
Plimpton Press, Norwood, Mass.	Cooke, Hathaway, Godfrey	1908-12
Remington Typewriter, Illion, N.Y.	Gantt	1910-17
Forbes Lithograph, Boston	Cooke, Barth	1910-12
Joseph & Feiss, Cleveland	Feiss	1910-
S. L. Moore, Elizabeth, N.J.	Barth	1911-12
Amoskeag Mills, Manchester, N.H.	Gantt	1911-12
Cheney Brothers, So. Manchester, Conn.	Gantt	1912-18
New England Butt, Providence, R.I.	Gilbreth	1912-13
Lewis Mfg., Walpole, Mass.	Keely	1912-13
Herrmann, Aukam, South River, N.J.; Lebanon, Pa.	Gilbreth, Hathaway	1912-15
Pullman Palace Car, Chicago	Barth	1913-19
Baird Machine, Bridgeport, Conn.	Barth, Keely	1913-14
Eaton, Crane & Pike, Pittsfield, Mass.	C. B. Thompson	1913-15
Eastern Mfg., Bangor, Me.	S. E. Thompson	1914-17
Winchester Repeating Arms, Bridgeport, Conn.	Barth	1916-
Watertown Arsenal, Watertown, Mass.	Barth	1909-13
Mare Island Shipyard, Vallejo, Calif.	Evans	1906-11

12. Alfred. D. Chandler, Jr., *The Visible Hand: The Managerial Revolution in American Business* (Cambridge, Mass.: Harvard University Press, Belknap Press, 1977), p. 277. The chief modification that many firms made was to eliminate functional foremanship.

A brief discussion of some of the first Taylorized plants illuminates not only the unusual character of these enterprises, but the methods by which Taylor gained entry. Both point to the idea that even when Taylorism was in its most technical stage, ideological elements were a strong influence in its diffusion.

It has been noted that much of the "success" of Taylorism depends upon a specific world-view, one that was not the common outlook of either management or labor in the 1880s. In spite of Taylor's attempt to "prove" success in dollar terms (the Taylor accounting system), the real superiority of the system could only be perceived by those whose aesthetic values resembled Taylor's. Those without positive empathy toward the vision of a neat, sober, individualized, hierarchical factory life, where all machines ran at the same speed and all effort was concentrated on the rapid performance of individual tasks, reacted with passionate enmity. Yet passion did not prevent such people from seeing in some detail the dysfunctions of the factory system. They saw the factory—in which men, women, and children spent over one-half of every twenty-four hours—as a place of personal interaction and affective, informal, group activity, where hierarchies were based on craftsmanship as well as on capital, social class, and the personal exercise of power. These two different visions of the factory could not coexist. Taylor's problem was the conversion of both traditional labor and traditional management, both subscribing to the latter view, to his own view. His efforts essentially revolved around the search for marginal individuals who did not subscribe to the common vision; he then cemented alliances with them.

In particular, Taylorism in the early stages needed management advocates in order to get a hearing; Taylor found them among those men with scientific interests, or former engineers, who had found a place among the big capitalists (termed "financiers" by the Taylorites) in management. Taylor did not hesitate to use old friendships and family connections to reinforce such bonds of common perception. Only men like Taylor, in the sense that they valued scientific investigation and the experimental approach above the common-sense truths and traditional modes of evaluation, had the blind spots (or vision, if you will) that kept them from perceiving the damage produced by the system, and kept their minds firmly fixed on the benefits. Such men could advocate Taylorism in spite of "class interest," and use their power to hold the organization together during the "hell period," which Taylor himself admitted was the first stage in the transition to Scientific Management.

It is interesting to note that this type of owner-convert very closely resembles the original "captain of industry" to whom Veblen attributes the growth and success of the industrial revolution. They were owner-inventors who combined mechanical, directing, and financial talents in a way that had been more common in the days of Boulton and Watt, and that was apparently vanishing in the era of "financier management."[13]

<h2 style="text-align:center">MIDVALE STEEL:
BIRTHPLACE OF SCIENTIFIC MANAGEMENT</h2>

In listing the companies which first employed Scientific Management, we must begin with the Midvale Steel Company, which was the last word in management in 1878 when it hired Taylor, then aged twenty-two, as a common laborer. The company was jointly owned by a banker, E. W. Clark, an old family friend of the Taylors, and William Sellers, a highly competent engineer who had not only made a reputation as an inventor and designer of machine tools, but as head of the successful machine-tool manufacturing company which had bought out Midvale.[14] Sellers was deeply involved in the newest ideas of applying systematic science to production; he attracted a number of young and enthusiastic chemists and metallurgists to Midvale. Some of Sellers' own standardizations of machine tools looked much like the first technical elements of the later Taylor system. In addition, Taylor was a good friend of Clark's son. For many years they hoped to gain control of Midvale, with Taylor handling the technical end of the business. Taylor's supervisors were all scientifically trained and looked with favor upon his experimental efforts. This favorable environment at Midvale saw Taylor rapidly appointed as chief engineer, and provided an inspiration in terms of giving examples of *technological* systematization; it made it possible for Taylor to get a hearing when he proposed a new kind of *organizational* systematization of time study and piece rates to control soldiering among the work force. In addition to providing an atmosphere favorable to invention, Midvale, and the Sellers plant before it, brought together a coalition of technical people and technically minded financiers that

13. Thorstein Veblen, *The Engineers and the Price System* (New York: Viking Press, 1921), pp. 32-34.
14. Copley, 1:110-342, provides a detailed description of Taylor's employment at Midvale Steel.

provided a web of connections which was to supply Taylor with jobs and with assistants even when his "system" met with enmity and even failure in plant after plant. Gantt was recommended, via Stevens Institute, to be Taylor's assistant,[15] and Barth, Wilfred Lewis and Henry Towne (of the gain-sharing plan) were all employed at one time as draftsmen at Sellers.

Taylor's system of management was nearly fully formed by the time he left Midvale in 1890. It involved piecework backed by a special accounting system, techniques for the systematization of machine shops, Taylor's first experiments in metal-cutting, and a plan for "functional foremanship" which gave quasi-professional independence to foreman-specialists. The dualism in Taylorism's approach to power—absolute for Taylor, but weakened for those who directed him—ultimately emerged in the contradictory approaches toward functional foremanship by Taylor himself. Functional foremanship appears to have been a product of Taylor's early thought, when the principal drive of his career was directed toward professional independence. The operational style of the functional foreman appears to resemble that of Taylor; the "teaching" relationship that the foreman has with his men is stressed, as well as his independence of judgment within his technical specialty. This extension of technical supervision was purchased at the cost of dividing up line authority, thus arousing the criticism of management.[16] Later in Taylor's career, when he had succeeded in freeing himself from line authority in the plant by establishing himself as a professional consultant, he gave less emphasis to functional foremanship.

THE LESSONS OF TAYLOR'S EARLY FAILURES

The pattern of violent internal dissension which followed Taylor's entry into a company was established as soon as he left the safe shelter provided by a management of engineers and went to work for "financiers," for whom he conceived a lifelong hatred. Not only were these gentlemen intolerant of Taylor's quarrels with the established powers in their plants, but they lacked the engineers' understanding of why Taylor spent so much money on long-range technological improvements. Taylor, in his turn, did not understand the business

15. Alford, p. 79.
16. See Luther Gulick and Lyndall Urwick, eds., *Papers in the Science of Administration* (New York: Institute of Public Administration, 1937).

cycle. (Or rather, he did not *approve* of it, which amounted to the same thing.) Leaving Midvale for the Manufacturing Investment Company, he sank his savings into a stock option deal (one of the owners had promised to make him a millionaire) at the same time that he was employed to supervise technical operations and introduce his system. The system ran into the usual problems; the heavy expenses incurred in the change-over alienated management, and before any long-range benefits could be attained, the company went broke in the business panic of 1893. Taylor departed under mysterious circumstances, divested of both job and savings by the "financiers." His conclusion was an important one for Scientific Management as a system of free professionalism: he decided that *the systematizer must be independent of responsibilities as a manager*, and he turned to consulting.

Yet while Taylor demanded financial independence and patent rights, when he was engaged to install his system, he insisted on having absolute authority. These demands soured his relations with a number of companies, such as the Simonds Rolling Machine Company (where Gantt played so large a part), which was liquidated shortly after the introduction of Scientific Management.[17] Despite the death of the patients, the operation was hailed as a technical success among specialists. But the suspicions of businessmen about efficiency systems are not to be wondered at, given the circumstances.

BETHLEHEM STEEL: THE TURNING POINT

Taylor's next important operation was at Bethlehem Steel, where he was offered a job through one of his old Midvale connections. On arriving to systematize the Bethlehem machine shops and to introduce piecework, he found the plant and the town itself divided into opposing factions. His reputation as a dangerous crank had preceded him. Taylor brought in Gantt and Barth, and allied himself with the established engineers in the plant. Joseph Wharton (founder of the Wharton School of Business and Finance) was unusually interested in the business value of science; he was also one of the directors of Bethlehem. Taylor formed an alliance with him over the head of the president of the company, and got the approval for the heavy expenses of his experiments by a series of end-runs, in opposition to the business-minded management, which continually attempted to curb what they considered his excessive spending. The experiments paid

17. Alford, p. 81.

off; while investigating machine speeds, the experimenters discovered high-speed steel. So shrewdly did Taylor set up production, allying high-speed steel with Gantt's bonus plan and Barth's slide rule, that, in order for high-speed steel to be used at all economically, it had to be used in conjunction with the Taylor system. Bethlehem's new tools, exhibited internationally, became a sensation,[18] and Taylor got the opportunity to advocate his system to every delegation of astonished foreign specialists that visited the plant.

In his wide-ranging activities, Taylor more than once crossed the president, who had hired a piece-rate expert, and got an agitator instead. The president complained to the directors that Taylor wanted higher wages for some of the piece-rate workers; Taylor wanted more money for his assistants; Taylor wanted expensive engineering changes in the equipment; Taylor fought with the bookkeeper; Taylor fought with *everybody*; in fact, this Taylor was nothing but trouble. When the costs he incurred appeared to be bringing losses in place of profit, the president went to see Wharton, and Taylor was fired. Salaries were then lowered, and all visible signs of the Taylor system forbidden. A few months later, the company was sold. Under the new regime, the "supernumeraries" (time-study men) were fired. Production dropped so drastically that the Taylor system was reintroduced in secret, by doctoring the books and hiding the slide rules and charts. When an accidental fire burned the records and tools, production again dropped, and the subsequent inquiry resulted in the official reinstatement of the Taylor system.

The differences between the previous and the reinstated version of the system, however, provided a forecast of Taylorism's brutal potential in the hands of management. The high wage differentials and shorter hours that Taylor advocated along with his system were dropped in favor of low standard wages, a twelve-hour day, and a seven-day week. In 1909 the workers went out on strike, and an investigating commission found conditions "a disgrace to civilization."[19] Taylorism had provided management with a technique of control that had no intrinsic limitations, making possible a quantum jump in industrial exploitation.

18. Urwick, *Making of Scientific Management*, 1:32, graphically describes the reaction of the British at this exhibition.

19. Taylor's work at Bethlehem Steel is described extensively in Copley, 2:161-80. The materials on Link-Belt and Tabor are summarized from Copley, 2:180-250, and from Urwick, *Golden Book of Management*, with exceptions noted below.

THE SHOWCASES OF TAYLORISM

Taylor's system had been born in the highly charged atmosphere of technological experimentation in the Midvale plant. Once exposed to the cold air of the business world, it crumbled, producing technological success and financial failure. In essence, the scheme was highly adapted to the types of organization where technology is the primary determinant of organizational values. Taylor's problems arose when he sold the scheme to plants where technology was not an ideological value in itself, but was in the service of other values—values set by other elements of the business or political community. One had to accept technological definitions of success to see the success of Taylorism; hence a "financier" could not look on the system with the loving eye of a godfather. Thus the series of "breaks" which led to the successful installation of the Taylor system were all provided by Taylor's old friends, the Midvale men—who were, in a sense, all godfathers of the system. Chief among these, for example, was William Sellers himself, who first bought the patents for high-speed steel and then sponsored Taylor's introduction of his system into the shops of William Sellers and Company. Taylorism collapsed at Sellers when its founder and his relatives retired, and his personal sponsorship came to an end.

The two great showcases of Scientific Management, Tabor and Link-Belt, were not originally converted to Taylorism on the grounds of rational inquiry. Although after the Scientific Management fad had begun, the example of these two companies helped to convert other businesses to Taylorite organization, Taylorism was accepted at the Tabor Manufacturing Company as part of a debt, and at Link-Belt as part of the ideological conversion of one of Taylor's personal friends. Wilfred Lewis, a boyhood friend of Taylor, who had risen from draftsman at Sellers to become a mechanical engineer, was one of the heads of the Tabor Company. Shortly after 1900, Tabor started to lose money; the process was accelerated by a series of strikes. With the new, higher wages, other companies were producing the same product at a lower cost, and the company went from selling stock to outright borrowing. Lewis went to his friends for money, among them Taylor. "Use my system," said Taylor, in effect, "or you shall have no money." In desperation, Lewis accepted, in spite of the fact that the genteel inhabitants of Philadelphia considered his friend a management crank. Straightaway, Barth, and then Taylor himself descended upon the Tabor plant, where they created the first showplace of Scientific Management. No Taylor lecture or tour was complete without a visit to, or at least a mention of, the advanced methods of the Tabor Company. From all accounts, the gratified Tabor management accepted their promotion to the status of management pioneers without regrets.

The second showcase of early Taylorism was the Link-Belt Company. Another of Taylor's personal friends, James Mapes Dodge, had founded a company which made industrial belting according to new designs which he had invented. Dodge was a fertile inventor, noted civic figure, and ebullient wit who had begun as a workman, after being forced to leave engineering school at Cornell because of lack of funds. Dodge was also an impulsive man, passionately fond of technological novelties. When his friend Taylor discovered high-speed steel, Dodge was stricken with speed mania.[20] He so infected his employees that the entire company undertook a prototypical Great Leap Forward, which ended with the breakdown of the machinery and the disruption of the machine shop. The profit from the increase in output was surpassed by the costs, and Dodge asked Taylor what should be done, thus becoming "the first purely voluntary Taylor executive." Taylor, of course, whipped out his instant plan and sent for Barth. Dodge promptly, according to one of his employees, "became enamored of the Taylor system." Thus the Link-Belt Company became the second of the famous Taylor "success" stories, which he used as a means of converting others. It was at this time that the tide began to turn for the Taylor system, and Taylor's biographer compares his record of conversion among mechanics and engineers to "the annals of Moody and Sankey." It is indeed no accident that the only way to describe the progress of Taylorism from this point onward is in terms of that honored American institution, the revival meeting.

The last of these crucial early conversions was at the Yale and Towne Company, manufacturers of Yale locks. Yale, the inventor, had died, leaving Towne, the technical and business brains of the partnership, to run the lock company.[21] Towne represented a unique combination of business ability, technical competence, and culture. Like the Taylorites, he had cut short his education (at the University

20. The effects of the first Scientific Management "speed-up" went generally unnoticed at the time, and were thus doomed to repetition. They closely resemble, for example, the disorders caused by Stakhanovism (see Chapter 4).

21. See also S. Giedion, *Mechanization Takes Command; A Contribution to Anonymous History* (New York: W. W. Norton, 1969), pp. 51-76.

of Pennsylvania) to become a draftsman and then an engineer. Unlike
the Taylorites, however, he had returned to school at the Sorbonne,
studying engineering and physics. Towne could, as an engineer and
employer, appreciate the Taylor system's goals, but his own inclina-
tions were somewhat less harsh and aggressive. He had invented a
profit-sharing plan for his own plant, and he felt that Taylor, in spite
of his friendship with him, was given to overstatement because of his
"very intense temperament." Towne was a cautious man: he did not
investigate the Taylor system for his own plant until he had seen it in
operation at the Tabor and Link-Belt plants. The careful studies he
insisted on before its installation were conducted by Barth in 1904.
Once converted, Towne put all his prestige and the prestige of his
company behind Taylor.

Not only was Towne instrumental in publicizing the system, but in
arranging Taylor's nomination to the presidency of the American
Society of Mechanical Engineers (ASME) in 1906, he assured the
Taylor system a national, and even international, forum. Taylor
guaranteed that his management system would forever be enshrined in
the profession of mechanical engineering by promptly reorganizing
the ASME itself according to his own principles, to the horror of its
conservative members.

THE EFFICIENCY FAD

*A very extraordinary thing has happened through a
Boston lawyer named Louis D. Brandeis . . .*

F.W. TAYLOR, January 1911
Letter to Admiral Goodrich[22]

In 1911, Taylorism was transformed overnight from an obscure
obsession of certain middle-class engineers to an amazing and highly
publicized nostrum for all the ills of society. The circumstances were
as follows. In 1910, in an emotionally charged atmosphere of opposition among the literate, muckraker-oriented middle class, the Eastern Railroads asked the Interstate Commerce Commission for an
increase in freight rates.[23] It is no accident that the leading sector of
expansion for the new big business economy, the railroads, was
labeled the "octopus" responsible for the price squeeze on the hard-

22. Copley, 2:367.   23. Haber, p. 51.

pressed farmers and older, urban middle classes whose political response had fueled the populist and progressive movements. The railroad increase represented the kind of parasitic middleman costs which were blamed for the increasing of prices to urban consumers at the very time that farmers, as producers, were receiving less. The moral fervor of the middle class was arrayed against the railroads, and so the Eastern Rates case was hot news, followed attentively in detailed reports in the daily press.

Louis Brandeis, who styled himself the "people's lawyer," serving without pay on the case, set about to prove that the rates should not be increased in spite of the railroads' increased costs. Remembering a conversation he had once had with Harrington Emerson, the "systematizer" of the Santa Fe railroad, he decided to base his case on the argument that, instead of raising rates, the railroads could cut costs by management reform. He spoke to Emerson. Emerson, who was not a Taylorite but a genial careerist who borrowed all the latest fashionable tricks, put him in touch with Taylor, Gantt, Gilbreth, Towne, and Dodge. Brandeis, from his first meeting with Taylor, fell under the spell of his "mesmerism" as thoroughly as any Gilbreth or Barth. In a series of meetings, he. mapped out his strategy with the Taylorites. Among other things, they needed a catchy, advanced-sounding name for their profession. After some debate, "Scientific Management" was hit upon. Thus was the Taylor system christened.

In this manner, the Eastern Rates case was converted from a trial of the railroads to a showcase for Scientific Management. Emerson took the stand and declared (sensation in the press) that the railroads could "save a million dollars a day."[24] Needless to say, the ensuing struggle of the witnesses for Scientific Management against those of the railroads was played up in the popular press as a struggle of light against darkness. Articles describing and explaining Scientific Management flourished not only in technical and semitechnical journals, but in intellectual magazines, ladies' magazines, and in the sensational yellow press. The boom was on.

The fashionable interest in Scientific Management was not without its unsavory side, however. So great was the demand for the services of the new scientific managers that a black market of get-rich-quick phonies of the most shoddy variety quickly sprang up. In the words of Professor Hoxie of the University of Chicago:

24. Urwick, *Golden Book of Management*, pp. 51-55.

The great rewards which a few leaders in the movement have secured for their services have brought into the field a crowd of industrial patent medicine men. The way is open to all. No standards or requirements, private or public, have been developed by the application of which the goats can be separated from the sheep. Employers have thus far proved credulous. Almost anyone can show the average manufacturing concern where it can make some improvements in its methods. So the scientific management shingles have gone up all over the country, the fakirs have gone into the shops, and in the name of scientific management have reaped temporary gains to the detriment of the real article, the employers and the workers.[25]

In the general enthusiasm for Scientific Management, the dysfunctions of the system were not closely examined. The quacks who brought strikes and organizational damage in their wake brought some popular revulsion, but not among the cognoscenti, who felt that "real" Scientific Management did not produce such consequences. This dissociation was encouraged by Taylor himself, who claimed that labor problems never occurred under "true" Scientific Management, but were instead caused by faulty management, impatience, or overeager assistants.

The documentation of the alliance between progressivism and Scientific Management provided by Samuel Haber, however, reveals that the bases of support for popular Taylorism were essentially middle-class "college men." These men of genteel pretensions and steadily decreasing financial and social influence saw in it a technique which would permit the expert professional to reassert control over a society that they had been pushed out of by a conspiracy of big capital and machine politics, which purchased the votes of the urban poor.[26] The middle-class backers of progressivism naturally supported the movement to "clean up" the factories and to reestablish the discipline of the working class that arose from the Scientific Management crusade. Efficiency in government and efficiency in industry went hand-in-hand.

When the working-class opposition to Scientific Management, in league with "corrupt politicians," managed to ban overt expressions of Taylorism in the installations of the federal government and its contractors, Taylorism survived because it had already become the private philosophy of "hardheaded businessmen." It had been built

25. R. F. Hoxie, *Scientific Management and Labor* (New York: D. Appleton Co., 1921), p. 117.
26. Haber, intro., pp. xii, and 116.

into business schools, and into the white-collar operations of government bureaucracies; it also comprised most of the scanty organizational training provided to professional engineers, thus gaining entry into the scientific, and especially military-scientific, operations that were to become a prominent feature of the new American technological society.

Haber follows the lead of many management historians who assume that Taylorism, while influential in its day, died with the formal end of progressivism.[27] Because Scientific Management gave rise to investigations of increasing sophistication into the nature of psychological interaction in organizations, it was assumed that management practice had evolved at the same rate as management theory,[28] leaving Taylorism as outmoded and abandoned as the phlogiston theory.

Yet as popular as it may be to assume that Taylorism vanished into the murky underworld reserved for dead pseudosciences, the notion that Taylorism is dead is quite mistaken. In the first place, while some of the original techniques of Taylorism, much like the early patents on high-speed steel, were indeed superseded, many of the practices first popularized by the Scientific Management movement continue in active use, under the original nomenclature devised by Taylor and his followers. Although many of the techniques are applied at increased levels of sophistication, they still form much of the foundation of efficiency in modern industries, and are considered neither peripheral nor quaint.

Not only have many of the techniques of the original Scientific Management system survived in continual use, but the discipline that grew out of the Scientific Management movement, and whose professional associations and training centers were founded by the original scientific managers, that is, industrial engineering, still exists, and has developed in the extent and variety of its applications. Its

27. Ibid., p. 74.
28. This change is, of course, exemplified by the increased psychological sophistication of Mayoism. Elton Mayo and his associates, noting the effects of informal groups on work, seem to negate Taylorism, but in the end, his discoveries were incorporated into broader "scientific" methods of control which one can only believe Mayo himself would have repudiated. William H. Whyte, in *The Organization Man* (New York: Doubleday & Co., 1957), describes how the entire apparatus of psychological testing and the manipulation of informal groups have been transformed into the scientific management of the white-collar and petty-executive classes themselves.

practitioners acknowledge with pride their intellectual origins in the Scientific Management movement, and they feel that the line of descent from Taylor and his associates is unbroken. Related disciplines derived from other sources, such as Operations Research (a series of complex mathematical techniques developed for decision-making in the Second World War, and known in its business application as Management Science), also acknowledge the pioneering role of Taylorism in some of the early approaches to the subject. And finally, Taylorism promoted the development of parallel schools of thought in government and general administration that incorporated most of its values, even when its techniques were not immediately applicable. In this latter sense, Taylorism indeed constituted a philosophy or "mental revolution" as its supporters claimed —it became a set of values concerning organization that spread far beyond the confines of factory organization and was not easily erased. Evolving beyond its technical and national origins, it became an important component of the philosophical outlook of modern industrial civilization, defining virtue as efficiency, establishing a new role for white-collar management experts in production, and setting parameters for new patterns of social distribution. Taylorism defined both the problems of industrialization and the solution in a single coherent system. Even if its techniques had entirely disappeared within a decade or two after its origin, which most decidedly did not happen, the mental revolution had been so deeply embedded in the structure of industrial society that it was a social philosophy that no longer could be casually abandoned.

A PERMANENT REVOLUTION
IN EFFICIENCY ENGINEERING

In assessing the impact of Scientific Management as a general philosophy of industrial society, it is essential not to overlook the immediate and permanent changes that the techniques of industrial management underwent with the efficiency craze of the 'teens and 'twenties. From this ongoing body of technique, the approaches and attitudes toward organization are continually renewed. It would have been surprising indeed if the scientific managers had failed to have a permanent impact on productivity assessment and industrial management, since this was the primary work of their careers. As any modern textbook on industrial engineering will testify, they were highly successful in founding a discipline that would have as its central concern the objective and quantified assessment of the impact of organizational and technical factors on industrial output.

For example, the *Industrial Engineering Handbook* depicts current practices in micromotion study and filmed motion study (begun by Gilbreth), time-and-motion study and wage-incentive determination (evolved since the days of Taylor's punitive piece-rate system but unchanged in its basic preconceptions), and flow-process charting and plant-layout analysis that show few departures from their turn-of-the-century models.[29] Another text, *Applying Industrial Engineering to Management Problems*, defines industrial engineering and describes its evolution and application in a number of leading American industries; it prefaces its prediction of the extension of industrial engineering's influence through constantly evolving techniques in the following manner:

> Industrial engineering is synonymous with change. Henry L. Gantt, Frank Gilbreth, and Frederick W. Taylor probably would not be surprised at the tremendous strides that have been achieved in industrial engineering since their early efforts. They would have demanded that the profession set its goals high because they laid the foundation on which they expected later generations to build. What will the future bring? It will bring change.[30]

This quotation and the examples that follow it make quite clear one of the problems in dealing with the history of Scientific Management, that of the internal change of the subject matter itself. This problem derives from the eclecticism of the original scientific managers and from their very success in creating a framework of stable values for incorporating new techniques. If a casual observer concentrates simply on technique without also looking at the stable framework of values in which technique is embedded, it is easy to overlook much of the continuity of the movement, despite the fact that many of the individual techniques generated by the movement have remained substantially the same in the intervening half-century. This point is illustrated in a standard management history text that details Taylor's contributions to Operations Research/Management Science, a discipline with many roots and one that does not directly owe its

29. H. B. Maynard, ed., *Industrial Engineering Handbook* (New York: McGraw-Hill, 1956), p. 4, fig. 1-1.

30. Alex W. Rathe and Frank M. Gryna, *Applying Industrial Engineering to Management Problems* (American Management Association, 1969), p. 33.

foundation to Taylor and the group around him. Giving Taylor credit as a pioneer in the operations-research, "mixed-team" approach, attributing to Barth the development of mathematic models for practical use in management, and citing the direct role of the management decision aids (Gantt charts, Gilbreth micromotion studies, aptitude tests, and so forth) developed by the scientific managers, the book deals with the problem of the general influence of Taylorism in this way:

> Taylor's work had importance in ways directly germane to operations research. His contributions, great as they were intrinsically, were even more valuable in revealing the merit of creating elements of organization whose object was not the *performance* of operations, but their analysis. It is difficult to overemphasize the importance of this first basic step: the formation of organizations for research on operations. The criterion for evaluating Taylor's work should not be the perfection which he seemed to claim, but only the degree to which his work led to *better decisions* than those which were possible, and in most cases, necessary before.[31]

Another problem for management historians tracing the fate of Taylorism is that of the fondness of management practitioners for devising new names for essentially the same set of techniques. This practice did not cease with the substitution of "Scientific Management" for "The Taylor System" in 1911, but continued with the development of the term "rationalization";[32] it is still common today, as this textbook example of governmental productivity analysis makes clear:

> In this concluding section, we are concerned with the more quantitative, systematic approaches to management; here and only here, the practice of management begins to resemble science rather than art. We shall term this particular approach *management engineering*. This term, I think, is preferable to "industrial engineering," which in too many minds produces the image of a steely-eyed efficiency expert, prowling an assembly line armed with his stopwatch and clipboard.[33]

The book goes on to present a set of standard techniques transposed

31. Claude S. George, Jr., *The History of Management Thought* (Englewood Cliffs, N.J.: Prentice-Hall, 1968), pp. 151-52.

32. Lyndall Urwick, *The Meaning of Rationalization* (London: Nisbet & Co., 1929), pp. 14-17.

33. Grover Starling, *Managing the Public Sector* (Homewood, Ill.: The Dorsey Press, 1977), p. 217.

from the private industrial to the public bureaucratic context. Yet neither name changes nor the most extensive changes in manufacturing and production technology obscure the fact that many of the devices first pioneered by Taylor and his associates have remained in active use. H. L. Gantt's familiar method of bar-charting a series of production outputs against different planning factors, known as the Gantt chart—although in fact it comprises a series of different kinds of charts—is still a highly useful industrial tool. Widely applied in both domestic and industrial settings from the earliest days of the Scientific Management movement, the Gantt chart saw use in the Russian Five Year Plans, the German rationalization campaign, and in many other industrial and governmental planning operations in Western Europe and the United States. When the developers of the PERT/CPM chart sought a method to depict the complex interrelations of project management over time, they turned to the Gantt chart, and by transposing it into a systems analysis net, created a method of charting the planning and control process which was suitable for computerization.[34] The supplanting of the Gantt chart by the PERT chart is a comparatively recent phenomenon, and one which is far from complete at this time. More important in terms of the extension of the Scientific Management approach is the vast increase in planning and control that PERT/CPM makes possible, particularly in processes that would have been too complex for the Gantt chart alone—such as the completion of various NASA missions and the development of the Fleet Ballistic Missile system.

A similar continuity exists in the field of time-and-motion study, now called "methods engineering"; its history is well worth an entire book in itself. After the original enthusiasm for time-and-motion study, the reputation of the "efficiency engineer" declined precipitously with union opposition and the influence of numerous quacks and quick-money artists in the 1920s. The entry of the United States into war production in the late 1930s and early 1940s, combined with the patient efforts of industrial engineers to professionalize the field and restore its reputation, led to a vast proliferation of time-motion systems based directly on the Taylor-Gilbreth models and geared specifically to the needs of an expanding number of individual corporations and industries. Most significant to the management

34. Joseph J. Moder and Cecil R. Phillips, *Project Management with CPM and PERT* (New York: Van Nostrand Reinhold Company, 1970), pp. 7-8.

historian, these new systems, unlike their original models, were mostly proprietary, and so their use, though crucial to the often vast industries that employed them, is not publicized nor their details published. Typical examples are MTA (Motion-Time Analysis), administered by the A. B. Segur Company; the Work-Factor system, developed by Joseph H. Quick and associates at the Radio Corporation of America (R.C.A.); a system of quantifying therbligs, developed by W. G. Holmes at Timkin-Detroit Axle Company; DMT (Dimensional Motion Times), used at General Electric; and MTM (Methods-Time Measurement), a contemporary, nonproprietary method.[35]

Comparison of a typical modern time-motion study textbook such as Karger and Bayha's *Engineering Work Measurement* with traditional Scientific Management texts from the first two decades of the century show stopwatch and clipboard setups, instructions on the proper posture for time-motion study, and so forth, that are almost precise duplicates. Accompanying Karger and Bayha's detailed discussion of modern time-motion study techniques is this interesting caveat:

> A word of caution is appropriate, however. Neither stopwatch time study nor motion study with therbligs have been superseded. In current methods engineering practice, either or both procedures are often used as the soundest approach to the most practical solution of a particular problem involving methods work and the establishment of labor standards.[36]

The conclusion that must be reached from the study of this and other industrial engineering textbooks from the 1940s on is that the time-and-motion studies most characteristic of original Taylorism never "died" with union opposition nor were they superseded by human relations methods. Among those practitioners, critics, and academics who have been in contact with engineering management, it is self-evident that Taylorist practices formed a continual part of the work environment from the time of their invention, and that their use extends far beyond that handful of firms that first hired Taylor or his associates. The "rediscovery" of Taylorism in certain circles of radical

35. Delmar W. Karger and Franklin H. Bayha, *Engineered Work Measurement: The Principles, Techniques, and Data of Methods-Time Measurement, Modern Time and Motion Study, and Related Applications Engineering Data* (New York: The Industrial Press, 1966), pp. 31-45.
36. Ibid., p. 33.

sociology in the mid-1970s was hardly a matter of interest in this context.[37]

New credit has been given to the work of the scientific managers in an often neglected area by Alfred Chandler in his recently published study, *The Visible Hand: The Managerial Revolution in American Business.* He stresses the contributions of Taylor and his associates in the development of modern cost accounting, particularly in the development of methods for calculating indirect costs and overhead. He notes their influence on General Electric and DuPont in this respect in particular. He points out that Taylorism, in the hands of middle managers, played an important role in substituting directed management planning for market processes (the "visible hand" of his title) in the process of integrating production and distribution in the newly merged companies that became the foundation of contemporary American business.[38]

Although it has been somewhat digressive to cite so much evidence at this point, it would be difficult indeed to examine the impact of Taylorism outside the factory and outside the United States without making it clear that Taylorism had a profound and permanent impact on American industrial management. It was to this end that the scientific managers devoted their careers. They wanted a "revolution" in management methods, and they were, to a surprising extent, successful.

TAYLORISM MOVES BEYOND THE FACTORY

The Scientific Management craze did not stop with industrial reorganization and articles in popular magazines dealing with its universal applicability. While ideas of personal efficiency techniques deriving from the Scientific Management crusade were amalgamated into the literature of the American mind-cure tradition,[39] the idea of public efficiency became the core of a political program. As Haber

37. In particular, one should note within this context Harry Braverman, *Labor and Monopoly Capital: The Degradation of Work in the Twentieth Century* (New York: Monthly Review Press, 1974), and the symposium review of Braverman in *Monthly Review: An Independent Socialist Magazine* 28, no. 3 (July-August 1976).

38. Chandler, pp. 272-81, 430, 438, 445.

39. See Donald Meyer, *The Positive Thinkers: A Study of the American Quest for Health, Wealth, and Personal Power from Mary Baker Eddy to Norman Vincent Peale* (Garden City, N.Y.: Doubleday & Co., 1965).

points out, Scientific Management almost immediately entered a powerful alliance with the progressive movement, as Taylor's "mental revolution" became the substance of a doctrine of governmental reform.

The significance of Taylorism's alliance with progressivism is that it moved Scientific Management from the purely economic and industrial realm to the political arena. It was an outgrowth of attempts to solve essentially political problems of social and economic distribution *outside* of the political arena. In the hands of the progressives, it became one of the techniques with which they intended to effect the depoliticization of politics. Borrowing from the British Civil Service reformers the concept of merit recruitment and promotion by objective examination, they were left with a need for a method of internal day-to-day civil service operations analogous to the objective "merit system" of recruitment—an efficient, objective, "merit management system." This was the need which was fulfilled by the discovery that in the industrial world there existed a newly developed method of "Scientific Management" that outmoded the "rule of thumb" and personalized management skills, replacing them with scientific technique. In the great campaign of the civil service reformers to define "administrative" problems as separate from "political" ones, the idea of the conversion of industrial scientific management into governmental scientific administration played an important role.[40] The teaching of the progressive reformers was that impartial administrative systems could be run "scientifically" for the benefit of "society as a whole," while "politics" favored special interests and must be contained. This apolitical stance was itself a political ideology, with the neutral, efficient, "administrative state" as its ultimate goal.

Administration, in this sense, should be run on the machine model of organization. Its separation from politics would guarantee merit principles of staffing over patronage, thus preserving efficiency by preventing outside political influences from interfering in the strict subordination of civil servants in the bureaucratic hierarchy. In the reverse direction, the separation of politics from administration would prevent the authoritarian patterns of bureaucratic efficiency from overflowing into the democratic structure of politics. American democracy could at the same time be efficient, and protected from the dangers of "Prussianism."

Taylor's article, "Governmental Efficiency," proposed the inclusion

40. See Haber, pp. 100-1, 104-6, 111, 117.

of an efficiency expert in the cabinet, as well as the immediate application of time study to bureaucratic work.[41] Woodrow Wilson and the Civil Service Reform League saw the preservation of democracy in the adaptation of patterns of European bureaucracy, and Scientific Management as the means of ending the spoils system.[42] The disgruntled members of Tammany Hall saw in this effort not the abolition of patronage, but the transfer of patronage to a new class, beyond their reach. While their idea that the reformers wanted the patronage for themselves is ludicrous, an echo of their excessive cynicism finds support in contemporary views that politics can never be banished entirely from administration, and that the pretense that it can is in itself a political view.[43] The legacy of Taylorism in government through progressivism is then ideological as well as technical, a credo of efficiency through unquestioned managerial control as the appropriate means of discharging government business.

The efforts of the progressives to introduce Taylor's "mental revolution" into the executive branch were never fully achieved, however. Much of the technological armory of Taylorism required for its proper application standardized measures of success, such as the profit measures of the business world. In the work environment of government, where outputs were frequently undefined and profit nonexistent, machine-speeding techniques, motion measurement, and the other secondary, quantifiable elements of Scientific Management frequently lost their significance. Divested of these mechanisms, the promotion of governmental "efficiency" meant simply the promotion of an ideology of unhindered control of operations by "experts" in organization, exercised through hierarchies built on the extreme division of labor. To the extent that such a structure required for its operations quantifiable measures of success, such measures would be invented and applied arbitrarily. Tied to a new technological elitism built on the Scientific-Management-oriented bureaucratization of government was an ideologically based drive toward "premature quantification."

41. Frederick W. Taylor, "Governmental Efficiency," *Bulletin of the Taylor Society*, December 1916.

42. Woodrow Wilson, "The Study of Administration," *Political Science Quarterly* (June, 1887, pp. 197-222; reprint ed, December, 1941, pp. 481-506).

43. See Herbert Kaufman, "Emerging Conflicts in the Doctrines of Public Administration," *American Political Science Review*, December 1956, pp. 1057-73.

Aside from the influence of Scientific Management on the programs of the progressives, the Taylorites themselves organized groups designed to carry out Scientific Management reforms directly in government. Such an organization was Gantt's "fighting university," the New Machine, which was supposed to be a "conspiracy of men of science" that declared war on waste in the financial and industrial system.[44] Influenced by the works of Veblen, which he read in 1916, Gantt turned from industrial organization to the application of his theories to government. He defined "real democracy" as the creation of full employment by organizing human affairs according to natural law rather than force, opposing his definition to the "debating society theory of government" usually implied by the term democratic. He advocated the scientific organization of society as "an engineer's way of eliminating the profit system" in 1918, predicting the Great Depression and advocating preventative measures of reform. The New Machine, in which he played a central and founding role, consisted of thirty-four members, primarily from the ASME. The organization dissolved in World War I, after sending one letter to President Wilson, in which it tried to apprise him of the social effects of large-scale production, and the danger it presented to science through the temptation to "Prussianization" or regimentation.[45] In its short life, however, the New Machine had profoundly influenced a younger group of individuals, who went on to careers in the New Deal, founded the Technocratic party of the United States, and aided in the development of the Soviet economic planning system.[46]

The mobilization of government for the First World War strengthened the influence of Scientific Management in American government, although not through the New Machine. Most of the important scientific managers donated their time and efforts to organizational work in the executive branch, particularly to the systematization of military logistics and the economic resources upon which they depended. Efficiency was equated with patriotism as a large part of the

---

44. Alford, app., includes a complete text of the charter and letter to President Wilson, and a full list of signatures of the members.
45. Ibid.
46. See Elsner, H., *The Technocrats: Prophets of Automation* (Syracuse, N.Y.: Syracuse University Press, 1967), p. 3, for the influence of the New Machine on the New Deal and Technocracy, Inc. The influence of Walter Polakov, charter member of the New Machine, on Soviet management is discussed below in Chapter 4.

Taylor Society went into government service, exercising special influence on ordnance and shipping.[47]

By the end of World War I, a great number of different influences had created a reservoir of Scientific Management philosophy in government, establishing the rhetoric of efficiency reform as a major part of the armament of crusading political figures and parties and, even more important, as a central part of the logic of military supply, resource control, and planning. The ideology and techniques of Scientific Management became those of the bureaucracies of the executive branch.[48]

THE ALLIANCE WITH HIGHER EDUCATION

If Scientific Management was integrated into government administration by the progressive movement and the First World War, it was its strange alliance with higher education that continually renewed its influence in society beyond its natural life span as a fashionable management innovation. The first scientific managers realized that one of their most important targets was the educational system. In part this was due to the fascination with higher education that was part of their character as "self-made" men; their own formal educations cut short, they longed for Establishment success, and for acceptance by the very "hard shell" and "old fashioned" professors they scorned so vehemently. But even more important in this alliance was the nature of the Scientific Management system itself, which they had created as a system for the intellectualization of complex manufacturing processes. Unlike the classical American use of the assembly line, which was built on the organization of a physical process, Taylorism was built on verbalization, or coordination through written work orders. Therefore, it greatly increased the number of white-collar jobs, while the cost of the increase was paid by the categories of

47. Haber, pp. 120-21.
48. The techniques of Scientific Management exerted their principal influence through the administrative management movement (Chapter 8), but note must be made of the revival of classical efficiency-measurement techniques in the recent productivity-assessment movement in government, as well as the revival of "old-fashioned" public administration in President Carter's Civil Service Reform Bill (*Public Administration Review*, July/August, 1978). The growing concern with controlling malfeasance and governmental costs appears to be giving rise to a climate of reform resembling that of the turn of the century when Taylorism in government flourished.

labor closest to immediate production, in terms of loss of control over, and alienation from, the increasingly fragmented jobs of the new system.

Nowhere are the contradictory elements of Taylorism more clearly illustrated than in the attitude of the colleges in respect to the new system. College professors objected to the Scientific Management reform of their institutions as strenuously as union members, and with more effectiveness. But as a system which created jobs through formalizing and monopolizing management skills, Taylorism was attractive indeed. The Taylorites needed a technique of certification, which the colleges could provide, while the colleges needed a technique for attracting tuition-paying students and disposing of a rising number of college graduates, which Scientific Management could provide. The professors did not want to *be* Taylorized, but they wanted to *teach* Taylorism.

From the start, the scientific managers had an interest in reforming higher education to conform to their own image. Taylor had strong ideas, not only about the inefficiency of colleges, but their impractical overemphasis on theory and their dangerous liberality in the handling of students. Students had too many "cuts," too many electives, drank and partied too much, and were intolerant of business discipline after graduation. These symptoms were all produced by the educational idea that was sarcastically summarized by Taylor: "The child and young man should be free to develop naturally, like a beautiful plant or flower."[49] The purpose of higher education in his view was not liberal education, but to feed manpower into industry.

In 1909, Morris L. Cooke, one of Taylor's original Four Horsemen,[50] was asked to analyze higher education by the Carnegie Foundation

49. Copley, 2:263. For a detailed discussion of the effects of Taylorism on primary and secondary education, see Raymond E. Callahan, *Education and the Cult of Efficiency: A Study of the Social Forces that have Shaped the Administration of the Public Schools* (Chicago: University of Chicago Press, 1966). He makes the point that the adoption of Scientific Management as the prevailing mode of school organization was a form of self-protection for administrators faced with adverse public opinion, and that its predominant effects were destructive, involving a descent into trivia, the growth of nonteaching staffs, the creation of "education administration" as an incompetent pseudoscience, the amputation of the teaching of various important subjects, and the subjugation of the public schools to business interests.

50. The only Taylorites with official recognition from the Master were Gantt, Barth, Cooke, and Hathaway.

for the Advancement of Teaching, one of the prime movers of national educational reform and standardization. The result was Bulletin Number 5, entitled *Academic and Industrial Efficiency*. In it, Cooke did all of the usual Taylorite things: he proposed a standard measure of efficiency (the "student hour"), attacked the academic committee system as inefficient, recommended "functional management" (a variant on functional foremanship), and recommended the removal of administrative duties from the teaching staff.

Writing on "The College Teacher as a Producer," he recommended that, as in the factory, the tools of production (in this case, lecture notes and "pedagogical mechanisms") be the property of the school or department, rather than the personal property of the professors; he also recommended that more class hours be taught per hour of preparation. The late and excessive hours of professors would be eliminated by determining a "fair day's work." Employment processes should be standardized and centralized, instead of depending on a long and tedious process of personal letter-writing. The teaching-research dichotomy was examined and found wanting, and separate chairs for notable teachers were recommended. Research itself needed more inspection and control to increase the efficiency with which it delivered correct answers. A relation between cost and product should be determined. In short, the Taylorites wanted a standardized teaching automaton, and the elimination of the contingencies of any research save their own.

The opposition of the "conservative professors" to this proposal of internal reform was extremely bitter,[51] but only in private institutions could the increasing popular pressure for efficiency reform be resisted in the long run. Public education, particularly primary and secondary school education, was heavily influenced by the Scientific Management revolution,[52] although public higher education was not immediately affected. The growth of specialized administrative staffs and efficiency reforms in public education burdened the "production" level of these organizations with a growing class of "professional" administrators, without producing the corresponding increase in quality and quantity of output that Scientific Management made possible in manufacturing production. The persistence of this growth despite the

51. Copley, 2:250, refers to professors of the "hard-shell" variety (in relation to the ASME). See also Copley, 2:260-80, for a more detailed discussion of the opposition.
52. See Callahan.

evident results illustrates the power of Taylorism as a management ideology in entirely incongruous settings.

The immediate effects of the Carnegie Report on Higher Education were negligible, and it was not until after World War II that the "managerial revolution" in university education got underway, pushed by the immense influx of new students and the development of automatic data processing and systems analysis.[53] Scientific Management methods had by then been installed in state governments, increasing the pressure on the state-supported institutions of higher learning to conform to the now-common ideology of internal structural "efficiency." The resistance of the professors to the Taylorization of education could not withstand the age of automation.

In part, the very universality of Scientific Management philosophy to which the colleges eventually succumbed had been promoted by those same institutions of higher learning. From the beginning, it was apparent that teaching Taylorism was good business. When Scientific Management hit the front pages, many schools rushed to get on the bandwagon with crash courses and conferences.[54] Professors suddenly found the movement a fertile source for learned articles, and a justification for the multiplication of departments and professorships. The Taylorites in turn made efforts to get Scientific Management accepted at the prestige universities and engineering schools; they managed to bring many key professors and deans of engineering and business into the regular group "lecture-tours" which Taylor gave at his home. As early as 1908, Barth got in contact with Harvard, bringing the future deans of the new business school to Taylor's house, where they came to the conclusion that Taylorism, as the most modern form of management, should be the core teaching around which all the courses in the school were to be organized.[55] The Taylorites were imported to give lectures and set up courses. The *pièce*

53. See Francis Rourke, *The Managerial Revolution in Higher Education* (Baltimore: Johns Hopkins Press, 1966).

54. Copley, 2:389, 390, 392-93.

55. Ibid. At one time or another, we find all of the foremost Taylorites lecturing, or even receiving professorial appointments (along with honorary degrees) at major institutions. Barth lectured regularly at Harvard and the University of Chicago; Hathaway was for years on the faculty of Business Administration at Stanford, and Taylor himself lectured at Harvard, the University of Pennsylvania, the Universities of Cincinnati and Illinois, and many other business and engineering schools. See Copley, 2:380-92; Urwick, pp. 83, 201.

de resistance of the undergraduate course offerings was Taylor himself, delightedly denouncing effete college students in the rude language of the factory floor.

Taylor himself would have preferred that his teachings be attached to the engineering schools,[56] but it was business schools such as Wharton and Harvard which recognized the value of Taylorism as a systematic and marketable body of knowledge over which only trained graduates could have an exclusive mastery. The engineering schools, such as Stevens, Pratt, and MIT, gave credence to Taylor as an engineer and systematizer, and were affected by his message of the engineer's right to exercise control in society. But they already monopolized a skill, and so did not seize on Taylorism as avidly as the business colleges. Thus it was not the engineers, but the academics purely in the business of organizational analysis, planning, and the teaching of management, who became advocates of the conscious message of peace through productivity at the same time that they absorbed the subconscious teaching to Taylorism: *the strategy of creating and monopolizing bodies of knowledge as a means of perpetuating and expanding professional job opportunities.*

TAYLORISM AND THE CHANGING RELATIONSHIP OF SOCIAL CLASSES

The process of organizational colonization by intellectuals appears to have been previously carried out extremely slowly, depending on almost spontaneous incidents to press it forward, as in the development of the "old professions" and of engineering itself in the nineteenth century. At the turn of the century, for reasons only partially known, this process operated with greatly increased speed as the multiplication of disciplines was force-fed by intensive academic activity. Taylorism certainly had an important part in the process, especially as it was related to industrial development. Looking at the expansion of Scientific Management at the turn of the century, it becomes apparent that Taylorism not only created new jobs, it made manifest a strategy for multiplying those jobs infinitely. The Scientific Management movement expanded the market for that formerly excessive commodity, the college graduate, for the Taylorites had made the amazing discovery that the industrial system, properly

56. Copley, 2:268-269.

cultivated, could absorb vast amounts of white-collar labor, far more than had ever been dreamed possible. The result was something like the neolithic revolution, when the potential number of people per acre was suddenly multiplied. When the formula permitting the increase of white-collar workers and professionals per industrial establishment was suddenly revealed, the way was opened to the almost explosive increase in organizers, communicators, and planners that we call the managerial revolution.

So successful was this technique that skeptical captains of industry, in a system of competition, were forced to beg for the services of men formerly thought superfluous. As one of the Taylorites remarked:

> Experience has shown that Johnny Pencilpusher is not an evil, nor is he unnecessary, and that it pays to employ him. Accordingly, he is now classed as "productive" and not as "non-productive" labor.[57]

This expansion, however valuable it was in releasing the pressure on the middle class, was bought at a certain price. The costs of sandwiching in a new layer of management between owners and labor were essentially carried by the working class. In proportion to the number of interesting new jobs opening up in management, the routine, dull qualities in laboring-class jobs increased.[58] The profits that came out of Scientific Management, as we recall, were the result

57. C. B. Thompson, ed., *Scientific Management* (Cambridge, Mass.: Harvard University Press, 1914), p. 69.

58. Hoxie, p. 134, describes how, after several decades of Scientific Management practice, the scientific managers, whose former concern was to develop workers with the mentality of oxen, came to lament the passing of high quality, intelligent labor!

An even more tragic, modern footnote to the progress and permanent dismemberment of skilled labor by Scientific Management is provided by the Joint Committee on Atomic Energy hearings on the loss of the *Thresher*. The continual complaint of witnesses is that it is impossible to replace the old type of craftsmen who could labor to exact specification, who took initiative to point out errors, and who could be trusted with complex work. As these skilled workers die off, it becomes impossible to complete with accuracy any complex piece of construction, in this case, a nuclear submarine. The hearings revealed that, in some industries, most of the work is carried out by seventy-year-old craftsmen, whom the owners fear to retire because they cannot be replaced.

Beginning with Veblen, there has been a strong argument that skill levels increase in newly organized industries, due to their ability to absorb techno-logical innovations. Thus, the Taylorites' claims that Scientific Management

of greater control exercised by the managerial class over all the materials needed on the job—including new techniques that increased control over labor so it could be treated as an inanimate material as well. The plan to break the unions was actually a plan to make labor inputs and costs predictable, as part of a stable calculation of profits by removing the discretion of the worker over his work. Neither the process nor the tools were to be controlled by the worker, who could then be made into an interchangeable and totally replaceable part in the work process, just like the standardized parts of the machinery with which he worked.

The relationship that Taylorism postulates between work and management is that increased control of employee functions makes increased management jobs; increased employee discretion or "whole job control" decreases management jobs. Labor controlled in this fashion can diminish at the same time that the scientific managers multiply. The expansion of the managerial class appears, therefore, to require a continual increase in control. And because jobs, systematized and simplified to a single motion for the purposes of control, lend themselves to mechanization, the search for control leads to the gradual transfer of work from fractious men to standardized machines. The result is a continual pressure to eliminate the laboring class from the place of work itself. This takes place without regard for

---

increases skill levels should not be neglected. Two phenomena occur with Taylorization: the increase in individual performance and output levels ("skill"), and the increase in the ability of the production organization as a whole to absorb technological innovations. Thus, in place of the craftsmen who once built naval chronometers, now, a more structured organization exists for the assembling of electronic timekeeping devices. This change represents a higher level of technology, but the electronic technicians who assemble the timepieces possess less "whole job" or craft skill than the aging masters of mechanical-chronometer construction. It was the opinion of these elderly craftsmen that one of the forces behind the change in technology was the difficulty in recruiting or training skilled manpower, coupled with the attractive increases in wages to unskilled workers made possible by the Taylorization of electronics assembly. As a by-product of the changeover, however, the craft skills involved in astronomical-observation-equipment construction were being lost, for they were similar to the skills practiced by the chronometer builders. "When we retire, this will be gone. The equipment now comes from Switzerland." (In conversation, U.S. Naval Observatory.) The relationship of wages, craft skill, and technological innovation is thus considerably more complex now than it appeared to be in Hoxie's time, before Scientific Management was a widespread social force.

the side effects in the outer society of the displaced classes; this was never a concern of Taylorism, which calculated efficiency in terms of internal organizational processes alone. Scientific Management, then, applied without check, becomes the first step on a new road to industrial peace: a peace derived from the continual extension of control over labor. And although Taylorism, in practice, was hindered from developing to the exaggerated degree of perfection advocated by its theorists, its widespread application was sufficient to publicize and promote its basic social orientation. The brave new world advocated by Taylorism had at its heart the vision of a social pyramid which, through a process of selection, training, and scientific uplift, would gradually absorb its lowest element: unskilled manual labor.

The faith of the Taylorites in the ability of industrial progress to erase social traumas prevented them from assessing the negative effects of evolving Taylorism on society outside of the factory. What happened, for example, to the girls who sorted ball bearings when they failed the new and systematized test of manual dexterity? What becomes of Schmidt, the human ox who lifts pig-iron in simple, easy motions, when those motions are transferred to an even more efficient machine? Taylor answered such complaints on the part of labor by pointing out that his system provided education in a trade, and new opportunity to rise into management via the openings he had created for functional foremen, planners, and time-study men. Indeed, he originally felt that such positions were most properly filled from the factory floor, although in practice they went to engineers and college graduates.

In the finest tradition of the anarchist prince, the otherwise practical Taylor is quite capable of waving an indolent hand over "the problems of the transition." Yet as the practice of Scientific Management spread, it became apparent that the One Best Way might have more immediate effects in the form of the pooling of a new lower-class exterior to the factory-created and maintained class structure. For the system begins by substituting repetitive and highly specialized tasks for craft skills, only to make the unskilled occupants of such jobs unemployable through its own encouragement of technological innovation. In raising productivity and the potential for social prosperity, it may very well define the lowest category of labor out of the marketplace, and hence out of the new prosperity. As the ideology of efficiency is transferred from industry to society, it leads inevitably to the argument that this class must be physically removed from society, as they were once displaced from production. It is, therefore, not at all surprising that some of the Taylorites were advocates of eugenics as a form of rationalization of the labor force.

As Scientific Management was transferred to the sphere of office organization it created parallel effects in the very heart of the white-collar revolution itself. The lower levels of office management lent themselves particularly to Taylorization. The arrangement of work centers around office machinery, and the design of secretarial desks according to arm length and the minimization of movement from a central point were classic applications of motion study. The development of elaborately quantified clerical subgoals and office planning demonstrates how time study can be applied to the movement of paper in place of machine parts. Yet Scientific Management, like Saturn, eats its own white-collar children, as office operation is first quantified, then systematized, and then reduced, as far as possible, to a minimum of mental and physical movements. The resulting fecklessness of the office "proletariat" of secretaries, file clerks, etc.,[59] is one of the important forces leading to the increasing mechanization of data processing. The need for stability and speed in processing paperwork sets up pressures for automation of routine procedures, eliminating the most repetitive forms of clerical work. Perhaps this is the simplest explanation for that commonly observed phenomenon of the

59. See Germaine Greer, *The Female Eunuch* (New York: McGraw-Hill, 1970), pp. 121-22, for a telling description of women as "temporary" labor.

It is, perhaps, appropriate to mention here a curious new study of worker control: L. Zeitlein, "A Little Larceny Can Do a Lot for Employee Morale," *Psychology Today*, June 1971.

The author states that employees steal from their employers because they are bored with narrow, routine jobs. He runs a comparative cost-benefit analysis of theft losses vs. costs of reorganization of the business, and concludes that it is cheaper to allow theft as a means of employee control.

Before its publication in *Psychology Today* the *Harvard Business Review* had previously turned down the article. It was, after all, a classic application of amoral Scientific Management techniques, and it offended the HBR down to its puritan roots. The interesting point is, however, that the control practices recommended in this article bear a close family resemblance to the working practices of Stalinism. Allowing theft, while keeping the rules against theft, certainly makes theft more thrilling, but it also opens up the way to arbitrary and discriminatory uses of power through the selective application of dead-letter rules. This is, of course, the first step in the destruction of the rule of law, and, in the long run, leads to the introduction of de facto totalitarianism.

growth of the reverse pyramid form of management, popularly called "all chiefs, no Indians."

Even a brief examination of business and governmental practice today reveals the legacy of Scientific Management technique in various forms. Yet it is clear that the legacy of technique is only a fragment of Scientific Management's broader influence on managerial thought, an influence that stems not from work blanks, routing systems, and Gantt charting, but from the general effects of the so-called "mental revolution" of which they were a part. Scientific Management was presented by its developers as a general philosophy for the resolution of labor-management problems, and for advancing the progress of industrial society. Examination of the unique way in which Scientific Management bound together various common themes of turn-of-the-century American culture into a coherent ideology of management will clarify the degree to which Scientific Management, as a general system of thought, influenced the philosophical outlook of modern industrial societies.

CHAPTER 3

A Passion for Order

Under first-class, non-political management, every jail in the country could be turned into an industrial unit, pay higher wages to the men than they could earn in outside industry, provide them with good food and reasonable hours of labour, and then turn over an excellent profit to the State.

HENRY FORD[1]

The Scientific Management movement was considerably more than a movement for the application of science in management. It was a means for converting industrial technology into ideology. In the universal application of the differential piecework rate, time-and-motion study, and the centralized planning of work routing, the scientific managers saw a true revolution in social relations, and the means of bringing rational order to a society destabilized by industry. From the hard reality of production technology, they derived the shakiest postulates: that social efficiency is the analogue of machine efficiency, and that the appropriate social order mimics the internal organization of machinery—designed by experts according to a pattern of minute specialization, rigid hierarchy, and absolute control. The claim with which they validated their social theorizing was that the social order which they advocated was the direct and inevitable organizational by-product of the use of machinery.

Yet the argument that the existence of machinery itself inevitably leads to a universal social order was made in the face of complete disagreement over the immediate effects of machinery on those who operated it. For example, when Thorstein Veblen discussed the discipline of the machine, he opposed the generally accepted opinion that the widespread use of machinery lowered the mental and cultural level of the workers who attended it. Rather, he said, the discipline of

---

1. Henry Ford, *Today and Tomorrow* (Garden City, N.Y.: Doubleday, Page, and Co., 1926), p. 90. I must thank Larry Spence for locating a copy of this amazing work in the dustbin of a local bookstore.

the machine makes man more intelligent and rational, introducing systematic, even scientific habits of mind. The basic lack of agreement underscored the inability of critics and social scientists of the period to depict, in a unified fashion, any universal set of social and political effects of machine technology. Alternative explanations for the varied use and effect of machines in different social orders would rely on the idea that the cultural setting of machine use is as relevant a determinant of social effects as the "innate" characteristics of the machine itself. How, then, could the prediction of a single hypothetical set of effects as inevitable serve any purpose other than that of propaganda for a desired social order?

Without a doubt, the social goals which Scientific Management attributed to the demands of machine technology were closely related to the general cultural setting of early American industry. Scientific Management was not drawn from the machine itself, but from cultural traditions about machinery and its use. Specific historical traditions that preceded the development of Scientific Management contributed much to its approach, in particular, to the social and organizational patterns which it built around machine use, and claimed to derive from the logic of the machine itself. These general patterns may be summarized as (1) the systematic application of scientific (and especially quantified) methods of study to industrial problems, (2) the invention of a new profession modeled on the role of the engineer for organizational design and maintenance, and (3) the use of machines for social control. These were all old ideas, the common heritage of Western industrialism, and many examples may be cited which were in no way connected with the Scientific Management movement. Yet Taylorism, while in this sense hardly new, was a unique amalgam of these ideas. By contrasting Scientific Management, as it developed from the work of Taylor and his followers, with those innovations and cultural movements that most closely resemble it, one may illustrate the degree to which scientific management, or the application of scientific ideas in management, is not Scientific Management, the social ideology derived from the technical rationalization of industry.

THE APPLICATION OF SCIENCE
TO INDUSTRIAL PRODUCTION

Taylor's efforts to depict work-routing accurately, to analyze and quantify work processes, and to compare the costs of production and various arrangements of the division of labor precisely, were neither the first nor the only such efforts. Yet nothing points up more clearly the social baggage of Taylorism, and how closely it was related to the turn-of-the-century American romance with heavy industry than the comparison of Scientific Management with similar developments in Great Britain and France, such as Matthew Boulton and James Watt, Jr.'s organization for the manufacture of steam engines, the statistical work of the French royalist financiers, and works of Jean Rudolphe Perronet and Charles Babbage on the division of labor.[2] While most of these efforts will be described elsewhere, the arguments concerning the "real" origin of Scientific Management in the works of Charles Babbage will be examined here.

Babbage and the Analysis of the Division of Labor

The statistical analysis of increased efficiency due to the division of labor is generally felt to have begun with the investigations of Charles Babbage, the famous British mathematician whose "Difference Engine" was the great-grandfather of the digital computer, although he had drawn to some extent on the work of Perronet, an eighteenth-century French engineer, and on that of Adam Smith, particularly in his choice of pin-making as the subject of analysis. Babbage's analysis of the processes involved in pin-making, the time required, and the means of determining efficient piecework rates based on a fair measure of output per man, is quoted in the report of a committee of the American Society of Mechanical Engineers with the object of discrediting Taylorism's claims to uniqueness.[3]

The fact that Taylor did not know of the work of Babbage refuted this argument, at the same time that it increased the evidence that scientific and industrial culture may give rise to similar ideas in different locales.[4] Taylor was, indeed, acutely conscious of his isolation from European technology; as an engineer, he found himself to be reinventing existing machinery, and he had joined the newly organized American Society of Mechanical Engineers in 1886 to remedy this problem. This experience led him to realize that the information

2. See, for example, Urwick, *Making of Scientific Management*, 1:20-21, and passim; and Erich Roll, *An Early Experiment in Industrial Organization: Being a History of the Firm of Boulton and Watt, 1775-1805* (London: Frank Cass & Co., 1931).

3. Urwick, *Making of Scientific Management*, 1:24-25.

4. Copley, 1:221.

dissemination system for management innovations, as opposed to technical inventions, was nonexistent; he decided to incorporate such a system into his management philosophy. A great deal of the "science" of Scientific Management consisted of systematically inquiring into and publicizing the methods and implements that had already been devised haphazardly throughout a given trade, with the intention of discovering the "best" ones.[5] Thus, because Scientific Management was conceived in partial isolation from the European scientific establishment, it was organized to help fill the information gap produced by the multiplication of complex technologies.

Dealing more directly with the question of piecework, it must likewise be stated that the general idea of timing piecework was as old as the division of labor that accompanied the factory system. It is therefore not surprising that many men besides Taylor and Babbage, separated by both distance and history, invented systems for calculating piece rates. The important difference between these schemes and Taylor's lay in Taylor's specific techniques for timing tasks and the manner in which he used them; however, this was a product of the cultural context in which it was devised, not of the machines for which it was devised.

Taylor and Babbage were both concerned with the objective measurement of work output, although Babbage could only anticipate methods available by the end of the century. Both men felt that such a system could aid in the reconciliation of capital and labor. However, the two differed radically in the use of objective measurement as well as in its actual definition. Babbage advocated automatic registry of output by machines; in examining the division of labor in the pin business, he came to the conclusion that timing with a watch increases the output abnormally. He decided that a better way to ascertain optimum production levels is to inquire of the worker "what quantity is considered a fair day's work." While fearing some negative consequences of workers' combinations, Babbage felt that one of the legitimate reasons for encouraging such efforts was to enable workingmen's organizations to set fair and objective standards for measuring output.[6]

Taylor's approach, on the other hand, was designed to combat worker control of the definition of a "fair day's work." The stopwatch,

5. Ibid., 1:193, 190-91.

6. See Urwick, *Making of Scientific Management*, 1:24; and Charles Babbage, *On the Economy of Machinery and Manufactures*, 2nd ed., enl. (London: Charles Knight, 1832), pp. 173-87, 291.

defined as an objective tool, was part of an armory of scientific and pseudo-scientific methods for putting the definition of a fair day's work entirely in the hands of management technicians so as to increase output systematically and, at the same time, combat unionization. Babbage applied science to the technology, organization, and accounting systems of the factory, trusting that good wages and steady work would provide sufficient motivation for labor efficiency. Taylor's scientific system of efficiency was built on the idea of measurement as a weapon. This constitutes a difference significant enough to explain why no "Babbage system" swept the industrial establishments of the world in the years preceding the rage for the Taylor system.[7]

Science in Management Versus a Science of Management

Another argument that supports the concept of Scientific Management as a universal by-product of machine technology derives from the history of American engineers in management. Engineers in the early nineteenth century frequently did hiring and materials procurement; they supervised the construction and accounts of their projects as well as their design. The thesis is advanced by one author that Scientific Management was not in the least unique; he says that it developed directly out of the American engineering management tradition, which applied science to industrial organization. He proposes as "the founding patriarch of the managerial revolution" a German-born American engineer by the name of Albert Fink, inventor of the "Fink truss" for bridge building. Fink, who became vicepresident of the Louisville and Nashville Railroad in 1870, has been called "the father of railway economics and statistics in the United States"; and contemporaries praised him for combining "the practical administrative qualities of George Washington with the capacity to compose the theoretical justification for revolution attributed to

7. An additional factor in Taylorism's popularity is, of course, the increased tempo of international industrial competition by the end of the nineteenth century. Babbage's earlier work reflects the easygoing spirit of British organizational efforts that was possible under conditions of market domination, plentiful and cheap labor supply, and the lower degree of trade union organization of the period. As the contemporary British press points out, the British never really outgrew the habits of this period, while by the first two decades of the twentieth century, the Americans, Germans, and Russians were full-fledged efficiency fanatics.

8. R. H. Merritt, *Engineering in American Society, 1850-1875* (Lexington: University of Kentucky Press, 1969), pp. 12, 75.

Thomas Jefferson." Also nominated for this honor, by the same author, is Herman Haupt, "a pioneer in scientific management," who served as general superintendent (1850-52) and chief engineer (1852-56) of the Pennsylvania Railroad, then leaving to serve as chief engineer on the Hoosac tunnel for the state of Massachusetts.[8]

Nowhere, however, does this valuable historical work contain a definition of Scientific Management apart from general references to the application of "science" in management by engineers. As will be shown in the section on French Scientific Management, such a general engineering tradition of applying science to management in Europe predates any American practice. The application of rational principles, and even new methods of accounting to management, is but one of the elements of the system of Scientific Management established by Taylor, however. And while in all of these engineering organizers the roots of the Scientific Management movement are visible—that is, the traditions from which Taylorism arose are clearly indicated—none of them incorporated the additional elements of Taylorism which contributed to its runaway popularity in the early twentieth century. The Scientific Management of Taylor was a system of social control designed to limit union influence, to train unskilled workers rapidly, to create a new professionalism and promote the interests of the middle class, as well as simply a system of applying rationality in great detail to the organization of work and management statistics. Its ideological elements and social influences are what differentiate Taylorism from simpler applications of rationality to organization. The application of "scientific" order to the acquisition and use of construction materials, characteristic of the work of the great European and American civil engineers, gives the Taylor system much in common with these earlier organizational inventions, but as a social innovation it clearly surpasses them.

A PATTERN OF PROFESSIONALIZATION

The historical causes of professionalization are unclear.[9]

A second important element in Taylorism was its technique of systematizing, and then professionalizing, a trade skill, and thus developing it as an effective vehicle for middle-class mobility. This

9. David Riesman and Christopher Jencks, *The Academic Revolution* (New York: Doubleday & Co., 1968), p. 202.

pattern, while important in explaining the popularity and rapid spread of Taylorism in the middle classes, is highly unoriginal. It is, in the management field, the clear duplicate of the process of the organization of engineering as a technical profession. Taylor himself was immersed in that process, since he began his work just after the engineering field was beginning to become less fluid, and a systematization of educational credentials was beginning to make things more difficult for the self-educated.

From this perspective, it is obvious what the techniques were for success: set down a body of arcane but marketable knowledge, gather disciplines, set up a school, establish certification, and found a professional society. Indeed, so impressed were the exponents of Scientific Management with this pattern of success that they tried to attach the movement directly to the influential societies and schools of the new engineering profession; failing in that, they copied the nomenclature ("industrial engineering," "management engineering," and so forth).

By some curious process, the word "engineer," once referring to a sort of technical handyman, rose to the heights of professional glory, only to degenerate most recently into an honorific for handymen once more. The early part of this history is of interest as a prototype of the pattern on which Taylorism, as an "ism," was established in the hands of engineers.

The idea of professionalization of a skill by the application of "science" to practical affairs was not a new one. The older professions in Europe had essentially set up "science" in its present form, lending it the gentility of their own class position, a gentility reinforced by the fashionable dabbling of aristocrats in the sciences. The international patterns of communication of the aristocratic class were duplicated by the new aristocracy of truth seekers, and much of this mystique carried over to the New World. The use of "science"—or the more overt elements commonly associated with science, such as laboratories, mysterious hardware and esoteric language—in combination with systematic processes of thought and a well-organized information exchange system had thus been used not only to ennoble the pursuit of common tasks, but the pursuers as well. For this reason, in the United States, as in Europe, the possessors of active minds who had their eyes fixed on middle-class gentility tended to pin their hopes for social mobility on their unceasing labors to create sciences out of services. Professional surgeons replaced barbers and midwives, pharmacists replaced herbalists, chemists replaced alchemists, and, eventually, engineers replaced smiths, as crafts were transformed into professions.

In many ways, the United States, with its high rate of social change, its legends of success, and its antitraditional "anything goes" notion of social development, tended to be at the forefront of this boom of scientific and technical professionalization. Both the numbers of new professions and the numbers of technical people in both the new and old professions grew amazingly in nineteenth century America. It has been estimated that, in 1800, there were no more than one or two dozen full-time scientists and engineers in the United States, while in 1900 there were forty-five thousand engineers, ten thousand chemists, and eight thousand other natural scientists. By 1950, there were one million engineers alone.[10] These numbers reflect not just the number of technicians, but a change in the definition of technical personnel related to the increase in professionalization itself. The number of "engineers" in 1800 is necessarily deflated, for it omits those who later could be called such; in 1800, they were only self-taught "inventors," whose skill was considered nothing more than an elaborate handicraft. The one to two dozen engineers included in the estimate are those whose education made them prominent, such as Thomas Jefferson, Benjamin Rush, and Benjamin Franklin, and not the unassessable numbers of mechanical innovators, of whom the foremost example was Oliver Evans.

Thus, while Scientific Management as a profession sprouted out of engineering, itself a part of the general trend toward professionalization in the nineteenth century, other movements derived from equally popular models. Osteopathy, chiropractic, and homeopathy derived from medicine, the "domestic science" (home economics) movement followed the lines of engineering and chemistry, and the American brands of the "social sciences" got their start from German models in this era. If anyone had cared to predict the paths of branching professionalization in the nineteenth century, it would have been an easy matter to foresee a "management science" created by engineers and developed along the same pattern as the engineering profession.

The Rise of the Engineering Profession

The impetus for the development of a formal profession of engineering in the United States began with the unprecedented demand for

10. Jay M. Gould, *The Technical Elite* (New York: A. M. Kelley, 1966).

roads and canals in the late eighteenth and early nineteenth centuries, which put trained supervisory personnel at a premium. The only school offering training related to these needs was West Point, founded in 1802, which taught military engineering to its officer candidates.[11] Work in the civil economy became so profitable that many resigned before graduation; the term "civil engineer" thus came to be applied to men skilled in nonmilitary surveying, and in the construction of dams, bridges, canals, docks, highways, and railways. The term "civil engineer" was also used in Europe, where more extensive, state training institutes turned out a larger, elite cadre of engineers, which gave rise to a strong "statist" tradition and intellectual emphasis in European engineering.

In the United States, apart from the small elite cadre of West Point men, engineers in that early era were self-trained people of the "ingenious American inventor" variety, who had only as much scientific and mathematical training as they could pick up on their own. Engineering for the most part, in these early days, grew on a system of apprenticeship, closer to the blacksmithing and construction trades than to the academies. As a result, specialization accompanied rather than followed the process of professionalization. Engineers of this type referred to themselves in terms of their specialties, and did not use the generic term "engineer" in the same manner as "doctor" until later in the century.[12]

Those few engineering schools founded before the Civil War did little to eliminate the rough-and-ready, homemade characteristics of American engineering. In 1825, in the wake of the construction of the Erie Canal, the first civilian engineering school was established at Rensselaer Polytechnic Institute. Special technical schools were established at Yale and Harvard in 1846, but remained poor cousins of the regular academic program. It was not until after the midcentury mark that the number of engineering schools and their graduates began to increase at an almost exponential rate. The Massachusetts Institute of Technology, for example, founded in 1861, had graduated two hundred men by 1900.[13] The ranks of the engineering schools were increased after 1862, when the passage of the Morrill Act began the process of establishing land-grant colleges in the various states. These

11. Samuel Cate Prescott, *When M.I.T. was "Boston Tech," 1861-1916* (Cambridge, Mass.: Technology Press, 1954), p. 10.
12. Merritt, p. 7.
13. Gould, pp. 41, 34-35.

colleges, founded to foster the "agricultural and mechanical arts," followed, in engineering, the lead of MIT and its sister institutes in the struggle for respectability.[14] While the institutes of technology took the lead in the development of a profession out of a craft, thereby coming to represent engineering's "high culture," the agricultural and mechanical schools were not far behind; without a doubt, their broader clientele accounted for much of the more extensive popularization of professionalization as a means of status improvement.

Although the egalitarianism, the new professionalism, and the iconoclastic support of science in the face of old social and religious "truths" were all basically revolutionary in their impact on American society, the polytechnic model of education which embodied these elements, and hence the profession of engineering, tended toward an amalgam of conservative belief, which included emphasis on private enterprise combined with faith in the efficiency and control of military organization, apparently contradictory ideas derived from its American heritage.[15] This combination was easily enlisted in support of the great construction projects of late nineteenth century American jingoism. Some authors trace this bias in the United States to the nature of professional engineering itself. American engineers were oriented to private business in a way that shaped their national characteristics. They were, on the one hand, not completely the free professionals they would have liked to have been; yet, on the other hand, they were not considered to be servants of the state as were engineers in Europe. Instead, they tended to become salaried professional executives of large construction firms, and hence, they thought of themselves as the servants of capital.[16]

The growth and success of the professional engineering schools established the respectability of engineering as a formal discipline; also, as they established a system of accreditation, and thus assured the class status of engineers, they, by definition, limited access to what was once a rough-and-ready inventor's technology, open to those

14. Riesman and Jencks, pp. 224-25.
15. MIT, for example, tried first to recruit Taylor himself for its president; failing in that, they settled on an army general.
16. Merritt, p. 3. Note must be made here of David Noble's recent work, *America by Design: Science, Technology, and the Rise of Corporate Capitalism* (New York: Alfred A. Knopf, 1977), in which a detailed historical picture of the transformation of science into a form of capital was accomplished through the systematic intervention of engineers as the servants of capitalism.

without formal schooling. The rise of these schools was paralleled by the establishment of formal engineering societies, modeled on the scientific societies already in existence. The American Society of Civil Engineers, for example, founded two years after Rensselaer Polytechnic Institute was converted entirely into a college of engineering in 1850, had emerged as a stable organization by 1870. During this period, about seventy established schools added engineering training to their curricula, and the American Society of Mechanical Engineers, of which Taylor was later to be president, got its start.[17]

The New Professional Mobility—A Model for Taylorism?

As the great polytechnic institutions matured and attained social respectability, they also marked the decline of their usefulness as vehicles of social mobility.[18] The certification required for success would henceforward lock out those without sufficient connections, time, and tuition money. New vehicles needed to be developed— marketable skills open to the ambitious outsider, which would enlarge access to the middle class by enlarging the middle class itself. Because the "old" professions had no desire to overproduce their own members and so lower the price for their services, as a profession became respectable, it tended to close. This closing was not absolute, but relative; it was accomplished by the equivalent of "unionization," limiting the members to the size of the market by erecting barriers to entrance. Foremost of these barriers was formal education, which socialized future members to correct attitudes, even as it controlled professional upgrading, an important part of maintaining any long-run monopoly on a specialty.

Professionalization, of course, has its vicious side as well as its benefits in terms of the systematization of knowledge; as it promotes opportunities for the "ins," it destroys those of the "outs" by redefining and monopolizing skills. For example, in the late nine-

17. Merrit, p. 3.
18. Prescott, pp. 229-324, includes a vivid description of the moving ceremonies accompanying the transfer of Boston Tech's record from its old inner-city building to its new "temple of science" in Cambridge in 1916. Fireworks, music, and dancing naiads accompanied the ceremonial rowing of the records—contained in a large gilded chest and carried on a replica of the state barge of the Venetian Republic—across the Charles River. No other symbolism could so clearly portray the aspirations of the new profession so recently risen from the grime of the machine shops of heavy industry.

teenth century, as the American Medical Association was formed, there was a systematic campaign for the destruction of rival theories and traditional practitioners, such as the class of female midwives. Since few or no women were allowed in the medical schools, the effective number of competitors practicing this most lucrative business was reduced. Similar processes of professionalization had comparable results in related fields. Technical advances were purchased at heavy class costs.[19]

If professions upgrade by closing, then one of the solutions to the problem of providing opportunities for social mobility in a society with an expanding and ambitious population is not to end the professional monopolization of skill, but to multiply the varieties of professionalism. Certainly in America the boom in new professionalism accompanied rapid technical innovation. The establishment of the profession of "industrial engineer" or "efficiency engineer" that grew out of the Scientific Management movement appears to be a very typical illustration of this pattern. Did Taylor consciously imitate this pattern or was he simply following the spirit of the age? Most clearly, his career was an example of the process of branching professionalism. He went into engineering at just about the time the closing-down process was beginning. He scrambled to get into the right societies, to get a night-school education—but the days of big successes for self-made engineers had already passed. Taylor's machine designs for big construction firms, like his pattern-making in the factory, could win him only the position of hired employee. On the other hand, the development of a managerial science for speeding up production advanced him to the status of independent professional. Given the ever-present pattern of engineering professionalization, the "new profession" approach that Taylor took directly copied what was happening in America to the profession of engineering. Like engineering, Scientific Management was oriented toward private business, and it promoted free professionalization by holding consulting to be the

19. The antiprofessionalism of the Cultural Revolution in China explicitly acknowledged this problem. The Chinese attempted, by the development of folk medicine, folk agronomy, and so forth, to break the "unionization" of the professional classes and their schools while maintaining technical progress. The cost of "professional" services was to limit their extent to the well-off population in urban areas, and to give disproportionate social benefits to a technical elite. The revolution required, then, a diffusion of technical knowledge such as occurred with the "barefoot doctors."

best occupation. But, more ambitious than its model, it aimed beyond state employment to the conversion of the state itself to its principles.

THE MACHINE AS A MECHANISM OF SOCIAL CONTROL

Most significant of the elements that Taylor molded into a new philosophy of organization was the idea of using machines for social and organizational control. The notion that design might replace supervision, as Jeremy Bentham's Panopticon reminds us, is certainly not confined to machine-age America. But the ever-present idea of using mechanical invention to control human nature and human interaction certainly flourished side by side with the American fascination with machines and the legend of the Yankee inventor.[20] As a natural consequence of the short labor supply on the unsettled Continent, the habits of invention that had flourished in Britain were intensified. For Americans, the invention of, and tinkering with, every sort of practical device that might multiply the effect of human labor became something of a national pastime.

The driving compulsion for machine control likewise became an important part of the American dream, which was built around the exploitation of a vast frontier. The pastoral ideal that shaped America, as Leo Marx points out, is not one of wilderness, but of settlement.[21] The endless, untamed spaces of the North American continent, and the apparently anarchic and "savage" Indians represented a fearful picture of chaos, a never-ending succession of tasks with too few people to accomplish all that needed to be done. The machine was the answer to manpower shortage, and therefore the shortcut through chaos to pastoralism. Invention would make one man capable of doing the work of ten, and hence push back the darkness. The railroad and the repeating rifle "opened" the West; invention subdued a continent. The irony of this process was that it opened the land to speculators, breaking the slow, nonmechanized patterns of settlement that would have realized the pastoral dream by creating a nation of farmsteads.

20. The perusal of nineteenth-century patents in this respect is not only humorous but instructive; Taylor's "nightmare machines" are not in any respect unique. See, for example: Bernard Nagler, ed., *Patent Pending* (Los Angeles: Price, Stern, Sloan, 1968).

21. See Leo Marx, *The Machine in the Garden; Technology and the Pastoral Ideal in America* (New York: Oxford University Press, 1956).

In this setting, a premium was put on technical and organizational innovations designed to push back a dark and chaotic environment, and to civilize ugly tasks by arranging machine intervention between man and nature. The assembly line was born in the slaughterhouses of the Middle West, where inventor after inventor turned his mind to the development of a means to kill and flay animals that would eliminate the use of human beings. Machine systems to avoid distasteful tasks, to move faster, organizational systems to pass work through more swiftly, these were all part of the American creative landscape. The new twist which Taylor offered was a mixed machine-organization system aimed not against an anarchic *environment*, but against an anarchic *society*. The Indians, of course, had been defined as part of the physical environment, and could, therefore, be regularized, rationalized, and incorporated into the pastoral image by simple elimination. No such technique could be used against the internal "chaos" of the urban slum or tenement dweller, for this was the work force of the economy.

Taylorism offered a way to make the factory worker, via the work process itself, into a neat, industrious, individualistic, thrifty, and sober Anglo-Saxon ideal. In this sense, its goals paralleled those of settlement workers when they trained children, as well as those of contemporary political reformers who tried to eliminate bossism as an effective form of political leverage and distribution of largess. In its advancement of the new version of the Protestant ethic, Taylorism was both the product of its times and one of the greatest innovations of its times. The factory system had created the proletariat; now it could eliminate it.

Taylorism and the Assembly Line

The culmination of the vision of machine control of human activity is not usually equated with the industrial rationalization process introduced by Taylor, but with the assembly line as it emerged from the Ford Motor Company in 1913. If Frederick W. Taylor's definition of efficiency was to organize work as the analogue of the machine process, Henry Ford's version of efficiency moved beyond this; it replaced the human imitation of machinery with machinery itself. In the Ford assembly line, machines, not men, controlled the tempo of production. The "continuously moving line" that became Ford's obsession was the product of a long history of American experimentation; as he said, "The idea came in a general way from the overhead trolley that the Chicago packers use in dressing beef."[22] The great difference between the systems was not in the use of the increasing division of labor, but in the means by which the organization and routing of work took place. Taylor's system relied on written records, and the use of management experts for planning, coordination, and experimentation; Ford's assembly line was a nonverbal process in which the timing of the production process was built into the speed of the line; the organization of the work process between machines was invested in the design of the line itself.[23]

Taylor's emphasis on the use of the written word ("printed work forms") as the controlling element in production routing and timing differs starkly from Ford's bald pronouncement that neither the keeping of records nor the use of experts was promoted in his plant.[24] Some worker would always remember how things had once been done, he said; records of experimentation and the operations of "experts" would promote pessimism about innovation, and interfere with the authority structure in the plant (that is, Ford's personal control). Yet this very difference gave Taylorism an immense advantage in its ability to absorb new technologies and to adapt itself over time, while "Fordism," carried to its logical extreme, had little adaptive capability.

The profits of the Ford line are built on speed, developed by a heavy investment in control through machine design. Once set up, the system operates by itself, not needing the continual tinkering, human control, and realignment that is built into the Taylor system. Yet as the history of the Model-T shows, the line could be adapted only under tremendous external pressure and with great internal dislocation. The costs of retooling the line are then most properly compared with those of Scientific Management's open-ended, information-gathering techniques and its investment in free professionals whose duties were to continually assess the production control system in terms of new knowledge. It should be apparent that Taylorism could be used to rationalize the assembly line, but that the reverse was not the case.

It should also be noted, however, that Ford could not resist setting himself up as a philosopher of industrial society with the aid of ghost

22. Henry Ford, *My Life and Work* (Garden City, N.Y.: Doubleday, Page, & Co., 1923), p. 81.
23. Giedion, p. 118.
24. Ford, *My Life and Work*, pp. 85-86.

writers—and, it is to be suspected, ghost thinkers as well. To read
Ford's works, one would suppose Ford's line to be the entirely original
and unique product of his monomania, with minor assistance from the
folk artisans he hired as workers. Yet while Ford never acknowledged
it, his debt to Taylor was great. At each stage of the development of
the assembly line for the production of automobiles, Ford indicates
that time-and-motion studies were employed, although not by professional scientific managers. Stopwatch timing and the "principle" of
reducing steps and motions are mentioned frequently as indicators
that the next stage of development of the line was more efficient than
the last. As a prophet of mass production and rationalization, Ford
follows Taylor's model closely; it is in his single-minded advocacy of
the cheap car as a "family horse" that he strikes off in new directions.[25]

In his investigation of the history of the Ford plant, Allan Nevins
came to the conclusion that Taylorism exercised considerable influence in the development of the assembly line. Detroit at that period
was steeped in Taylorism; Taylor had made speeches there which met
with enthusiastic approval. Taylor was surprised to find, however,
that his ideas were popularized by amateurs, who applied them
without systematic training or resort to professional scientific management experts. Many of Ford's assistants were students of Scientific
Management, and the originator of the idea of putting the whole car
on a moving line, Clarence W. Avery, was both university-trained and
an active advocate of Taylorism and modern industrial engineering.[26]
This view contrasts most distinctly with Ford's advocacy of folk
wisdom and avowed dislike for professionals, book readers, and other
types of city slickers. Some authors find the explanation in Ford's
personality—an authoritarian, ignorant, backwoods mechanic, he
compensated for his fear of intellectuals by hiring professionals and
laying claim to their ideas. With the craft of the semiliterate, he
promoted his status as an oracle by confining himself to brief, cryptic
sentences.[27] And, most importantly, he invested all his energies in a

25. For a description of "scientific study" that corresponds to Taylorism,
see Ford, *My Life and Work*, p. 81. One of Taylor's favorite examples, the
social effects of the mass production of shoes, is described on p. 153 of the
same work. Other examples abound, constituting testimony to the degree of
penetration of Taylor's ideas into the industrial world by 1923.

26. Allan Nevins, *Ford: The Times, the Man, the Company* (New York:
Charles Scribner's Sons, 1954), pp. 468, 474.

27. Jonathan Leonard, *The Tragedy of Henry Ford* (New York: G. P.
Putnam's Sons, 1932), p. 107.

system of nonverbal, mechanical control of production organization that could eliminate the challenge to his authority by a professional class of managers. To a certain extent, the modern assembly line (as opposed to the slaughterhouse trolley) should be classified as an extreme development of certain aspects of Taylorism in conjunction with pre-existing American traditions. Certainly, the assembly line's development under Ford would have looked considerably different, and possibly would have been a good bit less rational if Taylor's techniques of work measurement and passion for efficiency had not been well-publicized in Detroit before Ford began his work.

Despite a certain degree of relationship between the two systems, they have major differences which are instructive. While both derive their control from the integration of men and machinery, they differ considerably in their approach to control, and in their application of the scientific method. Taylor saw the machine as the embodiment of rationality; he considered rationality to be infectious. If systematic habits were introduced through working with rationally designed production systems, he thought that they would automatically spread from the working force through society. Social control was thus the by-product of the spread of the scientific method into everyday life through the medium of Scientific Management. Ford's passion for control, on the other hand, outran his faith in the scientific method; it led him to the espousal of active methods of espionage and coercion of workers in their private lives, as an adjunct to the control he exercised on their working lives through the assembly line.

While both systems espoused "efficiency" as their aim, the primacy of the scientific method of recorded experimentation in Taylorism led to its increasing sophistication, and culminated in the development of views of human motivation which are almost the reverse of Taylor's mechanistic and strictly economic vision, the views of the "human relations school." The downgrading of method and the exaltation of a fixed, mechanical definition of production efficiency led the Ford system to real losses in efficiency that had to be made up for by increasing the elements of coercion that were, for the most part, only latent in Scientific Management. For example, when Frank Gilbreth, originator of motion study, visited the Ford plant, he was horrified by the much heralded assembly line. Most of the motions made on the line specifically induced fatigue. Workers had to stretch or stoop excessively; motions were single, but not simplified. Gilbreth's motion system derived efficiency from the elimination of fatigue and waste motions—he did not even depend on the piece rate, Taylor's device.

When the Ford people told him that the line was efficient because people "got used to it," Gilbreth felt they had revealed the ruthless coercion that backed the effective functioning of the line. Its speed could only depend on the gradual physical destruction of the workers.[28] The vices of Fordism were a caricature of those which the unions once attributed to Taylorism. Undermining the image of rational enlightenment so carefully nurtured by the scientific managers, they reinforced the picture of "ruthless American efficiency" so often encountered in domestic and foreign analyses of modern industrial production.

A TECHNOLOGY OF SOCIAL CHANGE

Scientific Management was clearly a synthesis of ideas that were common in American culture. Its specific characteristics were inherent not in the ideas, which it united into a single plan, but in the organizational matrix in which these ideas were presented. The notion that the scientific method might be applied to the study of management, the idea of creating a new class of professionals for that study, and the application of the machine as a means of social control were none of them original ideas. Many examples of their application in various forms can be cited. Yet Taylorism was unique in that it combined all of these elements into a single solution that could be offered as an answer to the great social problems created by advancing industrialism. Taylor proposed to reconcile capital and labor on the grounds of middle-class professionalism, increasing available goods through the very means of rational production that would themselves control the working class. Neither Taylor's predecessors nor his imitators offered so broad a formulation. The power of Taylor's arguments dwarfed alternative management plans of that period; profit sharing, decentralization, workers' control, and other schemes fade and then reappear after the great era of the Scientific Management movement is over. During that era, one great idea was woven into the fabric of industrial society: that an increase in industrial efficiency would produce a corresponding increase in social efficiency.

28. Yost, pp. 246-47. It is to Gilbreth's credit that he immediately saw through the sham of the Ford "guided tour" that was specifically designed to cover up the destructive aspects of the system, and present a picture of spotless, automated efficiency. (See Leonard, p. 231, for a description of this technique.)

Social justice would be the product of technical rationalization. Was Taylorism original? In this respect, it appears that both Taylor's detractors and his followers were right. Split into its component parts, Taylorism held nothing original, either technically or organizationally.[29] Nothing it contained was alien to the culture from which it arose; in that sense, Taylorism was pure Americana. Yet Taylorism as a whole was an innovation of genius. The pattern by which it combined elements of industrial technology and organization was unique. Its novelty was in the combination of planning, accounting, systematization of workrooms, unification, technological advance, time-and-motion study and pay incentives into a systematic package with "guaranteed" results, which could be marketed to manufacturers in a manner that other management competitors could not outperform. By the same token, it was the synthesis of a growing technology of "social engineering," fueled by class mobility and fears of labor unrest, that was the truly new "secret of organization" that made the technique such a success.

Siegfried Giedion's approach to the problem of defining significant innovation is particularly applicable in the question of defining Taylor's "inventions"—so few of which were things, and so many of which were abstract relationships between men and materiel. Giedion separates the invention of physical machinery from the invention of new ways to organize the space between machines. The former are patentable, but the latter became more important as technology progressed. He cites, for example, the argument by Thomas Jefferson for the grain interests, which was used to break the patent on the first

29. Of all the arguments for the European invention of high-speed steel, for example, the most convincing is that of Emile Pouget in *L'Organisation du surmenage* [The Organization of Overwork] (Paris: Librarie des Sciences Politiques et Sociales, 1914), n., pp. 9-11, which emphasizes the importance of Taylorism as an entire system. He cites the invention of a high-speed steel several years before Taylor's Bethlehem Steel exhibit at Paris, which languished for want of an appropriate system of machinery and organization to make use of it. "In 1900, at the Vincennes Exposition, the Bethlehem Steel Works exhibited tools, lathes, etc., of an extraordinary strength; huge driving wheels, huge belts . . . everything indicated force! Besides, a very American setting emphasized their worth. These tools were equipped with Taylor high-speed steel.

"This unaccustomed spectacle interested the specialists above all and made them understand all the advantages of high-speed cutting tools, used by powerful machinery."

automated grist mill. Because its separate elevators, conveyors, and so forth, were based on principles known in antiquity, it was held to be unpatentable. Yet, by the very act of breaking the patent, the social significance of this unique innovation was emphasized.[30] Such, too, was the fate of Taylorism at a later date. But its value as an innovation reached far beyond its technological components, which were easily replaced. As a way of integrating ideas about industrial organization, it was a unique contribution to industrial society.

Scientific Management, which appeared at first glance to be a technology of organization, contained, in fact, a statement of the goals of that technology within the complex of ideas by which it was created. It was actually an ideology *about* technology—an ideology that defined the correct place of technology in society, and that advocated the replacement of traditional politics with a rational technology of political and economic choice. In this sense, it was a new contribution to industrial society.

It was as an ideology, and a foreign one at that, that it was recognized by its exponents in non-American industrial settings. These societies had seen the parallel invention of many of the component parts of what was described as "American efficiency." They had produced in some form the technical elite that was the natural carrier of this ideology; they were experiencing the class upheaval and civil disunity that encouraged the application of the new methods. Yet the unification of these factors into what has been called "the second industrial revolution"—the reorganization of world industry on an integrated, planned, mass basis for the promotion of broad-scale social efficiency—was not simply the result of the introduction of this or that technique of organization, but rather the spread of a new world vision of the proper goals for industrial and industrializing societies. It is with the results of this crusade for world order through industry that modern national politics must deal today.

30. Giedion, pp. 79-84.

PART II

FROM SCIENTIFIC MANAGEMENT TO RATIONALIZATION

That these principles are certain to come into general use practically throughout the civilized world, sooner or later, the writer is profoundly convinced, and the sooner they come the better for all the people.

FREDERICK WINSLOW TAYLOR,
The Principles of Scientific Management, 1911

CHAPTER 4

The Taylor System in Soviet Socialism

Prekrasny obrazets teknicheskogo progressa pri kapitalisme k sotsializmu.
[*An excellent example of technical progress under capitalism toward socialism.*]

LENIN, marginal note on Gilbreth's
"Motion Study as an Increase of National
Wealth," 1915.[1]

The concerns of Scientific Management—centralized planning to promote the efficient use of resources, worker betterment through rationalization of working conditions, and the natural right of a guiding sector of society, or vanguard, to reform national conditions on this model—have more than a coincidental relationship with Marxism-Leninism. One of the most curious episodes in the history of Taylorism is how this philosophy of private business came to be absorbed by its bitterest enemy, the first socialist state. The results were not only the creation of an apparently universalistic organizational technology in two diametrically opposed political systems, but the diffusion so achieved appeared to reinforce certain statist tendencies of Scientific Management in the country of its origin, the United States. The practical fusion of socialism, centralism, and bureaucratism that was effected under the aegis of Taylorism was to shape, by example, the organizational patterns for economic development and recovery in all states that learned from the Soviet experiment.

The history of Russian Taylorism begins with the attempt to establish a revolutionary proletarian state according to the Marxist blueprint. Karl Marx, acutely aware of the increase in industrial scale

1. V. V. Adoratskii, V. M. Molotov, M. A. Savel'er, V. G. Sorin, eds., *Leninskii sbornik* (Moscow: Partiinoe Izdatel'stvo, 1933), 2:226. Annotations on Frank B. Gilbreth's "Motion-Study as on (*sic*) increase of national wealth," *Annals of the American Academy*, May 1915, p. 9659.

and technical rationality in the middle years of the nineteenth century, as well as its by-product of increasing misery in the lower classes, developed a "scientific" theory of history which predicted that the working class would seize the industrial establishment at its highest level of development. Given this high level of scientific and productive development in the revolutionary society, he thought that it would be a simple matter for the working class to use the machinery of the state to establish fully rational patterns of egalitarian distribution of the industrial society's plentiful industrial output. The formula was simple, reasonable, appealing, and needed little elaboration of the postrevolutionary phase because the historical development of the advanced industrial countries was not yet at the point of revolution, or at the point where an even more advanced science would make childishly simple the technical means by which advanced societies could rationally plan production and distribution.

The problem was, however, that the "chain of capitalism broke at its weakest link," to paraphrase Stalin. In the country most demoralized and disorganized by World War I (by the very reason of its weak development of industry), popular uprisings overthrew the monarchist government, and a subsequent *coup d'état* by the Bolshevik faction of the relatively small Social Democratic party established the first "dictatorship of the proletariat." The first Marxist socialist revolution had occurred in the country least able, of all the industrial powers, to provide the industrial preconditions for socialist redistribution. The Bolshevik faction, therefore, changed its name to Communist Party and proceeded to wait for the world revolution to put the industrial apparatus of Western Europe at the service of the world proletariat.

The failure of the world revolution left the Russian socialist state and the Communist party isolated in a hostile "bourgeois" world, and faced with the terrible tasks of securing power in the process of fighting a civil war, rebuilding a war-torn economy, and developing industrial production to a level considerably higher than that of tsarist Russia. None of these tasks—not even the Russian revolution itself—had been included in the early Marxist blueprint; they complicated the vaguely defined problem of building a truly socialist state almost beyond understanding. The search for organizational and technical solutions to these problems led the Communist party to the very system on which they had declared war: the Taylor system for the organization of bourgeois factory production.

How had the Russians discovered the Taylor system? What advantages led them to overcome their distaste for it? The compatibility of Marxist scientism with Taylorite scientism was impressed upon Soviet communism by no less a person than Lenin himself. The works of Taylor had been introduced into prerevolutionary Russia via the international communications network of the engineering profession.[2] During the first big international publicity wave around the turn of the century, French, German, and Russian translations of Taylor's major works were published. The theoretical possibilities of Taylorism in industrial organization had been recognized by Russian specialists. (It must be remembered, also, that most of the big factories in prerevolutionary Russia were run with the aid of foreign specialists, and many industrial establishments were in foreign hands.) Little or no headway had been made in introducing Taylorism into Russian industry, due to near-explosive social conditions which made owners fear any substitute for the most direct forms of coercive control, added to a heavy-handed, conservative anti-intellectualism at the upper levels of society and government. In a country where labor appeared to be so plentiful and cheap, and few legal controls on even the most extreme forms of labor exploitation existed, there appeared to be little reason to make the investment required to change the system over to one of complex and often substantial financial incentives for labor. In this situation, Lenin, while studying the most advanced forms of capitalism in preparation for his work *Imperialism: The Highest Stage of Capitalism*, became acquainted with the writings of Taylor.

LENIN DISCOVERS TAYLOR

In 1916, Lenin prepared a series of notebooks on the detailed working of capitalist finance and production, as part of his search for new conditions in the organization of capital that would explain the delay of the once imminent proletarian revolution in the West. His finding, that the imperialist exploitation of colonial areas had permitted the "buying off" of the working class of the imperialist power, led him to elaborate a theory of nationalist revolution as the key to the destruction of world capitalism. However, his researches into the very latest methods of capitalist organization also increased his appreciation of the skillful methods of financial and psychological coercion

2. Urwick, *Golden Book of Management*, p. 108.

which had been developed by scientists, in the pay of the industrialists, for the purpose of exploiting the workers while, at the same time, decreasing their revolutionary spirit.

Lenin did not trust the motives of capitalist authors, but his faith in scientific data appears to have predisposed him to believe Taylor's results, if not his statements of purpose. The thousands of metal-cutting experiments performed by Taylor apparently impressed Lenin profoundly; *Tetrad' beta*, one of Lenin's preparatory notebooks, contains lengthy excerpts from the work of F. W. Taylor, with marginal notes indicating his appreciation of the sinister competence which science gave to capitalism. He appeared particularly impressed by the more ruthless but effective methods of Taylorism, which increased production by wringing the most labor from workers through imposing "scientific" control techniques that simultaneously co-opted the most talented (and hence most dangerous) workers away from unionism. Lenin was also fascinated by the lowered costs of production which Taylorism offered, the installation time ("two to four years!!"), the vast multiplication of white-collar jobs and, especially, the increase in paperwork ("*printed* work forms!").[3]

Exploring further the literature of Scientific Management, often through the medium of German translations and commentaries, Lenin apparently found in Gilbreth's works on motion study important answers to the problem of capital accumulation in a nonexploitative fashion suitable to the workers' state. Indeed, French socialists in 1914, bitterly opposed to Taylorism per se, had, nevertheless, found Gilbreth's version of Scientific Management acceptable. Gilbreth, formerly a manual laborer himself, sought to simplify motions rather than to intensify the speed-up under the rule of the stopwatch; this made his work more appealing to the European socialists than that of Taylor.[4] It is difficult to imagine that Lenin, well-acquainted with the works of both Taylor and Gilbreth, as well as with the European commentaries of them, did not perceive, in the difference between the techniques of Taylor and Gilbreth, potential grounds for developing a new technique of Scientific Management suited to socialism and yet as productive as the more exploitative means used for the increase of national wealth under capitalism. Scientific Management, as he

3. V. I. Lenin, *Polnie sobranie sochinenii* (Moscow: Gosudarstvennoe Izdatel'stvo Politicheskoi Literatury, 1962), 28:126-32.

4. Pouget, pp. 42-51.

remarked on the margins of a Gilbreth article, was the technique for the transition between capitalism and socialism.[5]

If the precision, competence, and effectiveness of the writings of the scientific managers first attracted Lenin's attention, it was the ability of Scientific Management to provide solutions for the immediate problems of Russian production that held his interest from the time of the preparation of *Imperialism: The Highest Stage of Capitalism* until the October Revolution. On the overt level, Taylorism offered a way to simplify work so that peasant workers could easily be taught the newly routinized factory work in shorter periods of time. Expensive and dangerous bourgeois specialists could be eliminated after the initial transitional period during which industry would be fully systematized. But not only could Scientific Management make the transition to full industrialism quicker, it could raise production to the point where the surplus, if not dissipated into profits, could be used to enrich the workers instead. If work went faster, then presumably one could accomplish the necessary production in ever-shorter amounts of time. The practical means of achieving an immensely shortened working day under socialism had been discovered. Then again, given the vast task of training masses of unskilled labor, and adding to it the problem of controlling the opportunists and other corrupted remnants of the old regime in the proletariat, the increased potential for control of the industrial establishment that Taylorism offered was not entirely unwelcome. Of course, this control would be entirely different from capitalist control since it would be exercised by the workers' state.

On a deeper level, however, Lenin's personality contained many qualities that attracted him naturally to Taylorism. His success as a revolutionary had been built on his puritanical discipline of both himself and others. In place of nihilistic excesses, he had stressed tight, secret, highly disciplined organization, and his own austere dedication to the revolution had been unquestionable. At a time when other revolutionaries had dissipated their energies in sexual excesses and vague (often gloomy) metaphysical discussions, Lenin was practical, direct, and "goal-oriented." The formation of his unusual and strong personality was related to a number of incidents in his own life which appear to form a biographical pattern similar in many respects to that of the other Taylorites.[6] For example, Lenin was the product of a

5. Adoratskii et al., p. 226, and pp. 104, 254, 262, 264.

6. See such biographies as Leon Trotsky, *Lenin* (New York: Minton, Balch & Co., 1925); Edmund Wilson, *To the Finland Station* (Garden City, N.Y.:

successful, bourgeois, intellectual family; his father died when he was sixteen, and his education was blocked not only by straitened family circumstances but by the execution of his much admired elder brother, which caused Lenin to be expelled from school as a political risk. The pattern of blocked schooling and career opportunities was a common one in Russia, for not only had there been a growth in modern education similar to that in the United States in the last half of the nineteenth century, but the government attempted to suppress revolutionary agitation by preventing all but the upper classes from obtaining schooling (for example, in the famous "cooks' sons" ukase), and by cutting down on employment opportunities for the new intelligentsia.[7] The pressure of the ambitious *raznochintsy* ("men of various origin") on higher education and the scant intellectual employment available was even greater than that in the United States, where an open, actively industrializing economy provided greater opportunity for class mobility. In the United States, organizational innovations promoted by such people as Taylor made greater room for the professional technician in the industrial economy, opening the way for the "white-collar revolution." In Russia, active governmental repression of these members of a would-be middle class drove them underground and marked the beginning of widespread revolutionary activity. Not until the revolution destroyed the aristocratic tradition and the reactionary government was the way clear for the substitution of an ideology of industrial development for one of stagnation in support of traditionalism.

A certain contradiction could be observed, however, between the classless democratic pattern of industrialism, advocated by the Bolsheviks before 1917, and the natural tendencies toward "commandism," exhibited by the intellectuals who directed the operations of this "vanguard of the proletariat." While on the one hand, the institution of democratic centralism with its strong party discipline made it clear

Doubleday & Co., 1940); and Bertram Wolfe, *Three Who Made a Revolution* (New York: Dial Press, 1948).

7. L. Tikhomirov speaks of this in 1892, as do most modern historians. See his *Russia, Political and Social*, vol. 2 (London: Swan Sonnenschein & Co., 1892). Also see M. Florinsky, *Russia: A History and an Interpretation* (New York: Macmillan Co., 1947), 2:1113 ff. See also a letter sent by V. A. Dolgorukov, head of the Third Section, to the Governor-General of Moscow in May of 1958, quoted in Franco Venturi, *The Roots of Revolution* (New York: Alfred A. Knopf, 1960), p. 232.

that the leaders of the party expected to exercise the strictest control over postrevolutionary development processes, on the other hand, they advocated the control of industry by proletarian soviets and trade unions, which would eliminate the need for direction by white-collar intellectuals and lead to the "withering away" of the state itself. In this situation, the adaptation of particular elements of the American Taylor system to Russian conditions had a certain air of theoretical and practical compromise between the two extremes.

FROM *THE STATE AND REVOLUTION* TO THE DECREES OF WAR COMMUNISM

While Lenin's notes reveal a distinct fascination with Taylorism, his published works prior to the October Revolution certainly give no indication of this. Indeed, having condemned Scientific Management in 1916, he advocated in the following year the complete democratization of the state apparatus through the elimination of bureaucracy built on specialized and technical functions. Only after the revolution did he openly promote the installation of the Taylor system in industry and government. However, in Lenin's prerevolutionary treatment of the sources of bureaucratic power in *The State and Revolution* (1917) certain echoes of the Western management literature with which he was acquainted may be found in what has been called a predominantly anarchistic statement.

Central to Lenin's definition of the "withering of the state" is the idea that the state's essential functions can be reduced to methods of accounting and control so simple as to allow their carrying out by any ordinary citizen without special training. These simplified duties can then be performed on a rotational basis by all citizens, and housewives will rule the state on their day off.[8] The democratic control of the *soviets*, egalitarian councils of workers in all phases of production, is thus assured over this truncated version of what was once a "state." The dominance of bureaucrats and experts, as well as their claim to special social rewards, will thus be broken by the standardization of public duties according to a rationalized and simplified pattern.

While this pattern of breaking down the state is vaguely reminiscent of the ways in which the introduction of new management methods

8. V.I. Lenin, *The State and Revolution* (New York: International Publishers, 1954), pp. 83-84.

broke down monopolies on craft skills and redistributed power in traditional manufacturing organizations, it also contains two mistaken assumptions common to the great mass of industrial and political literature on management that appeared in the West during this period. In the first place, it is assumed that methods of "accounting and control," despite their origination in the capitalist superstructure of the West, are value neutral. This is, of course, the claim of American civil service reformers, who developed from this idea of neutrality the notion of the "politics-administration" dichotomy. The second assumption is that of the imminence of the development of a science of management suited to statecraft, which is the burden of much of the administrative literature of the period. If this were indeed the case, the Bolsheviks had only to borrow and install these objective and simple methods; but the slowness with which the "science of management" evolved practical techniques suited to state operations was destined to be a source of disappointment to both Russians and Americans alike.

But, whatever the general implications of this plan, Lenin's advocacy of standardization and rotation of state duties at workmen's wages was soon to disappear in the turmoil of revolutionary reconstruction. The Soviets had originally planned that the spread of world revolution would bring the more industrialized powers to their aid. Instead, the war with Germany continued, and to the civil war was added the threat of Western intervention. Survival required reorganization. But the communists had broken the power of the government to control by dispersing it among the people; they had destroyed the Russian army with internal propaganda; they had broken down industrial production by chasing out the bourgeois engineers and technicians; they had given away huge sections of prime farmland by signing a separate peace with imperial Germany. To rebuild civil order and Russian military capacity, the Bolsheviks set about to establish a dictatorship of the proletariat which was in fact a dictatorship of the party, indeed, of simply the Politburo and Lenin himself.

National survival required the immediate establishment of a series of priorities: (1) the reorganization of the Red Army under firm party control; (2) the reconstruction and mobilization of industry to support the military effort; and (3) the establishment of techniques of procurement of the surplus required to keep the army and industry running from a devastated agricultural sector. These priorities, essentially in effect from 1918 until 1921, went under the euphemistic name of "War

Communism." They included forced grain confiscation, obligatory overtime, and the resurrection of the political police. And in spite of the short duration of this period, it set the pattern for sacrifice to attain social goals which seemed to form some sort of ideal model to which party leaders would refer in subsequent decades.

Reassessment of the period of War Communism shows that it contained more than the traditional Russian technologies of coercion in service of the revolution. The influence of the Taylor System of Scientific Management, filtered through the specific theoretical understanding of Lenin, Trotsky, and other party leaders, appears to have been pervasive in the new and superior control techniques that the party developed at this time. The preconceptions of these party leaders appear to have been bolstered by the data of both American Taylorites and Russian Taylorites trained in America whose reports seemed at times to form the outstanding information link between the party's policy centers and the lower levels of industry. The party leaders, hampered in their understanding of industry by lack of direct experience, hampered essentially by their background as revolutionary theorists-in-exile, were greatly dependent on the kind of theoretical "summing up" that the Taylorites could make of the messy reality of actual production; thus, because Taylorites controlled statistical information about technical organizations, their suggested solutions appear to have been influential. Taylorism, added to the turmoil of postrevolutionary Russia, seems to have set the Soviets on the path that led to the Kronstadt revolt.

Although this influence of Taylorism has frequently been denied by later authors,[9] examination of the major debates over the reintroduction of bourgeois specialists and "one-man leadership" reveals that the party's position on these questions was heavily influenced by the

9. Such as Maurice Dobb, *Soviet Economic Development Since 1917* (New York: International Publishers, 1948), p. 429. More specifically, there is a problem of determining how much of the impetus toward a planned "command economy" is Marxist in inspiration and how much has been read back into Marx by Soviet advocates of the new transplanted management technologies. Bukharin wrote in 1920, for example, that Marx and Engels (who had in fact little to say about planning), in predicting the end of political economy after the proletarian revolution, had implied that the end of the spontaneous forces of the market would require conscious and prearranged control of an organized national economy by national plan. George R. Feiwel, *The Soviet Quest for Efficiency: Issues, Controversies and Reforms* (New York: Praeger, 1976), p. 18.

hopes of Lenin and his adherents that Taylorism offered a solution to the problems of socialist organization, and by the insistence of the Taylorites upon specialization, and upon high levels of discipline from above. The general outlines of party policy during this period are well-known; they consisted of reestablishing power by a ruthless policy of force. The details of the application of that force in many areas, however, are frequently pure Taylorism, consciously derived, and applied in new and more brutal ways than ever before.

By the spring of 1918, conditions in industry had reached hitherto unknown depths of demoralization and disorganization. War casualties and the retreat of workers to the villages had created a labor shortage that was to become more severe with the civil war and famine. The breakdown of the money economy and intermediate economic organizations left workers to barter factory output, spare parts, and equipment on the black market in order to obtain the means of survival. The Congress of the Supreme Council of Public Economy met in May of 1918 to set up commissions to deal with the most urgent problems of restoring the economy. These problems had been presented by the Central Soviet Executive, following a series of speeches by Lenin in which he demanded that the economy be rebuilt by making capitalist science serviceable to a socialist regime. In particular, strong administrative measures were required to eliminate shortages by raising labor productivity through the reestablishment of labor discipline. As he stated in his speech, *Immediate Tasks of the Soviet Government*:

> We must *ponder over the fact* that *in addition* to being able to conquer in civil war, it is necessary to be able to do practical *organizational* work in order that the administration may be successful.[10]

This organizational work, which was crucial to the success of the revolution, involves a number of steps, as Lenin made clear, among them differential high salaries for specialists, and bonuses, which were crucial in overcoming the industrial backwardness that was costing the proletariat far more than the bonuses would cost. In particular, however, Lenin said that productivity must be raised, and that this could be done only by improving *labor discipline*—the intensity, skill, and organization of work.

---

10. V. I. Lenin, *Selected Works* (London: Lawrence & Wishard, 1937), 7:316.

In a passage which set American industrialists to crowing when its translation first became available in the United States, Lenin went on to say:

> The Russian is a bad worker compared with the workers of the advanced countries. Nor could it be otherwise under the tsarist regime and in view of the tenacity of the remnants of serfdom. The task that the Soviet government must set the people in all its scope is—learn to work. The Taylor system, the last word of capitalism in this respect, like all capitalist progress, is a combination of the subtle brutality of bourgeois exploitation and a number of its greatest scientific achievements in the field of analyzing mechanical motions during work, the elimination of superfluous and awkward motions, the working out of correct methods of work, the introduction of the best system of accounting and control, etc. The Soviet Republic must at all costs adopt all that is valuable in the achievements of science and technology in this field. The possibility of building socialism will be determined precisely by our success in combining the Soviet government and the Soviet organization of administration with the modern achievements of capitalism. We must organize in Russia the study and teaching of the Taylor system and systematically try it out and adapt it to our purposes. At the same time, in approaching the task of raising the productivity of labor, we must take into account the specific features of the transition period from capitalism to socialism, which, on the one hand, requires that the foundations be laid of the socialist organization of competition, and on the other hand the application of coercion, so the slogan "dictatorship of the proletariat" shall not be desecrated by the practice of a jelly-fish proletarian government.[11]

This method could not be adopted, however, without directly overriding the workers' committees in the factories and the trade unions; like their Western counterparts, these had been bitterly opposed to Taylorism, and they sensed the imminent betrayal of labor interests and union independence by the party. This argument, published in *Vperyod*, April 1918, was scornfully quoted by Lenin in his denunciation of the Menshevik opposition:

> The policy of Soviet power, from the very outset devoid of a genuinely proletarian character, has lately pursued more and more openly a course of compromise with the bourgeoisie and has assumed an obviously anti-workingclass character. On the pretext of nationalizing industry, they are

11. Ibid., p. 332. This translation soon became available in pamphlet form and was widely quoted in the United States in the early 1920s—frequently by conservative business circles.

pursuing a policy of establishing industrial trusts, and on the pretext of restoring the productive forces of the country, they are attempting to abolish the eight-hour day, to introduce piecework and the Taylor system, black lists, and victimization. This policy threatens to deprive the proletariat of its most important economic gains and to make it a victim of unrestricted exploitation by the bourgeoisie.[12]

The trade unions, through their leader Ryazanoff, raised strenuous objections to the adoption of Taylor piecework norms; they proposed a system in which industry trade unions would have collective responsibility for government-set minimums of production. The union representatives argued that workers in the West had fought piecework and Taylorism for years and that, if the soviets adopted such a system on the plea of raising production, they would have sacrificed all the conquests of the revolution. The Taylor system would exploit the swift and break the weak. With deep emotion Ryazanoff addressed the meeting:

> Do not, I beg you comrades, commit this terrible mistake, which the organized workers of Western Europe, with greater experience than you, have spent years trying to avoid.[13]

The Bolshevik leaders rose to denounce collective responsibility as a cover for industrial sabotage. Only the Taylor system could establish the individual discipline in each worker which the revolution had failed to give him. Lenin himself wrote a powerful polemic against the "Left Communists" who opposed the introduction of labor discipline, and, specifically, Taylorism, into Russian industry, and he compared their anti-Taylorite "theses" with those of the Mensheviks, who had claimed that the introduction of Taylorism amounted to handing back the country to the bourgeoisie. The use of capitalist "management" is not capitalism, Lenin said, when it is used only in the organization of work, and when the workers' commissars "watch the manager's every step."[14] Taylorism became the labor policy of the Soviet State as Lenin dictated the final form that the decree on labor discipline should take:

---

12. V. I. Lenin, *Selected Works* (New York: International Publishers, 1971), p. 450.
13. M. Philips Price, *My Reminiscences of the Russian Revolution* (London: George Allen & Unwin, 1921), p. 283.
14. Lenin, *Selected Works* (New York), "Left-Wing Childishness and the Petty-Bourgeois Mentality," pp. 450-51.

In the decree it is essential to make a definite statement on the introduction of the Taylor system, that is to say, to use all the scientific methods of labor, which this system suggests. Without it, it will be impossible to raise productivity, and without this we will not introduce Socialism. For the construction of this system, [we should] attract American engineers. Naturally, in its introduction it is indispensable to take into account bad nourishment, therefore we ought to establish famine norms of manufacture. The further organization of manufacture . . . in the transition to socialism will give us the possibility of shortening the working day. In the decree it is necessary to refer to accounting and the printing of accounts, relating to the production departments of enterprises. . . .[15]

TROTSKY'S PROMOTION OF TAYLORISM

While Lenin's theoretical espousal of Taylorism, and his orders to import American engineers trained in Taylorism were important in setting Russia on the path toward big-government Scientific Management, the influence of Trotsky appears to have had greater effect in actually impressing Taylorism upon the day-to-day operations of Soviet organization. More than Lenin (who concentrated on party organization) Trotsky influenced actual state and economic organization, first through his position as Commissar of War and his organization of the Red Army, and then through his interest in logistical support for the army, which led to his attempts to influence factory management and his takeover of the transport industry. His ideas of organization, long considered a manifestation of his secret Napoleonic leanings, as well as the foundation of Soviet bureaucracy, were, in truth, direct outgrowths of the demands of Taylorism in the Russian situation, influenced (as he later ruefully admitted) by the data on industry supplied to the largely ignorant, new Soviet leaders by Taylorite engineers with their own ideological axes to grind.[16] Many authors point out that Stalin first discredited Trotsky and then

15. Lenin, *Polnie sobranie sochinenii*, 36:212-213. "Statement to the Meeting of the Presidium of the Supreme Council of the National Economy" concerning the project of labor discipline, and made during a period of famine—hence the reference to lowered norms of production.

16. ". . . during the following months the situation grew steadily worse. There was cause enough in actual conditions, but it is also very probable that certain engineers were making the transport situation fit their diagrams" (the "death" prediction in 1920, that is). Leon Trotsky, *My Life* (New York: Charles Scribner's Sons, 1930), p. 463.

stole his ideas. In the sphere of industrial organization, what he stole was Taylorism, ready-made, and forced into Russian industry by all the coercive power at the command of a totalitarian regime.

Trotsky's reorganization of the Red Army out of the disintegrated fragments of the Russian army not only established, by its success, certain patterns of operation in Soviet society, but impressed Trotsky himself to the point that he espoused the systematic transfer of the techniques involved as the solution to the problem of postrevolutionary chaos in industry and labor relations. Men and regimes both tend to repeat the pattern of their first successes. Coming to the army with no previous military experience, Trotsky at once saw the inadequacy of traditional methods of keeping order in a period when revolutionary enthusiasm was the only motivating force left for organization. At the same time, however, that enthusiasm had to be balanced with expertise and adequate logistical backup if it were to succeed against the traditional armies of the Whites (Russian counterrevolutionaries) and of Western Europe.[17]

For the revolutionary army, then, Trotsky established a new mix of charismatic leadership, propaganda, and strong discipline. Taking over the Commissariat of War in early 1918, he came out in direct opposition to previous Bolshevik military propaganda in his speech, *Trud, distsiplina, poriadok, spasut Sotsialisticheskuiu Sovetskuiu Respubliku* [Work, discipline, and order will save the Soviet Socialist Republic], in which he called for a return of the bourgeois specialists, the "technicians, engineers, doctors, teachers, and former officers" because "in them is invested our true people's national capital, which we are obliged to exploit, to use, if we want to resolve the basic problems which stand before us."[18]

Both in the army and in the armaments industry, the luxury of eliminating the technicians as ideologically unfit had to be foregone. Trotsky brought the "bourgeois" officers back into service, and to insure their loyalty, established a parallel system of ideologically reliable, political commissars, whose countersignature was required on every order. Of necessity, he found that he had to hold the balance of power between these two hierarchies himself. The essential element in this organizational plan, however, was not the mechanics of control

17. Trotsky discusses this problem in depth in chs. 34-36 of *My Life*.
18. Leon Trotsky, *Trud, distsiplina, poriadok, spasut Sotsialisticheskuiu Sovetskuiu Respubliku*, Monograph (Moscow: Izd. "Kommunist," 1918), p. 15.

but Trotsky himself. Relying upon his oratorical gifts, he appeared to be everywhere at once on the front, urging, exhorting, and inspiring the makeshift army as his special train crossed and recrossed Russia. Commanders begged for his presence as "worth a division," while his charismatic stature grew.

But even as the success of this military organizational effort was becoming apparent, the industrial establishment that supported it was decaying at an ever-increasing rate. A fuel crisis had been developing since 1915, and even if the Germans and then the Whites had not captured the Donets basin, source of most of Russia's coal, transportation difficulties would have drastically cut the supply available. Agriculture had been devastated by war as well as by government requisitions. The result was a severe decline in industrial production, not only because of the material conditions of industrial supply, but due to the breakdown of "labor discipline." Absenteeism, lateness, and strikes not only accounted for a sharp drop in actual work hours by 1919, as opposed to 1914, the beginning of the World War, but a severe labor shortage arose when the semipeasant work force fled to the countryside because of food and fuel shortages in the city.[19]

In the fall of 1919, engineer Lomonosov, in charge of the transport system, made a diagram of the "locomotive epidemic" for the government. Locomotive repair was declining to the point that the railway transportation system of Russia, upon which the war and the economy depended, was doomed. Sixty percent of the engines were already "sick"; twenty-five percent were needed to transport the bulky wood fuel required by the railways themselves, so that as the number of inoperative locomotives reached seventy-five percent, actual transport declined to zero. As Trotsky was later to recall:

> Indicating a mathematical point in the year 1920, he [Lomonosov] declared: "Here comes death."
>
> "What is to be done then," asked Lenin.
>
> "There are no such things as miracles," Lomonosov replied.

19. L. Pasvolsky, *The Economics of Communism* (New York: Macmillan Co., 1931), pp. 168-73. The author deplores the lack of figures on lateness, but cites extensive numerical data which show that absences approach 80%, as opposed to a prerevolutionary average of 15%. Strangely enough, this numerical data, published in the Russian press from 1919-20, pertains to transport workers and railroad shops. One suspects that the availability of this type of data bears a direct relation to the influence of Taylorites in the transport industry.

"Even the Bolsheviks cannot perform miracles." We looked at each other, all the more depressed because none of us knew the technical workings of the transport system, nor the technical workings of such gloomy calculations. "Still, we'll try to perform the miracle," Lenin muttered dryly through his teeth.[20]

To restore transportation and industry, Lenin turned to Trotsky, who advocated the tactics that had worked so well in the army. The Commissariat of the Army should be converted into a Commissariat of Labor, and transport in particular should be singled out for restoration by new methods. The army passbooks should be converted into labor passbooks; the entry for "occupation before entering the army" should be used for determining the amount and disposition of labor available. Labor should be conscripted and transferred when needed, and "labor deserters" (those who had fled to the countryside) put in concentration camps. All possible coercive and psychological management-control devices should be put to work to raise labor productivity and break down all obstructions. The trade unions, once necessary to protect the worker against his capitalist bosses, were no longer needed to protect him against the workers' state; therefore, the independent power of the trade unions should be broken, and they should become arms of the state. "Socialist competition," stringent piecework rates, bonuses for the despised "bourgeois specialists," and "shock brigades" composed of *udarniki* were advocated. (This military terminology for "rate breakers" or exceptional workers was introduced into the language by Trotsky.) The plan, backed by Lenin but put forth by Trotsky, was the celebrated "militarization of labor" advocated at the Ninth Party Congress.[21]

The proposal evoked a storm of opposition within the party (categorized as "left S-Rs") and Trotsky defended it in the following way: "militarism" is a bad word to the left S-Rs, symbolizing barbarism in their minds, but this, he said, should only refer to *bourgeois* militarism. In advanced countries, the military hinders progress, but, in backward countries, with its demands for advanced

20. Trotsky, *My Life*, p. 463.

21. Summarized from Leon Trotsky, "Khozyaistvennoe stroitel'stvo Sovetskoi Respubliki" *Sochinenii*, vol. 15 (Moscow: Gos. Izd., 1927). See also, in the same work, "Osnovye zadachi i trudnosti khozyaistvennogo stroitel'stva," 6 January 1920. Trotsky's innovative terminology is discussed in I. Deutscher, *The Prophet Armed: Trotsky, 1879-1921* (New York: Oxford University Press, 1954).

technology, the military is a force for advancement. (This argument, too, is one we hear repeated to this day.) He goes on to equate his concept of the militarization of labor with Taylorism:

> The whole list of characteristics of militarism, *not* in the Left S-R sense of the word, merges with that which we call Taylorism. What is Taylorism? On the one hand, it is a refined form of exploitation of the labor force, the most merciless, when every movement, each breath is accounted for and watched for by the henchmen of capital, in order to convert this breath into profit. On the other hand, it is a system of wise expenditure of human strength participating in production ... This side of Taylorism the socialist manager ought to make his own, and if we take militarism, then we will see that it had always been near to Taylorism.[22]

How did Trotsky come to this curious espousal of "militarized" Taylorism? The answer lies in those engineers who provided the sources of data for his analysis of industry. In his defense of Taylorism, he points to the disorganization of industry, the loss of the best manpower to the administrative soviets and to the army; he gives the source of his apprehension:

> The American engineer Kili [*sic*: Kelly?], a Taylorist, who came for the Taylorization of our economy, hoping that a nationalized economy would serve as a favorable base for Taylorization, for its scientific wise construction, now paints the condition of our industry in the darkest colors. According to his account, loafing occupies about 50% (of all productive time) and the general expenditure of energy of the worker in the procurement of food he counts at 80%, while 20% remains for actual industrial work. I did not check these data, but Kili—this man, who has an excellent reputation in America, who came to us of his own free will in order to be of assistance, is accounted by everyone to be an absolutely honest and dedicated man. He is, in America, accounted to have great authority in matters of production. All these data force us to regard his numbers with no less faith than those of our Soviet statisticians—the more so because there are no contradictions between them.[23]

But according to engineer Kili's report, Trotsky goes on to state,

---

22. Trotsky, *Sochinenii*, vol. 15, p. 92. Gramsci also stresses the identification of Trotsky's "militarization of labor" with "Americanism," or Taylor-style rationalization. Antonio Gramsci, *Americanism and Fordism*, in *Selections from the Prison Notebooks* (New York: International Publishers, 1971), pp. 301-302.
23. Trotsky, *Sochinenii*, vol. 15, p. 85.

transport is in a worse state than industry as a whole. Here we find that Lomonosov's "death" pronouncement was Taylorite in origin and Taylorite in its aim:

> Engineer Kili in his report says that the fate of the country is linked with industry, the fate of industry with transport, and this is linked in its turn with the repair of locomotives; consequently, it is possible to say that the fate of the country depends on the repair of locomotives. I think that he is unconditionally correct.
>
> He says, according to the information of engineers, that our railroad network will come to a stop at the end of this winter. He does not say that he has the means [to combat] against this, but he says that he cannot imagine how this country will live without transport . . . Comrade Lomonosov, who is a big authority in railroad matters, a theoretician and specialist [who] arrived from America with Kili, is now occupied with the matter. In the Defense Soviet he demonstrated a scheme from which it concluded that if the falloff in engine repairs continues at the same tempo as now, then in the course of 1920, in the fall or the winter, we will not have one "well" engine.[24]

Continuing his recital of industrial conditions, Trotsky declared that the party must put the facts before the masses, telling them that the Soviet Republic is menaced with total ruin, examining the means of survival as a nation under these conditions and in the face of an endless blockade which prevents the import of the necessary machinery. The means he preferred, of course, was the "militarization of labor," whose details corresponded to an enlarged plan of Taylorism, applied on a national scale. The Taylorites had at last come within reach of their dream of a scientifically managed state: an entire nation run as a huge Taylorite factory, rationally, without waste, friction, or dissension. The Taylorites had shown the Bolsheviks the ultimate weapon against chaos.

Opposition to this program of action formed quickly. Apathetic and exhausted from the long war, the masses wanted to see some sort of materialization of the promises of the revolution, and in this they were supported by certain factions among the Bolsheviks, who wanted a strengthening of the systems by which labor and the conditions of

24. Ibid., p. 86. American aid for Russian transportation was not a brief interlude, but continued long after Trotsky's exile. During the First Five Year Plan and the Second Five Year Plan, Ralph Budd, president of the Great Northern Railroad, became transportation advisor to Soviet engineers. See W. H. G. Armytage, *The Rise of the Technocrats: A Social History* (London: Routledge & Kegan Paul, 1965), p. 223.

production could be controlled by the trade unions and other workers' groups. Trotsky had, in fact, foreseen this exhaustion; he had suggested to Lenin the prototype of the New Economic Policy (NEP), a period of somewhat more liberal relaxation; he had plunged to the opposite extreme when Lenin vetoed the scheme.[25] As the opposition formed to the latter plan, however, Lenin disassociated himself from Trotsky and took a middle-of-the-road stance in the trade union and labor question. The liberal opposition to militarization, known as the "Workers' Opposition," formed within the party—at first informally, and then as an organized group, headed by Shliapnikov and Mme. Kollontai, which operated on the slogan "Soviets without Bolsheviks." As the Ninth Congress was in session, a workers' revolt against the Bolshevik regime broke out. The naval base at Kronstadt, which had played such an important role in the revolution, was now pressing for the continuation of the revolution. Trotsky's troops put down the revolt by force as Lenin backtracked to present the New Economic Plan to the Tenth Congress. Later, the Workers' Opposition was condemned and factionalism outlawed. The Kronstadt revolt marked the turning point in the consolidation of Communist authoritarianism. It also marked a tactical retreat from War Communism to the looser system of the New Economic Plan.

THE INFLUENCE OF SCIENTIFIC MANAGEMENT ON SOVIET PLANNING AND LABOR DISCIPLINE

The defeat of War Communism and the plan for militarization of all labor did not end Russian Taylorism, but rather forced it deeper into the fabric of Russian organization, giving it, eventually, the appearance of a native phenomenon. Trotsky had, in fact, taken over all land and water transport, and got the railways running again by means of systematization and standardization of locomotive repair and operations along Taylorite lines, the takeover of the transport workers' union, and the establishment of centralized bureaucratic control.[26] And as the history of the United States arsenals shows, Taylorism, once established, can be dislodged in name only. During

25. Trotsky, *My Life*, p. 464.
26. Trotsky, *My Life*, p. 465, describes this process, leaving no doubt as to the technology employed. The year of work in Taylorizing the railroads was like a year in school, said Trotsky, for "all the fundamental questions of socialist organization of economic life found their most concentrated expression in the sphere of transport."

the NEP period, agriculture and petty industry were left to the private economy, but the "commanding heights"—industries of national importance—were still run by the state and the party. Lenin never considered the NEP more than a temporary expedient, designed to allow an increase in the supply of goods and services prior to the reestablishment of total state control and a more ambitious program of national economic development through the application of the general systems of social planning which Soviet economists attributed to Marx.

Thus, during the 1920s, the party, from its position on the "commanding heights," prepared the First Five Year Plan, using the services of foreign Scientific Management specialists and all of the multitude of techniques in the Taylorite armory. Such services, by this time, were indeed extensive—for as Stalin estimated twenty years later, two-thirds of Russian industry had been built by Americans. Not just transportation, but electrification was to play an important role ("Communism equals Soviet power plus the electrification of the whole country"), and American influence was strong in this field as well. Charles Steinmetz himself, later to become one of the early movers in the organization of the technocracy movement, aided the Russian electrification effort, and a constant stream of engineering exchanges to train Soviet engineers in American methods was a feature of the period.[27]

Walter Polakov, formerly a disciple of Gantt's and a member of the "New Machine" which had once aimed to reorganize American government on Scientific Management principles, came to the Soviet Union, and, serving as consulting engineer to the Supreme Economic Soviet, gave valuable aid in shaping the form and content of the Plan. He had the entire First Five Year Plan drawn up on Gantt charts, and he served in general as a link between the Russian and American Scientific Management movements.[28] The Marxist dictum that national planning should replace the capitalist market economy was being fleshed out with Taylorism.

27. See Armytage, pp. 223, 219-39. For an excellent discussion of the key role of the Goelro Plan (electrification) in the formation of the Soviet planning system as a whole, see Eugene Zaleski, *Planning for Economic Growth in the Soviet Union, 1918-1932* (Chapel Hill: University of North Carolina Press, 1971).
28. Alford, p. 215. Polakov seems to have been one of the main links in this process. He made the Russian charts available for publication in the United States, and did the translation of Clark's *The Gantt Chart* into Russian.

The 1920s complete the shift of Russian Taylorism from the organization of factory production to a generalized administrative technique via its introduction into the heart of the economic planning apparatus. The publicity for Taylorism and for American efficiency, along with the official worship of Ford, rather than ceasing with War Communism, went to an all-time high, as the party attempted to convince an entire nation that Scientific Management was identical with Scientific Marxism. Taylor's books were reprinted and numerous commentaries published. Scarce foreign exchange was used to purchase Scientific Management movies (most probably Gilbreth's pioneering films on motion study).[29] Clark's book on the uses of the Gantt chart was published and republished beginning in 1925;[30] the cadre of domestic experts on Taylorism grew through the recruitment of the old bourgeois technical specialists, using a combination of incentives and strict party control.[31] The Scientific-Technical Committee of the Supreme Soviet was set up, apparently with the help of American specialists, to conduct continuous scientific experiments related to the setting of industrial output norms, to investigate standards, to do fatigue studies, and to carry out all the other operations of a Taylorite scientific planning department.[32]

The Soviet apologists for Taylorism echoed Lenin in claiming that Taylorism was not exploitative in the socialist context, but only when it was established in bourgeois society. Such authors make it clear that the Russians were already acquainted on a wide scale with the works of Taylor, Gilbreth, Gantt, Barth, Hoxie, and even of Hugo Münsterburg and Walther Rathenau.[33] Gantt's system of piecework premiums, which involved special premiums for supervisors, foremen, and specialists, especially impressed them.[34] This very system, indeed, turns up in the abuses of the 1930s and is frequently castigated as a Russian invention.

29. F. Barghoorn, *The Soviet Image of the United States: A Study in Distortion* (New York: Harcourt, Brace and Co., 1950). This source was suggested, in conversation, by S. N. Silverman.

30. See Wallace Clark, *Grafika Ganta*, trans. Walter Polakov (1st trans. ed., 1926; Moscow: n.p., 1931).

31. Chakhotin in 1923 speaks of having taught Scientific Management in Russia; see Sergei S. Chakhotin, *Organizatsiia: printsipy i metody v proizvodstve, torgovle, administratsii i politike* (Berlin: Izd-vo "Opyt," 1923).

32. I. Rabchinskii, *O sisteme Teilora* (Moscow: Gos. Tech. Izd., 1921).

33. Chakhotin mentions all of these authors, along with the original Taylor-White experiments. They are also cited by Rabchinskii, *O sisteme Teilora*.

34. Rabchinskii, *O sisteme Teilora*, pp. 60-61.

Most interesting of all of the work of the apologists is the attempt that takes place in the 1920s to use Taylor as a justification not only for the victorious policy of "one-man command," but to explain the role of managers and specialists in terms of functional foremanship, thus laying claim to the preservation of principles of collegial leadership. Even the multiple controls on bourgeois specialists, including the parallel hierarchies of party "political specialists" could be explained as a return to "collegiality," thus countering the complaint that the party had abandoned democratic control. Functional foremanship, claimed the party, was going to be the basis of an emerging rule of interlocking councils of technical specialists. Conciliar government did not mean that *everyone* ruled, but that the qualified ruled. This was the true meaning of socialist democracy.[35]

The industrialization drive of the Stalinist era picked up and magnified the themes of the early 1920s. Lenin had died in 1924, with the NEP still in operation. Not until Stalin had finally triumphed in the subsequent power struggle was the way clear for him to attempt to solve the problems of inadequate agricultural supply and weak industrial development by the implementation of the First Five Year Plan, in 1928. The plan called for the raising of agricultural productivity by collectivization—the replacement of petty landholders by large-scale operations—and mechanization. At the same time, priority in the industrial sphere was given to the large-scale development of heavy industry: coal, steel, hydroelectric power, and so forth. The influence of the American model of mass scale and bigness was highly visible in this scheme; it had been consciously chosen by the planners on the grounds that it was more suited to Russia's broad expanse and abundant, if untapped, natural resources, than the Western European model of smaller and more flexible industries.[36] While the collectivization plan was a domestic creation, the projects of labor discipline and rapid technical training (the replacement of old bourgeois experts with Red experts) bore the marks of the Russian experience with Taylorism. Stalin's opening speech on the project of labor discipline was a verbatim reproduction of one made by Trotsky during his infamous attempt to militarize labor.[37]

35. Ibid., pp. 66-68.

36. Lincoln Hutchinson, *American Engineers in Russia, 1928-1932*. Unpublished manuscript survey in Hoover Library, Stanford University, Palo Alto, California.

37. Deutscher, *The Prophet Armed*, p. 515, shows that Stalin's 1929

The shortage of engineers at the beginning of the plan, and the later depression in the West meant that during the initial, or training, phases of the plan, the Soviets could import great numbers of foreign specialists who were unemployed at home. Some specialists were German, British, and Swiss, but most were American, and well-versed in Scientific Management techniques. This second influx of American-trained engineers had far less influence than had the first, however. Imported into what was essentially a going operation, the foreign experts, however needed they might be in setting up industries and training Red experts, ran almost immediately into an impenetrable wall of Russian chauvinism and professional jealousy. The Shakhty trials and subsequent trials of engineers for "wrecking" and "sabotage" indicated that the respect for technology and for the genuine difficulties of applying the plan were not primary factors in the industrial drive. The visiting Americans, both professional men and laborers—many of whom were convinced communists—recognized with amazement the grotesque methods of Taylorism that prevailed in factory management. Just how had the fad for Scientific Management during the period of "War Communism" been transformed into Stalinist techniques?

An examination of the Stalinist techniques indicates that none of the internal control mechanisms which Taylorites claimed for their system actually functioned; the only limits on Scientific Management as a disastrous form of exploitation of the working class were provided by external environmental controls, these being a product of American culture and government. In the Soviet Union, where policy removed these controls, Taylorism assumed a monstrous form. All the potential flaws of the system became visible, and the consequences were suppressed by force. The source of power for a "new class," the suppression of trade unions, and the potential for worker association were all present. Amazing combinations of techniques uncovered new potential for deranging skilled production. For example, the Gantt bonus system, combined with an excessive passion for piecework in a context of extreme worker deprivation, brought about extensive damage to capital equipment, which was noticed over and over again by foreign engineers who were powerless to stop it.

The piecework system became the fetish of the Soviet industrializa-

---

Sixteenth Party Conference resolution on "socialist emulation" is identical to Trotsky's resolution of 1920.

tion effort; it was extended to all possible, and some impossible, types of application. With piecework came the speed-up—ostensibly from below, by a combination of scientific setting of rates and worker enthusiasm, but actually from above, by setting exaggerated quotas from the central planning system, and placing responsibility for their fulfillment with party members who were mostly without technical expertise. These party managers and ratesetters were given monetary awards for success (the Gantt plan), or shot for sabotage in case of failure (the Stalin plan). In this way, such procedures as machine maintenance, for example, were put on piecework. The machine requiring repairs was disassembled; the parts went to a white-collar, rate-setting specialist who set a time and rate for the repair of each piece, usually without understanding the different types of labor involved. If the time set was decreased, the rate setter, but not the repairman, got a bonus. The result was, of course, exaggerated estimates of the speed and savings on machine repair. Frequently, however, when the time came to reassemble the machine, vital parts were missing; they had been stolen by the workers and sold on the black market in exchange for food. The whole fiasco would be covered up by the management, understandably anxious to avoid charges of wrecking; as a result, the quota would be too high for the remaining machines to fulfill.[38]

Observers repeatedly noticed machinery (usually valuable American, German, or Swiss imports) either rusting outside the factory for lack of spare parts, or screaming and smoking as the workers tried to fulfill their quotas on piecework rates set so low that they could not take time to fill the oil cups and still make a living wage. Workers, desperate to meet their daily minimum, exasperated the technical advisors by taking bigger cuts than the machinery could make without damage. Disillusioned foreigners would estimate (as the Russian technicians themselves complained years later, when on loan to the Chinese during the Great Leap Forward) that the loss in machine damage was greater than the value of factory output.

The techniques of mass production, so highly touted by the official party line, were undermined even further by immediate needs in a situation of weak economic coordination. The five year plans ap-

38. Andrew Smith, *I Was a Soviet Worker* (New York: E. P. Dutton, 1936), p. 45, describes this system. Smith wrote a letter directly to Stalin to inform him of the condition of the machinery and the high rates of injury. These conditions were, however, commonly observed, and Stalin appears to have been uninterested in such details.

peared to encourage the multiplication of paperwork and of supervisory levels at the same time that the effectiveness of the organizational underpinnings of such growth was lost through enthusiastic overapplication. By 1931, the Ford plant at Gorky, for example, which had been established with such fanfare, had degenerated into a management nightmare. The much-heralded Ford assembly line was in operation, in conjunction with Taylorite controls, but under conditions which negated many of the benefits of these systems. Instead of mass-producing the same model, the factory was turning out individual trucks, buses, and passenger vehicles. No two vehicles on the line were of the same type![39]

If Taylorism did not, in this disordered context, show positive results in the form of lowered production costs, it nonetheless had advantages that compensated for these immediate losses in efficiency. It was still a valuable scheme for the rapid training of workers through the simplification and recording of tasks. It was a useful form of control over labor that went hand in hand with the extension of government control over the trade unions. In addition, it elevated the place of the white-collar planner and technician in industry; just as it had done in the United States, it increased the number of advantageous positions in factory management that might be offered to party members.

TAYLORISM AND STAKHANOVISM

Nowhere are the social and disciplinary advantages of Taylorism (as opposed to its cost efficiency) more clearly illustrated than in its application to labor discipline in the Soviet Union. These are particularly clear in the campaign of speed-up and labor discipline known as Stakhanovism, which became one of the most important features of the Second Five Year Plan.

The Second Five Year Plan brought with it an intensive campaign to "master technique," continuing the drive for the development of heavy industry by emphasizing remedies for those conditions which had presented unforeseen difficulties in the First Five Year Plan. Coordination was the theme; one-man command was the guiding principle, and an increase in labor discipline was first among the new priorities. Severe penalties were now laid down for lateness and absenteeism.

39. Ibid., p. 189.

Labor-books, on the Trotsky model, were established as a control on labor turnover. Given the general condition of the economy, these measures look rather like draconic attempts to repair major social defects by fiat and coercion. A delay of twenty minutes in arriving at work resulted in a transfer from remunerative to forced labor, and absence without a medical excuse was punished similarly. Admittedly, many Russian workers were villagers lacking habits of punctuality, and so forth, but at this late date, much of the "labor discipline" problem came from a profound disregard for the quality of life of the working class because of the Stalinist policy of single-minded investment in industrial development.[40] Workers were late on cloudy mornings because they rose by the sun, having no clocks. Mothers were absent caring for sick children—the promised nurseries and medical care were nonexistent. Labor discipline under conditions of want took on a sinister new meaning. But more than punctuality was needed to raise labor productivity beyond the levels of the First Five Year Plan; in 1935, a systematized form of piecework speed-up, backed by extensive government propaganda, was introduced. This system, known as Stakhanovism, in honor of a coal miner who mined fourteen times the normal amount of coal in a single shift, was soon recognized to be based on an intensive application of Scientific Management methods. Yet the style of this movement was authentically Russian in many ways. Specifically, it outreached the farthest excesses of Taylorism itself, pushed on by Slavic zeal in a national environment now freed, thanks to Stalin, from the counterpressures of organized labor.

Several common questions arise in relation to Stakhanovism. First, what was its relation to the older "shock worker" system? Next, was it an extension of Taylorism, or was it domestic, invented and promoted by ingenious workers, as advertised? And last—did it really work? The answers to these questions indicate to what extent Scientific Management had penetrated the official thinking of the Communist party of the Soviet Union.

The old *udarnik* ("shock worker") system was set up under Trotsky, borrowing its glamour and nomenclature from the practices of the Red Army in the field. But it appears to have had, originally, a group

---

40. Victor Kravchenko, *I Chose Freedom* (New York: Charles Scribner's Sons, 1952) describes in detail the effect of these well-known directives in the context of day-to-day operations.

basis: a "shock brigade" of advanced, high-output workers would be established in a factory as a model of action and new work techniques. Subsequently, norms (the standard piecework rate) would be raised, ostensibly because of emulation and the effects of the teaching of this advanced experience. In practice, foreign engineers found that the system really did work more or less as intended, in the first phases, "because of the novelty,"[41] the Mayo "human relations" effect, in other words. But the practice was applied ever more widely, wherever a shortage existed that needed to be caught up (in short, everywhere), in factories, in whole industries, and as a widespread technique for increasing the rewards to higher-output workers in general. When every worker and every group that could manage to do so became a "shock worker" or a "shock brigade," then the special output effects of having first priority were dissipated. The term passed into generalized use, and while it had some value as a job classification entitling special ration privileges, it lost most of its specific effect on labor productivity.

Stakhanovism came to have elements resembling the shock brigade practice, but in its original conception, it stressed *individual* achievement. While high output was in fact attained by a better division of labor and the trimming off of superfluous functions in approved Taylorite style, the rewards, as in Taylorism, went to individual "rate breakers," setting them in competition with their fellow workers. Stakhanovism ideally tapped the hitherto hidden abilities of workers, who, being close to production, could spontaneously invent techniques enabling them to double and triple their output without excessive physical strain. As in the *udarnik* movement, the thrust for improvement of standards, officially speaking, came from below—as did the subsequent raising of norms.

This official emphasis on the movement's grass-roots origin is the source of the dissassociation of Stakhanovism and Russian Taylorism. Not only did the Russians themselves insist that there was no connection, but some Western authors, following their lead, concluded that this was indeed the case. Maurice Dobb, in his authoritative history of Soviet economic development, states:

> When the Stakhanovite movement began to develop, it was commonly discounted abroad as a propaganda-facade; while some dismissed it as simply Taylorism in Russian clothes. But subsequent events as well as closer enquiry into the movement show that it cannot be so lightly

41. Hutchinson, pt. 1, pp. 33-34.

dismissed as this. The methods used in the main introduced no new principle, and it is true that few of them will surprise students of American Scientific Management. . . . [W]hat was novel about it was that it represented a movement to rationalise working methods that arose from the initiative of individual workers themselves; and as such its achievements came as a definite surprise to the management of industry.[42]

Dobb goes on to contrast this picture with that of the forceful introduction of Taylorism in Western countries by "efficiency engineers"; he indicates that the new types of rationalization devised made possible permanently higher levels of production without excessive stress on the workers. This is as fair a summary of the Russian sources as exists.

The social context of Stakhanovism—Russia in the mid-1930s, subscribing to a doctrine of capitalist encirclement and on the brink of a new era of bloody purges within the party, having just emerged from the wholesale slaughter of collectivization—makes it apparent that the official sources would do nothing *but* stress the authentic grass-roots ethnicity of the system. The fascination with things American, at its height during War Communism, faded gradually until it was destroyed by the failure of American machines and engineers to bring about the miracles expected during the early years of the First Five Year Plan.[43] In this early period, even Stalin himself had spoken enthusiastically about the American example:

American practicality is an antidote to such phrase-mongering and "flights of revolutionary fancy." It is "that indomitable force, which knows and recognizes no obstacle, which by its businesslike perseverence washes away all and every impediment, which simply must go through with a job begun even if it is of minor importance, and without which any serious constructive work is impossible." But American practicality, Stalin maintained, runs the risk of degenerating into narrow and unprincipled commercialism, unless it is fused with the wide outlook of the Russian revolutionist. Only a combination of both, he concluded, produces a finished type of Leninist worker, the Leninist style of work.[44]

But when it became apparent that the Americans possessed no extraordinary secrets, anger followed disillusionment. The "Leninists" (including Stalin himself in his younger days) had stressed learning from capitalism and stealing its thunder; the latter-day "Stalinists" stressed

42. Dobb, p. 429.   43. Hutchinson, pt. 1, p. 19.
44. Barghoorn, pp. 28–29.

self-sufficiency to the point that the Soviet Union tried to lay claim to most of the major inventions of technological society. It could not be much different when organizational techniques were the subject of debate. In addition, to stress the Russian, and, indeed, the popular origins of Stakhanovism was to avoid the ticklish problem of the denunciation of the Taylorite speed-up made by Lenin and organized labor—and most of all to exorcise the spectre of the Workers' Opposition. Stalin might borrow Trotsky's words, but he could not do so without being reminded of the fate of the project for the militarization of labor which they espoused. Some appearance of "spontaneity" was essential. But even the stress on worker innovation was not "un-Taylorite," for Taylorism's specific work techniques frequently relied on the recording and propagation of techniques evolved by talented workmen. Gilbreth stressed the importance of developing regular channels for the centralization and transmission of the innovations of individual workers. The difference in the Russian system was only one of emphasis, a more strident populism.

The argument that Stakhanovism is Taylorism, then, rests on several factors. First is the recognition by foreign engineers and workmen then employed in Russia. American workers recognized, frequently with dismay, that Stakhanovism represented the techniques of piecework and speed-up which their unions had taught them to combat.[45] Visiting engineers immediately felt a familiarity with many of the methods of labor control, and used the common American names for them; yet at the same time they complained that their grandiose application in such a desperate economic situation totally undermined any pretense of scientific rationality.[46] While they felt that the older generation of engineers was competent and cultured, it had been too abstract and theoretical. The new Red experts inherited the older engineers' traits of impracticality and hatred of manual labor; to these weaknesses they added arrogance, envy, and a penchant for big ideas whose failure would be covered up by systematic lying. Thus, visiting technicians despaired at the conditions the Russian specialists created, referring to them, for example, as lessons on "how not to run a blast furnace," and stating flatly that "labor efficiency is a joke."[47]

45. See Peter Francis, *I Worked in a Soviet Factory* (London: Jarrold's Publishers, 1939), p. 103, and Smith, *I Was a Soviet Worker*, p. 294.
46. Hutchinson, pt. 1, pp. 7-8, pt. 2, p. 46.
47. Ibid., pt. 2, pp. 19-25, 48.

Yet while the joke was Russian, the common opinion was that the lines had been borrowed, in all seriousness, from the West.

The second argument for the Taylorite origin of Stakhanovism is the continuity of institutions set up under War Communism for the training of personnel, the continual revision of organizations, and the general dissemination of Scientific Management. These institutions never seem to have ceased functioning, even in what appeared to be entirely inappropriate and even hostile environments. In the 1930s, for example, with sixteen to seventeen-hour days and "voluntary" work on holidays the rule, institutes for the scientific study of management problems were turning out fatigue studies with a remarkable resemblance to those of the Gilbreths.

Third is the direct connection of the techniques of Stalin's plan of labor discipline to the proposals made for the militarization of labor made by Trotsky in 1920, which Trotsky himself did not hesitate to call Taylorite in inspiration. This connection, it must be emphasized, is so close that Stalin used long passages from Trotsky's proposal verbatim when introducing Stakhanovism into the five year plans.[48]

Yet, even though the guiding techniques of Stakhanovism were those of Scientific Management, they were not those of Midvale and Tabor, but were distorted tremendously by official sponsorship on a nation-wide scale in a command economy. In this distortion, as in a caricature where the disagreeable features of the subject are enlarged, the most unpleasant of the implicit organizational assumptions of Taylorism were made apparent. The Russian speed-up was Taylorism with teeth; the punitive piecework rates were dropped below the level necessary for the minimal decencies of life, and supplemented with legal penalties. Worker resistance having been destroyed, no set of inner controls prevented the rates from being set beyond the levels of physical endurance. Worst of all, in conditions of industrial disorder, the line between legitimate gains due to reorganization and outright fakery became rather indistinct. This tendency had, indeed, been present in Taylor's first experiments, and it is difficult to imagine how Soviet management specialists, under pressure to duplicate Taylor's results, could resist the temptation to turn to his occasionally dubious methods. Pressure from the center for Stakhanovite achieve-

---

48. I. Deutscher, *Russia in Transition* (New York: Grove Press, 1960), p. 134.

ments could actually lead to an overall decline in production, and subsequent coverups.

A former chief engineer of a newly built steel plant at Nikopol had this to say about the difficulties that the Stakhanovite campaign presented:

> Orders began to pour into Nikopol from Kharkov and Moscow headquarters. Every order was a blunt threat. We must instantly create Stakhanovite brigades, as pace-setters. . . . Engineers or superintendents who raised objections would be treated as saboteurs.
>
> Our plants had been operating less than six months. They worked on three shifts under many handicaps. Neither the amount nor the quality of the steel and other raw stuffs was adequate. The workers were mostly green, the staff mostly inexperienced. . . . Rhythmic teamwork, rather than spurts of record-breaking, was the key to steady output. More than fifteen hundred workers engaged on a common task, in which every operation meshed into the next, couldn't speed up arbitrarily without throwing the whole effort into chaotic imbalance.[49]

Had Taylor himself been in the place of this Soviet engineer, he would have stated no differently the problems involved, particularly after his experience with the disastrous speed-up at Tabor. Constraints of time, lack of skilled technical manpower in the planning apparatus itself, and the threat of dire legal penalties produced their inevitable effects in the Soviet plant:

> In the end, in my own sub-plant, I was obliged to resort to artificial speed-up. . . . On direct orders from the Party Committee, I regrouped my labor, putting the best workers, foremen, and engineers into one shift. Then we selected the best tools and materials, setting them aside for the special shift. . . .
>
> At eleven o'clock one evening, with reporters and photographers present, the "Stakhanovite" shift got under way. As expected, it "overfulfilled" the normal quota by 8 per cent. . . . Congratulations arrived from officials in the capitals. . . . As the responsible technical leader I was given a lot of credit.
>
> But this "victory" . . . was, at bottom, fraudulent and must boomerang. The other two shifts, deprived of their best personnel and their best tools, lost more than the favored group had won. By contrast they seemed ineffective if not actually "lazy." They naturally resented being made the scapegoats.[50]

49. Kravchenko, p. 187.
50. Ibid., p. 188.

The end result of the campaign, according to this witness, was that the sharply graded system of rewards and legal penalties drove a wedge (certainly not Taylor's "hearty spirit of cooperation") between, first of all, the technical staffs and the workers, and then between the different categories of workers themselves. This individualization and division of labor was characteristically Taylorite, and must be considered one of the purposeful outcomes of the Stakhanovite campaign, made possible only by the destruction of autonomous trade unions.

Stakhanovism, only one of the elements of Russian postrevolutionary Taylorism, did not disappear with the death of Stalin. A recent resurrection of the publicity on Stakhanov himself indicates the nostalgia of the Brezhnev-Kosygin regime for the earlier, heroic days of industrialization.[51] Increasing prosperity and popular weariness with stern measures of labor discipline resulted, in the post-Stalin world, in a relaxation of the original patterns of industrialization. The five year plans lengthened into seven year plans; consumer goods industries increased. But it cannot be doubted that, within the system, the pattern of Taylorism, so flamboyantly institutionalized, remained.

THE LEGACY OF SOVIET TAYLORISM

Although the influence of Taylorism on the development of Soviet management practice is an important, if neglected, chapter in Russian industrial history, the general influence of Scientific Management on Soviet government should not be overemphasized. Scientific Management did not cause the emergence of so-called Soviet state capitalism, but reinforced certain characteristic patterns that were already present. To the centralism, autocracy, and paternalism typical of the "command economy" of the czars, Taylorism added techniques of statistical control, planning methods, and an increased capacity for the training of specialized industrial labor. Its influence, then, was confined to the development of systems of rationalization that adapted what was, in many ways, an essentially Petrine system to the demands of mass technology.

There was also in Scientific Management a vein of latent pseudo-scientism that reinforced similar tendencies in Marxism-Leninism. And the postrevolutionary introduction of Taylorism, with its powerful arguments for the dominance of a technocratic class, finished the

51. *Pravda*, 24 September 1970, p. 2.

work that Lenin had begun when he advocated the direction of the "spontaneous" sentiments of the proletariat by a more enlightened and systematic vanguard. The vision of the governance of industrial society by a system of interlocking councils, or workers' soviets, could not withstand this double onslaught of the advocates of expertise. Several decades were to pass before an active system of workers' control was again to be advocated by a national Communist party; in the meanwhile, the powerful influence of the Soviet model of planned and centralized economic development dominated both communist and capitalist models of industrial development. Besides influencing the process of five year planning in such disparate nations as China and India, Soviet patterns of industrial mobilization left important traces in the West, from the platform of the American Technocratic party to Hitler's Four Year Plan.

In a somewhat indirect way, then, it may be said that through its influence on Soviet planning, Scientific Management has added considerably to the world legacy of statism, both in theory and in practice. And this elevation and advancement of the most authoritarian elements in Scientific Management, most ironically, has not been carried out in the name of conservatism, but in connection with a model of workers' revolution.

CHAPTER 5

Romantic Rationalism and the Growth of French Scientific Management

Êtes-vous certains de ne pas vous tromper en reprenant, contre le système Taylor, les arguments de vos aïeux? . . . en vous opposant, comme eux, au développement des moyens de production?

LE CHATELIER to the workers
of Paris, 1913[1]

At the turn of the century, Scientific Management found in France a ready-prepared ground for expansion. The concept of the technical professional as the architect of the rational society, met with subliminally in the works of Taylor, was entirely congenial to that class of technocratic managers that had emerged from the great French tradition of rational administrative reform. Quick to recognize the implications of Taylorism, the engineers and technicians of France espoused the doctrine of Scientific Management with enthusiasm. But even as they translated, disseminated, and taught the works of the scientific managers, they altered them to fit French social concepts, converting Taylor and his followers into somewhat soberer versions of the Saint-Simonians, engineers of the new production utopia. The resulting version of Scientific Management, while it attained a certain popularity in French management and even in intellectual circles, was not altogether successful.

The great tradition of revolutionary rationalism in France had indelibly marked all thought about state organization. The penchant for systematic order reflected in the legal foundations of the empire, the *Code Napoléon*, and that nearly indestructible backbone of government, the French civil service, had its parallel in the realm of

1. "Are you certain that you are not deceiving yourselves in taking up again, against the Taylor System, the arguments of your forefathers? . . . in opposing, as they did, the development of the means of production?" Cited by Pouget, p. 15.

speculation. Traditions of scientific utopianism advanced ideas of centralism, hierarchy, and rationality as the proper solution to the inequities of the human condition. This heritage of scientific utopianism, deriving much of its impetus from the synthesis of science and Christian social idealism created by Henri de Saint-Simon, had profound effects on the social outlook of the technical intelligentsia of France.

Historically, then, the scientists and technicians of France were systematizers on a broad scale: many could easily project their image of order on a series of ever grander social futures; they anticipated that organizations imbued with rationalism would spread in ever greater circles, eventually resulting in the attainment of universal harmony. Taylor saw an orderly factory creating orderly men, and orderly men creating, in the long run, an orderly world. But the French engineers, Paul Devinat tells us in 1927, saw Taylorism as the beginning of a new network of rationally unified enterprises: their ultimate vision was of a United States of Europe, brought together by the ties of multinational, rational, production planning.[2]

The French heritage of rational reformism fused with Taylorism to produce a vision broader than any created by Taylor himself. In the pattern of centuries-old tradition, the rationalists planned to capture the state, and convert it into a center of rational planning; from the center, they would impose order on a nation. From this vantage point, the romantic vision of order would inspire the whole of Europe. This grander vision explains the passion with which Scientific Management theory was embraced in technical circles in France, and, in the end, the weakness that kept it from reforming management practice by keeping it at the top of the organizational edifice.

THE PREREVOLUTIONARY TRADITION OF RATIONAL ADMINISTRATION IN FRANCE

In no country in Europe were social reformers more cognizant of the realities of administrative operations and their place in achieving order than in prerevolutionary France. The reason is not that the great French philosophers were more practical, but that many of them were administrators, and carried into their work their personal experience

2. Paul Devinat, *Scientific Management in Europe* (Geneva: International Labor Office, 1927), p. 143.

with the greatest centralized power in Europe. Even when the practice of systematizing great schemes of political order out of existing elements was not carried out by those directly experienced in governmental operations, it was influenced by the work of those who were; Vauban figures in Voltaire even as the *parlements* impress the *Président à Mortier* Montesquieu, and all things turn on the monarchy.

Thus, in the midst of the great French tradition of social criticism, we find a narrower tradition of rational, central administrative reform with close ties to general theory (vastly different, for example, from the pragmatic approach of the British) that at the same time motivates and reflects this wider French Enlightenment tradition. British administration grew like a coral reef, accumulating successive medieval offices; British philosophers built their theories on other political institutions. But in France, the monarch worked to build a more trustworthy administrative machine from the center out, cutting away the tangle of medieval offices and seeking to draw all things to himself. French philosophers made the mechanisms of state administration an important target of their endeavors.

The rational organizational reforms deriving from the Bourbon monarchy's attempt to establish its control over a powerful aristocratic opposition through a strong centralized government appear to be the first such successful attempt in Europe, and they serve as the chief contemporary model of centralized control. Dating from the sixteenth and seventeenth centuries, these centralizing reforms began with the destruction of the fortresses of the aristocracy and included the system of *intendants,* described by Tocqueville, that established a group of king's servants whose active efficiency undermined the power of the aristocratic landowners and attacked feudal prerogatives in the person of the *parlements.*[3] These and other reforms propagated by the king helped to establish in France a tradition of practical rationalism in dealing with the problems of social order. Specifically, this tradition centered on the idea that centralized reforms emanating from a powerful government could make society operate more effectively by eliminating the possibility of class conflict.

In this view, society was potentially, if not actually, a great pyramid

---

3. The journals of Louis, duc de Saint-Simon, clearly indicate contemporary awareness of the uses of the monarch's centralizing reforms of the state for class control. See Louis, duc de Saint-Simon, *Versailles, the Court, and Louis XIV,* comp. and trans., Lucy Norton (New York: Harper & Row, 1958).

of specialized classes (estates) and functions, at the apex of which the great rationalists wished to see "Reason enthron'd." Originally, this Reason was believed to be embodied in the figure of the monarch; only later, when this became clearly impossible, did Reason become an abstraction served by new institutions. The chief business of the rule of Reason was to reconcile the difference between rewards and functions in society, for the growing disjunction between them, however described, was seen to be the source of increasing grievances between classes, and the source of some impending cataclysm whose magnitude could not be predicted.

Thus, a pattern developed which characterized the grand, rational administrative tradition in France. The "legislator," or administrative reformer, tried to develop a scheme from the top of the great state organization that embodied the new principles of rationality which he had discovered, and his strategy for having them adopted relied upon somehow influencing the king to carry them out under his royal edict. He memorialized the king directly, and wrote in such a way that he might influence the very narrow "public opinion" that surrounded the king and hence could sway him. In the last resort, he might even write as if he had projected himself in the place of the king, in the hopes of eventually influencing persons in equivalent positions to identify with the author, and thus to carry out his great design. This tendency to look toward the centralized reforms of the national administrative machinery as the means of establishing a beneficial equilibrium in society is the last great living monument of Louis XIV, at once the philosophical predecessor of the international Scientific Management movement and its diametric opposite.

To illuminate the significance of the great French conference which in 1925 reconciled, with deep emotional effort, the theories of Fayol and Taylor, we must look to the evolution of the ancient French tradition of rational administration, which bound government and the roots of scientific logic into one complex in a fashion unique in the Western world, and whose latter-day descendents first opposed and then embraced the factory reforms of F. W. Taylor. The sequel—what effects this adoption *actually* had in the workings of the French industrial establishment—can only be explained in reference to this traditional approach, and to the areas of society in which it found adherents.

Curiously enough, this prerevolutionary fusion of science and administration was advanced, in many cases, by the great engineers of the period. Among these were Perronet, the bridge-builder, the engineer de La Jonchère, whose *Système d'un nouveau gouvernement en France* appeared in 1720,[4] and most important of all, Vauban, the chief engineer of Louis XIV's fortifications system, whose work on tax reform inspired a century of debate, but failed to bring about the universalistic fiscal reforms considered essential to the preservation of the economy of France. While the debate on taxation included a host of financiers and pamphleteers, few offered the vision of sweeping rational reform of feudal French duties, the insistence upon universal laws of taxation applicable to all classes in society, or the idea of administrative change as a tool for the wide-scale manipulation of the French economy and society as did the great engineer-administrators, headed by Vauban.

ENGINEERING LOGIC AND THE EFFECT OF VAUBAN'S "ROYAL TITHE"

Vauban's most important work, the *Projet d'un dixme royale*, appeared in 1707, and constituted a turning point in the application of strictly derived rational methods to the affairs of state.[5] For Sebastien de Prestre de Vauban, marshal of France, president of the Royal Academy of Sciences, inventor, soldier, and engineer, predicted nothing less than the collapse of the French economy due to the inadequacy of the system of taxation. His proposed remedy for the coming disaster was a unified proportional tax (in effect, the first income tax) which would include all of the exempted classes, would be based on the model of the church tithe, and would depend on a reformed and rationalized central accounting system.

The element of Vauban's proposals which made them truly unusual for their time was not just his proposed redistribution of tax burdens, but the great detail with which he presented his mathematical computations of revenue, his proposals for types and percentages of

4. This work, cited repeatedly in M. Vignes, *Histoire des doctrines sur l'impôt en France* (Paris: V. Gérard et E. Brière, 1909), appears to be unavailable in the United States.

5. Sebastien le Prestre de Vauban, *Projet d'une dixme royale. Qui supprimant la taille, les aydes, les doüanes d'une province à l'autre, les décimes du clergé, les affaires extraordinaires; & tous autres impôts onereux & non volontaires* (etc.) (n.p., 1707).

taxation, and his discussions of the calculations upon which he based the entire plan. And while his system had the advantage of consolidating a multitude of conflicting feudal duties, it had an additional advantage of being simple to publicize and to understand, thus adding another check upon the fraud of local tax collectors, who used every discrepancy in the tax law to their own private profit. Furthermore, he pointed out two major deficiencies, almost incomprehensible to modern statecraft: first, that the king had no single record of his total income and expenditures, and second, that there was no way of estimating the general taxable resources—not even an accurate census.[6] In short, Vauban proposed creating the statistical apparatus of the modern state as a means of routinizing the exercise of power and promoting economic growth.

While the immediate effects of Vauban's *Dixme royale* were comparatively minor, its long-range influence on French administrative philosophy and statecraft is considerable. And it had powerful, indirect effects on the state and society: it shaped the terms of the debate about reform for generations to come, centering it on the question of tax reform, and elevating the use of mathematical argumentation and practical documentation as the chief weapons of egalitarianism and utilitarianism in the debate against mystical, theocratic arguments about the God-given duties of various classes.

As one commentator points out, Vauban's work had a powerful influence on the physiocrats that followed, on the thought of those who prepared the *cahiers* of 1789, and even on subsequent postrevolutionary governments. The catalogue of authors whose own work takes into account that of Vauban is extraordinarily lengthy. It includes de La Jonchère, Coussin, l'abbé de Saint-Pierre, Condorcet, Rousseau, le duc de La Rochefoucauld-Liancourt, Mirabeau père, Quesnay, Turgot, DuPont de Nemours, and even Necker.[7] And although many opposed the details of the plan on philosophical grounds, they supported its general outlines. It is only fair to conclude that Vauban's *Dixme royale*, bristling with a new rationality that was to drive the mysticism from statecraft, heavy with elaborately calcu-

6. S. Vauban, *Essay for a General Tax: Or, a Project for a Royal Tithe, Submitted to the House of Commons*, 2nd ed. (London: John Matthews, 1710), pp. 71-91.

7. S. Vauban, *Projet d'une dîme royale*, ed., E. F. Coönaert (Paris: Librairie Felix Alcan, 1933).

lated, fold-out charts and, although ultimately conservative, destructive of aristocratic class sentiment, is rightly cited as the first "Scientific Management" document in Europe.

The last great representative of this prerevolutionary movement for rational fiscal reform, Turgot, while not technically trained, was a physiocrat who, as a leader of the *philosophes*, drew heavily on the thinking of this engineering tradition. As Controller-General for Louis XVI, he made the final attempt to reform the finances of the French state according to a plan based on a rational, universal system. Following Turgot, the history of financial administration in France is a dismal record of the piecemeal destruction of Turgot's reforms until the very eve of the revolution itself.

But by their failure, the prerevolutionary fiscal reforms indicated to the inheritors of the French government not that such rationalized and centralized reforms were impractical, but rather that the old regime was too far gone in decay and squalid upper-class selfishness to change. The result was that the postrevolutionary society equated this type of general reform with social virtue. In this manner, the classical configuration of elite-sponsored, centralized, bureaucratic, and scientific reforms came to form the basis of French utopianism as well as the direction of governmental evolution—a twin theme with that of revolution itself, permanently embedded in the French national consciousness.

RATIONAL MANAGEMENT
AND SCIENTIFIC MANAGEMENT

The work of the great French prerevolutionary rational administrators, then, is important to the study of Scientific Management in France because it establishes the first paradigm of national reform based on the great Enlightenment model of pure rationality. The pattern is one which repeats itself, establishing one after another grand scheme of state planning, legislation, and scientific social reforms. When Taylorism finally arrives in France in the early twentieth century, it is recognized as a cousin of this great model, enthusiastically adopted and spread through France by the technological elite as a sort of industrial missing link required by the classical model: a methodical elaboration of the conditions of perfected industrial rationality, as well as of the methods by which industry may be linked to the state.

While some of the specifically American aspects of Taylorism did not resemble the French model of statist rationality, and were thus discarded when the system was propagated in France, in some of its most general patterns of reform it followed closely the more ancient tradition. In Turgot's plan to convert "nonquantifiable" feudal duties to standardized, accountable taxation procedures in the hands of the state, with the object of rationalizing the tax burden on various classes, we see, perhaps, the first incarnation of the conversion of the "rule of thumb" to standardized, written management procedure. It is the pattern of public accountability of previously "invisible" organizational functions which strengthens at one time the formal organization, those specialists who monopolize the accounting process itself, and the leader(s) of the organization. It is the core, for example, for major statistical and accounting reforms from Vauban to Robert McNamara, and it is, of course, the central technique of Taylorism.

But what Taylor did was put the emphasis on the specialists as carriers of reform, while the French tradition, as we have seen, put it on the leader and his "servants." Taylorism as self-propagating professionalism spread farther and faster than could a king's word. No servant could serve as well as a self-interested, independent professional. And yet the French had, in fact, devised the basic organizational formula in the eighteenth century. Returning to France embedded in the powerful machine technology of the nineteenth century, Scientific Management was recognized and welcomed for what it was: the classic technology of power of the centralized state.

POSTREVOLUTIONARY BUREAUCRATIC RATIONALISM AND TECHNOLOGICAL UTOPIANISM

The late nineteenth century saw the development not only of a French brand of industrialism, but of a new breed of industrial and scientific rationalizer who was to seize on and popularize the first works of Scientific Management. Both were products of the great prerevolutionary tradition of rationalism born anew through each successive revolution. In the "century of revolution" that followed the Great Revolution, the ideals of the eighteenth century rationalists continued to play a significant social role. But rationality, even that of science itself, took on a mystical, ardent quality in this era, partaking in the general romanticism as it lent its name to a number of undertakings not strictly rational.

As Tocqueville has pointed out, the Revolution did not destroy, but consolidated the administrative organization of the old regime by sweeping away its feudal inconsistencies and uncovering its logical structure.[8] The completion of the old system of king's administration, through the installation of the rational fiscal and legal systems proposed for so many decades, required the physical destruction of the feudal aristocracy. The brief euphoric period in which Reason was enthroned in place of the Deity gave way to militarism and to statism. But these latter were in a new form, marked by the preceding mania for rationality; Napoleon was not only the archetype of the romantic concept of power, the Great Patriot, General, and eventually Emperor, but he took for himself the role of Great Legislator awaited by France for a century. Rationality as centralization was to take legal and bureaucratic form in the *Code Napoléon*, foundation of the state administration which was to learn to govern France without ever losing continuity through successive periods of revolution.

In its technical incarnation, Rationality as an abstract or social goal became bound up with utopianism through the works of Saint-Simon and his followers. Napoleon, in taking power, had also usurped the fascination of the intellectuals for a Rule of Science incarnated in a new philosopher-king. The "religion of science" with its prefabricated rituals, so pre-eminent at the time of the revolution, disappeared with the republic itself. But as one of Saint-Simon's biographers has pointed out, in spite of the embarrassed rapidity with which the scientific religion disappeared from a newly centralized society, it lived on in the writings of Saint-Simon—perhaps precisely because he was a crackpot left over from the ancien régime—and revived after his death to take the idealistic children of the stolid bourgeoisie by storm. Its influence left a generation of French engineers and financiers with a passion for scientific political reforms at the center of the more common impulse of the era, which was toward national expansion.[9]

The works of Saint-Simon, marked by the dilettantish interest in science of the prerevolutionary salons, coincided with the growth of new industry in France, and through some freak of insight (or, as his

8. Alexis de Tocqueville, *The Old Regime and the French Revolution* (New York: Vintage Books, 1964).
9. See Frank E. Manuel, *The New World of Henri Saint-Simon* (Cambridge, Mass.: Havard University Press, 1956), and also the same author's *The Prophets of Paris* (New York: Harper Torchbooks, 1962).

contemporaries claimed, of madness)[10] overlooked the dominant trends of commercial and aristocracy-encumbered French industrialism to postulate, in the grand tradition, a technocratic world order above both politics and commerce, staffed by experts, and based on the universal application of science and rationality. The utopian synthesis of technology, morality, and politics proposed by Saint-Simon appeared to be lunatic ravings to the famous scientists of the early nineteenth century to whom he addressed a constant stream of pamphlets and letters. As isolated and somewhat secondary figures in the social landscape, they did not appear to fit Saint-Simon's description of them as the new elite.

By the middle of the nineteenth century, however, the rising class of technicians and engineers sponsored by the growth of French industry was in a position to take Saint-Simonianism not as a description of contemporary society, but as a blueprint for the future, an ideology of rational social allocation of goods according to scientific planning. Thus, in an era dominated by the Napoleonic bureaucratic order, the link between rationalistic utopianism and scientific socialism was forged. Believing that the old military and religious elites had been decaying since the middle ages, Saint-Simon predicted that in place of the crumbling Catholic church, science would dictate a new moral order for Europe, ruling as the New Christianity. This order would be a functional one in which everyone worked, being fully employed according to his natural talents, while at the top of the society, those with the most talent would exercise the controlling functions. "A chacun selon sa capacité, à chaque capacité suivant ses oeuvres," is the familiar statement of Saint-Simonianism.

The new ruling classes would be a working elite, unlike the old aristocracy, composed of scientists, industrialists, and artists. And unlike the old elite which commanded, the new would administer, for a society of science and industry would be one of basic harmony. The

10. Anecdotes illustrating Saint-Simon's madness form an entertaining chapter in the history of French philosophy. Most famous among them is his proposal to Mme. de Staël on eugenic grounds, and his suggestion that they have their honeymoon in a balloon. His previous marriage of convenience lasted only a year; he dissipated a fortune entertaining impecunious scientists, lost an eye in a suicide attempt, and was committed, at one time, to an insane asylum. Rumor had it that his family had long been interested in science; his grandmother was supposed to have asphyxiated herself in her laboratory along with an assistant who was also her lover.

industrialist was already practicing the administration of large enterprises, and would soon take control of society away from the old, unfit, aristocratic elite. At one stroke, Saint-Simon revived the old French idea of the engineering-administrative order, for in this great beehive-like society of harmony and production, a key role was to be held by the engineer, the only one capable of communication with both the scientist and the industrialist, who could act as intermediary because he was able to translate thought into action. A new Europe and a new social order would rise out of the organization of the forces of production that were even then creating the industrial revolution.[11]

Besides advocating scientific rationalism as the key to a new, unified, European political order, the Saint-Simonian movement managed to confuse science and religion by establishing a "church" complete with sacred rituals, hysterical meetings, and a "sacred college of the apostles," whose hierarchy was depicted by uniforms of varying shades of blue—much as the technocracy movement of a century later used the color gray.[12] But while the organized Saint-Simonian movement, exhausted by these and other excesses, soon collapsed, it left an important moral and visionary heritage among the ranks of French technicians. For if Saint-Simon was Christ, the advent of Frederick Taylor could have been no less than the Second Coming; the mystical engineer had come to reform society by unifying science and industry.

Saint-Simonianism was long dead by the time of the Third Republic, when Taylor's writings had just begun to make their appearance in France. Saint-Simon's followers, changed by age into prominent bankers, scientists, and industrialists, apparently had rejected by this time their youthful excesses; never again did they publicly espouse the Saint-Simonian cult, although they frequently played key roles in the design and construction of some of France's greatest public engineering works of this period. Almost all of the influential publicists, engineers, and financiers responsible for the planning of France's railroad system were Saint-Simonians, and they were particularly influential in the construction of the Suez Canal. Utopianism had given them a valuable vision of the importance of a united and

11. See Georges Weill, *L'École Saint-Simonienne: Son histoire, son influence jusqu'à nos jours* (Paris: Ancienne Librairie Germer Baillière et Cie., 1896), especially chs. 3-4.
12. Manuel, *The Prophets of Paris*, pp. 152-55.
13. Ibid., p. 152.

coordinated system of communications and transport for France.[13] By the time the news of Taylorism had traveled to Europe, the general ideas of Saint-Simon, divested of their more fanciful elements, had become the common property of the technical class. Frank Manuel states that they provided, in the Catholic countries, the equivalent of the Protestant ethic, spurring their adherents to serious labor for a future good, preaching the moral value of work and of order in the form of science.[14]

But the heritage of Saint-Simonianism was not the property of the dispossessed; other forms of socialism better satisfied their needs. In preaching scientific utopianism, the raising of the poor through the increase of production, but the maintenance of control by the industrial and technical specialists who supervised production, Saint-Simonianism was the philosophy of an elite class. The privileged middle and upper middle classes of the technically trained professionals were its natural adherents. It was they who busied themselves with general questions of national methods of coordination and control in the industrial world, and whose activities very naturally appeared to further an alliance of technology and the more advanced forms of business. Thus, in seeking to advance Truth and Rationality through the extension of science in all its forms, this technical elite seemed to enhance the natural statism and centralism of French organizational thought.

Such a class of people was fully prepared for the theoretical and even the technical aspects of Scientific Management control; they were, in fact, in the process of seeking to develop analogues of this process when the news of Taylor's experiments came across the Atlantic. But there would be in such techniques, native or borrowed, subtle differences of tone, conscious rather than unconscious messages of elitism, general and theoretical impulses rather than specific, detailed, and dispersed techniques of education, infiltration, and propaganda. In short, because the way was prepared by Saint-Simonianism in a more severely hierarchical, bourgeois society, the adaptation of Taylorism could very easily fit into the same pattern. It could become simply another enthusiasm of the intellectuals, a fad of the technically-minded elite, profoundly offensive to the unified and highly conscious French working class, failing to the extent that it was only suitable for dissemination by force.

14. Ibid., p. 153.

TAYLORISM AND FRENCH SCIENTIFIC MANAGEMENT

In the great French heritage of rational administration and technological utopianism, Taylorism appeared to be the missing piece in a
complex jigsaw puzzle of technician-sponsored statism. In his 1927
survey of European opinions of Scientific Management, Devinat
concludes that it is the technicians who are the "first apostles" of
Taylorism; won over unanimously by their study of its methods, they
form a hardy corps of propagandists.[15] Their interest had first been
kindled at the Paris Exposition of 1900, when the news of Bethlehem
Steel's exhibit of high-speed steel burst on the industrialists of Europe
like a bombshell. At first, no one had believed the extravagant claims
of the Bethlehem works, "but we had to accept the evidence of our
eyes when we saw enormous chips of steel cut off from a forging by a
tool at such high speed that its nose was heated by the friction to a dull
red color."[16] The French, in particular the celebrated metallurgical
pioneer Henri Le Chatelier, hailed high-speed steel as a great scientific
discovery; investigating further, they were delighted to find Taylor's
experiments a model of the classical scientific method. They became
ardent partisans of Taylor's "science," and combatted the rumors
started by the British that high-speed steel had been discovered by a
careless workman who had overheated his tools by accident. From
that date, Taylor's ideas began to circulate in France, as these "first
apostles"—not simply technicians, but industrial engineers and scientists of the highest reputation—began the study of his publications.

Taylor's works first became known in France through their circula-
tion in the original editions among technical circles. *Shop Management* had appeared in 1903, *On the Art of Cutting Metals* in 1906 in
the United States; it was these papers, especially the latter, which
attracted attention first to the technical aspects, and then to the
organization of the Taylor system. While the British were more interested in keeping their competitive edge in tool-steel production,
the French immediately seized on Taylorism not only as a technique
for organizing to use high-speed steel, but as a revolutionary system of
technical organization with broad implications, not only for all of

15. Devinat, p. 139.
16. Le Chatelier, as quoted in Copley, 2:116. Also, Pouget, n., pp. 9-11,
describes the controversy in detail, offering a third version, i.e., that the
fascination with the exhibit led French specialists to rediscover a long
forgotten variety of high-speed steel invented by a M. Fattelay.

production, but for society as well. Le Chatelier, first introducing Taylor's works, commented that at last "the scientific method is now about to receive the crown which it deserves, thanks to the generous publication of the President of the American Society of Mechanical Engineers."[17] (It must be added that these florid philosophical embellishments are typical of early French Taylorism.) Later, contemplating the relation of social and industrial problems, he voiced conclusions that a generation of classically trained French scientists could scarcely avoid:

> One can apply to these problems (unemployment, co-operation, etc.) the scientific management method recommended by F. W. Taylor, that is to say, the method of experimentation. We are too prone to treat these questions by reason or by sentiment; all of our politico-social laws have been established in this way; that is the reason they are so often ineffective. The systematic use of experience will bring about a complete change in our mentality.[18]

Le Chatelier, noted industrial chemist, professor at the Sorbonne, and member of the Academy, had been deeply moved by the first writings of Taylor, and had decided to devote his influence to the propagation of Taylor's ideas in France. He was not, we should note, a classical Taylorite in the American sense; he came from a family distinguished for generations in technical fields, and he himself had made a brilliant academic career before his thirtieth year. An innovator in metallurgy, he was known as the father of high-temperature measurements; in fact, Taylor had tried unsuccessfully to get a Le Chatelier pyrometer for his first metal-cutting experiments.

Le Chatelier was fifty when he first read Taylor's writings. He had recently founded France's leading publication of the iron and steel industry, the *Revue de métallurgie*, in 1904. Impressed by the elaborate scientific method displayed in *The Art of Cutting Metals*, he decided to use the *Revue* as a forum for Taylorism. He himself made the first translations into French of Taylor's papers, and published them serially in his journal, accompanied by extensive commentaries on the industrial applications of Taylorism. By the time that the United States had given itself over to the efficiency fad following the Eastern Rates case, French technical men were deeply involved in

17. Copley, 1:xiv. Pouget, p. 13, calls Le Chatelier (quite fairly, it seems) "Le barnum français de Taylor."
18. Urwick, *Making of Scientific Management*, 1:94.

study and experimentation of the Taylor system. Not only had Le Chatelier's full translations of *Principes d'organisation scientifique* (1911) and *La direction des ateliers* (1913) appeared, but, from 1909 on, the pages of the *Revue de métallurgie* were full of research notes, records of experimentation (such as those at the Renault factories) and theoretical essays on the bases of production and economy in industry, the "human machine," and similar topics.[19]

A significant addition to the list of noted early converts to Taylorism was the former chief engineer of the Paris-Orléans Railway, Charles de Fréminville. As an engineer and technical director in the automobile industry, he was a colleague of Le Chatelier, a regular contributor to the *Revue de métallurgie* from its founding, and fully acquainted with the first French literature on American Scientific Management. The pattern of his conversion fully illustrates the typically French pattern of the early diffusion of Taylorism: solid membership in the bourgeois-technical elite, personal and theoretical inspiration. Classic French centralism and rationalism play a much larger part than do the social mechanisms of the American movement: class and population growth, the aspirations of the declassed, and the powerful impetus of Protestantism. Fréminville had received the finest technical education that the country had to offer; he had served with distinction in the highest posts available to technical people. He became an enthusiastic and persistent promoter of Taylorism not through his early acquaintance with the translated writings, but through a personal meeting with Taylor.

In 1912, when Fréminville first met Taylor, Taylor was fresh from the Eastern Rates case, and the center of a wave of publicity. Taylor's mesmeric intensity as he explained Scientific Management as a philosophy of rationalism, revolutionary in its impact, as well as a series of techniques for efficiently organizing industrial work, is said to have inspired in Fréminville a passionate enthusiasm to spread the new philosophy. Soon after, Fréminville began not only written contributions to the French journals, but a campaign of lectures to industrial and economic societies, thus launching the French management movement, which was to gain impetus and formal organization during and after the First World War.

19. See Devinat, pp. 211-15, for a full bibliographical listing. Biographical details on Le Chatelier and Fréminville were drawn principally from Urwick, *Making of Scientific Management.*

While a long history of centralized rationality and technological utopianism may have prepared the French technical elite for their rapid conversion to Taylorism, it did considerably less for the conversion of the employing classes, not to speak of the working classes themselves. Not only did employers fear that Taylorism, by redistributing the work, would weaken the authority of the head of the enterprise, but other objections, more specifically derived from the nature of European industrialism and ultimately from the nature of European society, were raised. There were, of course, the usual fears of medicine-show management reformers, and objections to the expense and time required for the reform of a business on the principles of Scientific Management.[20]

But in particular, European industry, and especially French industry, differed from its American counterpart in important ways. To begin with, the industrial revolution made slow progress in France before the Second Empire. Industry tended to be small and family-dominated; for a number of reasons, French industry was slow to pick up the technical advances made by the British after 1800. Geographical differences, the isolation and strain of war, the remnants of the old internal tariff system, and a comparatively more prosperous agriculture, in better balance with the population of the nation, conspired to retard industrialization. Most conspicuously, the French, while masters of science, possessed a society of strong class differences in which the devotion to a high culture of taste and refinement militated against the mastery of the technologies of mass production. Since the time of Jean Colbert, French industry was attuned to the manufacture of elegant, individualized, and craftsmanlike products for the very rich: silks, tapestries, crystal, fine china, and furniture. Mass production—either the first machine techniques of the British, or the later standardized organization of Scientific Management— required the output of uniform products for large markets which would, of necessity, have a lower common denominator of taste.[21]

The French manufacturers scorned the vulgarity of the British; even in spite of the later growth of great iron, steel, and manufacturing industries, a vestige of this argument colored upper-class executive attitudes toward early twentieth century Taylorism. Was not Scientific

20. Devinat, p. 130.
21. A.L. Dunham, *The Industrial Revolution in France, 1815-1848* (New York: Exposition Press, 1955), pp. 420-34.

Management better suited to the scarcity of labor in America, to the demands of mass taste in a society which preferred standardization to high quality and individualism? A concomitant of this individualism in production was the existence of "business secrets" in manufacturing upon which the unique nature of the product depended. Businessmen feared that such secrets might be revealed when labor and manufacturing processes were systematized in written record form under Taylorization.[22] The erosion of this attitude required the large-scale demand for manufactured goods created by the First World War, and the extensive business and industrial contacts with American manufacturing brought about by the war and continued through the postwar era. Through this process, efficiency became less of a sin against taste.

Two of the most important pre-World War I converts, exceptions to general executive apathy, whose gregariousness and enthusiasm meant much to the postwar Taylorite movement, were the Michelin brothers, André and Edouard. They were themselves renowned inventors, educated but self-made industrialists, who had patented the first detachable rubber automobile tire, and had subsequently gone into an eminently successful business manufacturing pneumatic tires. In 1912, Edouard first read of Taylor's work in Le Chatelier's *Revue de métallurgie*, and almost immediately got in touch with Taylor. When Taylor came to Paris in 1913, Le Chatelier gave a dinner for him at a Paris restaurant at which André met the great man for the first time. Wild with enthusiasm, he left the restaurant to purchase two stopwatches, one of which he sent off to his brother at the factory in Clermont-Ferrand.[23] The industrial eminence of the brothers' enterprises, which, during the war, grew to include aircraft manufacture, made their adoption of Taylorism in production a crucial model for French industry.

The period of prewar Taylorism in France, its beginning marked by Le Chatelier's serialization, in 1907, of *L'art de tailler les métaux*, ended violently at the close of the year 1913, in a series of strikes by the workers in the Taylorized industries around Paris. A spate of unfavorable publicity suddenly appeared in the papers, including commentaries on the evils of the Taylor system most probably drawn

22. Devinat, pp. 130-31.
23. Urwick, *Golden Book of Management*, p. 56.

from similar publications of the American trade unions;[24] even the Taylorites were forced to admit publicly that Taylorization had been carried out too hastily, and, in some cases, with the wrong employer motivation. Although Devinat states categorically that the French workers simply followed the lead of the American trade union protest out of solidarity and a general hatred of anything new, Georges Bricard, writing in the same period, leads us to believe that, in some cases, the protests may have been derived independently from the hasty and premature application of the Taylor system itself. He gives an example of the abuses of "Taylorism" growing out of intellectual fascination, the profit motive, and lack of skilled Scientific Management personnel:

> It (the fundamental principle of Taylor) had been at times misunderstood, notably in the application that had been attempted in one of the great automobile factories in the region of Paris. The principle that the management wanted to adopt was to determine by experience the best method for making a piece. This result once acquired, a special worker would labor as fast as he could for three hours, using the work procedures thus studied. His production would serve as the base for the determination of tasks. This system was not accepted by the workers in the factory who went out on strike until the management returned to its previous practices.[25]

Other observers agree that clumsy handling and executive misunderstanding had turned Taylorism into a particularly ugly form of speed-up.[26]

It is a difficult task indeed to disentangle the degree to which the violent protests of organized labor were in fact homegrown, or inspired by the arguments and protests communicated so actively and effectively by the international labor and socialist movements of America and England. Regardless of the original source of protest, however, the organized elite of French labor, much as workers elsewhere, complained that Taylorism reduced craft skill and forced them into a mechanical and uncreative type of labor. They feared the

24. Devinat, p. 211. (See also H. Dubreuil, *Standards: Le Travail americaine vu par un ouvrier français* (Brussels: Bernard Grasset, 1946). He equates prewar Taylorism in France with the speed-up.)

25. Georges Bricard, *L'Organisation scientifique du travail* (Paris: Librairie Armand Colin, 1927), p. 185.

26. Dubreuil. See especially Pouget, ch. 8, for a bitter description of the speed-ups engendered by the misapplication of Taylorism.

speed-up and its accompanying fatigue and drop in takehome pay. In addition, they feared that the application of a technique derived from a labor-scarce economy such as that of the United States would result in a permanent increase in unemployment in a society with plentiful labor. Under the influence of Scientific Management proselytizers, stopwatch timing as an element of a new speed-up was introduced at Lyon (*Berliet*), at Ivry (*Compagnie Générale d'Electricité*), at Douai (*Arbel*), and at Paris (*Renault*), to be followed almost immediately by strikes.[27] In December of 1912, following the introduction of "time study" at Renault, the workers demanded that the time-study men work side by side with them for the same number of hours per day before setting the rates; they met management's refusal with violent objection. The French workers, radical and organized, moved to protect not only their right to employment but their domination over their own "professions," their independent craft skills. Taylorism retreated, vanquished, until France entered the First World War.[28]

The best retort to the workers' fears of unemployment that the supporters of Scientific Management could muster was to point out that, although reorganization caused a drop in overall employment, Taylorism increased the overall production of society and hence the workers' living standard itself; in addition, those retained in the Taylorized industries would work under better conditions. The French, in fact, appear to have taken the claims of Henry Ford to "socialism" (remember the "profit-sharing plan"!) at face value, and Bricard quotes Ford's prognostication that soon all American families will be able to afford a car as an augury of the increased social well-being that would result from the spread of Scientific Management in France.[29] Workers, rather than opposing it, should rejoice that, in return for a reasonable period of "mechanical" labor, they will be able to purchase their own automobiles. Tahitians, after all, refuse to do all work, and as a result, never rise above subsistence. Such advocates categorized labor opposition as instinctive and sentimental, similar to their opposition to the introduction of machinery earlier in the century.

It is apparent that the argument of skilled, organized labor was, in fact, right, for the increased goods of the new society would be unavailable to those unlucky enough to be dismissed in the reorga-

27. Pouget, pp. 63-64.
28. Bricard, p. 185.
29. Ibid., p. 201. Devinat also finds Ford's (ghost-written) works influential in Europe, where they are seen as "primitive socialism"!

nization process, given the continued existence of the same forms of social distribution that were then in effect. The Taylorites were pleased to point out, after the terrible strikes of 1913, that gradually labor became "converted" in Europe—not the trade unions, it is true, but rather the individuals exposed to superior working conditions and wages in well-run Taylorized enterprises, especially those run by the French government in World War I.[30] It becomes obvious, however, that to the degree that Taylorism was accepted, under these conditions for the "good of society" in terms of higher productivity, that it set up a logic driving inexorably to a theory of centralization of productive organization and the redistribution of benefits to all members of society, including those laid off by the reforms.

"Taylorism" in the sense of universal rationalization could not be applied nation-wide under classical, or dog-eat-dog, capitalism without seriously increasing the level of exploitation of a highly volatile, well-organized, and numerous working class such as that in France. With the spectre of the World Revolution in the air after October of 1917, the only moral (and safe) way to apply Taylorism was under conditions of general social benefits increasingly supervised by the state. Taylorism plus capitalism appeared logically to equal crises of "overproduction" and social dislocation on a wide scale. Additional rationalization of a society required the gradual evolution toward socialistic welfare reforms as the price for higher productivity and political stability.

While the capitalists who were busy adopting Taylorism were perhaps the last to see this logic, the "technicians" who followed the rules of rationality saw it very soon; as early as the end of World War I such "scientific managers" as Gantt in the United States, Rathenau in Germany, and Le Chatelier in France were increasingly turning their thoughts first toward the general social problems of industry, and then toward the integration of industry in national and international societies, toward the development of rational forms of organization and distribution of human productivity. Given the heritage of European socialist thought from Saint-Simon to Marx, the pretensions of Taylorism to be a new and revolutionary "philosophy," and the continuing violent protests of the working class, this general trend was, in a sense, inevitable.

In the development of this type of technocratic, quasi-socialist,

30. Bricard, pp. 150-51.

almost utopian thinking, the French were, of course, among the first
and greatest of the pioneers. Heirs of Vauban, the French rationalizers
saw the wealth of society as a product of the hand of man. Two
questions were important for the uplifting of the poorest classes; first,
the creation of wealth and second, its distribution.[31] Taylorism
augmented the total sum of goods put at the disposition of all
humanity, thus fulfilling the first need at the same time that it made
the second logically inevitable.

THE WARTIME CONVERSION OF INDUSTRY

In 1914, France entered the First World War, and within a short
time, the conditions that had caused the retreat of Scientific Management were almost completely reversed. With the demands of war
production in France, Taylorism came into its own. To begin with, the
maintenance of the old "rule of thumb" method of operations, which
preserved both the worker's sense of artistry and his monopoly over
actual production information (which in turn preserved his job),
proved to be fatal under conditions of the rapid mass production of
armaments. Shells, cannons, and airplane engines required precise
work that could not be speeded without new forms of organization.
Shells, for example, had been made by hand methods. The workman
judged by eye the heat of the shell casing according to its color,
preparatory to tempering it. No standardized measurements or tests
were made. Haste or lack of skill produced faulty shells which
exploded in the cannon barrel. Victory required methods of routinizing and standardizing the production of armaments of uniform
quality.

Added to this difficulty was that of loss of manpower. This ag-
gravated considerably the difficulties of an industry which relied on
highly skilled craftsmen working "by rule of thumb." As the skilled
workmen were drafted to the front, presumably taking their thumbs
with them, the continuity of production on the home front required
the quickest possible substitution of written records for the old
techniques *du pouce et de l'oeil.* Taylorism not only codified and
standardized the production process, but preserved it in written record
form, establishing conditions for the rapid teaching of entirely
unskilled replacements the techniques of complex industrial production. It sped production on the home front by making possible the

31. Bricard, pp. 197-201.

immediate utilization of noncombatants and women to replace the vanished, skilled workmen.[32] At long last, conditions of labor scarcity had been produced similar to those which Europeans said had been originally favorable to Taylorism in the United States. The additional benefit was that such scarcity undermined the union position; reinforced by patriotism, the nation went to work Taylorizing its war industries.

Much as in the United States, the Taylorites in France plunged into war work. The wartime Scientific Management reorganization of a central automobile repair workshop, charged with transforming auto bodies into motor machine-gun cars, became celebrated through a series of lectures offered in 1918 by the Society for the Encouragement of National Industry. In 1916, powder production was reorganized according to the Taylor system. A certain Mr. Nusbaumer was called on to reorganize a large state enterprise for the manufacture of gunpowder; since he had studied with Taylor in the United States, his organization was remodeled totally along Taylorite lines. During the war, the government sent groups of French engineers to the United States (itself not yet at war) to learn the secrets of American production. They returned home converted to Taylorism; not even the Taylorites themselves, surveying the situation less than a decade later, were able to count up the number of enterprises converted to the Taylor system. The Taylorites of France, called on by the state, also provided pamphlets of methods for wartime reorganization; the government, to aid the rapid transmission of organizational information, established the *Bulletin des Usines de Guerre* in 1916.

A particularly important wartime reorganization—one of many in the maritime industry—was that carried out by Fréminville in the Penhoët shipyards. Penhoët, the best yard in France, had just built the great French liners the *Paris* and the *Ile de France*. During the war, they were required to change their entire plant in order to conform to the requirements of the French admiralty, at the same time that they had lost most of their shop foremen and skilled workers to the military forces. Given these problems, only "American methods" would serve. Fréminville, then chief engineer of the shipyard, designed the conversion as the entire enterprise, under his direction, began the study of Taylor, Gantt, and Harkness.

But most important of all during this period was the official

32. See Bricard, pp. 186-87, and Devinat, for application of Taylorism in the First World War.

recognition that the French government gave to Scientific Management, using its techniques of centralization, rationalization, and planning in its own organization, particularly that which had to do with the mobilization and coordination of industry. The growing tide of Taylorism in war industries was finally given official recognition in a circular of 26 February 1918, signed by Georges Clemenceau, in which he emphasized that all heads of military establishments must study methods of work suitable to the exigencies of the moment, in particular, the works of Taylor. In addition, he ordered the creation of a Taylorite "planning department" in every plant as a means of installing the Taylor system.[33] To some extent, however, the name of Taylorism was removed from processes of rationalization as a concession to worker sensitivity, although it did not occur to such a great extent as in the United States.[34] Especially in intellectual circles, the word "Taylorism" remained, and still remains, in vogue, symbolizing at one time the French preference for intellectual heroes, and the somewhat brash, even ruthless flavor of rigorous application of "American-style" rationalization.

FAYOLISME: THE VIEW FROM THE TOP

One of the reasons that Taylorism tended to maintain a distinct identity in France was that it was not the only great theory of industrial rationalization. The great rational heritage of France had produced independent currents of thought on the matter of systematization. A Captain Ply in 1888 had attempted to rationalize methods in arms factories in France; his work, however truncated, is regarded as the legitimate predecessor of Taylorism in France.[35] More specifically, however, the work of Henri Fayol in industrial management was long regarded as an authentically French theory which rivalled Taylorism; *Fayolisme* was marked by a generalism, an immediate resort to broad theoretical implications in state organization, and a concentration on the heroic mental qualities of the directors of enterprises which were all regarded as particularly French in nature.

Fayol's great work, *Administration industrielle et générale*, first appeared in 1916, in the third issue for that year of the bulletin of the *Société de l'Industrie Minerale*. While it may have reflected the rising engineering interest in systems of rationalization after the turn of the

33. Copley, 2: xx-xxi.   34. Bricard, p. 186.   35. Devinat, p. 94.

century, it would be difficult to argue that it was not independently evolved, for it was based on Fayol's years of experience as a mining engineer and director of a great mining and metals combine; also, it was preceded by two lesser papers, the first delivered at the *Congrès international des Mines et de la Métallurgie* in 1900, and the second in 1908 at a congress of the *Société de l'Industrie Minerale*.[36] Fayol's book speaks somewhat testily about the works of Taylor; already challenged as to his scheme's originality, Fayol addresses himself to the crucial differences between Fayolism and Taylorism. Fayolism addresses the problems of executive leadership; Taylorism only addresses the problems of worker organization and the technical elements of production. Taylor's work is useful to the extent that it speaks of the need to have a staff of experts to help the foreman; it has a fatal flaw in the system of functional foremanship, which undermines the principle of the unity of command. Brief quotations of some of Taylor's more lurid one-liners on contemporary "military" organization of factories (Taylor never actually did understand military organization) complete his general portrait of Taylor as an ingenious, but intellectually lacking, engineer-from-the-ranks.[37]

Fayol's work, we are told, attracted more French employers with its "big picture" generalizations about efficient management through command capabilities than did the first articles on Taylorism, with their seemingly excessive attention to technical detail. Devinat declares that in pleasing the "Latin mind," however, it eventually led many of the most enlightened manufacturers to Taylorism.[38] A glimpse at Fayol's work shows why it was the natural organizational philosophy of employers, as Taylorism was of engineers, in France. Besides avoiding painful detail, Fayolism avoided the core of Taylor's teaching, the rearrangement of the duties and know-how in the factory to promote the growth of a technical middle class. Rather, it reinforced the class system as it already existed in the factory, assigning "technical" know-how to the workers themselves, and stressing the growing need for management skills in manufacturing organizations grown almost beyond comprehension in size and complexity.

For a long time, French handwork had exceeded machine-made

36. Henri Fayol, *General and Industrial Management* (London: Sir Isaac Pitman & Sons, 1949), foreword, p. v.
37. Ibid., pp. 68-70.
38. Devinat, p. 32.

goods in quality; the French were reluctant to shift to machine manufacturers in many cases until World War I, for reasons mentioned above. As a consequence, the overall quality of machine-made goods was behind that of the United States at the turn of the century. The result of this general technological and cultural situation was that factory work supported an interdependent, but highly differentiated, class structure; there was an important worker subculture which monopolized skills, and there were engineers with a highly theoretical training, including higher mathematics, but much less practical connection with the "nuts and bolts" of production than their American counterparts.[39]

In the management, or rather, "directing" classes, the result was almost a caste system of command, oriented toward personal inspiration rather than expertise, justifying its special position on the basis of loose concepts of grandeur and charisma inborn in the executive which only naturally set him apart from the rest of the organization— even the technicians. Fayol reinforced this class structure in the factory, and through his teachings added to the dignity, self-knowledge, and theoretical means of justifying the position of the "directing" class. In doing so, he justified the class structure of the France of the Third Republic. He flatteringly compared the qualities of the industrial leader with those of the minister of state, relegating mere technical expertise to the bottom of the heap.

The accompanying table of comparison of Fayol's and Taylor's assignment of Fayol's basic tasks of organization to different categories of labor indicates the social biases of each system. Fayol's science of administration represented his stable, successful life pattern and his secure place in society as a scientist and industrial executive, just as surely as Taylor's was related to his own more erratic life, his drive for success and domination.[40] But there was more than a simple difference in direction or style in the two approaches. *Fayolisme* was a doctrine of leadership, suited to stable societies with fixed class differences; in appealing to those at the top, it circumscribed the area of its own success, limiting its spread to executive personnel. Taylorism, the faith of the technicians, grew in unstable, disrupted societies, where the relative position of classes was in constant motion, and where losses of manpower called into question old social relationships.

39. Fayol, p. 84, on "The Misuse of Mathematics."
40. Urwick, *Making of Scientific Management*, 1:39.

In a situation of traditional order, then, Taylorism appeared to the vested interests to be a disruptive element, while in a situation of disorder, the reverse was apparently true, and Taylorism appeared to be a ready-made recipe for order. Spreading as a philosophy of those who believed in their own social betterment, and who not only required order as a confirmation of their new position, but who, with proper organization, possessed the technical capability to assure order, Taylorism became the key to the reorganization of the war-torn nations of Europe on a new social and productive basis. The disorder of World War I gave way to even greater postwar changes in society. The balance of French society shifted to favor Taylorism, and it was almost inevitable that the Taylorites would assimilate *Fayolisme.*

During the war, the emphasis on reorganization for the war effort rooted both Taylorism and Fayolism firmly in French productive and governmental organization. Fayol was an important consultant to the French government, and later his attention to the specific problems of the administration of the affairs of state paid off in an invitation to help the French government reorganize the postal system. Fayol was actively interested in improving the administrative and practical training of engineers; this interest branched into a general attempt to develop a curriculum of formal administrative studies, suitable for future directors of technical enterprises and state servants.[41]

The active participation of management specialists of all varieties in the war effort developed, in the postwar era, into a management craze reminiscent of what had happened a decade earlier in the United States. Everywhere, nations were rebuilding damaged industries and planning new ones; this clean start demanded the latest in productive and organizational methods. The members of the international management movement saw great opportunities in this effort at rebuilding; they spent great efforts attempting to inspire and organize it, in essence, providing it with its theoretical backbone. Their documents and writings at this period reflect infinite pride and faith in the progress of mankind through organization, as they recite the growing list of societies both technical and popular, modeled on the old Taylor Society, sprouting up to spread Scientific Management in Russia, Czechoslovakia, Germany, and France.[42]

In this European organization movement, the French, with their

41. Fayol, pp. 81-97; Devinat, pp. 53, 78.
42. See Devinat's list, pp. 74-90.

THE DIVISION OF ORGANIZATIONAL FUNCTIONS: FAYOLISM AND TAYLORISM COMPARED

	Fayol					Taylor		
Fayol's Six Functions	Percentage of Talent Required					Assignment of Functions**		
	Worker	Foreman	Head Technician	General Manager	Head of State	Worker	Foreman/technician	Employer
1. Technical, production, manufacturing; adaptation	85	60	30	10	8	0	ALL	0
2. Commercial; buy, sell, exchange	—	—	10	10	8	0	0	ALL
3. Financial; search for and use of capital	—	—	5	10	8	0	0	ALL
4. Security activities; protection*	5	10	10	10	8	built into system; therefore zero		
5. Accounting; stock-taking, costs, statistics	5	10	10	10	8	0	special planning dept.	0
6. Managerial; planning, organizing, command, coordination, control	5	15	35	50	60†	0		formal right of command only

* Fayol does not hesitate to say that protection services in large organizations are not provided by the organization, but by the state, through the army and police—thus making himself a firm supporter of the Marxist concept of the state (Fayol, *Administration industrielle et generale*, p. 4). As for the problem of strikes, internal discipline, etc., Fayol states categorically that "French workers are obedient and loyal if well-led" (ibid., p. 23).

† Note the close resemblance of executive and ministerial talent. The "percentages" of talent required in each type of worker in the organization are apparently arbitrarily derived so that the shaded portrait of each type of "brain" will add up to 100% (that is, vertically, although they do not necessarily add up horizontally).

** The left-hand portion of this chart is an abridged version of one provided by Fayol as a central element in his teaching (ibid., pp. 8-13). Needless to say, Taylor does not present his ideas in similar fashion, but makes it very clear throughout his work who gets what, where, when, and how.

predilection for scientific and learned societies, played an important role. And in France itself, the really great propaganda efforts followed the war, cashing in on the popular acquaintance with Taylorism in wartime industries. In 1920 Le Chatelier founded the French Conference on Scientific Management, which was dedicated to the propagation of Scientific Management. The Michelin brothers, old converts to Taylorism in their own industries, set out in 1918 to make Taylor's work known throughout France in the interests of national prosperity. In 1921, their efforts resulted in the creation of the "Taylor-Michelin Committee," in collaboration with Le Chatelier. The committee devoted itself to popular agitation and professional training. In the next ten years, 860 students from engineering and technical colleges were sent on training courses; movies, press releases, and pamphlets were prepared and distributed. The most important of these were the *Prospérité* pamphlets, distributed free by Michelin and Company. At the end of the decade, convinced that their effort had borne fruit, they ceased their efforts at propaganda, concentrating only on the revision of the long standing Scientific Management systems in their own plants.[43] American specialists, too, are to be seen in this decade of hyperactivity. Taylor had died in 1915, but not before inspiring many of the most important French converts to Scientific Management through personal meetings; in the postwar era, the Gilbreths, in particular, were extremely active in the European movement.

In this general postwar trend toward the organization of Scientific Management societies, Fayol did not remain inactive. In 1919 he established a center for the spread of Fayolism, the *Centre d'études administratives*, which very naturally was seen by all parties concerned to be the heart of a rival philosophy. The center was, in fact, a mirror of Fayol's approach, being described as somewhat small and restricted.[44] Of course, Fayol was no longer young—now seventy-eight, he had retired from business the previous year to supervise the spread of his philosophy to military and governmental affairs, rather than simply to the higher echelon of business. Not only was he reorganizing the posts—in the best tradition of Turgot—but he was drawing up a proposal for a Prime Minister's Department, something like an executive office, coordinating the activities of the members of

43. Urwick, *Golden Book of Management*, p. 56.
44. Urwick, *Making of Scientific Management*, 1:109.

the cabinet. The interesting effect of Fayolism in this period of its great popularity was that it appeared to work backwards: first it led executives to Taylorism, and then it increased the interest in applying Scientific Management in the upper echelons of large commercial enterprises, such as banks, insurance, and even public service rather than in its original sphere of the management of the technical end of production.[45]

In the meanwhile, the Taylorites of the French Conference on Scientific Management, more numerous and active in publicizing their works, were meeting once a month to discuss every aspect of management, much as the old Taylor Society had done, familiarizing many with every aspect of Taylor's "mental revolution," and leading, in 1923, to the first French Management Conference in Paris. A year later, the second French Congress was held, and in that same year Le Chatelier led the French delegates to the first International Management Congress, organized at Prague.[46] At the same time that the Taylorite enthusiasm was sweeping Europe, Fayol's center, although small, was doing important work in getting schools to teach administrative methods.[47] The celebrated rivalry, in many ways a half-hearted creation of Fayol's pique and his followers' enthusiasm, could not last under these conditions. In 1925, Fayol, invited to speak at the second International Management Congress at Brussels, paved the way for a unification of the rival organizations in a speech in which he recanted his heresy, declaring that Taylor's work and his own were the same. Fréminville, president of the French Conference on Scientific Management at the time, "grasped the hand thus extended," and the reconciliation was complete.[48] From the two organizations, a single, unified, and more powerful organization was created: the *Comité de l'organisation français*, center of the widespread propaganda movement for Scientific Management in France.

What Fayol had said, in fact, was that Taylor dealt with the lower, or technical elements of management, and his own system with the higher, or administrative elements, relegating Taylor to the bottom of his own pyramid, and not actually reconciling the two systems.[49] Even this grudging attempt, however, was sufficient admission for the

45. See Devinat, pp. 31-32.
46. Urwick, *Making of Scientific Management*, 1:95.
47. Devinat, p. 78.
48. Urwick, *Making of Scientific Management*, 1:108.
49. Fayol, pp. 69-70.

Taylorites to announce that the reconciliation was complete, and to move to swallow up Fayolism and its executive schools into a new system of Scientific Management, one most characteristically French.

TAYLORISM AND FRENCH TECHNOCRACY

The new French school of Scientific Management that arose after 1925 had both a different configuration and different results than its American cousin. Fayolism, representing a trend of organizational thought which reached back through the traditions of the *Code Napoléon* to prerevolutionary administration, could not be merged with Taylorism without outweighing it in the resulting synthesis. Such a synthesis, while containing a wealth of detailed plans for order, left enough ambiguity about the directorial role that traditional French management patterns were allowed to survive. These patterns, resting on general inspiration and financial control, had a precise counterpart in the autonomous and skilled French working class. Neither directors nor workers could basically approve of a plan which destroyed their independence as it built the control of a class of technocratic managers.

The result was that Scientific Management penetrated many French industries in form, but not in substance. In those most traditional, it was blocked by the traditional class structure; numerous accounts testify to the informal, if not formal, adherence to traditional organization based on both worker and director autonomy in prearranged, almost traditionally dictated, spheres of influence. In the late 1920s, H. Dubreuil, an eyewitness to labor conditions and organization in both French and American factories, indicates that while Scientific Management had not fully penetrated even American enterprises, it was, in many cases, nothing more than a gloss in the operations of French factories supposed to be scientifically managed.[50] Michel Crozier's investigations in post-World War II France indicate much the same thing, that the organization of work in production enterprises is frequently a matter of tying together autonomous spheres of work in which technically trained workers make use of information monopolies and uncertainty to guard their independence.[51] As for

50. Dubreuil, pp. 10-11.
51. See Michel Crozier, *The Bureaucratic Phenomenon* (Chicago: University of Chicago Press, 1964).

management itself, Roger Priouret informs us that the traditional concept of "boss" (*patron*) still reigns supreme in most French enterprises of 1968. The old notion of the boss as master, rather than manager, persists in spite of the preoccupation of the French with Taylorization, he says, referring to "la persistance du patronat de droit divin."[52]

Formally sponsored by the state, Scientific Management moved into war industries as it had into establishments owned by inventors rather than financiers. Yet state sponsorship emphasized those organizational elements most closely resembling, and expanding upon, the traits of traditional French bureaucracy. Taylorism brought new forms of technological and industrial planning, linking industry and the state. But French government had been no stranger to the concepts of centralized planning in the times of Turgot, or even of Colbert. Only techniques were new, not the idea of their use. The types of centralized planning growing out of Taylorism in France differed profoundly from those in Russia, however. Not only was this difference due to the persistence of the more traditional bourgeois class structure of France through the stress of World War I which had resulted in massive social upheaval in Russia, but to the commitment of French society to parliamentarism—a commitment never developed by the weak *Dumas* (parliamentary assemblies) of prerevolutionary Russia or the abortive postrevolutionary Constituent Assembly. Even Gaullism, one of the most active modern sponsors of state economic planning, never lost sight of the ultimate democratic goals of the state. It can never be said that the French allowed rational-technical state economic planning to usurp the political process, or rather, the basic elements of popular government, in the way that planning and control had, in Russia, swamped the operations of the soviets. In this sense, it might be said that the bureaucratic heritage of 1917 was even greater than that of 1789.

We must ask, then, what happened to the "technocratic" classes of France? For one thing, the older technical professions in France, as has been pointed out, had a long history of formal education and state sponsorship, unlike their self-educated counterparts in Britain and the United States. As a result, they were not so much educational entrepreneurs as accepted members of the privileged, intellectual,

52. Roger Priouret, *La France et le management* (Paris: Denoël, 1968), p. 19.

salaried class. They sponsored Scientific Management, in many cases fervently, but because of its attraction as an intellectual approach rather than as a lever for social betterment. Rational, centralized control of the working class was, in a sense, aesthetically attractive, since it was not directly tied to visions of personal aggrandizement. The results of being attached to such advocates soon showed up in the structure of French Scientific Management itself, for it soon became possessed of an elaborate philosophical superstructure more rigorous and developed than its U.S. equivalent. The sponsorship of technical control by the scientific intellectuals resulted in the growth of formal theories about Scientific Management which tied it into the broader intellectual traditions of France.

The greatest effects of Scientific Management in France appear to have been precisely where it had the least effects in the United States: on the theoretical appreciation of industry by the intellectuals. Le Chatelier's persistent publicity efforts for Taylorism as the crown of the scientific method, the incarnation of the French Enlightenment in machinery, bore strange fruit in the intellectual world. For the American efficiency fad, never really rising above the level of "pop" culture at home, was enshrined, albeit negatively, in the highest intellectual circles of Europe. Taylorism, being a foreign import, presented itself very early as an identifiable culture complex to the intellectuals—not just to those oriented to science, but to those oriented to literature as well. The French Taylorites of the 1920s denounced the opposition of those intellectuals who, they claimed, placed aesthetic considerations above production and would rather see the noble workman free, but poor.[53] Hardly a complaint of American Taylorism!

It appears that even in the 1920s (French Taylorites to the contrary) that worker unrest in response to Scientific Management had touched off a sympathetic response among the more radical categories of French intellectual, and that this was at least as important as aesthetic revulsion *à la* Rousseau. Borrowing from the terms of the propaganda of the French Taylorites themselves, they repeatedly argued that the alien culture complex represented not only speed, efficiency, and high productivity, but also American-style disregard for all elements of grace and tradition in European culture. It was rationality armed— destined to take over the world by virtue of superior productivity. A

53. Bricard, pp. 197-201.

tone of admiration and repulsion marks this trend of thought, which reaches a peak of development after World War II, with the evolution of various approaches to the coming rule of Americanized "technocracy" in Jacques Ellul, Jean Meynaud, Jean-Jacques Servan-Schreiver, and others.

In the development of this school of thinking, early Leninism and the leftism of the brand of the Workers' Opposition and, later, anti-Stalinist Trotskyism appear to have exercised continuous influence. In particular, James Burnham's *Managerial Revolution* is often cited and seems to have actually influenced, in a seminal way, the postwar school of criticism. Burnham's book, drawing on the thesis of the separation of management or control from ownership, expands the concept through the application of Marxist categories of thought into a world-historical phenomenon: the development of a "new class" of managers and bureaucrats.[54] While this thesis had been a common topic of debate in the United States since the appearance of Berle and Means' *The Modern Corporation and Private Property* nearly a decade previously, it appears to have had more influence on the development of the French intelligentsia's attitudes in its later Marxist garb.[55]

In a sense, the accolade accorded by a former Trotskyite, linking together the administrative philosophies of Leninist-Stalinist Russia, Nazi Germany, New Dealism in the United States, and the American Technocratic Party, made a specifically *technocratic* menace (as opposed to fascist, bureaucratic, etc.) a respectable part of varying shades of leftist philosophy. From the postwar period (Burnham's book appeared in the early part of the war), the French developed increasingly subtle theories of bureaucratism and technocratism at the same time that the totalitarian thesis and its technocratic components, which relied on the existence of similar organizations for mass control and terror in the Soviet Union and Germany, gradually dissipated in the United States, with the evolution and/or disappearance of its real-life models. As a result, Ellul, as early as 1949, adapted the new theories of cybernation into the general thesis that a wave of

54. J. Burnham, *The Managerial Revolution* (New York: John Day Co., 1941), pp. 7-8.

55. A. A. Berle and G. C. Means, *The Modern Corporation and Private Property* (New York: Macmillan Co., 1933). Only J. Meynaud gives Berle and Means as a source; the others, including Burnham, do not.

"technique" was sweeping over the world; his theory had to be "rediscovered" a decade later in the United States, when the translations of his work appeared.[56]

A great part of the postwar upsurge in technocratic theory in France may have been the result of the shift in organizational patterns in industry during the economic recovery, carried out in an atmosphere of increasing American influence. Granick states that the French technocrat only gained his rightful place in industry after the Second World War. The 1950s saw fierce "carnage" among the French family-type firm; the new giant firms that resulted "have long been headed by the men whom the French themselves call the 'technocrats.'" These are men of middle age, for the most part graduates of the handful of great technical and engineering schools of France, who combine with their technical training classical humanistic studies— frequently Latin and Greek.[57]

The result was only the beginning of the erosion of what Granick calls the "Napoleonic" philosophy of management, in which the directors abhor organization charts in direct proportion to their "insistence on centralized authority" because "an official organization chart of a company has the great disadvantage of clarifying managerial relationships and lines of authority." This clarification, in the French view, only limits the freedom of command.

This slow pace of organizational change inspires the warning of J. J. Servan-Schreiber in *The American Challenge*, in which he predicts that unless Europe learns the American lesson of large scale organization and management, it is destined to become nothing but an American market, a colony made dependent by its needs for advanced electronic goods. The most important skills to learn are management skills—the efficient combination of resources. American neo-Taylorism, the combination of management skills with an expanding education and innovation system, is leaving France far behind in the technological race:

> In America today the government official, the industrial manager, the economics professor, the engineer, and the scientist have joined forces to develop coordinated techniques for integrating factors of production.

56. Jacques Ellul, *The Technological Society* (New York: Vintage Books, 1964), intro., pp. i-viii.

57. D. Granick, *The European Executive* (London: Weidenfield & Nicholson, 1962), pp. 72-73, 261.

These techniques have stimulated what amounts to a permanent industrial revolution.[58]

In a sense, Ellul's discussion draws on the same data, although somewhat earlier, and the original masters of technique that he cites are, of course, Frederick W. Taylor and Gilbreth, whose motto "the one best way to do work" is purposely quoted as the core itself of "technique" in the sense that it grows out of machine-type rationalization. (In a more general sense, it can be traced to the sixteenth century origins of science, according to Ellul.)[59]

Meynaud's "technocratie" draws directly on the classical American definition of Veblen and later, of Howard Scott, which derives from the essential world-view of the Taylor society and views the technocrat as a master of expertise which saps the foundations of parliamentarism (or "politics") in the name of efficiency. It symbolizes rational production and *distribution* of resources presided over by the "technocrats"—the scientifically trained. Meynaud analyzes the degree to which technocracy is invading the political sphere, predicting its further expansion to the extent that democracy will be preserved only by the existence of rival systems of science, or of industrial societies.[60]

While the debate about "technocracy" continues world-wide, there is no doubt that the greater sophistication of the French in description and philosophical development in this matter is part of the old heritage of French Taylorism, which was seriously noted by the intellectual community at the time of its introduction at the turn of the century, and which thenceforward took care not to lose track of its development and application. This attention, paradoxically enough, was fostered by a type of detachment; concern with the future of industry, concern with the condition of the French working class led to the consideration of Taylorism, both pro and con, but in a studied fashion appropriate to the academic, not to the type of management-education entrepreneur that had pushed the early application of Taylorism in the United States. To the extent that the French retained the old stability of classes—though there were many periods of short-term instability—the French fascination with Scientific Management remained intellectual.

58. J. J. Servan-Schreiver, *The American Challenge* (New York: Avon Library, 1969), pp. 53, 92.
59. Ellul, pp. 38-39, 133.
60. See J. Meynaud, *Technocracy* (1st ed., Paris, 1964; New York: Free Press, 1969).

CHAPTER 6

Scientific Management
and German Rationalization

*An Stelle des Klassenkampfes sollte und muss endlich
die Klassenverständigung treten, und das Taylorsystem
weist einen angenehmen und gangbaren weg dorthin.*

GUSTAV WINTER
*Das Taylorsystem und wie man
einführt in Deutschland,* 1919[1]

The Taylor System of Scientific Management met with a certain sympathy in Germany, not the least of whose causes was the German tendency to confuse Taylor's birthplace with his national origin. Despite Taylor's birth in Germantown, Pennsylvania, one German convert to Taylorism cautions his readers, Taylor "was born and is a full-American and not a 'German-American' as people like to assert repeatedly."[2] Nor does it appear that these German enthusiasts were aware of Taylor's detestation of the Germans, which took the form of racial caricature on more than one occasion. In Taylor's passion for order and planning, his advocacy of the scientific rationalization of work, and most of all in his promotion of a new method for suppressing the class struggle in industry, German managers saw a kindred soul. The means by which Taylorism was adapted to the needs of German industrial management itself constitute an important illustration of the influence that management theory may exert on social and even political change.

The turn-of-the-century German social and industrial setting into which Scientific Management was introduced had much to do both

1. "Class understanding shall and must, in the end, step into the place of the class struggle, and the Taylor system is an easy and pleasant way to this." Gustav Winter, *Das Taylorsystem und wie man einführt in Deutschland* (Leipzig: Verlag Carl Findeisen, 1919), p. 96.
2. Gustav Winter, *Der Taylorismus: Handbuch der wissenschaftlichen Betriebs-und Arbeitsweise für die Arbeitenden aller Klassen, Stände, und Berufe* (Leipzig: Verlag von S. Hirzel, 1920), p. 6.

with its continued popularity as an industrial doctrine, and with the emphasis on the authoritarian and what might be called the social-organic aspects of Taylorism, aspects that had been severely limited in the United States. The powerful aristocratic, bureaucratic tradition derived from Prussia was highly compatible with the rigorous austerity, rational planning, and bureaucratic elements in the Taylor system; at the same time, it easily led German readers of the period to overlook a certain zany, technocratic egalitarianism that emanates from the writings of Taylor. The German neo-feudal ideal of the corporate state, emphasizing the functional harmony of estates and crafts, the antithesis of Marxist class war, clearly predisposes its adherents to the acceptance of Taylor's plan for imposing industrial peace through the functional integration of industrial classes. And finally, the German drive for high productivity, in a situation of competition with the earlier established industrial powers, made the Taylor system seem most attractive, because of its efficiency in the combination of men and materials, its great increases in productivity through rationalization, and its reputation as the most advanced of modern management methods.

A brief survey of these general factors behind the rapid diffusion of Taylorism in Germany makes it clear that the borrowing of Taylorism did not mark so much a turning point, as a speeding up or reinforcement of elements already present that were creating social change. In particular, Taylorism shaped German hopes and plans for the future by making it appear that the specific tools required to engineer the administrative and industrial base of a new order were now at hand. The threads of Scientific Management planning and industrial reorganization are seen in the mobilization of war material from 1914 to 1918, the resurgence of German industry in the postwar rationalization period—the first *Wirtschaftswunder*—and in the construction of a new synthesis of industry and society that followed 1933. In all of these settings, such threads are inextricably bound to what outsiders consider typical German bureaucratism and technologically based authoritarianism. A brief survey of the latter may clarify the characteristics of German Scientific Management.

NEW AND OLD WORLD BUREAUCRACY

The debut of Taylorism on the American scene and its role in the support of Progressivism's continued attack on the spoils system presents a great contrast to the entrance of Taylorism into the highly structured, class-dominated, bureaucratic milieu of post-Bismarckian Germany. Because German unification was the product of Prussian military activities, the image of Prussian militarism was eagerly taken up by the big industrialists of the non-Prussian area. While in Prussia itself a class-based constitution preserved the dominance of the conservative Junker elements, the Prussian synthesis of the state and military through bureaucratism influenced Germany as a whole. From the era of unification dates the passion of the industrial leaders for self-aggrandizement through military reserve commissions, the wearing of military uniforms, the purchase of landed estates, and the general imitation of the backward Junker, agrarian upper class.[3] In industrial organization, the military model predominated, and many employers insured military discipline by hiring only men who had first served in the army.[4] The general ambience of industry and administration in Germany at that time was military and aristocratic, in contrast to the original environment of Taylorism. If the development of Scientific Management marks the beginning of American bureaucratism, it must be pointed out that Scientific Management entered the German bureaucracy essentially at a midpoint in its development.

The pre-1870 configuration of Prussian military-state relations and the preeminence of Prussian bureaucratic studies, notably Cameralism, are, therefore, important elements in the German acceptance of Taylorism. Certainly the notion that organizations were amenable to scientific study and improvement was a distinct contrast to traditional Anglo-Saxon "know-nothingism" in administration, and the worship of the "instinctive" modes of organization and leadership that Taylor had set out to combat in the United States. By the first half of the nineteenth century, the Prussians had achieved a synthesis of merit and patronage in the construction of the aristocratically based state bureaucracy that was necessary to maintain military effectiveness in a relatively poor state.[5] Prussian public thrift through tight organization stands in contrast to the private thrift and public spoils of the post-Jacksonian era in America. No further poles can be imagined

3. E. J. Feuchtwanger, *Prussia: Myth and Reality: The Role of Prussia in German History* (London: Oswald Wolff, 1970), p. 208.

4. Gerald D. Feldman, *Army, Industry, and Labor in Germany, 1914-1918* (Princeton, N.J.: Princeton University Press, 1966), p. 37.

5. See Hans Rosenberg, *Bureaucracy, Aristocracy, and Autocracy: The Prussian Experience, 1660-1815* (Boston: Beacon Press, 1966).

than the world of the uniformed aristocratic administrator and that of the backroom American patronage boss. Yet both worlds were, for different reasons, open to Scientific Management's message of efficiency and the One Best Way. Successful militarism not only elevated cultural values of commandism, but required the development of thought about both systematic organization for planning, and the arrangement of logistical support. By the first decade of the twentieth century, the Prussian general staff concept was sweeping the military establishments and large industrial organizations of Western Europe and America at the very time that Taylor was pressing his plan for higher levels of "staff work" in industry. The two approaches in the industrial setting dovetailed very neatly indeed. The First World War permanently fixed these techniques in the military-industrial mobilization plans of the major powers. In the German context, militarism elevated the virtues of rational planning above popular politics in ways to which American industrial planners such as Gantt could only aspire in their most extravagant theoretical pronouncements. For example, under Bismarck the military budget was agreed on for first a four-year and then a seven-year term, with a corresponding decrease in control over the military by parliamentary institutions.[6] Yet not for another century would a similar, if short-lived, proposal for five-year appropriations be advanced by budgetary planners in the American Department of Defense. In the latter case, the logic of rational planning was forced to retreat before the demand for popular institutional control of appropriations. While militaristic bureaucratism was not, perhaps, perfectly congenial to every aspect of Taylorism, in planning, control, the willingness to study organization, the love of efficiency, and a passion for rules to the point of red tape, the two systems had important elements in common.

ADVOCACY OF A FUNCTIONAL CLASS
ORDER IN THE INDUSTRIAL STATE

Scientific Management, as we have seen in previous chapters, incorporated a number of broad social ideals which may be roughly summarized as anti-Marxist in character; it established a three-tiered class structure in the factory in place of a bipolar one, and through

6. Feuchtwanger, p. 194.

various mechanisms integrated that structure into a harmoniously functioning whole. In this interlocking mechanism, productivity would rise, and strikes and the violent manifestations of class antagonism would be unknown. These social ideals, derived from and inherent in Taylor's rational methods of factory organization, were highly compatible with a longstanding tradition in German thought, that of the corporate state, or *Ständestaat*.

This corporatist tradition, stressing organic social unity through the organization of functional estates, was preeminently conservative and nationalistic in its roots. And when it emerged after the First World War as the conservative answer to postwar chaos and the threat of Marxism, it had become so entangled with the Taylorism that many of its advocates had espoused, that it was impossible to say precisely where the influence of one left off and that of the other began. Thus, from lesser figures in the history of corporatism such as Goetz Briefs, to the great advocates of post-World War I *Planwirtschaft* such as Walther Rathenau or Wichard von Moellendorff, the example and teachings of Scientific Management can be shown to have been a real and a lively force that gave new strength to old German doctrine.[7]

The roots of the corporate state tradition can be found in Germany's late industrialization and the formation of German nationalism. Late industrialization left the feudal organization of the economy in place longer; the guild structure, suppressed in France in 1791, flourished in Germany until the middle of the nineteenth century; not until 1869 was complete freedom of occupation established by law. The anti-Napoleonic character of German nationalism put a premium on the development of a theory of society which drew on native German organizational tradition and opposed the French revolutionary tradition and its emphasis on individualism and equality. The response was a conservative neo-feudal theory of the state and society that emphasized the "organic" structure of functional or occupational estates in place of "atomistic individualism," as well as stressing natural hierarchy and the inherently unequal distribution of rights, duties, and rewards.

Schools of thought varied within this general corporatist tradition:

7. See Ralph Henry Bowen, *German Theories of the Corporative State; with Special Reference to the Period 1870-1919* (New York: McGraw-Hill, 1947), especially pp. 9-11, for a classification of the schools of corporativistic thought.

a functional parliament coordinated society in what has been called the "occupational estates" school; early Nazism favored a version dominated by the Viennese professor of political economy, Othmar Spann, in which all human activity was to have been arranged in a hierarchy of estates, crowned by a state which would itself be the most general estate, and leader and judge of all the other estates.[8] In this most reactionary form, many of the corporate state concepts dovetailed neatly with Taylor's vision of the role of the technocratic and managerial "estate" in industrial society, although his theory as a whole, with its emphasis on individualism and rationalism, must be seen as the precise opposite of the mystical, romantic, hazily neofeudal notions of much of the corporate state literature of the same period.

THE TRANSFER OF THE TAYLOR SYSTEM TO GERMANY

Three distinct phases mark the development of German Scientific Management. The first began at the turn of the century, when the techniques of Taylorism were transferred directly into German factories by engineers who were converts of the new efficiency method. These advocates met with direct opposition from the highly organized German working class, as well as with general cultural opposition to this "foreign" system. The latter sentiment was obviously intensified by the First World War which led, among other things, to the cessation of the engineering exchanges that were publicizing Taylor's methods in Germany. The renewal of engineering exchanges in the immediate postwar period led to a resurgence in the borrowing of American efficiency techniques. This second phase involved the "nativization" of Taylorism, in which its general social message was amalgamated with the traditional philosophy of the corporate state, and its specific efficiency techniques presented as no different than the traditional, ingeniously thrifty work habits of the German craftsman. Finally, there emerged in the period after the war the highly significant and internationally influential German rationalization movement, fueled by the desire for national reconstruction, the renewed infusion of American mass-production techniques, and the heritage from the previous period of a unified German philosophy of planned state-

8. Ibid., p. 10.

industrial development, the modern industrial corporatism of Walther Rathenau and his associates.

It was the Bethlehem Steel exhibit at the Paris Exposition of 1900 that aroused the immediate interest of the engineers of the highly competitive German steel industry. In 1901, following the example of the Taylor-White experiments with high-speed steel, a committee of the *Verein Deutscher Ingenieure* (VDI) undertook metal-cutting experiments in association with the managers of some of the larger engineering works in Berlin.[9] In a brief period of time, German variants of high-speed steel appeared on the market to compete with those of the British and the now surpassed American variety. The VDI maintained a central role in the introduction of Scientific Management reforms in Germany analogous to that of the ASME in the United States; it popularized Taylorism among the members of the engineering profession, founded organizations designed to promote efficiency in industry, and encouraged communication and exchange with the Scientific Management movement in the United States.

The immediate effect of the technical exchanges with the United States was the presentation of Taylor's most important written works to German industrial and technical audiences. The Wallichs translation of *Shop Management* appeared soon after its American publication, and went through many German editions in a short period of time. Its college-professor translator had visited the United States and Bethlehem Steelworks; he had become an active advocate of the Taylorization of German industry. The often-cited translation by Dr. Roessler of *The Principles of Scientific Management* appeared in 1913, only two years after its U.S. publication date, and was very popular. Rudolf Seubert's *Aus der Praxis des Taylor-Systems* appeared for the first time in 1914 (it was reissued in 1920 during the postwar Taylorism boom) after its engineer-author had spent eight months studying the Tabor Manufacturing Company. A wave of popularizing articles appeared in the technical journals, including those of mechanical engineer Wichard von Moellendorff, later one of the architects of Germany's wartime planning system and active advocate of the full unification of the postwar industrial economy through state planning and coordination on a Scientific Management basis.[10]

9. Copley, 1:65, 246.
10. See Rudolf Seubert, *Aus der Praxis des Taylor-Systems; mit eingehender Beschreibung seiner Anwendung bei der Tabor Manufacturing Company in Philadelphia* (Berlin: Verlag von Julius Springer, 1920), pp. v, 154.

The effect of this German interest in Taylorism went far beyond Germany; in exile in Zurich, Vladimir Ilich Ulyanov obtained and read with profound absorption the Wallichs translation of *Shop Management* and Seubert's work, as well as Gilbreth's discussion (in English) of his work with the chronocyclograph. It is clear from his marginal notes that he was impressed not only with Taylor's and Gilbreth's method for increasing productivity and their espousal of a more practical curriculum in the schools, suited to training the new type of worker, but also by Seubert's passionate advocacy of the Taylor system as a scientific means of reordering German industry as a whole, and his insightful assessment of the role of class division in delaying and damaging the application of the system. Lenin's insight, that a Taylorism-based increase in productivity was exploitative under conditions of class conflict, but constituted a transition to socialism under postrevolutionary conditions, clearly owes as much to the German literature as to the American.[11]

Seubert's work appears to be representative of the opinions of the well-informed German technical advocate of Taylorism. He sees Taylorism as a means of putting the entire study of industrial organization on a scientific basis, as well as simply a specific set of organizational techniques. Although he is well aware of American trade union resistance and the ways in which Taylorism could be used to manage labor, he feels that, nevertheless, Taylorism, when fully established, does indeed fulfill its claims to show employer and employee their common interest in overcoming the natural barriers to higher productivity. Because Taylor's works were first introduced into Germany by college professors, resistance to Taylor's ideas was engendered by the class barriers to communication between academics and those engaged in industry. Seubert feels that, to correct the tendency of German academic advocates of Taylorism to speak from the heights in hazy generalizations, what is needed is an accurate, technically based description of Taylorism's successes in American plants; an attempt must be made to present the system as a whole, rather than as a few individual, sensational techniques, such as time study or differential piecework. The success of German Scientific Management will depend equally on the development of both efficiency *and* class cooperation, in the manner that Taylor himself advocates.[12]

11. Adoratskii et al., 22:254-68.
12. Seubert, intro. to 1st ed., 1913, and pp. 153-55.

During this early period, German technical advocates of Taylorism persisted in seeing the labor resistance to the system as the result of the incomplete application of Taylor's ideas by German industrialists. Following the same line of argument that Taylor himself used in the United States, they saw "false Taylorism," "half-Taylorization" and the incomplete application of a few badly understood techniques of Taylorism as the source of labor opposition; the remedy would be the establishment of a more complete system and the growth of understanding about the principles of Taylorism as a whole. In fact, the German critics were well aware of the American Congressional investigations of the Taylor system. The anti-Tayor propaganda of the British and American trade unions had also moved rapidly to the Continental labor movement. "The Taylor system kills the soul," was the criticism; it was a resurrection of the piecework system and "murder-work," systematically designed to make a profit at the expense of the workers' health. Sarcastically referring to the American origin of "ein neues soziales Wunderding, das Taylorsystem," Taylor's critics pointed out that with its inevitable progress in Germany came an equally inevitable brutalization of labor. One of the deepest tragedies of human history, the rendering lifeless of physical labor, would be the end result of the introduction of Taylorism. It converts man into a machine, and replaces muscle-work with nerve-work through its forced work tempo, monotony, and noisy bustle. A serious body of criticism, equally important after the war, when Lenin's early opinions were included, was developed by the socialists on the theme of physical depletion and the destruction of native craft skills.[13]

The answer of one early advocate of the Taylor system, Gustav Winter, to the strikes that met the Taylorization of industrial plants was to pronounce them the work of "demogogic labor leaders," aroused by the clumsy application of "half-Taylorization" incompletely adapted to German conditions. The solution he advocated was the development of a German variety of Taylorism more suited to the German style of work, or "full Taylorization."[4] The nativization

13. See Winter, *Der Taylorismus*, especially pt. 1, ch. 4, "Fremde und deutsche Kritik." See also Gustav Frenz, *Kritik des Taylor-Systems* (Berlin: Verlag von Julius Springer, 1920), and Günther Reiman, *Das deutsche "Wirtschaftswunder"* (Berlin: Vereinigung Internationaler Verlagsanstalten, 1927).
14. See Winter, *Der Taylorismus*, ch. 4, and Winter, *Das Taylorsystem*, pp. 46-47; also, Frenz, ch. 1.

of Taylorism was one response of the technical advocates of the Taylor system to the strong nationalist resistance that they encountered in prewar Germany. Complaints that the system was "American," unsuited to German methods of labor and the traditional intellectual craftsmanship on the model of Hans Sachs, the medieval cobbler-philosopher, were met with arguments showing that standardization and rationalization were only good sense, already incorporated in German industry, indeed, that they originated in German craftsmanship (besides, Taylor was a German), and therefore did not constitute foreign influence. This, too, was the response to Taylor's "utopianism"—the argument that the scientific method could reconcile class conflict in industry. Was it not inherently similar to the reconciliation of classes for the national good on strict hierarchical lines as proposed in the quintessentially German philosophy of the corporate state? The Taylor system was simply a detailed industrial plan for putting into practice general philosophical principles which were German in origin.[15]

As in the United States, the opposition to the Taylor system led to the coining of new, innocuous language to refer to the reorganization that was taking place. French engineers, hoping to avoid trouble in the factories into which they were introducing Scientific Management, changed the term, *"l'organisation scientifique du travail"* to the apparently less dangerous *"l'organisation rationnel du travail,"* which the Germans borrowed when they faced similar labor problems, and, in addition, wished to refer in a more systematic fashion to reorganization of industries beyond the plant level. According to Lyndall Urwick, they coined the term, *die Rationalizierung* ("rationalization"), which was to come into international usage in the 1920s as a way of referring to the systematic introduction of Scientific Management reforms; with the success of the German rationalization movement, "rationalization" was eventually transformed into a generic name for all systematic reforms in management.[16]

In general, the arguments against the Taylor system resulted in an emphasis on the part of pro-Taylorists on the separate natures of "true" (good) Taylorism, or fully adapted and Germanized Taylorism on the one hand, and "pseudo-Taylorism" on the other hand, which was the cause of every bad effect on labor and society. This dichot-

15. See Winter, *Der Taylorismus*, ch. 4, and Winter, *Das Taylorsystem*.
16. Urwick, *Meaning of Rationalization*, pp. 14-17.

omy was revived and reemphasized after the First World War in response to the revival of the "Taylor question" by the German government under the influence of the Leninist example of national reconstruction. Influential in this renewal, among other things, was the appearance of R. F. Hoxie's work in the United States, which discussed in detail the damage done by charlatans in the Scientific Management movement.[17]

In January of 1914, Taylor, enraged by reports that two German engineers for whom he had written letters of introduction were engaged in dishonest commercial practices, wrote that the incident confirmed his dislike and profound distrust of Germans, and swore off further recommendations for German nationals.[18] By this time, however, the practices of Taylorism were already very much a part of the German industrial scene, and the engineering exchanges were to resume almost immediately after the war. A survey of Taylorized trades that appeared in the period immediately after World War I indicated the extensive influence of the writings of Taylor and Gilbreth in the ongoing reorganization of bookbinding, weaving and knitting, bricklaying and stonemasonry, as well as a wide variety of other types of work, including housework, agricultural organizations, schoolwork, and various white-collar occupations.[19] The significance of direct exchanges in providing personal contact and experience with American Scientific Management during the postwar period well into the 1930s should not be underestimated. When, in the early 1960s, David Granick interviewed the leaders of German industry, he found corporate officials with uninterrupted tenure who had spent considerable periods of time in the 1930s studying American factory rationalization firsthand, and had been recruited to take top positions in German industry upon their return.[20]

17. See I. M. Witte, *F. W. Taylor, Der Vater wirtschaftlicher Betriebsführung* (Stuttgart: C. E. Peoschel Verlag, 1928).

18. Copley, 1:65, 246.

19. See Winter, *Der Taylorismus.* This work includes extensive descriptions of German reorganization and its American counterpart, as well as illustrations of various production forms, correct versus incorrect motions, and the time-and-motion study of typesetting in German book production.

20. David Granick, *The European Executive* (London: Weidenfield & Nicholson, 1962), pp. 278-90. The author points out that that the standard German pattern of recruitment of top corporate managers in their late twenties and early thirties is designed to provide long periods of continuity in leadership.

THE RATIONALIZATION OF THE CORPORATE STATE

The First World War saw the emergence of national resource and industrial planning in Germany, as it had in wartime France and America. This process in Germany extended in scope with the postwar reconstruction and the coordinated "New Economy" proposed by the most important of the wartime planners, and culminated in the German rationalization movement of the middle and late 1920s. The foundation of this "economic miracle" was a coherent philosophy that unified traditional German corporate statism with Germanized Scientific Management. The campaign to install Scientific Management at the plant level, and the systematic rationalization of trades, as we have seen, went on continuously from its point of origin, never losing its influence in shaping the opinions of practical men about the appropriate means of day-to-day organization in production processes. But from this practical foundation, broader conclusions could be drawn about the nature of economic and social organization. These broader conclusions entered the realm of competing political philosophies, and consequently had a considerably bumpier history than that of technical plant organization.

Traditional corporatism's elements of utopianism, welfarism, and hierarchy, in combination with the modern industrial planning, rationalization, and detailed industrial standardization that derived from the Scientific Management movement, formed an advanced and modern version of the "conservative socialist" formula whose development had been pioneered by the supporters of German autocracy. The chief figure in the movement that unified these disparate elements into a coherent modern order was the celebrated philosopher-industrialist, Walther Rathenau, while the principal architect of the fusion between the narrow elements of Scientific Management and Rathenau's broader philosophy was one of his closest associates in the *Allgemeine Elektrizitäts Gesellschaft*, and an ardent convert to Taylorism, Wichard von Moellendorff.

This fusion, which ended with the full development of the rationalization movement, did not take place all at once, but moved forward through a series of increasingly broader applications from a tiny base in the military planning apparatus. Extending into a mixed public-private state planning system for war material that involved and assisted the growth of the great cartels, this new form of planning became the center of intense debate at the foundation of the Weimar

Republic, when the nature of economic reconstruction in the new government, including the merits of institutionalizing overall planning on the Bolshevik model and the proper method of applying American efficiency systems in the German setting, became a source of great controversy. The final step in this process, the mass-scale systematization and reorganization of German industry, began after the Dawes Plan assisted monetary stabilization in 1924, and continued until the world depression of 1929.

The Role of Military Planning

The First World War saw the transfer of techniques of large-scale industrial and scientific development planning from the private to the public sphere. While military planning had had an old history in Germany, it did not have a counterpart in industrial planning, coordination, and rationalization, even for industries crucial to military logistics. This was in part due to the conviction of the chief of the German General Staff, Count von Schlieffen, that long wars were impossible in an age of industrial and world trade interdependence, and that the coming war would be brief and decisive.[21] On 8 August 1914, Wichard von Moellendorff, a mechanical engineer already active in popularizing Taylorism, who was also a high official in the metals division of Germany's great international cartel, the General Electric Corporation (AEG), wrote to its managing director, Walther Rathenau, to warn him that, if there were a successful English blockade, there might be shortages in the German supply of metals. Rathenau discussed the situation that very evening with the head of the General War Department, and was the following day summoned to an interview with the War Minister himself. At this meeting it was agreed to establish a raw materials administration within the War Ministry with Rathenau as its head. Rathenau brought von Moellendorff with him from the AEG, and in the next few days the Kriegsrohstoffabteilung (KRA), consisting of five people and no clerical staff, was established.[22]

The KRA is credited with keeping Germany from losing the war in the first few months, due to the impending collapse of the supply of imported nitrates needed for munitions manufacture. Using their

21. Feldman, p. 6.
22. Count Harry Kessler, *Walther Rathenau: His Life and Work* (New York: Harcourt, Brace & Co., 1930), pp. 172-76; Feldman, pp. 46-47.

knowledge of raw materials supply in European industry, and their excellent technical-industrial contacts, the KRA staff first commandeered the available nitrate supply, including fertilizer, before it was dispersed for nonmilitary uses, and then pressed for the establishment of full-scale nitrogen fixation plants based on a newly discovered process. Making Germany independent of foreign imports of nitrates and planning the expansion of the ammunition supply based on the steadily increasing supply of nitrates, as well as controlling scarce commodities for military-industrial manufacture, made enemies as well as friends for the agency. Most notably, the promoters of the Hindenberg plan, with its vast and unrealistic propaganda goals, felt that the more realistic planning of the KRA in respect to ammunition manufacture was timid to the point of sabotage. It was easy to hint that soldiers at the front were being deprived of needed ammunition by activities of an agency that had been founded by a Jewish industrialist.[23]

Nevertheless, Rathenau's war work resulted in laying the organizational foundations for a national planning and economic control system through establishing a structure of interlocking public and private corporations controlled by the government. One of the innovations produced by his intervention in raw materials distribution was quite characteristic of his thought: the *Kriegsrohstoffgesellschaften* ("War Raw Materials Corporations") were a system of private stock companies created under government auspices to handle the commercial management of commandeered raw materials, to set prices, to store, and to distribute them to military industries in a manner that would maintain control with a minimum of displacement in the national industrial structure. Rathenau induced top industrialists to contribute their aid and expertise to the corporations, which he considered a step toward the self-directed unification of industry and industrial planning that would prepare the way for eventual state socialism. ". . . They [the war companies] occupy," said Rathenau in 1915, "a position between a joint-stock company, which embodies the capitalistic form of private enterprise, and a bureaucratic organization: an industrial form which perhaps foreshadows the future."[24] An additional effect of this increased fusion of public and private economic organization was the tendency to press smaller companies

23. Feldman, pp. 55-61, 494-95.
24. Kessler, pp. 176-77.

out of competition with the larger government contractors, increasing cartelization to a certain extent.

Although Rathenau resigned from the KRA a scant six months after its establishment, in favor of a military officer, his influence continued to be felt in government and civil life. Having inherited the presidency of the AEG, he remained one of the greatest industrialists in Europe; he continued both to consult and advise the government on the war effort and to write increasingly influential and popular works on economic organization. Moellendorff, however, continued in government service, actively contributing to the military planning effort and using every available opportunity to advance the construction of the organizational basis for the postwar technocratic state that both he and Rathenau envisioned.

The Influence of Rathenau's Thought

Long before the end of the war, both Rathenau and Moellendorff had begun to investigate the means for postwar reconstruction of German economic and industrial life according to a more unified and efficient pattern, both in terms of production and human relationships to productive labor. Rathenau's writings on industrial reconstruction were the more numerous and celebrated, establishing him as one of the most significant thinkers on industrial organization in the twentieth century. In 1917, he published *Von kommenden Dingen* ("In Days to Come") and *Probleme der Friedenswirtschaft* ("Problems of the Peace and Industry"), in 1918, *Die Neue Wirtschaft* ("The New Economy," also the title of a pamphlet by Moellendorff), and in 1919, *Der Neue Staat, Die Neue Gesellschaft*, and *Autonome Wirtschaft* ("Autonomous Industry"), the latter being in response to Moellendorff's efforts to establish a practical base for state economic planning, with whose timing he did not agree.[25]

Rathenau felt that society had been permanently changed by the development of mechanization in industry. The world was becoming amalgamated into one compulsory association, through interlocking industrial dependencies. The joint-stock company depersonalized

---

25. English translations were made only of *In Days to Come* (London: G. Allen and Unwin, 1921), *The New Political Economy* (n.p., 1918), and *The New Society* (New York: Harcourt, Brace, & Co., 1921), for these were considered in the period representative of a more extensive body of work in economic philosophy.

ownership, creating industries no longer private, but "autonomous"—
managed entities like the state in form, with their own independent
existence. Their size and influence, he argued, rendered their control
and organization a matter for state concern, and not simply a private
matter at the whim of nominal owners. The inefficiencies of private
competitive industry, of production and consumption, would be controlled in the national interest.[26]

At the same time that industry was becoming autonomous and
bureaucratized, the nation, through this process, was being divided
into two permanent classes, not so much through exploitation in the
Marxist sense but by the division of mental and manual labor inherent
in mechanization. Mental labor enjoyed the luxuries of life, maintaining itself through inherited private property and through its monopoly
on education. Manual labor, on the other hand, lived in a fictional
state of liberty and equality of opportunity, but its free contract of
services and equal access to education was a myth in the face of
inequalities in property. In addition, the manual laborer, thus trapped
in the lower class, was even robbed of the joy of work itself by the
increasing microdivision of labor. While this progressive division of
labor tended to convert manual into supervisory work (a point that
Taylor had stressed as justification for the increased inequality of his
system), Rathenau felt that this process was too slow and erratic to
carry out the first moral duty of the industrial order: the technical and
psychological elimination of the proletariat.[27]

Rathenau thought that the only appropriate remedy was the
evolutionary development of state socialism. He advocated the elimination of hereditary wealth through a progressive income tax, the
amalgamation of industries into self-governing bodies in which both
workers and the state participated in managerial councils, and the
development of comprehensive industrial planning under state control
as a means of increasing national production efficiency and greater
equality of distribution of the national product.[28] The war, he pointed
out, had advanced the process of state intervention in production and
consumption already; now the postwar government needed to advance the process systematically.

The state itself would take on a new form with the growth of the

26. Rathenau, *In Days to Come*, pp. 121-23.
27. Ibid., pp. 35-36, 54-60.
28. Ibid., pp. 123-28.

new, unified, and rationally planned, self-directing economy. The centralized, bureaucratic, parliamentary state would be replaced by a purely "political state" at the summit of an organic hierarchy of functional states. Shorn of its economic, cultural, administrative, and other extraneous tasks, the political state is reduced to its own essential function, that of giving direction and making final decisions. R. H. Bowen points out that the details of Rathenau's "collective economy" bear more than a passing resemblance to the teachings of the pre-1914 British Guild Socialists, and cites textual evidence as well as Rathenau's own tendency to avoid acknowledging intellectual indebtedness to others to support this point.[29] The important difference, however, is that the Rathenau-Moellendorff state socialism is, to use a term later applied to it, "conservative socialism."

Moellendorff shared most of Rathenau's views, and while he contributed specific innovations and government programs to the jointly evolved plan of state socialism, it is generally agreed that the theoretical outlines and general inventions of the system are Rathenau's. One great difference separated them, however; while Rathenau dealt with the social by-products of the introduction of Scientific Management in his plan for industrial reorganization, and it is clear from his discussion of the division of labor that he was acquainted with the Taylor system, his most recent biographer, Donald George Sanford, points out that Rathenau specifically omits references to Taylorism. Sanford believes that Rathenau's plans for rationalization and standardization follow a pattern he calls "Fordism," specifically because Rathenau wished to avoid the negative connotations that mention of the Taylor system would have on the promotion of his own plan for the restoration of "joy in work."[30] In contrast, Moellendorff was an ardent convert to Taylorism, an engineer who had done much to publicize Scientific Management in Germany, and an enthusiast for the application of engineering models to society. His work constitutes proof of the ease with which the Taylor system and its social and

29. Bowen, pp. 178-79, compares *The New State* (1919) to G. D. H. Cole's *Self-Government in Industry* (1917).

30. Donald George Sanford, "Walther Rathenau: Critic and Prophet of Imperial Germany" (Ph.D. diss., University of Michigan, 1971), pp. 337-340. Kessler cites a passage indicating Rathenau's awareness of Scientific Management and its claims, p. 198. Rathenau was not, however, averse to forced labor, as his wartime memorandum to Ludendorff, advocating the deportation of Belgian workers for German industry, indicates. See Kessler, p. 232.

political message could be merged with the German corporatist tradition. Indeed, Moellendorff's characteristic fusion of technocratic language with romantic, Prussian, and mercantilist ideas was to remain influential in the language and style of administration long after the demise of the Weimar government.

Moellendorff's "New Economy"

The 1918 revolution left a socialist government in command of a series of ministries staffed with uncooperative bureaucrats from the Imperial period at the same time that it had on its hands a war clearly lost, and a program that included the hazy goal of "socializing" the economy by means as yet unspecified. A socialization commission designed to develop plans was formed; it included the foremost politicians, republican advocates, and socialists. But when the leader of the Economic Ministry, Dr. August Müller, was passed over for the chairmanship of the commission in favor of Karl Kautsky, Müller and his ministry went its own way, passing laws without consultation with the committee, and independently developing its own plan for socialization.

The only plan that was in any sense developed enough for immediate application was the war plan of Rathenau. In November of 1918, Moellendorff was named undersecretary of the ministry, and he had, as we have seen, well developed and forceful ideas about the appropriate direction of the economy. In 1916, Moellendorff had published a small pamphlet, *Deutsche Gemeinwirtschaft*, in which he advocated the organization of a "military collective economy" for the postwar period.[31] The new economy would preserve in peacetime the communal spirit of industrial organization during the war, a spartan, highly productive, and disciplined order in which private enterprise would be dominated by national purpose. But rather than have these changes imposed by the bureaucratic state, Moellendorff proposed that they be carried out through organizations of industrial self-government. Bowen points out that he did not specifically state by what means these "self-governing bodies" would coordinate their operations in the absence of state interference, because he had privately come to the conclusion that coordination should be achieved through a resurrection of a "National Economic Council modeled

31. Wichard von Moellendorff, *Deutsche Gemeinwirtschaft* (Berlin: Verlag von Karl Siegismund, 1916).

after the ideal of a Stein or Bismarck," and he felt that the time was not yet ripe to advance publicly this potentially unpopular idea.[32]

Moellendorff, in 1919 in *The New Economy*, advocated the replacement of traditional economic individualism with the collective economy. Whether it was called *Gemeinwirtschaft* or, as some had named it, "capitalist technique under the control of society," was immaterial to him: the traditional economy left no way out "between Marx, Malthus, and emigration."[33] His other economic writings of this period are credited with introducing the term *"Planwirtschaft"* ("planned economy") into common usage, as well as advancing a concept later considered by non-Germans to be a typically Nazi management term, *"Gleichschaltung,"* the streamlining of, or bringing into line the various parts of economic and political life.[34]

At the time of Moellendorff's appointment to the *Reichwirtschaftsamt* ("State Economic Ministry"), he was given a free hand to prepare the plans for national reconstruction. He filled his department with sympathetic former colleagues from industry and proceeded to develop the practical plans necessary to transform the "new economy" into reality. The work of the government in the economic sphere was given special emphasis by the Russian revolution and subsequent industrial reconstruction along the strict lines of "War Communism," which appeared to be a contrast to the weak and erratic Weimar government. The revolution in Russia, in addition, had been followed

---

32. Bowen, p. 185. W.R. Bruck, in his *Social and Economic History of Germany from William II to Hitler* (Cardiff: Oxford University Press, 1938), pp. 155-62, was perhaps the first to publicize widely the significance of Moellendorff's career. Bowen, pp. 187-206, offers a lengthy discussion of his life and work, particularly his role as Undersecretary of State for Economic Affairs, based on archival resources and correspondence. His memorandum of 1919 was published in 1971 (Hagen Schulze, ed., *Akten der Reichkanslei: Weimarer Republik*) and forms the basis for Charles Maier's analysis of the conversion of the working-class-managed, planned economy of the socialists to "a class-neutral technocratic concept." See Charles Maier, *Recasting Bourgeois Europe: Stabilization in France, Germany, and Italy in the Decade after World War I* (Princeton, N.J.: Princeton University Press, 1975), pp. 142-43, and nn. 10, 11, 12.

33. Wichard von Moellendorff, "Die neue Wirtschaft" in *Auf der Schwelle der neuen Zeit* (Berlin: Verlag Dr. Wedekind & Co., G.m.b.H., 1919).

34. Bowen, n., p. 191, points out that the administrative use of this term was coined by Moellendorff, although it later came into common usage among the Nazis and was considered (by non-Germans at least) to have sinister overtones.

by the Spartacist rebellion in Germany, and had given rise to a large and vocal class of Bolshevik sympathizers whose influence did not fully cease with the defeat of the Spartacists. The radical talk of some Weimar politicians and the intensification of economic reform attempts were directly related to the attempt to undercut this radical agitation. In March of 1919, Moellendorff managed to secure the adoption of a "basic socialization law" that allowed the government to go ahead with the organization of the "collective economy." He then moved to reorganize the coal and potash industries as semipublic cartels according to the pattern of self-governing industrial unions described by Rathenau.

In this stormy political atmosphere, Moellendorff drafted a confidential memorandum for the cabinet, urging the immediate adoption of a detailed plan of economic and political reorganization that would establish the "new economy." In this document he advocated a "perfectly unitary economic policy" in which all elements and subdivisions of economic life should be "brought into line" (*gleichgeschaltet*), in the same way that electric currents are coordinated through a switchboard. Expressing grave doubts about the ability of a Bolshevist-type system to support the entire population in the conditions of economic chaos that would be the immediate result of a Bolshevik takeover in a highly industrialized nation, he argued for a highly controlled, planned economy organized through duty and compulsion. This *gebundene Planwirtschaft* would create a people's community that would provide social justice and the strict apportionment of rewards according to achievement, but it would not be a "paradise for weaklings." The structure would be built from below on the basic tendencies for association already demonstrated by certain vocational groups. With its advocacy of national patterns of rationalization, its emphasis on a nationalistic, guild-like structure, and its stress on the beauties of labor, the document might be perceived, perhaps, as chief among the writings of the period that represented a fusion between traditional German corporatism and Germanized Scientific Management.

The memorandum was leaked to the press in May of 1919, before the cabinet could act on it, unleashing a bitter public debate over the acceptability of *Planwirtschaft*. Its class collaborative base was anathema to the extreme left. Socialists feared it was delivering the nation over to the great trusts. Organized labor opposed the proposal for a "holy year of toil" contained in the plan, which would allow strikes only if nine-tenths of the affected workers approved. Small commercial interests feared the elimination of middlemen and independent traders in the face of the absorption of distribution by the "rationalized" sales and purchasing syndicates of the great cartels. Conservatives opposed the plan's heavy redistributive taxation. Rathenau quarreled with Moellendorff for acting prematurely and thus jeopardizing the entire scheme for gradual transformation of the economy. In July the cabinet rejected the plan of the Ministry of Economic Affairs, calling it the "forced cartelization of all branches of our economy." The minister of Economic Affairs resigned, as did Moellendorff. Eventually, Article 156 of the Weimar Constitution established a National Economic Council, but it bore little resemblance to the original concept, and was scornfully denounced by Moellendorff as neither Bismarckian (conservative) nor Lassallean (socialist).[35]

A Renewal of the Efficiency Campaign

The debate on the new economy was accompanied by a renewed debate on the employment of foreign industrial organization methods for the rebuilding of German industry. A revival of the never-extinguished interest in Taylorism was very much in evidence with the reissuing of Seubert's work, the renewal of engineers' visits to Taylorized plants and Ford's assembly line, and the subsequent publishing of many works describing and advocating American management methods, particularly Taylorism. Above all, Lenin's promotion of Taylorism and the apparent success of his draconic measures in restoring Russian industry made a reassessment of American methods the center of a national debate paralleling the American "efficiency fad." Taylor's German biographer divides the critics of the period into several categories that are similar to those groups in the United States. First of all, there were the workers and "students of economics" who opposed its exploitative use by entrepreneurs, and who asked how it was possible to put Taylorism to work in a socialist setting, a question not yet clearly answered even by the Russian experience. Then there were the doctors of physiology and psychology who opposed the system for "social and hygienic" reasons. Finally, employers and industrialists opposed the system because of the great cost of its introduction. According to its opponents,

35. Bowen, p. 204. See also "The Debate over *Planwirtschaft*," pp. 195-206.

Taylorism, as pushed by extremists and dogmatists, had a "shady side."[36]

Taylor's advocates responded with Taylor's arguments; Gustav Winter, writing on the "so-called shady side of Taylorism," points out that the fear of technological displacement on the part of the workers in Taylorizing industries does not take into account the increased number of jobs that have always been produced by mechanization, nor the rise in consumption that accompanies technical increases in productivity. The problem of crises of overproduction, used by Marxist critics of Taylorism, may be solved, he suggests, by barring women from employment and assisting them to develop their true vocation as housewives and mothers. One need only contrast the "Taylorist *Planwirtschaft*" with the bankrupt policies of the Bolsheviks to answer the Marxist criticism, says this commentator. He concludes that an efficient Taylorized economy will not only support heads of households but speed recovery from the lost war.[37]

Ford's assembly line, devised in 1913, fascinated the Germans. It seemed to be the physical manifestation of Taylorism, and of American efficiency—the foundation of America's emergence as a great industrial power. As before the war, a differentiation was made between "bad" Taylorism (foreign, punitive, promoting the soulless microdivision of labor) and "good" Taylorism (Germanized, simplifying work, shortening the hours of labor). But this difference was sometimes equated with a perceived difference between "Taylorismus" (bad) and "Fordismus" (good). Taylorism was seen in this view as emphasizing the personnel management side of work organization— labor control through piecework schemes, time-and-motion study, and the increasing division of labor—while Fordism was seen as emphasizing standardization, plant rationalization, the industry-wide specialization of plants, and the flow planning of work, or the assembly line.

The actual relationship between Taylorism and Fordism in the United States shows that the German view tended to be oversimplified. Neither system had a monopoly on "murder-work" or the "soulless" division of labor. Indeed, the tendency to emphasize "Fordismus" in the immediate postwar era appears to be part of the

---

36. I. M. Witte, *F. W. Taylor, Der Vater wirtschaftlicher Betriebsführung* (Stuttgart: C. E. Poeschel Verlag, 1928), pp. 86-87.
37. Winter, *Der Taylorismus*, pp. 231-33, 235 et passim.

general European campaign to placate organized labor by eliminating the label of Taylorism from management systems that drew directly on Scientific Management technique and literature. In Germany, at least, Ford was regarded as less tainted by antilabor sentiments. The German translation of *My Life and Work* apparently lent an aura of genuine social concern to Ford's ghost-written prose and compared favorably with Taylor's now infamous "Schmidt" episode, and his pronouncement that the laborer must "dumm und stark wie ein Stier." Many German technical authors appear to have been unaware of the common American opinion of Ford's writings and to have taken them literally. Like the French, the Germans for a certain period believed Ford's claims to be a "profit-sharing" utopian dreamer and saw Ford as a reforming quasi-socialist industrialist, on the model of a Rathenau or an Abbe.[38] An additional and more sinister appeal of Ford was his virulent anti-Semitism: the German translation of his work of 1920, *The International Jew*, had been through twenty-nine printings by 1933.[39] Some sources claim, citing records of the Bavarian government, that Ford bankrolled Hitler's Beer Hall Putsch.[40]

Despite the collapse at the national level of the New Economy, and the often unfavorable debate on Taylorism, at the practical level of plant rationalization German progress in the widespread application of Scientific Management was rapid and uninterrupted. The engineers who calculated piece rates, conducted motion study, and laid out floor plans—often direct copies of methods they had personally observed in America—formed a reservoir of potential supporters for some form of national rationalization. German Scientific Management did not disappear with the attack on Taylorism, but regrew on the strong roots of continued practical application, developing into what was to become the national rationalization campaign.[41]

38. See, for example, Gustav Winter, *Der falsche Messias Henry Ford* (Leipzig: Verlag "Freie Meinung," 1924). Antonio Gramsci's radical criticism of Taylorism echoes the common European understanding of the period that equated Fordism, Taylorism, Americanism, and rationalization at a general level, but identified Fordism specifically with the direct management of the distribution and transportation of industrial output (not simply production) and the overall impetus toward a planned economy in modern capitalist industrialism. Gramsci, p. 279, pp. 285-87.

39. Henry Ford, *Der internationale Jude: Ein Weltproblem* (Leipzig: Hammer-Verlag, 1922 and later editions).

40. See Leonard, *The Tragedy of Henry Ford*, and N. Belyaev, *Genri Ford* (Moscow: Zhurnal'no Gazetnoe Ob'edinenie, 1935).

41. Charles Maier offers a fascinating explanation for this apparent collapse

In the immediate postwar period, Carl Köttgen, an electrical engineer for the great German electrical equipment firm of Siemans, and later president of the *Verein Deutscher Ingenieure*, became convinced that Germany's future lay in the mass-scale application of the practices of Scientific Management that he had observed while touring American industry. By converting Carl Friedrich von Siemens to his cause, and enlisting the support of the German government and other important industrial firms, Köttgen brought about the creation in 1921 of the National Board for Efficiency (*Reichskuratorium für Wirtschaftlichkeit*, RKW), a mixed private-public endeavor that enlisted the support of high state officials, influential industrialists, engineers, and academics. Meeting in Berlin, it declared itself the central organizational agent of the postwar rationalization movement. Thus, the impetus for centralized industrial planning, standardization, and rationalization passed from government to the great cartels, which were able to carry out, with the stabilization of currency after the Dawes Plan in 1924, a massive and highly productive reform of the industrial basis of the German economy.[42]

Other groups appeared in the early 1920s to forward the progress of German rationalization. Some of the most significant included the Standards Board of German Industry (*Normenausschuss der Deutschen Industrie*), the Committee for Efficient Manufacture (*Ausschuss für wirtschaftliche Fertigung*), the Committee for Efficient Administration (*Ausschuss für wirtschaftliche Verwaltung*), the National Specifications Board (*Reichsausschuss für Lieferbedingungen*), the National Board of Work and Time Study (*Reichsausschuss für*

---

and revival of the Scientific Management movement in a broader form and under new nomenclature. Taylorism, he points out, had radical-utopian elements that were potentially too upsetting to the bourgeois order; therefore, it collaborated with critical leftist elements in denouncing "Taylorism." But, by stressing only the conservative elements of Scientific Management under the labels of "Fordism," "rationalization," or "Americanism," bourgeois industrialists could carry forward the Scientific Management campaign without threatening the basic class structure in Germany and France. See Charles Maier, "Between Taylorism and Technocracy: European Ideologies and the Vision of Industrial Productivity in the 1920s," *Journal of Contemporary History*, January 1970.

42. For a full membership list of the RKW, as well as addresses made by Köttgen and others on the significance of the enterprise and its intellectual origins, see *Reichskuratorium für Wirtschaftlichkeit E. V.* (Berlin: Selbstverlag des RKW E. V., 1926). See also Urwick, *Golden Book of Management* pp. 152-54.

Arbeitseitermittlung), and a spinoff organization of the VDI specifically charged with the promotion of scientific thinking in industry, the Study Group of German Industrial Engineers (*Arbeitsgemeinschaft Deutscher Betriebsingenieure*). Among the members of these and other groups associated with the RKW were many who had been involved in the popularization of the works of Taylor, Gilbreth, and other American efficiency engineers, who had observed United States industry firsthand, and who were key figures in the Germanization of the Taylor system itself.[43]

The German Rationalization Movement

Although the renewed efficiency and standardization campaign had begun immediately after the war as part of the reconstruction effort, economic instability and the burden of reparations kept it from flowering into the full-scale social and industrial movement that could significantly change Germany's productive efficiency. The German rationalization movement proper thus dates from 1924, when currency stabilization was achieved; it was only then that this extensive internal set of organizational and technical reforms could be undertaken by the major German industries. It came to an end in 1929, when the world depression caused a general collapse of the German economy. It left, however, a significant heritage in the form of huge rationalized cartel structures whose upper reaches were interwoven with government, an armory of economic planning and control techniques that were not yet fully integrated with governmental organization, the passion for "efficient" operational and linguistic styles applied to every conceivable activity, and an implicit demand for a political order sufficiently stable and efficient to support the stable and efficient operations of the great cartels.

Robert Brady's extensive 1933 survey of German industrial rationalization and cartelization divides post-World War I rationalization as a whole into two phases, the "negative phase" of the immediate postwar period, and the "positive phase" that was its natural out-

43. See *RKW*, pp. 30-33, and Urwick, *Golden Book of Management*, pp. 152, 184, 229. The membership list of the RKW (see n. 42) contains some interesting names in addition to the well-known advocates of Scientific Management, among them Dr. R. ("Finance-Capital") Hilferding, whose work was borrowed in Lenin's *Imperialism, The Highest Stage of Capitalism*, in V.I. Lenin, *Selected Works*, 1 vol. ed. (New York: International Publishers, 1971), and industrialist Fritz ("I Paid Hitler") Thyssen.

growth. The negative phase involved "rationalizing" production in the overexpanded heavy industries at the beginning of reconstruction following the inflation and the Ruhr invasion, and led directly to plans for the drastic reorganization of physical plant and business organization, including realignment of technically related industrial units, increased plant specialization, the closing down of inefficient units, and the scrapping of old buildings and machinery. This reorganization was the natural transition to "positive" rationalization: the systematic introduction of scientific methods into all aspects of production, distribution, and consumption.[44]

The rationalization process was not only carried out as an interlocking process between industries, but gradually and automatically extended its sphere of influence in all types of operations. For example, technical developments in power transmission brought about realignment of the electric power industry, which in turn required major reorganizations in those plants utilizing purchase current. More significant, rationalization expanded from production to physical distribution, marketing, and finally even into consumption of ultimate-consumer goods. According to Brady, once rationalization expanded beyond the confines of old plant and equipment, it collected a host of enthusiastic propagandists who saw it as a panacea for all the ills of industrialized society; all personal and collective problems could be solved through the extension of rationalization into every corner of economic, social, and governmental life. This passion for efficiency as a cure-all "possessed many of the mystical, juvenile, and naive properties of the recent 'new economic' era in the United States."[45] Indeed, given the exchange of ideas and personnel, there is no reason why it should not.

There is no serious question that the original model and inspiration for the self-conducted rationalization of the German cartels was the work of Walther Rathenau, and that the movement was heavily influenced by the example of the Scientific Management movement in the United States. The movement itself was coordinated to a large extent by the work of the RKW, which promoted efficiency methods and standards, conducted experiments, and carried out the various practical and propaganda tasks necessary to coordinate and advance

44. Robert A. Brady, *The Rationalization Movement in German Industry: A Study in the Evolution of Economic Planning* (Berkeley and Los Angeles: University of California Press, 1933), p. xii.
45. Ibid., p. xx.

the national industrial movement. The rationalization movement was characterized by a smooth interweaving of academic, technical, and corporate personnel, all of whom saw in industrial reform and national rationalization the salvation of the social order.

Among the most advanced of the rationalizing cartels were, of course, the AEG and Siemens in the electro-technical industries, I. G. Farbenindustrie A.G. (dyes and chemicals), to which Moellendorff was a consultant after leaving government, Vereinigte Stahlwerke A.G. (steel), and important elements of the machine industry, a major target of the standardization and reform efforts of the RKW and the VDI.[46] Combination, rationalization, and standardization with significant long-range planning efforts were also pushed through in the German transport system—railroads, air and ship transportation—and in the national postal system.[47]

The connection between the rationalization campaign and the American efficiency movement was clearly recognized by the participants, one industrialist indicating, for example, that rationalization was generally equated with "Americanization."[48] It was in overtly linking mass-scale rationalization to nationalistic goals and the ideals of corporatism and social stratification that the Germans had gone beyond what the most enthusiastic American efficiency engineers had only dared hint at. The uplift and occasional hokum of the American movement appears to have been taken literally and applied seriously by Scientific Management's German interpreters: "national efficiency," a watchword of both movements, simply looked different on the other side of the Atlantic.

The great success of rationalization, the first so-called "economic miracle" of German industry, reinforced similar efforts that were going on in Europe at the time, leading directly to the resolution on rationalization of the World Economic Conference at Geneva in 1927. Declaring that rationalization increased productivity, reduced costs, and improved both the standard of living and the conditions of labor, the International Economic Conference urged governments, industries, and professional organizations to work for the rationalization of all spheres of life and production; they advocated that the work of rationalization, standardization, labor training, and reform be carried

46. Ibid., p. 154.
47. Ibid., p. 259.
48. R. von Holzer, *Systematische Fabriks-Rationalisierung* (Munich: D. von Oldenbourg, 1928), p. iv.

out on an international basis. Rationalization, in this statement, was clearly identified with Scientific Management—not in the narrow sense of the Taylorization of individual machine shops, but in the generalized social and economic sense which had been developed by the individual and organizational exponents of the international Scientific Management movement in the years since Taylor's death in 1915. In this sense, the resolution was a formal statement of the international goals of the "mental revolution."[49]

In advancing these goals, the great rationalizing cartels of Germany were as much pioneers as the centralized planners of Soviet Russia. The machine shops of the world, while not yet harmonized like Barth's musical pitches, were no longer alien to each other, and the structure of industrialism in the advanced nations was growing to look increasingly similar. Such national variation as occurred was not so much in the concept of rationalization itself, but in the manner in which national rationalization movements found accommodation with very different types of political environments. The resolution of tension between the political order and the growing pressure from the rapidly expanding Scientific Management ideology was achieved in ways sufficiently different to render impossible the universal, rational, and pacific order that the early scientific managers believed would be the inevitable outcome of their efforts. The years that followed were to see the participants in the Geneva economic conference hurling the output of their newly rationalized production processes at each other across the European and Asian fronts of the Second World War.

AFTER EFFICIENCY

The so-called "totalitarian" economic system of the Third Reich, involving a combination of public control and planning with the maintenance of private ownership in the form of huge cartels, was a direct descendant of the longstanding operations of the rationalization movement and the "New Economy" proposed by Rathenau and Moellendorff. For that reason, it showed strong Scientific Management influence, as should be expected. The question of whether the German Scientific Management movement merely preceded the demise of Weimar or was a contributing factor has never been satisfactorily resolved. For example, Robert Brady's history of ra-

49. Urwick, *Meaning of Rationalization*, app. A, pp. 151-53.

tionalization concludes that the rationalization movement influenced the change of government particularly through its negative effect on employment.[50] His opinion on the role of rationalization was similar to that expressed by Hitler, in his January, 1932 speech before the Duesseldorf Industry Club. Hitler stated there that rationalization led inevitably to unemployment and to a crisis of overproduction in the rationalized industrial states. An Asian-Bolshevik conspiracy against the superior white states had intensified competition, rationalization, and the unemployment and economic crisis in order to hasten the collapse of the industrialized West, and put its immense production plant at the service of Asiatic political dogma. He spoke, therefore, specifically against the commonly held view that rationalization could put Germany in its rightful place among nations by increasing productivity; he stated that the unification of political will must occur *before* the intensification of the rationalization campaign if Germany was not to fall prey to the world Bolshevik-Jewish conspiracy.[51] As opposed to this "contributing factor" theory, the majority of German authors stress political factors, and only indirectly the underlying economic situation, as responsible for the shift in regimes. The question, although thoroughly debated, remains unresolved, despite general agreement on the sequence of events.

The direct influence of the earlier Scientific Management movement on the organization of Third Reich administration and production controls often appeared ironic to observers. For example, there is no question that the organization of armaments production planning was directly descended from the methods and plans first put into operation in Walther Rathenau's little Raw Materials Department in the War Ministry of imperial Germany. Albert Speer, the "wizard" of armaments production and master of Germany's war economy, attributed his success to the extension of patterns of organization, first used by Rathenau, into a plan of "industrial self-responsibility." Explaining that Rathenau's principles involved increasing production by exchange of technical experiences, division of labor from plant to plant, and standardization, Speer quotes his opinion that such methods would guarantee "a doubling of production with no increase in

50. Brady, p. 418.

51. Adolf Hitler, *My New Order* (New York: Reynal and Hitchcock, 1941), pp. 92-124. This speech was delivered privately to the Duesseldorf Industry Club on 27 January 1932 before an audience of financiers and big business men who financed Hitler.

equipment and no increase in labor costs." Dr. Fritz Todt, Speer's predecessor in the Ministry of Armaments, had discovered one of Rathenau's assistants on the top floor of the ministry, who had drawn up a memorandum on the structure of raw materials organization, and, in Speer's words, "Dr. Todt benefited by his advice."[52] Yet, as late as 1931, Hitler had personally denounced the corporatist and rationalizing principles of Rathenau and his disciples.[53]

Many of the inventions of the form of modern corporatism developed in Rathenau and Moellendorff's "New Economy" saw their full realization in the economic structure of the Third Reich. The combination of welfarism and forced draft labor, disguised under euphemistic and symbolic nomenclature, the "streamlining" (*Gleichschaltung*) of all elements of society, particularly the control of trade unions and other potentially dissident groups, the development of state-controlled planning, especially the Four Year Plan of 1936, and the formal Nazi espousal of corporativism all owed much to the work of this earlier period. Rathenau and Moellendorff had not foreseen the rapidity and ease with which their war-born economic model of fused state and private production could be reconverted to the service of militarism. And, too, neither of them lived to see the final application of their innovations. Rathenau, identified by the right wing as one of the Jewish architects of the "stab in the back," was murdered by nationalists in 1923, while Moellendorff, despondent over the distortion of his own ideals by the National Socialists, committed suicide in 1937.[54]

Yet until Nazi Germany actually entered a self-defeating war, military mobilization, or "pseudomilitarism" as some authors call it, appeared to make good sense in terms of making an early and rapid recovery from the world depression of 1929. With a militaristic neo-feudalism to take the place of shattered market ties, Nazi German corporativism appeared far more efficient in its use of social resources than a demoralized France, England, or United States. Pressure on the labor market was relieved by drafting youth for unpaid labor service, and by driving women and Jews from the professions and other attractive forms of employment. Contracts for military goods,

52. Albert Speer, *Inside the Third Reich* (New York: Macmillan Co., 1970), p. 208.
53. Peter Drucker, *The End of Economic Man: A Study of the New Totalitarianism* (New York: John Day Co., 1939), pp. 124-25.
54. Bowen, p. 206.

road construction, and the "motorization of the German people" stimulated industrial production. As employment rose, potential inflation was controlled by various techniques of enforced savings such as the Winterhilfe fund or required time payments on Volkswagens that were never delivered, as well as by preventing labor from bidding up wage structures by forbidding workers to move geographically or even from plant to plant to take advantage of shortages of skilled labor.[55]

An essential element of Nazi statism, both for economic reasons such as wage and productivity control, and for ideological reasons such as the prevention of Bolshevism, was the absolute control of labor. This control embraced a range of devices from welfarism to slave labor; in all of them, traces of the heritage of the international Scientific Management movement's mechanisms of labor control were visible. On the positive side, there was a Mayoistic concern for the reimposition of organic unity on that formerly isolated unit, the factory worker, through group determination of physical conditions in the factory (the "Beauty of Work" program), and management-sponsored, cut-rate group vacations and spare-time activities (the "Strength through Joy" movement). Throughout these efforts, the attempt was made to substitute group and official "reinforcement" for money incentives by symbolically recognizing the sacred and ennobling aspects of labor in ways that ranged from the promotion of the Hans Sachs image to the ironic "Arbeit Macht Frei" over the entrance of Dachau. Indeed, Robert Brady, discussing typical fascist approaches to labor relations, quotes the argument of Elton Mayo, one of the founders of the "Human Relations" school of management, that industrial and social discipline create security through the understanding of the nonrational response, and Brady points out that the denial of any differences between labor and capital in this manner is the beginning of fascist-style labor control.[56]

The doctrine of the corporate state, officially adopted but for the most part a dead letter, was useful in "streamlining" the trade unions

55. See such works as B. H. Klein, *Germany's Economic Preparations for War* (Cambridge, Mass.: Harvard University Press, 1959), J. Kuczynski, *Germany: Economic and Labour Conditions Under Fascism* (New York: International Publishers, 1945), or N. Y. Wollston, *The Structure of the Nazi Economy* (New York: Russell and Russell, 1941), especially ch. 1, "War Economics in Peace Times."

56. Robert A. Brady, *The Spirit and Structure of German Fascism* (New York: Viking Press, 1937), pp. 384-92.

and in forming state-controlled groups of various occupations and professions as "transmission belts" of governmental policy. Labor movement was prevented by a series of Trotsky-style labor passbooks. These labor systems were reinforced by an exploitative apprenticeship system which further attached workers to specific industries and plants; the system looked even more like neo-feudalism when techniques of buying and selling labor, officially attached to one or another plant, developed among industrialists as a means of reallocating this increasingly scarce resource. Inside these plants, the speedup was applied, in classical Scientific Management fashion, through the manipulation of differential piecework rates in the most punitive way. In the most negative version of this system, the modern Scientific Management techniques of control through the microdivision of labor made possible the use of foreign forced labor in complex technological tasks such as missile assembly.[57]

The efficiency craze that had originally been generated by the Scientific Management movement also continued through the change of regimes, which appeared to bring out the latent emphasis on efficiency of form above efficiency of results, and, in addition, to provide new objects on which to exercise the mechanisms of efficiency. While the use of stopwatch timing in increasing the efficiency of mass gassing is well known, perhaps the most *outré* manifestation of the efficiency cult applied to social theory was seen in the German adaptation and application of the "science" of eugenics for racial betterment and increased social efficiency. This pseudoscience, long identified exclusively with the Nazis and seen as an offshoot of outdated genetic theories and racism, had an influential Scientific Management component, and was represented in the United States by a very lively movement that combined racism, conservation, anthropology, and efficiency faddism under the aegis of progressivism. For many decades, close ties were maintained with the German eugenicists, who were seen as superior practitioners in this area. In both countries, the eugenics movement led to state intervention in birth control and to forced sterilization laws, as well as to various experiments designed to raise the reproduction rates of the "superior" races.[58]

57. Speer, pp. 370-71.
58. See Donald K. Pickens, *Eugenics and the Progressives* (Nashville, Tenn.: Vanderbilt University Press, 1968). The U.S. movement dated from the turn of the century, when genetics and efficiency were pressed into service to develop a social response to an apparent paradox discovered by the progres-

The Nazis, however, brought the eugenics arguments into permanent disrepute by carrying them to their logical extremes. They attempted to mass-produce a master race in "mothers' homes"; they established Hereditary Health Courts to apply sterilization laws to physical, mental, political, and racial deviants; they systematically applied euthanasia on a forced basis, first to the sick and crippled, and then to "parasitical" races. As they stretched notions of social efficiency to include the withdrawal of insulin from general availability, the gassing of polio victims, and finally to the practice of genocide, the praise of American eugenicists for National Socialist methods dwindled and was finally extinguished.[59] While the efficiency craze generated by Scientific Management was not the sole cause of this campaign of murder, its elevation of efficiency and rationality as virtues above common morality, its pseudo-scientific language and organizational techniques, and its early entanglement with ideas of racial and social efficiency certainly assisted in legitimating a developing climate of opinion that allowed administrators of the efficiently bureaucratized Aryan reproduction and minority liquidation campaigns to function with a sense of duty well done.[60]

---

sive movement: as civilization advanced, unchecked welfarism would lead to the excessive multiplication of the poor and unfit at the expense of the less rapidly multiplying, superior, Anglo-Saxon middle class, thus reversing Social Darwinism and leading to the collapse of modern civilization. The only way to preserve the "genetic" qualities of the superior classes (thrift, intelligence and ambition—all reflected in a lowered birth rate) was to stop the reproduction of the unfit and enhance that of the fit by social and governmental intervention. The battle for birth control, fought in terms of fundamental democratic freedoms, was the positive side of the eugenics campaign. The passage of forced sterilization laws for the poor, the insane, epileptic, criminal, and feebleminded, broadly enforced in a manner that had overt racist and class warfare overtones, was the darker side of this picture. The most famous attempt to merge Scientific Management and eugenics was the demonstration project of Frank Bunker Gilbreth, who was the son of a stockbreeder as well as a famous scientific manager. The low reproduction rates of the intellectually superior Anglo-Saxon middle class could be explained by the desire to conserve the economic basis of the children's class status. The principles of efficiency, however, could make superior, Anglo-Saxon children "cheaper by the dozen," as Gilbreth put it. The failing intellectual and racial balance of modern society could be restored by modern industrial methods of mass production applied to human breeding and education.

59. Ibid., pp. 98, 99 ff.

60. See Hannah Arendt, *Eichmann in Jerusalem: A Report on the Banality of Evil* (New York: Viking Press, 1963).

Perhaps the central problem of the Scientific Management legacy in the Third Reich was that, in promoting efficiency of form, or the appearance of efficiency as high virtue, it did not, as its original inventors once had hoped, penetrate the irrationalities of political and economic life, creating genuine social effectiveness. Rather, it provided techniques for enhancing the total control of the economy and society without leading to any serious reexamination of the basic aims of that control. In this sense, post-mortems on the Third Reich provide ample evidence of the failure of international Scientific Management in its self-appointed civilizing mission to provide a common logic of worldwide rationality that would uplift the quality of human life. The active promulgation of Scientific Management techniques of efficiency often promoted unintended inefficiencies, as well as different interpretations of efficiency that worked at cross purposes. One example would be the use of characteristic management procedures to promote the continual centralization of power, a task justified not only by the demands of "efficiency" but by the application of the doctrine of the *Führerprinzip*. Luther Gulick, in his *Administrative Reflections on World War II*, expresses the surprise with which American military managers, so convinced that European despotisms were better organized, discovered that the appointment of a "czar" in an area—apparently the most efficient course—would lead to snafus and bottlenecks in the administration of the war effort. On the other hand, "democratic" teamwork, although less centralized, produced higher efficiency in the organization of modern, high technology, war administration.[61]

In the case of National Socialist administration, "czardoms," or absolute and centralized leadership posts, promoted the growth of private kingdoms and rivalries that undermined the organization of military production. More important, these lucrative technical management kingdoms were prizes frequently grabbed off by the corrupt "old boys" of the Nazi party's early days. These were ignorant and vainglorious party organizers whose political credentials and lifestyles had little in common with the technocratic efficiency engineers supposedly promoted by the installation of Scientific Management processes. The most egregious example is that of the Four Year Plan for economic autarky, begun in 1936. On the surface a coordinated

---

61. Luther Gulick, *Administrative Reflections from World War II* (Birmingham: University of Alabama Press, 1948).

economic plan in the Bolshevik-Scientific Management tradition, it became an instrument for the personal enrichment and enhancement of the power position of its chief, Reich Marshall Hermann Goering. Goering, a corrupt, self-seeking heroin addict, used his position to deal in the black market, shake down industrial leaders for "gifts," misappropriate funds for his immense palace, and in other ways to misdirect and undermine the economic planning apparatus of which he was head. Even Hitler himself, at last seeing some of his minister's inadequacies, separated out armaments production from the Four Year Plan and put it directly under the competent Albert Speer.[62]

This combination of efficiency of form with nonrational ideology led to other paradoxes of inefficiency. Despite the fact that women formed a reserve labor pool of patriotic, literate, and potentially skilled German-speaking workers, and that the Western countries had pressed women into war production, for some time the Germans resisted the use of women workers in industry, believing that the morals of German womanhood would be affected by leaving wifely duties, and that their "ability to bear" would be decreased. Forced labor was thus not only used in factories, but diverted into domestic service to relieve the German housewife of her burdens at the very time that England, for example, had reduced the number of maid-servants by two-thirds.[63]

In the end, the course of the war itself illustrated that the pseudo-efficiency of language and "streamlined" organization and politics provided no intrinsic check on the increasingly irrational policy choices of the leadership itself and, indeed, may have even increased its isolation from reality. Poor estimates of American production efficiency, of English sympathies, and the Russian will to resist led to entanglement in a disastrous two-front war. In a pattern entirely unforeseen by the early advocates of Scientific Management, rationalization had become at once the tool and the victim of the irrational polity.

> Zum Geleit
> Arbeit! Arbeit! Segensquelle!
> Heil und Ehre deiner Kraft,
> Die aus Finsternis die Helle,

---

62. See Klein, ch. 2, and Speer, pp. 200-1; Speer outlines in detail his rivalry with Goering and its consequences.

63. Speer, pp. 220-21.

Edles aus Gemeinem schafft!
Aus dem Wirken quillt das Rechte,
Aus dem Schaffen keimt das Echte,
Wehe, wenn die Tat erschlafft!

Mensch, was dich auch immer quäle,
Arbeit ist das Zauberwort,
Arbeit ist des Glückes Seele,
Arbeit ist des Friedens Hort!
Deine Pulse schlagen schneller,
Deine Blicke werden heller
Und dein Herz pocht munter fort.

Völker! Lasst das Murren, Klagen
Über Götzendienerei!
Wollt ihr einen Götzen schlagen,
Schlagt den Müssiggang entzwei!
Nur die Arbeit kann erretten,
Nur die Arbeit sprengt die Ketten;
Arbeit macht die Völker frei.

A.W.

Introductory poem, Gustav Winter, *Das Taylorsystem und wie man es in Deutschland
einführt*, Leipzig, 1919

CHAPTER 7

Management and Traditionalism in Great Britain

We often hear, nowadays, of what is called "Scientific Management," by which some American "Efficiency Engineers" claim to work marvels.

SIDNEY WEBB, 1917[1]

British management attitudes in the nineteenth century appear to have been shaped primarily by the stability of the class structure and by the generally pragmatic approach which characterized British political thought. To begin with, the general stability of the British government and class structure created a climate of pragmatic conservatism. Britain passed through no great revolution as it entered the nineteenth century, but responded instead to the revolution in France by formalizing previously latent theories of conservative politics. The old, highly differentiated class structure of feudalism remained in place, evolving at a slow pace, but still relating classes in terms of a pattern of leadership and deference, even in the face of the upheavals of the industrial revolution. The famous characteristic of British pragmatism was equally influential in shaping the British approach to management. Even in the eighteenth century, the British had accused the French of an excessive preoccupation with the spinning of abstract theories; when Montesquieu developed the theory of the separation of powers from his study of the English constitution, Macaulay accused him of building card-houses, preferring the insubstantial and amusing to solid experience.[2] The British experimental approach had created,

1. Sidney Webb, *The Works Manager Today* (London: Longmans, Green & Co., 1917), p. 131.
2. See the introduction to Charles de Montesquieu, *The Spirit of the Laws* (New York: Hafner, 1958).

in the sphere of government, a constitutional monarchy which gradually evolved into parliamentary democracy, in economic thought, theories which avoided centralized control for national coordination, and in the sphere of technology, a great tradition of practical invention culminating in the industrial revolution itself. The general results of this unusual and apparently contradictory combination of traditionalism and pragmatism were to be seen everywhere. The upper classes had, in common with the feudal classes of Europe, ideas of duty, leadership, and display that those aspiring to their status imitated; they lacked, however, the attachment to centralization from which French bureaucratism developed. Educational reforms in the great universities at the beginning of the century, followed later by reforms in secondary education, established common patterns for the training of the future governing classes. But these reforms were modeled on traditional classical education, and only grudgingly admitted scientific studies; practical technology and organization were considered beneath the attention of a gentleman. Reforms in the civil service, drawing on this educational tradition, and derived from the examples of the new colonial service organized to govern India as well as from the Chinese examination system for civil service entrance, froze this attitude of "gentlemanliness," by the late nineteenth century, into a type of neo-mandarinism which saw government of every type the fit province of the generalist and the classicist. So powerful were these attitudes that they were assimilated by those members of the middle, and later the lower classes, that were drawn into administration via the university and examination route.

In a similar manner, the laissez-faire economics of the British differed vastly from the elaborate French development of centralized economic controls. The notions of free competition and unencumbered domestic trade, with which the French had toyed briefly in the eighteenth century and failed to translate into reality, were elevated in Britain to the level of general ideologies of business, trade, and production. An overarching rationality was granted to this system by Adam Smith's "invisible hand," believed to produce a more finely tuned logic than any man-made scheme of centralized control. With the need for imposed rationality thus disposed of, the field was open to legions of practical and individual organizational and innovative efforts.

The developing technology and management of the great industrial revolution that had been launched by pragmatic inventors were governed by the same techniques; they were advanced by a series of practical organizational inventions devised to meet immediate needs. Individuals invented managerial plans appropriate to govern individual industries without the inspiration of a general plan for rationalizing industrial production in general. Although they might have lacked a general theory of rationality, such plans were nonetheless internally rational, individually systematic in the way in which they were designed to handle specific problems. The French appeared to take the lead in the formal assessment of national patterns of organization, while the British, although intensively concerned with practical applications of technology and the division of labor, tended to follow the French in theoretical analysis. So, for instance, the famous analysis of the division of labor by Babbage used the example of pin-making derived from the work of Perronet, just as Adam Smith had, in an earlier era, derived his example of the division of labor in pin-making from the *Encyclopédie* of 1755.[3]

But although there had been traditional connections between the British systematizers and the French rationalists, their work differed greatly. For the British amalgamated the high rationality of the French with their own brand of common sense, practical discussion, and regard for the intractable nature of the human material. The perceived lack of rationality in human affairs led the French to despair, and to hope that a great power could impose order; it led the British, on the other hand, to a respect for liberty and the hope that free choice would lead to rational action.

The practical nature of British production organization in the nineteenth century meant that much of the historical record of such forms would be lost in the archives of individual enterprises. Formal writings were few; the working plans of industrial organizations remained in the archives until the twentieth century when British management specialists felt the need to answer the Taylorites.[4] Great examples of systematic and rational organization existed, however, from the turn of the previous century and before, and a tradition of serious thought about management matters expressed in writing accompanied them. This could hardly have been otherwise in the foremost manufacturing nation in Europe.

3. See Charles Babbage, *Machinery and Manufactures*, and also Adam Smith, *An Inquiry into the Nature and Causes of the Wealth of Nations* (New York: Modern Library, 1965), p. 4.
4. See Roll, intro. Urwick also discusses this problem in vol. 1 of *Making of Scientific Management*.

RATIONAL MANAGEMENT AND
STEAM ENGINE MANUFACTURE

Perhaps the greatest example of the rational systematization of management in Britain grew out of the most advanced form of technology, that is to say, the steam engine, at the beginning of the nineteenth century. The operations of the Boulton and Watt engine works are particularly striking when compared with production enterprises of the twentieth century which put similar pressures on the "state-of-the-art," such as missile manufacturing. For there, too, the continual need for innovations in materials and manufacturing techniques creates great pressure for continual management innovation to integrate the new techniques in a timely manner. From these pressures comes the advance edge of managerial evolution. In short, not only were Boulton and Watt in advance of their time, but some of their techniques of flow charting bear a remarkable resemblance to independently devised methods in advanced contemporary industries which struggle with similar problems of procurement and manufacture of complex items according to a series of time deadlines.[5] This similarity underlines the unoriginal nature of many of the "technical" managerial elements of Taylorism, and emphasizes its importance as an ideology of control rather than as a neutral technical instrument.

The firm of Boulton and Watt owed many of its management innovations not to James Watt, Sr., the inventor, or his partner Matthew Boulton, but to their sons, who took over the enterprise. This was perhaps the first model of what was later to become a standard pattern in the development of industry, the "father" generation of inventors and entrepreneurs being succeeded by the "sons" who turned to pure management.[6] Originally, steam engines were developed for mine pumping, and James Watt's patents made possible their conversion to general power uses. The problem of manufacturing steam engines in quantity depended, however, on the maintenance of high standards of craftsmanship and exactness. Watt discovered such rare standards at the manufacturing works of Matthew Boulton, which specialized in fine luxury items such as silver and jewelry.[7] In

---

5. Urwick provides a reproduction of a Boulton and Watt flow chart (*Making of Scientific Management*, vol. 1) which is uncannily like modern systems diagrams, PERT milestones charts, and related systems of work planning.
6. Roll, p. xv.
7. Ibid., p. 6.

partnership, they set up an elaborate series of subcontracts designed to deliver "fire-engines"—steam engines still primarily destined for the mines, and designed individually. There was no actual engine factory at this stage. The organization grew according to the need to line up skilled subcontractors and reliable materials; the elaborate problems of costing, which came out of this basic manufacturing arrangement, were already developing accounting solutions. Even a rudimentary notion of spare parts was developed to prevent mines from flooding in the event of failure of certain highly stressed parts.[8]

The "son" generation at the Soho Engine Manufactory concentrated on the systematization of shop organization, wage payment (they developed an elaborate combination of day and piecework incentive wages), and plans for work routing, rather than on the simple extension of the business. Their shop records show that, contrary to common practice, the company repaired and replaced tools at its own expense, rather than leaving it to the workmen.[9] Yet the operations of the firm were not without certain paternalistic characteristics. The lack of strikes in the early stages is attributed to close contact between masters and men. Christmas presents, assorted bonuses, and factory insurance societies were important elements of the Boulton and Watt labor policy. The first strike of engine smiths, in 1791, occurred when a clerk left and his account book could not be found (hardly Scientific Management procedure); it was quickly settled when the book was located. In 1794, a bookkeeper was assaulted for enlisting apprentices in the army, and because of reduced piecework rates,[10] showing how successfully company policy had deflected worker hostility from the higher executive elements.

Although both Roll and Urwick credit the firm with being "pioneers" of Scientific Management practice in Britain, it appears that the rediscovered records of Boulton and Watt actually describe an island in general nineteenth century business practice.[11] And even were this not so, there are crucial differences between Scientific Management and the Boulton and Watt system: in the handful of poorly paid clerks and bookkeepers, some of whom acted for other Soho businesses as well,[12] we see no future "new class" of managers, but rather the traditional class-based pattern of organization that so

8. Ibid., pp. 85-86.
9. Ibid., p. 174. It was at that time customary for workers to pay for mending and replacement of tools.
10. Ibid., p. 222.   11. Ibid.   12. Ibid., p. 251.

closely resembled feudalism—lords, clerics, and peasants. In the "scientific" management of the Soho plant it *is* possible to see the pervasive influence of engineering logic, which by its very nature must have been quite limited in its extent through British society. Boulton and Watt was *in general*, by all accounts, an unusual, technologically based firm, which owed its technocratic organization to its ownership by technician-inventors. As such, it takes its place among the other uncommonly organized manufacturing systems of the day, including those run as educational examples by Quakers and humanists. The circumstance of ownership makes most of the difference, rather than the general progress of a social movement.

In drawing a parallel between the ownership of engineers in Soho, and the ascendance of nonowning engineers in the United States, both of which they claim created conditions for the advancement of Scientific Management, the historians of Boulton and Watt make an important error. Leaving aside, for the moment, the question of an organized engineering *profession* with a coherent vision of systematization (Boulton and Watt's "engineers" were self-taught machine *assemblers* with an unfortunate propensity to drink, much complained about by the partners),[13] we find that the very dynamic which tended to spread engineering influence in the United States tended to limit it in Britain. A loose class structure and a high regard for technology, on the one hand, contrasted with a highly stratified society which admired general culture and the man of easy circumstances on the other. Organizational engineering as a vehicle for class betterment certainly could not succeed where engineering skills themselves could not bridge the gap between working and executive classes without the aid of inheritance. Early British rational management did not develop a self-propagating class of merchandisers, and so remained isolated in those plants where "engineer" owners invented it. Britain may have lived by its engineering skills, but it was not governed by their possessors.

SCIENTIFIC ORGANIZATION AND THE "FOLK ENGINEERING" TRADITION

Apart from factory records, few formal statements concerning the general principles of rational organization exist with the exception of

13. The letters of Watt on the difficulty of finding engineers are excerpted in detail on Roll, pp. 60-61.

those made by Babbage. The differences in Babbage's treatment of the division of labor from the "classical" time study of the Taylorites, aside from the general ones of scale, have been treated in a previous chapter. Babbage's work, neglected as it was during that time, nevertheless represents another important, but submerged, trend in British thinking. Babbage is one of the most serious apologists for technology in Britain, in contrast to the more simple-minded advertisers of the glories of "progress" who lived on both sides of the Atlantic. In fact, he is perhaps the closest version of an Anglo-Saxon Saint-Simonian that one can find, differing mainly in his lack of mysticism, and in the scope of his proposals. (It is, of course, only natural that the inventor of the difference engine should approach the matter of scientific progress in a more specific manner than the visionary French scientific dabbler.) By midcentury, Babbage was pointing to postrevolutionary French state sponsorship of science as a model for England, noting the speed with which the Continental powers were developing science and technology. As early as 1830, he described contradictory forces in Britain, that of popular enthusiasm for science and technology contrasted with the lack of sponsorship, and the mismanagement of the Royal Society; he predicted that popular enthusiasm alone could not prevent Britain's science from future decline.[14]

Babbage's vision was shared, in the early nineteenth century, by other English scientists and educators, who feared that the wellsprings of the industrial revolution might run dry without systematic public education in the sciences. These men were influenced by the post-Napoleonic German push for scientific education, which had grown on the French model under the impetus of military defeat.[15] It was apparent that, if England could not improve public education in the sciences, it would lose ground to the Continental powers by the turn of the century. Class bias, ecclesiastical dominance of the universities, and a generalized Victorian complacency and ignorance about the sources of British innovative talent conspired to defeat the attempts at reform. At the great universities, the attempt to upgrade education

14. Babbage argues for state science in *The Exposition of 1851; or, Views of the Industry, Science, and Government of England* (London: John Murray, 1851). See also *Reflections on the Decline of Science in England* (1830) as cited in ch. 8 of the above reference.

15. A. Haines, *German Influence upon English Education and Science, 1800-1866* (New London: Connecticut College Press, 1957), p. 4.

resulted in a system of comprehensive examinations, begun in 1839, in which honors could only be given in classics and mathematics. While this underlay later civil service reforms, it shattered scientific education, as professors of anatomy, chemistry, physics, and so forth found their classes dwindling to a half-a-dozen or fewer students a year.[16] The upgrading of private educational institutions (the so-called "public" schools) for the upper class had the result of attracting the more ambitious of the middle class to private education, and undercut the development of good general primary and secondary day schools. Class bias preserved class schooling, and undercut the supply of members of the intermediate classes to the industrialization process, those "technologists and technicians" capable of translating scientific invention at the most abstract level into profitable manufacturing processes. These "technologists" were required in greater numbers and with better training as the industrial revolution continued, but British class separation wasted the talent to be found in the lower classes.[17]

It was from these classes of frequently illiterate craftsmen that the wonderful flow of British practical invention had its origins. Much of the industrial revolution derived from outside the "establishment" and the universities.[18] Yet, to advance beyond the first stages of the industrial revolution, this talent required cultivation—literacy and mathematics for a basic minimum—and even this was frequently denied by the narrow educational system of the day. When no mechanized industry existed, the wave of innovations which began the industrial revolution required a laissez-faire atmosphere to develop; in this type of "anything goes" environment, invention can flourish. As the industrial revolution continued, however, invention became cumulative, and that culture which could systematize the rules of discovery and establish general patterns for the training of its people could pull ahead in the race for industrialization. In England, the mercantile

16. Ibid., pp. 13-14.
17. Haines, pp. x-xi, develops the definition of "technicians" as products of mass education, the second "step" in a hierarchy of increasing need for abstract understanding: scientists, technologists, technicians, and workers.
18. Sir David Brewster, vice chancellor of Edinburgh, is quoted as saying in 1830: ". . . Mr. Babbage has asserted that the great inventions of the age are not, with us at least, always produced in universities but we go much farther, and maintain, that the great inventions and discoveries which have been made in England during the last century have been made without the precincts of our universities." Haines, p. 28.

classes who profited from technical invention began to feel that progress was inevitable, a fruit of their own virtue, and that national inventiveness was a sort of inexhaustible national resource. Neither the Germans nor the French, late to industrialize, were under such illusions.

Progress seemed to be in the air in England at the middle of the nineteenth century, in spite of the doom-sayers. The British had repeatedly proven themselves to be the most progressive nation in the world, outdistancing their rivals in both quantity and quality of production, time and time again. French statism, even under Napoleon, had been unable to equal the output of the British, even with greater control over the economy from the center.[19] Bearing in mind this contrast, the British cited free enterprise as the cause. Lack of control encouraged entrepreneurship, and this was the root of British business success. Only an economy operating without legal hindrance could produce such advances in practical and broad-scale technology. The counterpart of this laissez-faire philosophy for the general economy was, for individuals, the theory of "self-help." Between these two levels there was really no theory of organizations or groups, since all things took care of themselves if general freedom and individual character were supplied in sufficient quantities.

The primary exponent of "self-help" was Samuel Smiles, author of *Self-Help*, *Character*, *Duty*, and a host of similar works in which he enunciated the doctrine that success in the world of work was a matter of individual effort. In spite of the author's acquaintance with the industrial and engineering processes of the day, he does not deal with the question of the organization of resources as a factor in group or individual achievement, save for the minor exception of a few lectures on Thrift. Like Horatio Alger, he essentially celebrates the virtues of a bygone day: in *Lives of the Engineers*, the poor, illiterate mineworker's son who becomes the foremost railway engineer of England masters the design of the local mine's Newcomen steam engine by building models of it in clay while working as a cowherd. Later, as tender of the machine itself, he takes it apart at night to memorize the pieces. Not until adulthood, when he can afford to pay for reading lessons, does he unravel the mysteries of the Watt engine from books. His success enables him to educate his son, who then enters his father's profession. Smiles illustrates how, within a single generation, tech-

19. See A. L. Dunham, ch. 1.

nology had advanced to the point where engineers require at least a childhood schooling in letters and mathematics, on-the-job training no longer being sufficient in itself. And while Smiles rejoices in the increasing status of the profession, he does not mention that this very fact bars forever the working children from whom the "enginemen" were once recruited.[20]

The *Lives* unwittingly illustrates both the limits of "self-help" and the astoundingly high level of national talent and energy which backed the first half of the industrial revolution. The great reservoir of mechanical and experimental genius among the ordinary people can be summarized no better than by a contemporary, George Stevenson, the great railroad engineer himself: "The locomotive was not invented by one man; it was invented by a nation of engineers."[21] Much the same could be said of many other famous British inventions of that highly mechanical era.

The common man's fascination with machinery, however, while similar in the eighteenth century to that in America, met with greater obstacles, as in the cases in which illiterate designers found the rewards and patents going to the great men of the Royal Academy, or absorbed without comment by the upper-class owners of the mines and foundries. Yet this situation was an improvement over that in France, for the demands of commercialism were more potent patrons than royalty itself. The first steam-powered vehicle, for example, had been built in France in the middle of the eighteenth century, but it lost its noble sponsor when it failed to operate on the rough roads of the time. In England, steam vehicles were designed and abandoned for similar reasons until advocates suggested their use in place of horses on the railed tracks on which coal was hauled from the mines. The mine owners sponsored the test engines until their profitability was proved, and from there the invention spread to freight hauling, and finally to passenger service.[22]

The limits of individualism, self-help, and sanguine visions of progress were set by social forms of organization only vaguely hinted at in Smiles. The pitmen in the mines, he says, were formerly bondsmen, with a strange dialect of their own, and given to uncouth

20. Samuel Smiles, *Lives of the Engineers: George and Robert Stevenson,* vol. 5, *The Locomotive* (London: John Murray, 1904).
21. Ibid., p. 8.
22. Ibid., pp. 75-85.

ways until lately uplifted by Sabbath schools.[23] Other Victorian authors let us know that, until the late eighteenth century, the workers in the pits were in fact chained by the neck[24]—presumably in the very mines where the first Newcomen engines labored to lighten not the work of men, but of mules. The different dialects and customs of the workers, compared to those of the operators of these first mechanized, industrial establishments, create an image not so much of management or employee relations as of colonization itself, carried out among an alien people. Indeed, so strange were some of these dialects that in one case a judge tried to throw the testimony of a worker out of court on the basis of insanity, before a "translator" stepped forward to volunteer his services.[25] The subsequent conditions of labor in the first half of the nineteenth century, having been fully documented by the Parliamentary commissions which investigated them, need no repetition here. Suffice it to say that these indescribable horrors, fully equal, in their way, to the worst excesses of the oppressive regimes of this century, were hardly inspirations to individualism. Rather, group resistance grew so threatening that reforms "from above, before they come from below," to use the words of the Russian czar, were almost inevitable.

SYSTEMATIC MANAGEMENT
AS WELFARE MANAGEMENT

Alongside of this dominant ideology of individualism, another ideology of organization grew up almost as a reaction to the first. This was the welfare ideology of labor betterment, derived primarily from religious motives. The right to command men was not simply conferred by strength of character in jungle warfare, but was the opportunity to lead them to virtue and industry. The most famous exponents of this theory were Quakers such as Sir William Mather; perhaps the earliest and most famous example of factory organization on this model is Robert Owen's New Lanarck. Owen's model community combined the uplift-type of labor betterment with the roots of welfare-efficiency philosophy: he insisted that better working con-

23. Ibid., pp. 10-11.
24. Charles Knight, *Knowledge is Power: A View of the Productive Forces of Society and the Results of Labor, Capital, and Skill* (London: John Murray, 1855), pp. 77-79.
25. Smiles, p. 4.

ditions would pay off in higher quality labor and dividends to management. This conclusion, far in advance of its time, was rejected out of hand by the majority of owners until the end of the century. Other welfare and cultural experiments, consisting of model villages, libraries, and so forth—although not means of organizing labor— were carried out during this period, even though no direct relationship was established between profit and welfare. Many of the Quaker establishments were said to have operated at a loss. The thinking that went into the construction of these experiments was not lost, however, but formed the basis of British management theory in a way that laissez-faire could not. It provided an ideology of virtue and, as the century wore on, specific features of advanced factory management such as training and promotion plans, lighter work and hours, and even various schemes of copartnership to increase worker efficiency in the advanced Quaker-influenced industries, such as Hans Renold, Mather and Platt, and Lever's, which operated under the motto of "waste not, want not."[26]

BRITISH SLOWDOWN AND AMERICAN SPEEDUP: THE ATTACK ON TAYLORISM

The general picture of industrial organization during the period of undisputed British industrial superiority in the first half of the century was not visibly influenced by the slowly developing, religiously inspired trend of welfarism. In spite of these conditions, or some say because of them, British manufacturers of the period were first in the world. British textiles, British iron and steel, British machinery—all were superior. In particular, British tool steel was the best in the world, and the quality of British machinery and tool steel set the general pace of manufacturing. The American tool-making and steel production organizations in which Taylor started his career all looked to the industries of Great Britain as the most advanced models of manufacturing practice, and considered themselves in competition with them, working to surpass the British industrial lead with no less energy than the French and Germans.

Taylor's speed mania ran headlong into British practice from the first, when, in 1882, Midvale Steel began importing gangs of highly

26. John Child, *British Management Thought: A Critical Analysis* (London: George Allen & Unwin, 1969), pp. 36-37, gives a capsule description of the influence of Quaker thought on early British industry.

skilled British labor, because of the difficulty of obtaining enough skilled Americans for steel work. The British workers not only cultivated all sorts of exotic practices for the restraint of output, relying on the ignorance of American management to continue them after their emigration, but they began a campaign to convince the American workers in the plant of the wisdom of their course of action. Taylor, never understanding the source of the British workers' customary habits of self-protection, was forever convinced that British laborers were the arch-practitioners of "organized soldiering," responsible for the eventual loss of British production superiority. A typical Midvale occurrence was the importation of an advanced piece of British machinery for rolling locomotive tires, complete with a crew of skilled British laborers. The crew turned out fifteen tires a day, and the machine made no profit, to the despair of its owners. When general explanations and exhortations to speed failed, Taylor had the entire crew fired; he then trained American workers, put them on the differential piecework rate, and turned out one hundred and fifty tires a day. While British labor practices protected the British workman from management, they did not protect British industries from the new competition offered by their American rivals. Taylor saw British unionism and worker combination as the source of what appeared to be a growing difference between American and British rates of industrial production.[27]

American competition with the British for the tool steel market was directly responsible for the financial backing and organizational encouragement that Taylor received in his metal-cutting experiments. It was this competition in tool steels, more than anything else, that illustrated the problems inherent in the British approach to production. This approach had grown up in the early part of the century when Britain was the only advanced industrial nation; it was rapidly becoming insufficient to deal with the requirements of production in the decades of intense international industrial rivalry at the end of the century. For combined with great innovative talent was profound complacency about the uniqueness of that talent; British management traditionalism and ethnocentrism complemented perfectly the worker conviction that only the restraint of output would prevent labor exploitation. Both management and labor assumed that British industry would remain first in the world more or less indefinitely and

27. Copley, 2:315-16.

that, furthermore, the general level of world industrialization was more or less static, the markets for industrial goods being generally fixed in size.

Just after the middle of the century, Robert Mushet of the Titanic Steel Company in England had discovered a harder tool steel alloyed with tungsten and manganese which was air-cooled or "self-hardening," and within two decades it had replaced the centuries-old carbon tool steel in world use.[28] Mushet steel appears to have provoked a wave of experimentation in the industrial nations of the West even as it gradually attained a unique world pre-eminence. It would appear also, as the controversy after the development of high-speed steel indicates, that the predominance of Mushet steel was an article of patriotic faith in Britain. For when Taylor and White, in search of a tool steel that could hold an edge at even greater machine speeds than Mushet steel, discovered that chromium steel, when water-cooled, held its edge just below its own melting point, the British response was a curious one, especially in the traditional steel-producing areas of England.

The discovery of high-speed steel in 1888-89, as mentioned in a previous chapter, was not simply the outgrowth of a technical search for better materials, but a by-product of Taylor's compulsive speed mania, so enmeshed in his system of labor and materials organization that he could market his management system simply by promoting high-speed steel. Indeed, he took advantage of every inquiry about high-speed steel to remind his questioners that the invention was useless without the Taylor system. So great was the interest in the discovery that, according to Taylor's biographer, within a few days of the discovery, letters began to arrive from Europe, South America, Australia, and South Africa, thus widening the potential market for the Taylor System of Scientific Management.[29]

From the first moments of the Paris exposition, the British never took high-speed steel for anything but a purely technical invention, and they set about immediately to better it. Yet even as a simple technical invention it was upsetting enough:

> The feelings with which the Sheffield visitors to the Paris Exposition saw red-hot American tool steel turning castings at double the speed then practiced at Sheffield were the reverse of pleasant, for Sheffield tool steel

28. Ibid., p. 435.
29. Ibid., p. 111.

had been in unchallenged use in the engineering shops of the world despite prohibitive tariffs, and the possibility of Sheffield being compelled to yield her supremacy to America had never been contemplated.[30]

Taylor's biographer goes on to include in his account of the exhibition the fact of repeated British visits to the Bethlehem Steel exhibit, and he reports that other exhibitors in the building complained about the crowds of representatives of European industry at the Bethlehem exhibit that blocked their own displays.

Perhaps some of the glee with which the French praised Taylor's papers as models of scientific investigation, surpassing those of Sir Lothian Bell and Sir William Siemans, both British pioneers in the development of steel production, was a direct result of this British loss of face. The immediate outcome (besides an ongoing polemic between the French and the British on the subject) was that the British almost immediately set about duplicating the Taylor-White experiments in Manchester.[31] The Sheffield steel manufacturers were particularly bitter over the innovation, and when rival American firms tried to break the Taylor-White patents (Vickers had the English rights), Sheffield led the British efforts to aid them, raising money for the battle and sending delegations of experts, including members of the faculty of the University of Sheffield.[32] In the midst of personal attacks on Taylor, the British claimed that the discovery was the result of a clumsy accident—one, in fact, which had been made originally in Britain.[33] The court battle to void the Taylor-White patents took five years, and during this time the anti-Taylor propaganda generated by the interested industries became permanently rooted in Great Britain, although the French continued to write and speak against it.

Little competitive advantage appears to have been gained from this struggle, however, for by 1906 other German, American, and British varieties of high-speed steel had appeared in the world market, all of them superior to the original Taylor-White steel.[34] The important fact to remember is that, during this time, the output of Bethlehem Steel's principal machine shops *more than doubled*,[35] and presumably that of the other users of high-speed steel followed suit. Originally the output of Bethlehem's machine shops tended to be equivalent to or slightly higher than that of similar shops in Britain; now the British were engaged in a world production race which had increased in tempo,

30. Ibid., p. 112.   31. Ibid., pp. 246, 256.   32. Ibid., p. 86.
33. Ibid., p. 91.   34. Ibid., p. 109.   35. Ibid., p. 112.

and in which their technological supremacy no longer made them the undisputed leaders. Technological change had put a premium on innovation in production *organization* of the very type which British labor had learned to combat so effectively.

In duplicating high-speed steel as a technological achievement, the British tended to consciously reject Taylorism as an organizational scheme for increasing output. To some extent, organizational accommodation had to be made for the increased speed at which machine tools could run, as the Vickers representatives to Bethlehem found out from Taylor. Workmen could not putter about mending their own tools, storage and materials handling had to be accomplished more efficiently, and laborers themselves had to get used to working at higher speeds.[36] The Vickers Company rejected Taylorism as a package, but adopted enough of its specific features so that the "Vickers' System," as it came to be called, did not really look like indigenous British management practice; Taylor himself felt that it was so close to his own system that its "Made in England" label was amusing.[37] But, in general, Taylorism as a philosophy of organization was rejected most strenuously by the British. In the words of a British management historian:

> F. W. Taylor was to exercise a profound influence on British management thought, yet his writing made little overall impact on British industry before the First World War. Pioneering employers such as the Cadburys, Renolds, and Rowntrees gave scientific management an attention that was both receptive and critical. On the one hand, scientific management was equally at odds with laissez-faire indifference. . . . Yet, on the other hand, it lacked that sympathetic view of workers and their representative organization on which Quaker employers particularly insisted.[38]

36. As late as 1917, outmoded and disorganized patterns of work prevailed in British machine shops. Webb quotes the president of the Institute of Mechanical Engineers, Mr. Michael Longridge: "Except in a few cases, workshop organisation here has not received the attention given it in America or Germany. There are still shops without definite planning of the progress of the work, without adequate equipment of jigs and gauges, and without standard shapes of tools or a tool-room; where men drift about in search of tools or tackle, or wait in idleness for drawings and materials; where machinery is obsolete and light so bad that good work cannot be done if the machinery were up to date. Such shops must go. They cannot compete in price or quality of work with those in which what is known as "Scientific Management" or anything approaching it, prevails . . ." Webb, p. 134.
37. Ibid., pp. 324-25.
38. Child, p. 38.

Taylorism in this early period ran into a series of barriers once it crossed the Atlantic, of which chauvinism was possibly the least.

Much more was involved in the rejection and the ultimate conversion to Taylorism than simple national pride, although later attempts to "prove" that Scientific Management was a British invention became a standard part of the management literature by the 1930s.[39] Aesthetic revulsion over the "crude and harsh 'engineering' approach"[40] of American efficiency engineering likewise played a part, but not a large one. It would seem that much of this apparent "cultural" rejection of brash and unattractive American methods in favor of a British "leadership" approach had to do with the different situation of skilled labor in Britain, itself a product of the British system of feudal classes evolved to meet the problems of industrialism.

In particular, the comparatively strong organization of the working class, in addition to their specific opposition to Taylorism and all other types of piecework abuses, appears to have had a great deal to do with the final adjustment of the industrialists to Scientific Management. The class system, with its stress on the distance, technical ignorance, and moral leadership of the classes directing the industrial enterprise, had left the monopoly of practical skills to the working class, and even the development of an engineering profession was insufficient to fill the gap. For even when engineers had attended college, they were "social outcasts" in the words of Taylor, and he blamed this, along with governmental "flabbiness" (!) in the face of worker obstructionism, for the problems of British industrial production. When you herd workers into classes, he was fond of saying, you promote strikes and trade unionism.[41] Specifically, skilled workers had banded together into the most famous trade union organizations in the world at that time; it was far too late to rely on their ignorance to manipulate or bully them into increased speed at disproportionate financial rewards, as Taylor had the illiterate immigrant laborers of America. Taylor's famous example of Schmidt's handling of pig-iron, based on his ox-like mentality, was anathema to British labor, which started a rumor that Schmidt had died shortly after his labor had been increased on the Taylor system.[42] Even though the Taylorites were

39. See the works of such British authors as Urwick and Child.
40. Child, p. 40.
41. Copley, 1:100, 410, 404.
42. Another story spread by the British trade unionists, and picked up by the French (see Pouget, pp. 68-69) concerned a British visitor being shown

eventually forced to produce Schmidt to prove the contrary, the effort proved to be in vain.[43]

If organized trade unionism blocked Taylorism's conversion of the working class, it also hampered its progress among the industrial directors who were progressive enough to have considered the modernization and adaptation of their modes of organization. For managerial progressivism in Britain had developed out of the Quaker strain of thought that stressed the duties, as well as the rights, of the employer, resulting in the general philosophy that industry had broad social functions beyond profit-seeking. Such management pioneers as Joseph and B. Seebohm Rowntree, or Edward Cadbury, had investigated the evils of sweated labor, poverty, and drink; they had come to the conclusion that bad labor conditions had brought about lower standards of productivity and higher levels of force. It followed, then, that industrial conflict was not simply the product of "agitators," and that trade unions had a legitimate place in the industrial order.[44] This communal emphasis in industry led to a conscious rejection of Taylorite individualism, and of the differential piecework schemes that the unions had denounced as punitive.

BRITISH SOCIALISM PRE-EMPTS SCIENTIFIC MANAGEMENT REFORMISM

Chapter 1 illustrates the manner in which Taylorism was designed to meet the problem of the growing rift between capital and labor in America. Taylor and his followers had asked both management and labor to put aside their quarrel over the division of the rewards of industrial production and to concentrate instead upon increasing the returns to both sides through efficiency reforms. They preserved the traditional American emphasis on individualism and on private business in their organizational reforms and, to the extent that they succeeded in increasing productivity, wage levels, and control, postponed the clash between classes.

A most crucial consideration in the failure of Taylorism to make

---

around a modern American factory. Everywhere high production and efficiency prevailed. But the visitor saw only young men at work, and asked, "But where are your old workers?" The American capitalist conducted him to the cemetery: "Down there," he replied.

43. Copley, 2:55. Schmidt appears to have lived longer than Taylor himself.
44. Child, pp. 39-41.

much impression on British industrial organization at the turn of the century is that the British, with a much older industrial establishment, a militant trade unionism, and less class mobility, were already far advanced in the engineering of a solution to the same problems addressed by Taylorism. Specifically, this involved the development of a body of socialist theory which proposed the very answer that was anathema to Taylor: the redivision of the product of industrial society. British labor had organized the first movement in Europe to protest systematically against prevailing laissez-faire economic doctrine and exploitative industrial practice. The cooperative societies, trade unions, and syndicalism of the 1830s evolved into Chartism and violent protest which aimed not at the destruction of the government but at full working-class representation.[45] This early organization, generally "socialist" in aim (although not in the orthodox European sense), formed the roots for the later establishment of the Labour party. Indeed, European socialists at midcentury, particularly Karl Marx, saw in the organization of the British labor movement a model of the forces leading inevitably to the violent revolutionary redivision of the product of industrialism under the future world socialist order.

With the rise of European socialism, especially Marxism and "nihilism" (mostly identified in the British mind with Bakuninist anarchism and the later movement headed by Prince Kropotkin), English authors on the situation of labor in the late 1870s and early 1880s were amazed that the British working class adamantly refused to be moved by these powerful currents of thought. Edward R. Pease, the original secretary of the Fabian Society, stressing the absence of doctrinaire theory in 1883, the year of the founding of the Society, cites an article on "socialism" by a Mr. Samuel Smith, M.P.:

> Our country is still comparatively free from Communism and Nihilism and similar destructive movements, but who can tell how long this will continue? We have a festering mass of human wretchedness in all our great towns, which is the natural hotbed of such anarchical movements; all the great continental countries are full of this explosive material. Can we depend on our country keeping freer from the infection in our midst than the neighbouring European States? Emigration and temperance reform, he thinks, may avert the danger.[46]

45. Max Beer, *A History of British Socialism*, 2 vols. (1st ed., 1919; London: George Allen & Unwin, 1940), 2:23-37.
46. E.R. Pease, *The History of the Fabian Society* (London: Frank Cass & Co., 1963), pp. 15-16.

The efforts of the Fabian Society were to modify this picture considerably, and their theoretical work, popular education, and political campaigns encouraged a movement for nonrevolutionary socialist reform carried out piecemeal over the next eighty years. The Fabian Society, profoundly committed to constitutional democracy, was influenced, according to the account of its members, far more by Auguste Comte's *Positive Polity*, Herbert Spencer's Darwinism, and Henry George's American populist manifesto, *Progress and Poverty*, than by Owenism or Marxism.[47] Following a doctrine of "permeation," it maintained close ties with the Labour party after its founding and, through infiltration and skilled political exposition, it exercised a continuous influence on British governmental and social organizations from the time of its inception.[48] Taylorism, then, arriving after the turn of the century, and couched in the rude language of the factory floor, was in no position to substitute its industrial management solutions to social problems for those advanced with such wit by Shaw, Webb, and the other literati among the Fabians;[49] the building of a political compromise in Britain was already in progress.

In other ways, the antiquated class structure of Britain, with its stress on the cult of the amateur for the upper classes, and practical but humble expertise for the lower classes, proved to be a barrier to Taylorism. The high level of practical skill required by Taylorism appeared *declassé*, and therefore unattractive to those wishing to improve their status. The old professions over time gravitated upward to the lower levels of the upper class; the new professions lacked the formal recognition of schooling and status. Management professionalism and education were highly dubious when even engineering it-

47. Ibid., pp. 13-27.
48. The reprint record of the original *Fabian Essays* (London: George Allen & Unwin, 1889, 1908, 1920, 1931, 1948, 1950), by Shaw, Webb, Wallas, Olivier, Clarke, Besant, and Bland, attests to its influence. Pease points out that Fabians were encouraged to join and influence other social organizations.
49. The Fabians, especially Webb, rejected Taylorism out of hand as exploitative, and compared the efficiency expert in the pay of the factory owner to the hired henchmen of the medieval robber baron. (See Webb, pp. 17-18.) Webb and the Fabians saw efficiency as a product of welfare work and the elimination of *human* waste in society, especially sweated labor: see Fabian Tract no. 108, "Twentieth Century Politics: A Policy of National Efficiency" (London: Fabian Society, 1901). It was not until well into World War I that Webb came to advocate Taylorism in a limited way as part of the war effort.

self was suspect. And scientific training was so neglected in British government and official circles that, on the eve of World War I, the government was unaware that crucial ingredients for the manufacture of explosives were lacking in Britain, and were being imported from Germany.[50] With the battle for scientific education still raging in England, not only technical subjects, but "overspecialization" was suspect, following the classical Greek dictum that specialized practical knowledge was not the proper study of citizens, but of freedmen, artisans, and slaves. The civil service examinations, true to this ideal, favored the generalist and, in particular, the student of the classics. Science was not really in a position, then, to glamorize business.

The general oversupply of manpower in Britain had furthered the illusions of factory owners that profit rested on lower wages and the direct use of force rather than on the reorganization of resources, even reorganization involving the veiled coercion that characterized the "mechanization" of labor. "Herding in classes" was convenient and required little specialized knowledge of organization or technology on the part of management. Unlike the United States, where skilled labor was still comparatively scarce, and the social structure unfixed, the British system was not conducive to the elevation of a new middle class of would-be management professionals.[51] Added to the dislike of social climbing was the fear of charlatans, closely associated with specialization in the minds of the British management caste; both constituted a dangerous threat to gentlemanly dignity.[52] This, and the neglect of science and engineering as formal professions that had grown out of similar motives, prevented the formation of even a rudimentary version of that class in which Taylorism naturally flourished.

Without technocrats of uncertain social origins, there was no group whose greatest interest lay in the propagation of Scientific Management as a profession. It was due to this absence of carriers that the compromise between labor and industrial management could eventually be made. The very fact that a compromise could be engineered

50. D. S. L. Cardwell, *The Organisation of Science in England* (London: William Heinemann, 1957).

51. This thesis is developed by H. J. Habbakuk in *American and British Technology in the 19th Century: The Search for Labor Saving Inventions* (Cambridge: Cambridge University Press, 1962), although in relation to innovation in general, not management innovation.

52. Granick stresses this as a traditional characteristic of British management which persists to this day.

at all was the outcome of a situation where ownership and labor faced each other directly, without an intervening professional class. The immediate result had been that no group justified its existence by its ability to redirect the conflict, thus creating its own vested interest in preserving a situation in which it could be the eternal mediator. The ultimate result of the British situation was the handling of the conflict in more direct ways, involving first the recognition of trade unions, and ultimately the nationalization of industry.

The First World War marks a turning point in both labor relations and the evolution of British management thought. The wartime shop stewards' movement developed into a powerful challenge to private ownership and to owners' management as labor pressed demands for workers' control. The influential strain of thought deriving from Quaker industrialism emerged to the forefront of management thinking as slogans of workers' control drove the more traditionally oriented class of industrialists to fear complete worker overthrow in their own factories.[53] At this point they were at last ready to listen to the Quaker "welfare" employers and to make some sort of compromise with organized labor. By its very nature such a compromise would require the rejection of Taylorism. It involved a delaying action for the demands of workers' control and a search for alternative methods to undermine the labor movement. Such alternatives had certain requirements: they had to provide a new basis of legitimacy for owners' control (humanism and leadership led the list ahead of "dehumanizing" science as sources of legitimacy) and, eschewing visible techniques of control such as Taylorism, they had to provide subtle, psychological means of manipulation and propaganda in the interests of higher worker output.

The result was that British management began to cultivate a sort of proto-human relations school of management thinking even before the works of Elton Mayo appeared. With roots in prewar humanism, it had gathered momentum with the "brotherhood of the trenches," which brought members of separate classes together, often for the first time.[54] Prewar excesses of exploitation, often revealed in wartime health and fatigue studies for the first time, combined with the new activism of the labor movement and the shadow of Bolshevism to reinforce and speed up management's movement down the path of the

53. Child, pp. 42-45.
54. Ibid., p. 44.

"new humanism." Under these conditions, Taylorism in Britain did not pass the luncheon meeting stage, as the records of the International Management Institute (a sort of international Taylor Society) tell us, while at the same time, highly active and well-organized societies and business associations were promoting the rapid conversion of French, German, and Fascist Italian industry to Scientific Management.[55]

THE BRITISH HUMAN RELATIONS SCHOOL

The real growth of the indigenous British management philosophy based on the study of the health and psychology of industrial workers dates from the First World War. Its evolution and brief encounters with Taylorism illustrate the unique cultural and social conditions in Britain which prevented Scientific Management from taking root.

In 1891, when Cooke-Taylor described *The Modern Factory System*[56] in England, there is not the least hint of discussion of organizational techniques such as the controversy over various wage plans that was raging in America at the time. Technology predominates; organization is confined to the simple statement that men gather in large (factory) groups around a power source, and the surprisingly modern statement that electric motors will allow the decentralization of the factory system—perhaps even its dismantling into neo-cottage industry. Although there is no discussion of the organization of labor, the condition of labor forms an important secondary focus of the work, and is accompanied by an extensive discussion of the history of legislation for factory reform. This Victorian view of the march of Progress through centuries, with its curious blind spot in the matter of either worker combinations or the techniques of labor and materials organization as a resource, appears to be a common one.[57] The contrast with equivalent turn-of-the-century American works, replete with diagrams of wonderful new filing and routing systems, discussions of lady "typewriters," and the organizational potential of new

55. *Bulletin of the International Management Society*, vols. 1-2, 1927-28. (At this stage, the *Bulletin* was only a mimeographed newsletter.) Sample notice: In September of 1927 a lunch meeting on "rationalization" was held in Great Britain. Officers of forty industries adopted a resolution to promote science in industry.
56. R. W. Cooke-Taylor, *The Modern Factory System* (London: Kegan Paul, Trench, Trudner and Co., 1891).
57. See both Cooke-Taylor and Knight.

office machinery, is clear. And much like the early party organizations in American constitutional thought of the last century, the early trade unions in Britain appear to have been officially ignored in respectable circles.

Such writings as begin to appear about the time of the First World War appear to combine an extraordinary degree of paternalism with the general consideration that the poverty and alienation of the working class are poor foundations for modern warfare and modern war production. The great Taylorite crusade had made only a limited impact on a few of the most advanced industries, and one or two British texts on management techniques had appeared.[58] An advanced thinker such as Sydney Webb could predict the growing role of managers in all complex industrial orders "from now to Utopia,"[59] but works of two decades later despair over the fact that this idea has not yet penetrated the national consciousness.[60]

The general tendency was, under the stress of war, to return to the pre-existing ideas of health and betterment. In particular, the health conditions produced by factory labor and urban pollution had visibly undermined potential military manpower; a dramatic illustration of this problem with the military unit composed entirely of dwarves from London that saw action in the First World War.[61] More than the long-range effects of rickets and the terrible incidence of infant deformity were questioned, however. If skilled workers fell ill from dope fumes due to poor ventilation, aircraft production dropped; the production of TNT involved similar risks.[62] Inspection teams, in the name of war production, investigated health conditions, and forced compliance. Industrial health and fatigue studies came of age in the war; from the early nineteenth century's concern with child labor abuses, resulting in legislative reforms, the health movement had moved on to consider, within the framework of the new hours laws, specific conditions of work: anthrax in wool workers, open factory machinery, and the high incidence of worker mutilation, "phossy jaw" that ate away the bones

58. Child, p. 53.
59. Webb, p. 5.
60. See, for example, P. S. Florence, *The Logic of Industrial Organization* (London: Kegan Paul, Trench, Trubner & Co., 1933), ch. 8.
61. Farnham, p. 396.
62. T. M. Legge, "Occupational Diseases" in A. E. Berriman et al., *Industrial Administration: A Series of Lectures* (Manchester: Manchester University Press, 1920), pp. 81-82.

of the matchmakers, and various industrial poisons, especially lead poisoning. Prewar health legislation laid the foundations for yet another stage in the development of health investigation and the conditions of labor.[63]

The Taylorites' organizational work for World War I in the United States had influence in that it pressed the British to adopt scientific standards for the measure of labor productivity in terms of certain variables. But the variables they chose to measure were those that affected health and welfare. From this fusion was born a new scientific humanism which essentially quantified Quaker welfarism, a "science" with strong paternalistic and manipulative overtones. Because it was a science created by enlightened industrialists rather than by middle-class experts with something to sell, one of the most noticeable aspects of the new scientific humanism was its reliance on voluntary compliance of factory owners based on appeals to their good will and conscience, basically, on noblesse oblige. Merchandisers or private consultants, playing up fears of being left behind financially in some contest of competitive virture, were not a characteristic of the movement; bland moral exhortation was.

In 1919, the first important British work on Scientific Management was published by the Ministry of Reconstruction, which summarized the new management techniques in use elsewhere and urged employers to adopt them. Drawing on the new experimental literature proving that management "goodness" was profitable, it treated welfare as a necessity, thus illustrating how far British management thought had evolved into the area of industrial psychology.[64] The stress on virtue and unity in industry was emphasized when shortly thereafter employers established the Industrial Reconstruction Council and the National Alliance of Employers and Employed, with its journal *Industrial Unity*.[65]

No better illustration of the difference between the British and American approaches to management exists than the contrast between the well-known views of Taylor on wage determination with those systematized by B. Seebohm Rowntree in a lecture delivered on 12 November 1918. Here he calculates the necessary base wage on the

63. B. Seebohm Rowntree, "Social Obligations of Industry to Labor," in Berriman et al., pp. 2-15.
64. Child, p. 53.
65. Ibid., p. 96.

basis of industry's social obligation to labor, evolving a series of statistics that enabled him to calculate a living wage on the basis of standard living conditions. A man's wage should allow him to marry, support three children, occupy a decent house, and work with physical effectiveness (this latter requires a nutritional calulation). A woman's wage should be smaller because it should include no family allowance. The sticky problem of men with more than three children, and of women who had to support families is temporarily avoided, since Rowntree hastens to demonstrate that even minimum wage standards are not being met, and he quickly moves on to describe remedies. The basic way to pay the minimum wage is for industry to examine inefficient and costly processes and to reform them, using the savings thus realized to increase wages. Profits will follow because of increased worker efficiency under proper living conditions.[66] The conclusion one must draw is that the only motivation for Rowntree's proposed efficiency and social reforms is moral: thrift and welfare concern will lead to increased productivity and higher profits by and by. This is, of course, the completely opposite approach to Taylor's marketing of expert advice on techniques of profit increase which may eventually lead to welfare, thus giving moral justification for the "hardships of the transition."

Robert Brady points out that even in this early period of reform proposals, Britain was already losing ground to the Taylorized nations. Britain, he says, had begun to lose her preeminence as the major industrial country in the world in the late nineteenth century; in the early twentieth century, Britain experienced a decline in exported mass-produced lines of goods to Germany, America, and Japan. Since 1913, textiles especially had experienced such a decline, but other goods were represented as well. From the perspective of half a century, he characterizes Britain's declining balance of trade in this manner:

> One by one Britain lost the lead to her newer, more modern, and more enterprising overseas competitors in iron and steel products, many lines of machinery, cheaper woolens and rayon products, various lines of manufactured foods, etc. Part of this loss was the result of a shift to the production of higher quality products, but most of it was due to growing technological backwardness which had already become general by the time

66. Rowntree, in Berriman et al.

of the first world war in large segments of her industrial system. Between the two world wars Britain never staged an effective or sustained industrial recovery similar to that of the US during the twenties or to that of Germany with her "rationalization movement" after 1925.[67]

The crucial period of decline was in the 1920s, the era of the accelerating campaign for Scientific Management in Europe and America. As even war-torn Germany attained a comparative level of recovery, the contrast with continued depression in England grew greater. Just the reverse of the situation in which England had gained industrial predominance in Europe after the Napoleonic war now prevailed after the First World War. A hundred years before, the Continent had been starved for goods, and England had large supplies of cheap manufactured goods to sell. The equivalent situation recurred in 1945, after the Second World War, but then it was America with goods to sell, facing a European economy so exhausted that it did not even immediately constitute a market.[68]

Some rationalization did take place in certain specialized sectors during the 1920s, but it was neither extensive nor did it stress maximized production on the American model. A leading advocate of business rationalization, Sir Alfred Mond, advanced the model of English chemical industry rationalization after 1926 in his book *Industry and Politics*. Deriving many of his ideas from the American presidents of large concerns with whom, as the head of a great chemical combine, he was in natural communication, he stressed the role of management in the reconciliation of labor and capital over cost cutting, and cost-cutting techniques over the maximization of low per-unit-cost production. This model was important to the British chemical industry of the period, where the primary concern was that labor trouble not shut down expensive chemical equipment, and the secondary concern was that of developing the kind of cost cutting that fit into a stable cartelized economy better than maximized competitive production. Later British industrial authors, however, find this pattern of rationalization typical of the pattern of English productivity failure, where Scientific Management, when introduced, was put at the service of various kinds of welfarism, including the technical simplifica-

67. R. Brady, *Crisis in Britain: Plans and Achievements of the Labor Government* (Berkeley and Los Angeles: University of California Press, 1950), p. 9.

68. Ibid., p. 10.

tion of tasks and raises in wages and profits, through the emphasis on the cost-cutting side of Taylorism rather than on its output maximization side.[69]

Critics find that the era between the wars, thus marked as the turning point in the decline of British productivity, was the time when technical retardation began to be visible everywhere. The very techniques and social conditions which had once made British goods the best and cheapest in the world were now insufficient in the face of sustained innovative effort in other nations.

> Britain was in arrears, and . . . this technical retardation was paralleled on the one side by the swift proliferation of an efficiency-inhibiting growth of closely interwoven trade association and cartel controls the effects of which upon production were generally of a restrictionist character, and on the other—in the face of chronic mass unemployment—by a wide-ranging and deeply rooted aversion to job-destroying technical change in trade union circles. Along with this, compared with either German or American practice, went little attention to industrial research, scientific management, standardization in the field of consumer goods, or technical rationalization on an industry-wide basis.[70]

The Weimar rationalization movement, so crucial to the later successes of the Nazi war machine, was the direct outcome of the German Scientific Management movement.[71] Scientific Management's two greatest triumphs of the early twentieth century, outside of the United States and Russia, were the conversion of the Germans and the official connection that the Scientific Management movement developed with the Italian Fascist state, of which the Taylorites were especially proud. The same international bulletin which records these triumphs catalogues the failure of the campaign, month by month, in England. No organization in England, it states, corresponds to the American Management Association or the Taylor Society, but the Society of Technical Engineers has been organizing a Scientific Management movement in engineering, getting in touch with the universities, and arranging for the reading of papers on standardiza-

---

69. I. C. McGivering, D. G. J. Matthews, and W. H. Scott, *Management in Britain: A General Characterization* (Liverpool: Liverpool University Press, 1960), pp. 93-95.

70. Brady, *Crisis in Britain*, pp. 9-10.

71. See Brady, *Rationalization Movement*.

tion in its meetings as of December, 1927.[72] A significant step has been taken in the same year, it reports: a luncheon meeting on the general subject of "rationalization" has been held, and officers of forty industries who attended have adopted a resolution to promote science in industry.[73]

It would be wrong to assume that during this era stasis had been achieved in management philosophy. The now predominant school of human relations was extremely busy evolving tactics of industrial psychology designed, according to their advocates, to avert open industrial warfare.[74] Prominent among them were the pioneer managers Cadbury, Casson, Elbourne, and Renold. The best known management author among them, John Lee, stated in 1921 that the attention to industrial science had been caused by industrial unrest.[75] In *Management: A Study of Industrial Organization* (London, 1921), he advocated a "scientific approach" to the problems of management, but claimed that while Taylor's Scientific Management was important, it should be qualified by industrial psychlogy. "The truth is that human nature is too complex for the crude Scientific Management."[76] Although his work was akin to that of Mary Parker Follett, the American management theorist, his post as director of the London Telegraph and Telephone Centre and his advocacy of science in management lead the British to identify him as their first "scientific" manager.[77]

While to some extent the British rationalization movement was pushed by the new Institute of Industrial Administration, events in the development of American management studies had the result of accelerating the British industrial psychology movement. The works of Mary Parker Follett, which gained only limited influence (mostly in the Boston area) in the United States, were far more influential in Britain in the late 1920s, with their much more subtle view of human nature, their deemphasis of the "engineering" approach, and their humanistic approach to converting the industrialists. Elton Mayo's work of 1931, which established the American human relations school

72. *Bulletin of the International Management Institute*, no. 5 (Geneva, 1927), p. 4.

73. Ibid., no. 2, p. 1.

74. Child, p. 53, quotes Casson as saying that the main problem is "how to prevent industrial warfare—how to establish a right relationship between workers, managers, and owners."

75. Ibid., pp. 53-54.   76. Ibid., pp. 59-60.   77. Ibid.

of management thought, likewise had a profound influence in Britain, since it tied in with the type of thought already developed there. By the 1940s, the work of Mayo and Follett was taken up and expounded on a broad scale in numerous books and pamphlets, and later, Chester Barnard's congenial "leadership" doctrines were embraced.[78]

Yet, it truth, very little in the way of general education and practical reform of management practice, recuitment, or education appears to have taken place. In the 1930s and even after, volume after volume pleads for increased status for management specialists, and for the development of business education, accompanied by more acute observations about Britain's decreasing ability to compete and the cultural attitudes that underlie it. A typical example, *The Logic of Industrial Organisation* (London, 1931), draws on the works of Fayol, Taylor, and Urwick, pleading for more efficient organization of industry and better processes of recruitment for talented managerial personnel. "England is now in intense competition with other manufacturing countries, is no longer, by divine dispensation, the workshop of the world." English producers, the work exhorts, must abandon the attitude of the old days, which was one of "take it or leave it" with foreign buyers, growing out of the cultural attitude summarized by the Germans as "das gentleman ideal."[79] Many of the talented are lost forever to business through poverty, states the author, and the remainder are educated in the public (that is, private) schools and universities, which foster love of hierarchy and ritual, emphasize games, and teach scorn of business and profit.[80] The inexorable conclusion that this type of study reaches is that *industry cannot advance without major changes in the entire class and educational structure.*

A postwar election of the labor government and subsequent nationalization of large industries and health care represented, in a way, the culmination of the British "human relations movement," which had grown out of the dialectic of conflict and exploitation of a century and a half of British industry. At the same time that it had failed to stem the gradual decline in exports, it had, in conjunction with the labor movement which had so influenced it, focused the general discontent on a few targets, succeeding in blaming the ills of England solely on private ownership. The Labour party was the only logical outcome.

78. Ibid., pp. 114-16.   79. P.S. Florence, pp. 245-46.
80. Ibid., pp. 251-56.

TRADITIONAL FORCES
IN CONTEMPORARY MANAGEMENT

Despite the rapid evolution of modern industrial management in the postwar era, British practice and British management education preserved their prewar biases, with only some attempts at modification. The decades since the war, despite many advances in the study of labor psychology and the belated attempt to improve production efficiency, constitute a chronicle of decline. The list of British firms, especially in automobile and motorcycle manufacture, that have failed to compete against their American, German, or Japanese equivalents, reads like an honor roll of British industry. The failure certainly has not been in the area of craftsmanship, nor even just in productivity, but in the various market forecasting, sales technology, and other modern management skills that characterize the more successful foreign industries, as, for example, in the case of British motorcycles versus lightweight Japanese imports. Various observers point not only to old plants and old skills, but to old-fashioned management as a basic problem in the decline of British industry.

In the 1950s, for example, David Granick's study of British executives found the characteristics of the highest level of management little changed from the prewar era. The cult of the gentleman amateur had led to such fear of specialization as the creator of opportunities for charlatanry that managers surveyed rejected simple and old-fashioned proposals to increase research and development as too risky.[81] Yet, in the midst of this upper management stagnation, Granick found, a new movement was taking place at the lower levels of management:

> The single major managerial development of postwar Britain does not really violate the proposition that managerial professionalism is still rejected. For this development has been concentrated in the area of production efficiency and on the lowest level of the managerial hierarchy. It is old-fashioned work study, bearing the new name of "Organization and Methods" and now relating to office as well as to production workers. . . . While this doubtless is highly important for efficient operations, it represents a managerial movement which was revolutionary in American industry during the first decade of this century—but had been routinized into standard operating procedure in the United States by the 1920s at the latest.[82]

81. Granick, pp. 252-53.
82. Ibid., pp. 253-54.

A British survey of 1960 also testifies to the persistence of traditional management attitudes. British management is not yet professionalized, find the authors, but is still largely patrimonial. The extension of collective bargaining, industry-wide, has caused the surrender of some control over limited conditions of employment, but by doing so has allowed management to retain control over other matters in the plant, and to take a "neo-paternalistic" initiative. In this setting, traditional attitudes are still prevalent. Managerial overheads may be regarded as unnecessary costs just as frequently as they are deemed investments; new management techniques are dubbed "new-fangled" as often as they are adopted as useful aids, and many managements still prefer security to the uncertainties of development, a stable production level and "cost-cutting" to an expansion of output and reduction of unit cost, and a measure of cartelization to a measure of competition. The authors summarize this traditionalism in the following manner:

> At the risk of gross over-simplification, some of the relevant influences [on the slow development of professionalization] may be subsumed in the statement that social class factors, and related elements in the educational system, which derive from the pre-industrial order and from an earlier industrial stage, are still widely prevalent. Managerial qualities are often regarded as "inborn" or conferred by "right," rather than by the most relevant kind of education; in the educational system and elsewhere there are biases towards general and arts, and against "useful" or "vocational" subjects . . . ; many managerial and staff persons expect that their hours of work and other functional characteristics of their jobs shall be sharply distinguished from those of other grades, and this is still the prevalent practice; and the fairly widespread incidence of the managerial quest for security and stability, and of elements of cartelization in the economy, are partly attributable to the predominance of "class" over professional interests and criteria."[83]

There is no escaping the conclusion that Britain had chosen, in the years that followed the First World War, an alternative path to the reconciliation of labor and capital than the technocratically based

83. See Summary of Opinion Research Centre survey first published in early May of 1977 in *The Manchester Guardian Weekly*, 8 May 1977, p. 4. The article refers to a "revolution of falling expectations" and compares worker attitudes in Britain, West Germany, Japan, and the United States. The British proved "remarkably unambitious in the material sense," preferring leisure and a "pleasant life" to more money.

management solution offered by the extended version of Scientific Management. Direct democratic confrontation in the political sphere played a greater role than did the indirect manipulation of labor via the rationalization of the industrial workplace. Traditional class attitudes prevailed over the *arriviste* bustle of a rising class of Taylorite efficiency engineers. Cost-cutting and the maintenance of traditional markets prevailed over maximized production. The consumption of leisure and the limitation of demand came to be preferred over the stressful striving for wage increments derived from higher output. Whatever the costs and benefits of the arrangement, the skepticism, traditionalism and class relations that underlay British political institutions were sufficiently reflected in the industrial sphere to render Scientific Management's social missionary streak inert. In the short run, this meant that its practice in management spheres was reduced for many decades to the level of technical improvements only. The long-range consequences of this management strategy are only now becoming visible.

PART III

POLITICS AND
THE IDEOLOGY
OF MANAGEMENT

The application of scientific management to the machinery of government in the democracies, great and small, is a job that can be done and will be done. There is no mystery about Leviathan; he is merely an enlarged sardine.

LYNDALL URWICK, 1948

CHAPTER 8

Beyond Scientific Management

Indeed, Scientific Management is all but a systematic philosophy of worker and work. Altogether it may well be the most powerful as well as the most lasting contribution that America has made to Western thought since the Federalist Papers.

PETER DRUCKER, 1954[1]

No exact date marks the conversion of Scientific Management, the prescriptive theory of efficient machine-shop organization, into Scientific Management, an ideology of organization for industrial civilization. As the international Scientific Management movement pressed for the rationalization of world industry, it stressed the utopian and idealistic elements of its philosophy to overcome labor resistance to the elements of the speed-up that it contained. As different groups interpreted and developed the work of Taylor and his followers, the individual management gimmicks that appeared to be the trademarks of Scientific Management became the least significant part of the Scientific Management message; Taylorism emerged from the 1920s as a general philosophical doctrine of management—"scientific management" without capitals. It seemed to be the rational and natural way to prescribe the proper distribution of power in organizations, and to justify the dominance of the technically trained professional in organization and society as well. It used the language of science to propose that its broad-based, "utopian" social goals were the realistic and inevitable consequence of the applications of its principles. In short, it was a doctrine with universalistic claims and an influential political message.

The Scientific Management doctrine of technocratic control, cen-

1. Peter Drucker, *The Practice of Management* (New York: Harper & Row, 1954), p. 281.

tral planning, and high productivity, leading to a golden age of mass production in which high levels of material consumption would banish class enmity and create permanent social harmony, had a core of truth that made it a powerful doctrine in the political sphere. Scientific Management genuinely increased productivity, making more low-cost manufactured goods available for consumption, and it genuinely increased middle-class opportunity by redefining the role of the planner, systematizer, and white-collar worker in industrial production. Efficiency in the factory was a measurable commodity with a "scientific" basis and real benefits. It was only natural that Scientific Management, in the course of the campaign waged to install it in international industry, should leave the world of industrial management and become incorporated into political ideologies and movements. The way in which this process of increasing politicization occurred in the United States illustrates the power and persistence of Scientific Management ideology in locations far from the factory floor.

THE POLITICS OF SCIENTIFIC MANAGEMENT

The emergence of Taylorism within the factory, as we have seen in earlier chapters, paralleled the emergence of other social doctrines which were designed to cope with the social disorder of industrial development. These movements, demanding the reorganization of state and society, showed a natural affinity for one another, and Taylorism dominated the technical end of the coalition that resulted during the progressive era. The "One Best Way" demanded a rationalization of the political systems which increasingly interlocked with the industrial establishment in which the rationalization efforts had their origin. Scientific Management, translated into politics, advocated the development of the state as an organ of national planning and allocation according to a rationally derived system of priorities; it glorified a monolithic rational-technical order in place of the weak democratic forum that compromised among the interests of powerful groups. H. L. Gantt's denunciation of the "debating society theory" of democratic politics is typical of the Scientific Management ideological bias:

> I don't agree with the average politician's concept of democracy. His is the debating-society theory of Government; policies, according to him, must be decided not by demonstrated facts but by opinions; not according to the

laws of physics but by majority vote. Such democracy accomplishes nothing and leads nowhere. Real democracy consists of the organization of human affairs in harmony with natural laws, so that each individual shall have an equal opportunity to function at his highest possible capacity. . . . Voting upon a question of fact is the poorest way to settle it. Does water run uphill? . . . The best way, if we don't already know, is to find out. Let us do away with debating-society methods in both politics and industry and substitute demonstrated facts for the opinions of either an autocrat or the great majority. Until the people consent to such a change they will never attain to real democracy.[2]

In short, the scientific managers advocated an end to traditional politics and the transformation of the government into a technical operation. It was only logical to them that the bureaucratic reforms introduced into the executive branch by progressivism and the civil service movement be extended indefinitely.[3] The one exception to Taylorism's message of increasingly unified managerial control, and the only principle not inherently incompatible with constitutional democracy, was the divided power advocated by the plan of "functional foremanship." This system, which divided authority to allow the direct participation of different kinds of specialists in production, was designed to assure the dominance of technicians over the line command of financier-owners; it was gradually overshadowed by the increasing development of Scientific Management centralism when the right of the technical elite to dominate in their specialties could be taken for granted.[4]

An assessment of Taylorism's effect as a political ideology should not underestimate effects of the continued widespread assimilation of Taylorism in American industrial and governmental bureaucratic circles long after the initial enthusiasm of the Scientific Management

2. L. P. Alford, pp. 260-61.

3. The ambitions of the latter in respect to this aim were specifically disclaimed by the development of the "politics-administration" dichotomy (see Chapter 9).

4. Gulick and Urwick point out that it was essential to the development of Scientific Management to eliminate the "division of authority" of functional foremanship and restore "unity of command." The influence of Fayol's work should also be taken into account. The first English translation of *Administration industrielle et générale* appeared in 1929. Gulick and Urwick later attempt a formal compromise between the conflicting orthodoxies of functional foremanship and unity of command in *Papers in the Science of Administration*.

crusade had waned. Taylor's system of rationalization and standardization was well established in the large manufacturing enterprises of the United States before the First World War. Industrial practice and management schools continually renewed the pool of Scientific Management believers. The active opposition of organized labor did not succeed in eradicating Scientific Management from enterprises where it was already established, as, for example, the Watertown Arsenal case showed, even when it succeeded in banishing the formal nomenclature of Taylorism and its most hated symbol, the stopwatch. At the same time, the violence of union opposition forced internal changes in the Scientific Management movement directed toward a more careful consideration of how working conditions, in addition to wage payment scales, affected labor productivity. The Hawthorne experiments, conducted from 1927 to 1932, derived their original impetus from Scientific Management studies of the relation of fatigue and boredom to productivity, and led part of the Scientific Management movement into new directions, softening some of the harshness of its original impact.[5]

During this period, the early union opposition was gradually changed to support, as the Scientific Management movement proved that in practice it supported certain improvements in working conditions, and developed a less rigorous attitude toward organized labor. First compromising with Scientific Management and then incorporating its principles, the expanding unions recognized that

5. The classic account of these experiments in F. J. Roethlisberger and W. J. Dickson's *Management and the Worker* (Cambridge: Harvard, 1939) makes clear the relationship between the design of the studies and the pre-existing Scientific Management methodology for work study, and especially for fatigue study. Elements of the experimental context that were time-bound and culture-bound resulted in the misuse of the findings when managers tried to duplicate the "Hawthorne effect" by enforcing behaviors found in the original studies but inappropriate in the new context. For example, Roethlisberger and Dickson's account documents—although it apparently went largely unremarked at the time—that the high productivity in response to the specific social incentives of the experiment was demonstrated by groups composed of women, for the most part newly recruited to factory work from the farm. The use of similar incentives on groups of men, whose long work experience and union backgrounds made them wary of potential speedups, resulted in labor resistance and a decrease of productivity. Forty subsequent years of work experience and union membership may have brought the socialization of women workers much closer to that of the men in the study, thus increasing the potential for negative responses to the coercive management paternalism inherent in such misapplications of the "Human Relations" approach.

Taylorism, in reducing crafts and leveling all labor within the great industries that it had reorganized, had created a more broadly based community of interest in the working class, thereby establishing the basis for a new type of unionization. Union demands for security, high wages, and safe and hygienic working conditions overlapped to a certain extent with the effects of the newer versions of Scientific Management. To a degree, then, both unions and business had a common interest in furthering the establishment of Scientific Management systems within the factory in this later period. Until the recent emergence of job enlargement as a key issue, then, Scientific Management was an integral part of the compromise engineered between business and labor.

Scientific Management made good political propaganda long before its principles were incorporated to any great extent in government itself. The themes of national efficiency, conservation of resources, and the war against waste that were an important part of progressivism seemed all the more powerful when documented by the experiences of efficiency engineers in industrial practice. It looked businesslike and made good political sense to incorporate the views of efficiency experts in modernizing, reorganizing, and "eliminating waste" from government agencies. Thus, in 1905, Theodore Roosevelt, in keeping with his vigorous support of the extension of the merit civil service, appointed the Commission on Departmental Methods, or Keep Commission. In 1910, a successor commission, the Taft Commission on Economy and Efficiency in Government, which incorporated personnel and ideas from the new governmental efficiency movement, was appointed by the president.

The Taft Commission began a work considered to be monumental —the first comprehensive description of government organization, offices, and functions ever undertaken. As a sign, perhaps, of their optimism concerning their ability to bring permanent and fundamental order to government, the resulting organizational description was published in a loose-leaf binder, suitable for appropriate updating should the occasion arise. The commission's most significant proposal was the creation of an executive budget; cross-national data, the most significant being from England, France, and Germany, were introduced in support of the idea.[6] The budgetary research of the commis-

6. See U.S., Congress, House, Presidential Commission on Economy and Efficiency, *The Need for a National Budget*, 854 (Washington, D.C.: Govern-

sion clearly reflects the interests and work of F.A. Cleveland, its chairman, who was deeply involved in New York City budget reform through the New York Bureau of Municipal Research (and who was, incidentally, a friend of Taylor).[7] A great part of the impetus for the Taft Commission's work is clearly a result of ongoing, progressive, merit civil service reforms; some, also, is pure cost-cutting. But a serious new influence of the industrial Scientific Management movement is visible in the general approach and definition of efficiency, and in the attempt to render office work more efficient by adapting new methods and devices currently in use in business. The idea of "Taylorizing" government office work to save money, and cement the civil service reform's victory over workers, who were only recently rebellious patronage appointees, was definitely in the air. Efficiency required the elimination of local offices, which were protected by patronage; the extension of civil service hiring would make possible the substitution of efficient administration for inefficient politics.[8]

This first phase of popular enthusiasm for "business" efficiency and engineering methods can be said to have culminated in the election of Herbert Hoover as foremost representative of the cult of the Engineer-Administrator.[9] Hoover, like his predecessors, declared war on waste, his background adding moral weight to his own efficiency campaign. But the crash of 1929 buried his efforts and left large segments of the population blaming the business system, its ethic, and its representatives for the depression, precisely because these forces had claimed credit for the previous era of prosperity. The stock market crash can be said to mark the end of the social predominance of what might be referred to as first-generation Scientific Management theory in America—the cult of efficiency and business dominance which began with the efficiency craze of 1911.

---

ment Printing Office, 1912). See also U.S., Congress, House, Presidential Commission on Economy and Efficiency, *Message of the President of the United States on Economy and Efficiency in the Public Service*, 458 (Washington, D.C.: Government Printing Office, 1912).

7. Barry Dean Karl, *Executive Reorganization and Reform in the New Deal: The Genesis of Administrative Management, 1900-1939* (Cambridge, Mass.: Harvard University Press, 1963), p. 188.

8. House, 458.

9. Arthur Schlesinger, *The Crisis of the Old Order* (Boston: Houghton Mifflin Co., 1957), p. 155, quotes contemporary praise for Hoover from American industrialists: "For the first time in our history, we have a President who, by technical training, engineering achievement, cabinet experience, and grasp of economic fundamentals, is qualified for business leadership."

A central characteristic of the first-generation Scientific Management craze was that, while the central planning control and other mechanisms by which it increased the efficiency of organizations were considered essential for the development of the private businesses upon which national prosperity depended, the application of efficiency mechanisms to government would be limited to the kind of cost-cutting, accounting, and office reform mechanisms that would not, in fact, extend any control over private enterprise itself. The idea that greater social efficiency might involve the extension of an efficient government control over the private sphere, while a natural extension of Scientific Management thinking, was developed only by a few of its most devout engineer advocates, while the run-of-the-mill efficiency addict strictly compartmentalized business efficiency and government efficiency.

The search for solutions to the world depression made it not only possible to think the unthinkable, but desirable. At the close of the First World War, H. L. Gantt had expressed the then extraordinary view that the one-sided rationalization of the industrial sphere, by increasing the efficiency of production without correspondingly increasing the efficiency of distribution, would lead to a crisis of overproduction. Similar views were expressed by both Marxists and fascists, who had developed them as arguments against the rationalization campaign in Europe. In 1921, H. G. Wells, in town to report on the Washington Naval Armaments Conference, walked the streets of New York, imagining how they would look at the end of the decade in the grip of the coming financial catastrophe; he fantasized bodies hurtling off the upper floors of the skyscrapers, and the city in panic.[10]

The depression brought such previously unorthodox views to prominence, and ushered in the second phase of Scientific Management. Since the long-awaited crisis had come, it was now time to attempt to finish the introduction of Scientific Management's political views directly into government, to extend and rationalize the state so that it might be capable of rationalizing social distribution. The most extreme version of this second phase in the United States is represented by the organization of the Technocratic party, which rose to national view only to dissolve when its anticonstitutional and pseudoscientific bases were uncovered. More influential, in the long run, was the more limited influence exerted by Scientific Management in the

10. H. G. Wells, *Washington and the Riddle of Peace* (New York: Macmillan Co., 1922).

extension of the federal bureaucracy under the New Deal, as a product of its incorporation into the influential Brownlow report, and into the "administrative management" movement.

THE FANTASY OF MANAGERIAL CONTROL OF THE STATE: TECHNOCRACY, INC.

The clearest statement of Scientific Management's political ambitions, albeit in greatly exaggerated form, was made by Technocracy, Inc. This would-be elite advocated state planning and national standardization, and was organized in the form of a political party designed to integrate Scientific Management into government through an electoral revolution. Technocracy, Inc., was derived from academic discussions of general social efficiency reforms based on Taylorism and on Veblen's "Soviet of Engineers"; it indicated clearly the extraordinarily far-reaching nature of Scientific Management's political message when separated from its technical vehicle. While the American technocratic movement has been labeled the closest domestic variant of both fascism and Stalinism,[11] its resemblance is not so much a result of its very minimal borrowings from these movements, but rather of the mutual roots of all three in the international Scientific Management movement of the decade or two before.

The ideal of a rationalized, managerially controlled state had been a latent element of Taylorism until the period after World War I, when scientific managers began to generalize from their experiences in war planning and industrial mobilization. These experiences raised the sights of these crusaders: the creeping rationalization of private industry was less impressive than the idea that the mechanisms of the state might be rationalized, and then used to rationalize production and distribution on a national scale. French managers, with their ancient intellectual heritage of centralism and their dreams of Saint-Simonian technological utopias, were easily led to this vision. Similarly, Germans such as Rathenau, founder of the German rationalization movement, thought naturally in these terms. The example of Lenin's use of Scientific Management in national industrial rationalization fired the imagination of social reformers as well as engineers and technical managers the world over, despite the intense dislike of many of them for Bolshevism and for the Russian revolution.

11. James Burnham, *The Managerial Revolution* (New York: John Day Co., 1941), p. 73; and Elsner, pp. 157-58, cites contemporary press sources.

In America, unlike continental Europe in its strong heritage of political liberalism, it was not such a simple matter for native Taylorites, such as Gantt, to evolve general views of social reform out of the aggressive individualism of American Scientific Management. Perhaps because of a greater degree of laissez-faire ideology in the American environment, the purest ideological statement that evolved out of Taylorism became the political platform of a party on the lunatic fringe, rather than a respectable component of national management thinking. Centralized, rationalized, technocratic control of the state was, in the United States, a fantasy of petty clerks and draftsmen, rather than the political program of great technicians and administrators as it was in Europe. The relation of this vision to the original tenets of Taylorism, as well as to the less dramatic, ongoing influences of Scientific Management in government can clarify, however, the portrait of Scientific Management's inherent ideological message.

The American Technocratic party, which rose to prominence in the early 1930s, was derived from classic American patterns of problem solving. The alchemy by which the reputable ingredients of American liberalism, rationality, and technology were converted into a mass movement with totalitarian aims was based on the direct application of the ideological components of Taylorism, without the mediating influence of traditional American constitutionalism. It begins with the works of Thorstein Veblen, which formed a crucial link between the factory experience of the Taylorites, and attempts to apply engineering techniques directly to American society. Long before Gantt's postwar studies of "overproduction," Veblen pointed out in *The Theory of the Business Enterprise* (1906) that the increasing efficiency of industry in a capitalist environment (that is, one with a highly unequal distribution of wealth) meant that crises of "overproduction" in terms not of the goods people *needed*, but of what they could *afford*, and resulting depressions were inevitable. Only wars or other means of wasting the unsalable surplus could divert depression, and the increasing production of industry was gradually outrunning even this possibility. Big industry, said Veblen, became inevitably linked with the production of armaments and the making of wars.[12]

In 1919, Veblen wrote a series of articles later published as *The Engineers and the Price System*, which began by pointing out that the

12. Thorstein Veblen, *The Theory of the Business Enterprise* (New York: Charles Scribner's Sons, 1920).

capitalists and financiers sabotage the potential of their own plants to make the goods that the people desperately need, in order to maintain the style of living of their own class by freeing it of the pains of adjusting to economic fluctuations. What is really needed, he says, is for those who understand the techniques of raising production—the technicians and engineers—to take over and run the enterprises full speed ahead for the benefit of the entire people. Veblen discusses the potential for a general strike of technicians, their unity as a class, and so forth. The only possible government would have to be run on an "un-businesslike" (nonprofit) principle, that is, a soviet. And the American soviet would have to be one of technicians. The soviet of technicians would consider the welfare of the whole people, organizing society so as to eliminate waste and duplication and thus raise the overall standard of living. Before such a successful coup, however, a group of engineers would have to gather for purposes of planning, mapping out the actual operations of the system, and propagandizing the public about the vices of the profit system.[13]

The idea of forming an association of engineers dedicating their expertise to the rational solving of national problems actually dated back before Veblen's proposal, to Gantt's "New Machine," formed in 1916. Influenced by Veblen's earlier writings on the inefficiency of industry, Gantt proposed his "conspiracy" of "men of science" and "masters of arts and materials" to "socialize" finance and industry so as to prevent the emergence of "many Prussias" (including, by implication, the United States) and endless wars. At the end of the war and just before his death in 1919, Gantt published a series of articles warning of an impending economic catastrophe. But Gantt did not believe that governmental intervention would be an effective means of reorganizing business and putting those concerned with increasing productive efficiency in charge, in the place of the financiers. Although the group petitioned the president, basically it subscribed to the belief that only massive popular education could do the job. Because of this, the New Machine, while it lasted, remained only a talk group.[14]

At the end of the First World War, Veblen also organized a

---

13. Thorstein Veblen, *Engineers and the Price System*.
14. Alford, app., describes the New Machine in detail, including the petition to President Wilson; he includes a membership list which indicates the extent to which the New Machine influenced the later technocratic movement.

discussion group at the New School, where he taught; he hoped this group would eventually provide the nucleus of the soviet of engineers. Gantt was by this time dead, and the New Machine had lost its driving force, although its members got together again after the war to reconstitute it. There was an overlap in membership in the New Machine and the soviet of engineers, for qualified engineers with interest in social planning were few. Both the New Machine and Veblen's soviet gradually fell apart, but not before they had attracted and profoundly influenced a younger group of disciples, many of whom went on to the technocratic movement and to government careers in the New Deal.[15]

One of the hangers-on at the soviet meetings as well as those of the Taylor Society during this period was a young man in search of a great mission, Howard Scott. Profoundly influenced by the discussions he had heard, he began to develop his own theories of social and economic reform, based on half-digested fragments of Veblen, Gantt, and the Taylorites. By 1920, he had established a "Technical Alliance" as an offshoot of the now-defunct soviet; a number of reputable figures such as Veblen, later New Dealers such as Stuart Chase, various qualified engineers, and scientists joined the organizing committee of the alliance. Scott appointed himself as "chief engineer" of the Technical Alliance, which, as the direct predecessor of the Technocratic party, set for itself the goals of graphically determining the operations of the present production and distribution system, uncovering the waste therein, and working out a new design for production and distribution.[16]

Although the alliance had high-sounding goals of national service, Scott himself appeared to regard it as a consulting business, selling details of the "production system" for cash to all clients, including the Industrial Workers of the World (I.W.W.). This shady financial turn of affairs alienated some of the more respectable members, who nevertheless remained in the alliance's general orbit.[17] Throughout the 1920s, then, Scott's organization mounted a propaganda campaign that went almost unnoticed. The intellectual core of Scott's pamphleteering was the radical engineering literature of the 1915-1919 period, rewritten and popularized, with additions by such engineers as Polakov, who returned from his consulting work in the Soviet Union to write quasi-philosophical engineering works about power and the

15. Elsner, pp. 23-25.   16. Ibid., p. 23.   17. Ibid., pp. 27-31.

unity of everything.[18] Only a few odd groups of believers based in Southern California took notice of the works of the Technical Alliance in the 1920s and the term "technocracy" was coined in Berkeley to summarize its approach.[19] In the meanwhile, the more reputable Taylor Society had renounced its ideas of radical social "efficiency" reforms and had become deeply involved with the eminently successful "business system." Scott's parallel attempt to find a legitimate business market for his theories failed for want of buyers, and fixed his resentment of the business system more firmly.

The stock market crash brought profound popular disillusionment with the business system in general, intensifying public receptivity to plans for more humane social alternatives. The old alliance of Taylorism with business, which stressed the virtuous and socially beneficial results of unbridled individualism, and business control of society as structured through the new management techniques, went into eclipse with the collapse of the business system itself. However, the general Scientific Management approach to social reform suffered no such fate. The failure of business revived the old neo-Taylorite arguments that questions of social and economic distribution should be taken from the private sphere and placed in the public sphere, where a rationalized state might do a superior job of balancing production and distribution.

More immediately, the depression and the search for social alternatives to private enterprise put the technocrats in the position of prophets. Scott went to see Professor Rautenstrauch, one of the members of the New Machine, who was teaching in the Industrial Engineering Department of Columbia University, with his proposal for an energy survey of North America; the survey was designed to pinpoint the causes of the depression, which Scott could now claim that he had predicted. Rautenstrauch was impressed, arranging for rooms at the university to begin the energy survey. A few months later, there was a sensation in the press when Scott, with the apparent backing of a noted American university, announced the tentative

18. See Walter Polakov, *Man and His Affairs from the Engineering Point of View* (Baltimore: Williams & Wilkins Co., 1925), and *The Power Age: Its Quest and Challenge* (New York: Corvici, Friede, 1933). In this manner, Lenin's "soviets plus electrification" was enshrined in the Technocratic party's platform of control over the energy system.

19. M. D. Gutter, "The American Technocratic Movement" (M.A. thesis, University of California, 1967). See also Elsner, p. 2.

conclusions of the survey: industrial employment in the United States had reached its maximum in 1919, while total production had done so in 1929, and unemployment would continue until the collapse of the industrial system![20]

Scott now took to the road, offering broad political solutions couched in technical jargon, while vaguely hinting at a coherent program of reforms to be revealed at a later date. The only message that he offered was that the economy and state should be taken over by competent engineers (such as himself, of course).[21] His campaign, however, and the publicity that surrounded it called forth serious criticism of his efforts. Rautenstrauch's departmental rivals pressured him until he recanted, renouncing technocracy as misguided; the energy survey collapsed as a result. This severed Scott from his academic base. His critics, including engineers, businessmen, and political figures, then attacked (1) the undisguised element of dictatorship in the plan, (2) the feasibility of the proposed reforms of the "price system," and (3) the credibility of Scott as a leader. Scott's claims to philosophical originality and engineering expertise collapsed when it was publicly revealed that the source of his ideology was a series of odds and ends gleaned from Veblen, Marx, and a British physicist named Soddy, and that, worst of all, his claims to be the former director of a great engineering project were utterly false. In fact, he had been a cement-pouring foreman, fired from that very project for incompetence.[22]

Technocracy, Inc., did not disappear from the face of the earth with these revelations, but rather was converted from a caricature of the Taylor strategy of social mobility (engineering expertise, academic self-promotion of new professionalism, and the call for middle-class advancement) into a mass political movement. Photographs of mass meetings, attended by uniformly gray-clad technocrats, driving gray cars, and dispersing messages on gray stationery, were now featured with scare captions in the press. Public pronouncements on the evils of the price system became more shrill, until the campaign to substitute

20. Elsner, pp. 7, 37.

21. See *Pamphlets on Technocracy* (Binder's title) (New York: Technocracy, Inc., n.d.), which includes such titles as: "A Thermodynamic Interpretation of Social Phenomena," "America Must Show the Way," "The Plan of Plenty," and "Pax Americana."

22. Elsner, p. 5. Howard Scott also claimed a Ph.D. in engineering from the University of Berlin (Elsner, pp. 8-9).

the rule of the Technate for that of the business-dominated federal government came to look like a plan for violent revolution. The issue of violence added to the differences over strategy and tactics that were splitting the party, and the national structure of the Technocratic party collapsed into regional factions; in the end, all but a handful of its most crackpot followers deserted the movement.

Two interrelated questions are raised by the existence of the Technocratic party: first, who were the followers of the mass movement, and second, what were the explanations for its sudden collapse? When the respectable technical figures abandoned the movement, technocracy continued to draw support not from the professional middle class, but from the undereducated, recently impoverished, *lumpen*-middle class. It was a caricature of the Scientific Management movement, but with specific political goals in place of latent political ambitions. Eventually reduced to recruiting by mail order and matchbook cover, it offered its followers, who were frequently high-school graduates with thwarted ambitions to continue their schooling, a specialized "education" in the operations of the price system and technocratic systems of reordering it, heavily larded with impressive technical jargon, and it promised (in its esoteric councils, not in its public recruiting messages) offices in the coming Technate, or technocratic government, to those so trained.[23]

Taylor's reforms withstood close inspection, even as did his life, when hired detectives searched in vain for signs of insanity. Neither Scott's life nor his philosophy could withstand such scrutiny, and this lost him his competent technical following (although they turn up later, as advocates of the great legitimate "energy" projects of the United States, such as the Tennessee Valley Authority). Henry Elsner attributes the failure of Technocracy to the inability of the party to attract the very engineers whose rule it postulated.[24] This failure has more complex roots than Scott's quackery, it must be noted, since most of his most outlandish variants were evolved after the defection of the saner heads in the party.

From the very beginning, Technocracy postulated *only*, and somewhat cynically, the rule of the technically trained middle-class expert; it failed to produce a practical program of labor control that could have promoted an upper-class alliance, and was unable to ally itself

23. Conversations with former technocracy recruits in San Francisco area.
24. Elsner, pp. 187-88.

with the now politically active lower class, which had already had its fill of control by experts. When even the professionalized middle class failed it, no significant proportion of the electorate was left. From that point on, its membership dwindled as individuals came to realize that the Technate was a dead letter in terms of electoral victories, and that only the exercise of violence remained. Technocracy, Inc., did not die at that point, but converted, by the late 1940s, into a millennial religion of technological utopia. Having given up its aspirations as a viable political party, it lives on in odd corners of the Far West.[25]

THE REALITY OF MANAGERIAL INFLUENCE: SCIENTIFIC MANAGEMENT AND NEW DEAL BUREAUCRATIZATION

The Report [of the President's Committee on Administrative Management] is a great state document of the highest interest and importance. It is shot through and through with the ideas of Scientific Management. Thus, for the first time, *the philosophy developed from the work of F. W. Taylor and other pioneers has been applied practically to the government of a great nation.*

LYNDALL URWICK, 1949.[26]

The failure of technocracy as an organized Scientific Management-based political doctrine did not represent the failure of Scientific Management influence on politics and government in the United States. Technocracy, Inc., was an extreme—Scientific Management refined almost entirely to its political message, and without most of the active and practical technology in which Scientific Management's ideological core was usually embedded. The main body of Scientific Management doctrine, through its historical alliance with progressivism and its influence on the attempts to develop an "administrative science," exercised a direct influence on the organization and management of the federal executive branch. This influence was never as complete or as grandiose as the aims of technocracy—for it was felt through the day to day work of a more sober brand of government

25. As late as 1970, Technocracy, Inc., still maintained a San Francisco office.
26. Urwick, *Making of Scientific Management*, 1:154. Emphasis added.

officials, administrative specialists, and consultants, and was exercised in combination with other modern, technically based doctrines, most notably Keynesian economics. An additional source of continued Scientific Management influence on governmental organization derived from its embodiment along with other progressive reform elements in the "administrative management" school of public administration that dates from that period.

Both the high point of Scientific Management's influence in government and the turning point in its conversion from a factory-based engineering system to a bureaucratically based administrative system occurred in the year 1937, with the appearance of the *Report of the President's Committee on Administrative Management*, a systematic proposal for reform of the executive branch, and Gulick and Urwick's *Papers on the Science of Management*, a collection of essays that forms a key statement of the administrative management school of public administration. The president's committee itself, chaired by Louis Brownlow and including Charles E. Merriam and Luther Gulick, marked a significant change in the presidential use of advisors in the examination of federal management procedures, for these men were primarily academically oriented, rather than being leading representatives of the business community.

The great search for remedies for the economic catastrophe that had overtaken the nation had returned to prominence many of the reformers, ex-progressives, and socially oriented Taylorites who had been little heard during the complacent years of business prosperity before 1929. The intellectual currents which brought Scientific Management thinking to the very center of executive power were not quite as direct as Urwick's analysis of the Report of 1937 would appear to indicate, however. They appear, in fact, to have made a transit through Russia before returning, through dissident liberalism, to the American continent. If, as Schlesinger assures us, the New Deal brought the United States back from the very brink of revolution, then the role of the international descendants of the Scientific Management movement in the process is irony itself.

Although the idea of social engineering, so explicitly advanced by Veblen with conscious reference to the Russian model, was echoed by the architects of liberalism in the 1920s, this was in many ways simply a reflection of the general concern with the development of more socially responsible ways of handling the impact of industrialization. The Russia of the 1920s was the only experimenting ground where the state directly concerned itself with the kind of industrial and social reform that had long been discussed in the West. Isolated by distance and language, the Russian "model" of the 1920s (at that time not one, but many coexisting models) lent itself to foreign speculation, and each group of observers tended to see its own image therein, a confirmation of its own lines of thought.

Thus, in 1928 Charles A. Beard proposed that technological civilization, founded on science and power-driven machinery, should extend itself until its concepts of order ruled public policy. He challenged the engineers to create plans for a social technology.[27] John Dewey expressed the hope, in 1929, that a national economic council representing government, business, and labor might establish voluntarily forms of collectivism resembling those in the Soviet Union.[28] Technocracy, Inc., then, was not an isolated phenomenon, but a lunatic variant on a serious trend of social thought which, deriving from Veblen, stressed the imminence of the planned society, given the current development of the industrial system.

One of the elements in this support of planned order was the sense of foreboding which haunted those who had become closely acquainted with the effects of the new industrial technology. Scientific Management had created conditions for a phenomenal rise in industrial productivity; yet it had put this productivity at the service of the "financiers" so mistrusted by Taylor. In spite of Scientific Management's claim to increase the "size of the pie" for both business and labor to share, the immediate benefits of the increase in productivity went into business profits, with a corresponding discrepancy between the ability of society to produce goods and to consume them.

Scientific Management, stressing the rationalization of the production process, led those who subscribed to its logic, from Gantt on, to question the rationality of distribution and consumption in the United States. From 1919 through the early 1920s, the intellectual world was full of the notion that the disparity between productivity and consumption would produce economic ruin if the new techniques of production rationality were not extended to the economy as a whole. The list of Cassandras is extensive; it includes not only H. G. Wells, the great science fiction author, but Rexford Tugwell, later to become an important member of the "brain trust," who, completing

27. Schlesinger, p. 133.
28. Ibid., p. 132.

his dissertation in 1922, predicted that economic ruin would come about if the private planners of big business "wholly out of social control, . . . unbalanced the system in their own favor to the extent of destroying their own markets,"[29] and warned against the inevitable results of practices and policies which enlarged productive capacity without increasing and spreading purchasing power.[30]

During the late 1920s, a number of liberal spokesmen (among them John Dewey, Rexford Tugwell, Paul H. Douglas, and Stuart Chase) had visited Soviet Russia, there to be fascinated not by communism, but by the collectivity, the unity of social interest, apparently resulting from rational, centralized industrial planning.[31] In 1928, returning from Russia with an American trade union delegation, Chase and Tugwell wrote with some awe of the planning of production and prices by Gosplan—greater than the price-setting activities of Standard Oil, an order before which "even Mr. Henry Ford would quail!"[32] The system of state planning was an elegant one on paper, contrasting favorably with the business cycle and waste of capitalism. Time would illustrate, they felt, whether the practice matched the theory.[33]

While a number of these figures, among them Chase and Tugwell, toyed briefly with the technocratic movement, they came to real prominence in the New Deal when their ideas and energies were enlisted in the great search for democratic alternatives to the bankrupt pattern of relationships between government and the economy. With the professors, economists, and intellectuals drawn into Franklin Delano Roosevelt's "brain trust," new theories as well were drawn into the service of national reform. While the predominant economic influence was Keynesian, in administrative organization, a new concept of "state Taylorism" was introduced into the process of policy-making. Scientific Management, which had provided the tools for the rationalization and increase of industrial productivity, would, in the hands of the state, provide the tools for the renovation of the economy at the practical organizational level, for the overall rationalization so long awaited to

29. B. Sternsher, *Rexford Tugwell and the New Deal* (New Brunswick, N.J.: Rutgers University Press, 1964), p. 19.

30. Ibid., p. 20.

31. Schlesinger, pp. 141-42.

32. S. Chase and R. Tugwell, eds., *Soviet Russia in the Second Decade: A Joint Survey by the Technical Staff of the First American Trade Union Delegation* (New York: John Day Co., 1928), p. 29.

33. Ibid., pp. 53-54.

repair the damage done by an unplanned business order. Arthur Schlesinger, for example, describes the intellectual antecedents of economics professor Rexford Tugwell as follows:

> In the work of Frederick Winslow Taylor, the father of scientific management, Tugwell found the techniques by which society might achieve the ends proposed by Patten, Veblen, and Dewey. The greatest economic event of the nineteenth century, Tugwell liked to say, was when Taylor first held his stopwatch on a group of shovelers in the Midvale Steel plant. Only Taylor had not gone far enough. Tugwell believed that the logic of scientific management required the extension of planning from the single factory to the industry and then to the entire economy. "We need a Taylor now for the economic system as a whole."[34]

While no single figure emerged as the Taylor of the American economic system, Tugwell, as the last American governor of Puerto Rico in the 1940s, had a chance to bring about an "administrative revolution" based on concepts of state planning derived from the New Deal. Nicknamed "Everything Smells" by the islanders for his reforming zeal, Tugwell set out to undercut "Marxian socialism"[35] with his reform program, only to be attacked as a "fascist" by a congressional investigating committee seeking to cut off funds to the island. When the committee found Tugwell's organization and control "quite comparable to the pattern used by the Fascists in Italy,"[36] the accusation formed an interesting contrast to those of the 1930s that gave him the opposite labels of advocate of "Russian communism," "master romanticist and collectivist," and "Assistant Commissar of Agriculture."[37]

Such apparently conflicting accusations had been leveled at the New Deal as a whole, as evidence of borrowing organizational ideas and techniques not only from the Communists but the National Socialists was unearthed. Herbert Hoover, for example, claimed that the aim of the New Deal was the collectivization of the American way of life, and that its techniques had delayed the recovery of the nation until the Second World War.[38] The New Deal, in his view, fell little short of an attempted coup:

34. Schlesinger, p. 94.
35. Charles T. Goodsell, *Administration of a Revolution: Executive Reform in Puerto Rico Under Governor Tugwell, 1941-1946* (Cambridge, Mass.: Harvard University Press, 1965), pp. 16-17.
36. Ibid., p. 29.
37. Sternsher, p. 351.
38. Ibid., p. 76.

In Central Europe the march of Socialist or Fascist dictatorships and their destruction of liberty did not set out with guns and armies. Dictators began their ascent to the seats of power through the elections provided by liberal institutions . . . Once seated in office, the first demand of the European despotisms was for power and "action." Legislatures were told they "must" delegate their authorities. Their free debate was suppressed. The powers demanded are always the same pattern. They all adopted planned economy. They regimented industry and agriculture. They put the government into business. They engaged in gigantic government expenditures. They created vast organizations of spoils, henchmen and subsidized dependents. They corrupted currency and credit. They drugged the thinking of the people with propaganda at the people's expense.

If there are any items in this stage in the march of European collectivism that the New Deal has not imitated it must have been an oversight.[39]

From the previous discussion of Soviet and German planning mechanisms, it is apparent that the grain of truth upon which these accusations were founded consisted of the continual exchange of organizational techniques within what had become a common industrial—not political—culture; this international system of rational-technical organization rested on the foundations laid by the old international Scientific Management movement.

The weakest link in the logic of these accusations was the degree to which such organizational techniques were directly responsible for the excesses of the totalitarian regimes which they served, whether they led inevitably to massive bureaucratic growth, impersonality, and finally to the casting off of all social morality as an irrational barrier to the planning process, or whether they simply gave new life and strength to destructive political regimes. One of the reasons that it is impossible to disentangle such a historical relationship of administrative organizational technique to political operations in the 1930s is precisely because they were purposely welded together in the fascist regimes and scrupulously separated in the United States. Neither was a purely "administrative state," and so it is not possible either to exchange their virtues and vices for purposes of denunciation or to use these traits as a sound basis for the prediction of the behavior of more completely administrative regimes. Both were too far from the visionary, planned-

39. Herbert Hoover, "The Road to Freedom" (Address delivered 10 June 1936), in A. T. Mason, ed., *Free Government in the Making: Readings in American Political Thought* (New York: Oxford University Press, 1965), pp. 786-87.

distribution network that arose from the logic of state-centered Scientific Management.

The ideological role of Scientific Management thought in the New Deal, while a distinct presence, is likewise difficult to disentangle from other influences. Especially in the early phases of the New Deal, about all that any administrative planning or "Taylorization of the economy as a whole" could amount to was a general attempt to establish administrative organs designed to operate on the "underconsumption" theory, that is, to try to increase the purchasing power of the poor so that the products of the industrial system might be absorbed. Since this general aim intersected with a number of other major theories, such as those of Keynesian economics and with specific welfare claims (pensions and jobs for specific sectors of the population), it is impossible to say to what extent theories of social engineering inspired practice, or rather, simply provided broad justification for the hastily organized humanitarian activities that the situation demanded. However, even when the specific organizations thus established were not directly related to Scientific Management theory, the very fact of their multiplication created problems in terms of the traditional means of government organization. Thus, it was in the organization and control of the executive branch that Scientific Management was to leave a distinctive mark.

Disorganized growth in the number and extent of federal agencies had marked the government's attempt to deal with the problems of the industrial era since the Civil War. Various subsequent attempts to bring order into federal administration had foundered on the spoils system and on the lack of basic administrative and organizational technique. It was necessary, in a sense, to retreat to basics. Efforts at reform had to be concentrated primarily on the personnel system—establishing and extending the merit civil service—and secondarily on budgetary reform and the introduction of mechanisms of fiscal control and responsibility. Bringing order and organization to the structure, no matter how essential a task, fell into the category of "fine tuning," impossible to accomplish without the assurance that the officials who would carry out such a task were objectively chosen and competent, and that the funds with which the government carried out its programs were honestly and accurately disbursed.

By the time Franklin D. Roosevelt took office, the basic mechanisms of bureaucracy, the merit system and control budgeting, were largely in place. The problem of order and organization, however, was more intensified than ever. The overwhelming problems of the depression, coupled with Roosevelt's penchant for "fresh starts"—the establishment of new agencies to deal with tasks as they arose rather than the attachment of new functions to old agencies—caused an even more massive extension of government and increased the need for systematic reorganization of the executive branch. It is in this context that one historian of the Roosevelt administration characterized the New Deal as the cause for the need for executive reorganization "only in the sense in which the famous last straw 'caused' the camel's broken back."[40]

Roosevelt had indicated that he needed "broad executive power" to deal with the emergency, but in the course of his first term, he found that both Congress and the courts opposed the extension of his power. In the second term, he turned to extending the efficiency of the executive branch, believing that the clarification of executive organization would not only increase efficiency, but be a vehicle for the extension of effective presidential power. In March of 1936, he appointed a three-man committee chaired by Louis Brownlow to make "a careful study of the organization of the Executive Branch of the government . . . with the primary purpose of considering the problem of administrative management," stating that "many new agencies have been created during the emergency, some of which will, with the recovery, be dropped or greatly curtailed, while others in order to meet the newly realized needs of the Nation, will have to be fitted into the permanent organization of the Executive Branch." Privately, however, he made it clear to the members of the President's Committee on Administrative Management that its emphasis should be on the development of administrative means to give the president authority to carry out his responsibilities under the Constitution, rather than to stress the traditional cost-cutting and economy bias of reorganization.[41]

The task of reorganization faced by the President's Committee on Administrative Management had grown to monumental proportions, in terms of previous organizational structures:

> Of ten Independent Regulatory Commissions outside the normal machinery of the Departments, five were set up between 1934 and 1936. Of 93 "Governmental Corporations" in 1936, i.e., public authorities in the form of companies wholly owned by the Federal government, at least 83 had been set up since March, 1933. As of August 31st, 1936, the Roosevelt

40. Karl, p. 166.   41. Ibid., p. 27.

administration had issued 1,616 Executive Orders, an average of 38.47 per month, or nearly double the highest previous figure. Proclamations numbered 3.78 per month, exceeding all other averages except that of the Taft administration, which appears to have suffered from a fever of exhortation.[42]

The approach taken by the President's Committee on Administrative Management was broad-based, managerial, and rooted in the new academic discipline of public administration, rather than a simple business-oriented, cost-cutting approach. Their analysis and proposed redesign of the administrative processes of the executive branch were strongly influenced by progressive reformism, the evolution of social science away from the static examination of classic institutions, and by Scientific Management itself, as it had been modified through its application to urban reform and governmental budgeting. Louis Brownlow, the committee's chairman, was a pioneer in the city manager movement, which sought to replace corrupt local politics with nonpolitical, expert administration, and which was based partly on the German model of urban administration, and partly on the engineering model of dealing with subcontractors. He himself had served as a city manager as well as published the first popular book on the subject.[43]

The other members of the committee, Charles Merriam of the University of Chicago and Luther Gulick, generally considered a key figure in the transformation of Scientific Management into the "administrative management" approach to public administration, were also immersed in the neo-progressive reform currents of the prior period. Merriam, well-known as the founder of the movement to quantify political science, had, as president of the American Political Science Association, led the effort to establish the Social Science Research Council. Having studied in Berlin, he was strongly influenced by the German model of administration, and he sought to fuse public administration and political science at the University of Chicago. An urban reformer, he ran for mayor of Chicago in 1911 and lost; shortly thereafter, he refused an offer extended by Frederick A. Cleveland to serve on the Taft Commission on Economy and Efficiency, feeling that his proper sphere of action was in the University and the city of Chicago.[44] In 1929, however, he had accepted the

42. Urwick, *Making of Scientific Management*, p. 158.
43. See Karl, ch. 3.   44. Ibid., pp. 51-52.

position of vice-chairman of President Hoover's Research Committee on Social Trends, and so it was as an advisor to presidents, and pioneer in the application of social science research to the highest policy needs, that Merriam accepted Roosevelt's 1936 appointment.[45]

Luther Gulick, while completing his graduate work at Columbia, had shuttled between the university, and the Bureau of Municipal Research and its attached Training School for Public Service. Founded in 1906, the bureau was associated with the progressive urban reform movement; it stressed the rationalization of administration, concentrating primarily on budgetary reform and analysis. Its uncovering of financial irregularities in machine-dominated New York City government earned it the title of "Bureau of Municipal Besmirch" among its enemies; in 1913, it was responsible for producing a plan for budgetary reform, now celebrated by Alan Schick as the first attempt at program budgeting.[46] Frederick A. Cleveland, a professor of accounting at New York University, and friend of F. W. Taylor, assisted in setting up the original staff of the bureau and later served as its director; the influence of Scientific Management on its conception of efficiency was fully as great as the traditional Victorian concern with thrift. The bureau was involved in the preparation of the 1921 Budget and Accounting Act through its domestic and foreign research; in recognition of its widening scope of activities, it was reorganized in 1921 as the National Institute of Public Administration; Charles A. Beard, former head of the organization, named Luther Gulick as his successor. Gulick's work had been concentrated in the area of budgetary research and reform, and it was he who brought to the Report of 1937 language and a concept of governmental efficiency most closely resembling Taylor's old statements on the nature of the "mental revolution."[47]

Gulick's work had clear ties to the international Scientific Management movement, but the strands of Scientific Management philosophy in his thinking had been interwoven with his broader understanding of government and politics so that it would be most difficult indeed to say that he resembled the narrow-minded technocratic type of previous decades. Collaborating with Lyndall Urwick, a passionate

45. Ibid., pp. 37-39.

46. Allen Schick, "The Road to PPB: The Stages of Budget Reform," in Fremont J. Lyden and Ernest G. Miller, eds., *Planning Programming, Budgeting* (Chicago: Markham Press, 1972), pp. 21-23. See also Karl, p. 144.

47. Karl, pp. 151, 226.

advocate of international rationalization, in editing the historically significant *Papers in the Science of Administration,* he wrote advocating the development of an administrative science to replace the inexact, uncontrolled, and socially unprofitable machinations of old style politics. "In the science of administration, whether public or private, the basic 'good' is efficiency," he states.[48] The papers themselves, selected from scientific managers and progressive reformers interested in improving governmental efficiency, include essays by Elton Mayo and associates, Mary Parker Follett, John Lee, the British rationalizer, Henri Fayol, J. D. Mooney of General Motors, and, of course, by Gulick and Urwick themselves, who outline the current state of the science of administration. Taylor's work casts a long shadow over this new "science." Refuted, advocated, analyzed, or borrowed, the ideas of the old scientific managers are very much in evidence throughout the essays. They were clearly a formative influence on the most advanced academic and practical administrative work of the day, and as such it was unavoidable that they be assimilated into the management of the greatest bureaucracy of its time.

The report that the President's Committee on Administrative Management issued in 1937 began by summarizing the growth of the executive since 1789; it went on, in the most classic Scientific Management language, to indicate the need for efficiency reforms in the machinery of government:

THE FOUNDATIONS OF GOVERNMENTAL EFFICIENCY
The efficiency of government rests upon two factors: the consent of the governed and good management. In a democracy consent may be achieved readily, though not without some effort, as it is the cornerstone of the constitution. Efficient management in a democracy is a factor of peculiar significance.

Administrative efficiency is not merely a matter of paper clips, time clocks, and standardized economies of motion. These must be built into the structure of a government just as it is built into a piece of machinery.

Fortunately the foundations of effective management in public affairs, no less than in private, are well known.[49]

The findings of the committee are presented in six parts: The first

48. Gulick and Urwick, p. 192.
49. U.S., The President's Committee on Administrative Management, *Administrative Management in the Government of the United States* (Washington, D.C.: Government Printing Office, January 1937), p. 2.

part concerned the expansion of the White House staff to meet the expansion of the administrative system as a whole, as a guarantee that all matters coming before the president would have been examined beforehand from the "over-all managerial point of view, as well as from all standpoints that would bear on policy and operation," and to facilitate the flow of business to and from the president himself.

Section two dealt with personnel management, asking for the extension of the merit system, the reorganization and improvement of personnel administration, and, in order to facilitate recruitment, the revision of plans for compensation of civil servants, especially the higher posts, to levels similar to those in private industry.

The third section concerned fiscal management, suggesting improvement in the staffing of the Bureau of the Budget (founded in 1921) and the improvement of government auditing, especially the installation of a modern system of accounts and records. Budgeting, especially, should "provide in financial terms for planning, information, and control," as it was currently incapable of doing.

Section four addressed the problem of planning management which would require the establishment of additional "machinery for over-all planning management" for the use of the executive order and above that provided for budget control. Here was made the suggestion for a permanent "National Resources Board" to be set up to replace the temporary committee established by executive order in 1933. Planning would cover the categories of waste and the improvement of national living standards, as well as gathering data on the natural resources of the nation and planning for fair distribution among the working population. It is section four, in fact, that looks most like the old platform of the Technocrats.

The fifth section discusses an extensive plan for the administrative reorganization of the government of the United States.

"The Executive Branch of the Government of the United States has . . . grown up without a plan or design like the barns, shacks, silos, tool sheds and garages of an old farm," states the committee.[50] This ramshackle structure throws an impossible burden on the chief executive, as well as impairing both effective action and the constitutional separation of powers through confusion and multiplication of agencies. The bureaucracy must be put under the firm control of the president through the "modern arms of management in budgeting,

50. Ibid., p. 29.

efficiency research, personnel, and planning," while at the same time the principle of executive responsibility to Congress should be strengthened by the development of an independent fiscal audit, and through the simplification of the confusing structure of the government. Twelve streamlined departments are proposed to consolidate the duties of the multiplying agencies of the government. Most especially, this provision emphasizes the continuing executive responsibility for efficient organization, involving continual efficiency research and experimental adjustment.

The final section deals with the philosophy of the accountability of the executive, and it is here that the committee grapples with the problem of limiting the excesses of the administrative state while at the same time strengthening and modernizing the executive in the context of an eighteenth century constitution. The care with which constitutional safeguards are maintained in the proposals of the committee is a distinguishing characteristic of the administrative philosophy of the 1930s and 1940s which tends to disappear, at least in overt statements, with the progress of the Cold War in later decades. Scientific Management is a tool for executive efficiency *in the service* of Congress and the laws, rather than a prescriptive means of redesigning government as a whole:

> Under the American system the Executive power is balanced and made safe by freedom of speech, by elections, by the protection of civil rights under an independent judiciary, by the making of laws which determine policies including especially appropriations and tax measures, by an independent elective Congress, and by the establishment of Executive accountability.
>
> The preservation of the principle of the full accountability of the Executive to the Congress is an essential part of our republican system. In actual practice the effectiveness of this accountability is often obstructed and obscured . . .[51]

The essential quality of the executive reforms is that they will increase the accountability of the executive to Congress, especially when matched on the congressional side by the development of organizations for collecting, coordinating, and processing information and for conducting independent and reliable auditing of executive spending.

In summary, then, the study represents a faithful attempt to

51. Ibid., p. 43.

rationalize, if not to Taylorize, the Constitution.[52] But rather than imposing the unitary command mechanisms that the industrial model of rationalization appeared to demand, the incorporation of rationalization into the separation of powers scheme was stressed, not simply the lopsided growth of the executive. The hope was that the organization of the state would then be sufficiently developed to take on the planning duties and extended social responsibilities required in the increasingly technological atmosphere of the twentieth century.

Torn between the rising power of foreign autocracy and the image of domestic inefficiency, struggling against economic disorganization, and oppressed by the vision of the coming war, the committee finishes its argument for modern management techniques in the following way:

> It may be said that there is danger that management itself will grow too great and forget where it came from or what it is for—in the old and recurring insolence of office. But in the judgment of your Committee, based upon broad observation of the bewildering sweep of recent events here and elsewhere, the really imminent danger now is that our democracy and perhaps others may be led by false or mistaken guides to place their trust in weak and faltering inaction, which in the bitter end runs to futility and defeat. In the late war, democracies showed vast strength and tenacity in times of strain. . . . And now we face and will master the critical tasks of reorganization and readjustment of many tangled parts of our national life on many new frontiers. The injustice and oppression intertwined with solid good in our American system will not always yield without a firm display of our national constitutional powers. Our national will must be expressed not merely in a brief, exultant moment of electoral decision, but in persistent, determined, competent day-by-day administration of what the Nation has decided to do.
>
> Honesty and courage alone are not enough for victory, either in peace or in war. Intelligence, vision, fairness, firmness, and flexibility are required in an assembled, competent, strong organization of democracy. To falter at this point is fatal. A weak administration can neither advance nor retreat successfully—it can merely muddle. Those who waver at the sight of needed power are false friends of modern democracy. Strong executive leadership is essential to democratic government today. Our choice is not

52. The idea of modernizing the Constitution to suit the industrial era has been continued by Rexford Tugwell at the Center for the Study of Democratic Institutions. See "A Proposed Constitutional Model for the New States of America," in Rexford G. Tugwell, *The Emerging Constitution* (New York: Harper's Magazine Press, 1974).

between power and no power, but between responsible but capable popular government and irresponsible autocracy.[53]

Only a fraction of the committee's work could be adopted without congressional approval, however, and this approval was withheld for political reasons, some of them the very reasons foreseen by the committee itself. Roosevelt's extensive welfare reforms had already fallen under attack from the conservative business community, which had denounced his measures as (1) socialistic and (2) leading inevitably to Roosevelt's establishment of dictatorial powers for himself. The net result was that they balked at the idea that the executive branch, already grown in size, should reform itself so as to become more efficient as well. The Taylorization of the executive was a step on the road to the dictatorship of the president, they claimed, and, it is to be suspected, made a somewhat more vulnerable target than the more directly humanitarian reforms which so infuriated private enterprise. Roosevelt's defense of the proposed legislation, which repeated the arguments of the committee that a headless bureaucracy which could not be commanded by the president was also beyond the reach of the Congress and the electorate, was met head-on by the congressional fear that the reform legislation would lead to an excessive development of executive power.[54] The result was that much of the reform legislation was delayed for several years.

With the entrance of the United States into the Second World War, Congress granted the powers it had previously refused to the executive branch. Efficiency was justified in the name of defense mobilization; during the war nearly all of the work of the President's Committee on Administrative Management was institutionalized within the government.[55] Scientific Management influence, rejected in the "dictatorship bill" of 1937, had once again entered government, as it had elsewhere in the wake of military production competition. Symbolizing the new influence of the middle-class expert in the state, it formed a basis for the extensive development and improvement of applied systems of planning, statistical control, direction of contract production, and operations research, as the products of the business and engineering schools of the nation were drawn into military service. As in the First World War, the aftermath of this period of mass application and mass

53. President's Committee, p. 47.
54. Urwick, *Making of Scientific Management*, p. 156.
55. Ibid.

education in the use of these military production control systems left an indelible mark on society as a whole. Efficiency in organization had specific definitions according to technique in the minds of all those trained to work for the massive production victories of World War II.

The nature of the war itself, however, reinforced the need for constitutional safeguards with important moral considerations. Because the architects of the wartime executive were still imbued with the ethics of the previous decade's public administration, and in addition because they viewed the war as a contest between democracy and totalitarianism, they spared no effort to preserve the constitutional characteristics that distinguished the former kind of regime from the latter. The war could not be won, in truth, should the United States take on authoritarian characteristics in an attempt to contest the supposedly greater efficiency of the authoritarian regimes against which it fought. In rejecting the temptation to resort to that truism of the Cold War that "systems in competition become more like each other," they consciously refrained from the logical extension of the centralized and quantified national social and production control systems deriving from Scientific Management.

Luther Gulick, in his 1948 postmortem of wartime organization, examined the lessons of the war in relation to the supposed superiority of totalitarian regimes to "make adequate and far-seeing plans; to integrate and coordinate the economy; to act with vigor, intelligence and dispatch; to interrelate military, political and economic strategy; to master timing and surprise, protected by complete control over secrecy of action; and to develop fanatic national unity and enthusiasm."[56] As a consequence of the avoidance of the use of these techniques of centralized control, the American organizers of the war, according to Gulick, learned to rely on the vigor and intelligence of a democratic people, in the last analysis, and to be wary of "czars" and of the resulting excessive centralization that could lead to their abuse of power.[57] Postwar examination of the ruins of the German and Japanese war machines confirmed their belief that the inherent virtues of the state, run according to an ideology of centralization and control, were exaggerated.[58]

The victory, however, brought renewed competition with an au-

56. Gulick, p. 123.
57. Ibid., p. 119.
58. Ibid., p. 123, in reference to the strategic bombing survey of Germany and Japan.

thoritarian regime; the early triumphs of Stalinist Russia immediately after the close of the war, based on surprise and continued military mobilization during the period of relaxation and demobilization in the United States, revived the old arguments about the superiority of authoritarian state organization, particularly in foreign policy. At the same time, the techniques of authoritarian organization had been widely disseminated by wartime training; another generation of administrators, educated by the experience of war mobilization, was taking over the organization of the state and the economy. Speaking to the new generations of Cold War administrators, Gulick closes his course of lectures with an admonition that must have appeared as superfluous in prior administrative contexts as it appears sentimental and antiquated in the context of contemporary management:

> I want you to grasp the central fact which this war experience drives home; that good administration and democracy are not incompatible. They are inseparable allies; neither can exist or survive long without the other. I hope you will note and reflect on the administrative lessons I have endeavored to draw from our management of the war; but most of all, when men come to you with doubts over the administrative efficiency of democracy and over a large measure of freedom and private enterprise, I hope you will remember the experience of these war years.
>
> Don't sell Thomas Jefferson short![59]

The war years and the attempt to "return to normalcy" that followed had brought about a permanent change in American consciousness. And later, when it proved impossible to repeal the New Deal, the Republican attempt to eradicate "twenty years of treason" renewed the influence of classical business philosophy in government, including the old-fashioned business concepts of efficiency with all the organizational preconceptions that this entailed. Yet, even with the attempt to cut back bureaucratic expansion or "creeping statism," the bureaucratic bases of control were strengthened immeasurably during this period, as streamlining, centralization, and the extension of the control of the Executive Office of the President were all continued on the prewar model. The first and second phases of Scientific Management, business efficiency and centralized government control as efficiency, were merged in a new synthesis. Clever public relations, the involvement of the business community, and the gradual acclimatization of the American public to ideas of centralized bureaucratic

59. Ibid., p. 129.

control in government had, however, in the intervening decade shifted the public response from one of opposition to "dictatorship" to one of approval for "efficiency." The second "managerial revolution," carried forward in both the governmental and corporate spheres, was underway.[60]

In government, the postwar pattern of extending efficiency through increased control was developed through the massive, coalition-based reorganization of the executive branch under the two Hoover commissions.[61] In 1947, President Truman appointed the first of the two bipartisan commissions to reorganize and economize in governmental operations after the hasty expansion of the war years. The second commission, appointed in 1953, consolidated the changes that had taken place at the same time that it sought to audit and cut back those elements of government that were in direct competition with private enterprise. The first Hoover Commission proceeded through a series of extended studies conducted on a public basis, incorporated the work of leading business figures as well as academics, and handled the press with great care, hoping to avoid the pitfalls that had been faced by the small, confidential advisory group approach of the 1937 study.

Despite the active efforts of former President Hoover himself to keep the commission's work untainted by that of its New Deal predecessor, most observers felt that the first Hoover Commission in particular proved a true successor to the Brownlow Committee.[62] It extended the control of centralized agencies over dispersed power centers, eliminated duplication and overlap, and clarified lines of control from the presidency outward. It built on the organizational foundations of 1937, extending, for example, the Executive Office of the President and attaching to it the National Security Council. Its work led to the establishment of consolidated government procurement through the General Services Administration. Its advice was embodied in the 1949 amendments to the National Security Act that

60. One should note in this respect the conscious formation of the Eisenhower Administration as a "Management Administration" (Drucker, *Practice of Management*, p. 3), numerous articles in *Fortune* magazine during this period, and a number of well-known works that describe the phenomenon, such as William H. Whyte, *The Organization Man*, New York: Doubleday & Co., 1957.

61. Herbert Emmerich, *Federal Organization and Administrative Management* (Birmingham: University of Alabama Press, 1971), pp. 83-84.

62. Emmerich, p. 90, quotes in this context Herman Finer, "The Hoover Commission, and many of its collaborators, are Mr. Brownlow's children."

established the Department of Defense and its panoply of tri-service agencies, and that centralized and developed the intelligence community under the CIA. Yet, in putting into place the apparatus for the conduct of the Cold War, the Hoover Commission had absorbed, publicized, and made legitimate the administrative ideas advanced in 1937, and now no longer called "executive usurpation."

In the private sphere as well as the public one, automatic data processing and other technical means vastly extended the managerial areas open to quantification and rationalization, while the new human relations approaches developed as a result of the Hawthorne studies gave promise of routinizing and rationalizing even the organizational inputs of the managerial psyche. Creativity itself promised to yield up its secrets to systematic and routinizable techniques of the organization of group interaction and thought. The sphere of rationality, and hence of the calculable efficiency measurement in administration, appeared to be expanding indefinitely in the new era.[63] And while the content and technique of the postwar "managerial revolution" had changed vastly from its turn-of-the-century predecessor, there was nothing in the direction of its thought or organization that would seem alien to a Taylor, Gilbreth, or Gantt. The arrangement of new content was in the familiar Scientific Management pattern: an increase of efficiency relying, on the one hand, on the growth and dominance of elites deriving leverage from the multiplication of professionalized management subspecialties, and, on the other hand, from the rearrangement of complex tasks into microspecialized components suitable for close supervision and increasing mechanization or automation. The growth in management and the decline in individual autonomy from the 1950s on has been well and extensively described elsewhere. During this growth it is apparent that Scientific Management as a general approach to organization had, without exception, penetrated the industrial establishments, managerial training, and government of every major industrial power. It had become as much a part of the new industrial era as the machine itself.

63. For an interesting discussion of the cultural determinants of efficiency measurement, with emphasis on assembly line processes, see Daniel Bell, "Work and Its Discontents: The Cult of Efficiency in America," in *The End of Ideology* (New York: Collier Books, 1962). Victor Thompson in *Modern Organizations* (New York: Alfred A. Knopf, 1961) discusses the rush toward rigid quantification as a dysfunction arising from the need for security. Might one assume, then, that insecurity became endemic in postwar bureaucracies?

CHAPTER 9

Democratic Government
and the Technology
of Administration

To be the slaves of pedants—what a fate for humanity!

MIKHAIL BAKUNIN

Since the days of the great American crusade to reform the civil service by the use of "merit" examinations for recruitment, and the "science of administration" for its internal organization and operations, it has been assumed that administration is a tool which can serve many political masters. Politics is choice, runs the old argument, and administration is action; on this politics-administration dichotomy rests the conclusion that authoritarian techniques of administration are suited to the governance of democratic states.

"If I see a murderous fellow sharpening a knife cleverly," said Woodrow Wilson in 1887,

> I can borrow his way of sharpening the knife without borrowing his probable intention to commit murder with it; and so, if I see a monarchist dyed in the wool managing a public bureau well, I can learn his business methods without changing one of my republican spots.[1]

Yet even Woodrow Wilson was forced to admit that administrative action designed to carry out the law was more than simply action without choice, but an integrated structure of both choice and action dependent upon superordinate organs of political choice. For this reason he could not see the way clear to identify the difference between politics and administration with the difference between "the Will and the Deed."[2] As the national administrative machinery grew

1. Wilson, "The Study of Administration," p. 504.
2. Ibid., p. 496.

in scope and complexity, it became more and more apparent that highly specialized administrative organizations cannot be value-free "tools," analogous to the sharpened blade that serves surgeon and robber alike,[3] but rather that they are carriers of integrated values.

Modern specialized administrative structures are more appropriately compared with other highly specialized technical equipment, say, for example, an electric can opener, which by its very existence postulates a specific series of integrated artifacts of which it is but one interlocking part, and which has little use apart from its specific function in that network of social artifacts. An anthropologist of the future, finding an electric can opener in a kitchen midden, could hypothesize not only tin cans, but electrical distribution nets for the fueling of such a tool, complex machine tools for its manufacture, and even a "disposable" society that valued single-use containers above screw-top containers suitable for reuse. In short, the efficiency of such a tool, purchased at the price of extreme specialization and a reduction of adaptability, makes a statement about the type of civilization in which it exists and ultimately, about the social values of that civilization. This is not to say that some degree of moral or valuational flexibility of the implement is not inherent in its design as a tool; it opens the elderly arthritic's can of hash or the lazy sybarite's beluga caviar with equal ease. Likewise it may be pressed into service out of context to crack walnuts or weight papers. But the point remains that it carries a good deal of cultural baggage; it expresses priorities, and rests on an interlocking network of similar artifacts; its possessors tend to want to use it for the purpose for which it was designed. Both the can opener and the complex, highly specialized bureaucracy represent a social investment, or choice; while the technique by which they were constructed may be "value neutral," by the fact of construction they have absorbed resources and thereby limited alternatives. Thus, they represent a social priority or an element of social value.

Leaving aside this mechanical analogy, and the idea of specialized institutions as a whole representing value through the social choice that allocates resources to them rather than to their alternatives, it can be shown that such institutions must inevitably internalize value as well. The administrative hierarchy and its activities can be represented

---

3. Citation is omitted here of that recent literature which equates the two.

as a hierarchy of choice in successively smaller areas of jurisdiction, and for this reason cannot be freed either of the human political process or of human values with even the most stringent controls. Herbert Simon describes the integration of values into administrative organization in terms of the very means-ends dichotomy of traditional administrative thought. Rational organization consists of the construction of means-ends chains, logical sequences of actions designed to achieve goals:

> It is clear that the "means-end" distinction does not correspond to the distinction between fact and value. What then is the connection between the two sets of terms? Simply this: A means-end chain is a series of anticipations that connect a value with the situations realizing it, and these situations, in turn, with the behaviors that produce them. Any element in this chain may be either "means" or "end" depending on whether its connection with the value end of the chain, or its connection with the behavior end of the chain, is in question.[4]

Value orientations are therefore an integral part of all sequential human activity designed to attain goals, including those organized activities designated as "administration." Now if the claim of the administrative reformers, so ably stated by Wilson, is that administrative systems may be adapted from authoritarian uses to the service of democratic governments without adverse influence on democratic values, precisely because they are value-free creations of a "science of administration," then that claim must be re-examined.

If it is impossible for administrative organizations to be value-free, then the degree to which they execute the values allocated by superordinate organs of political choice depends either upon the ability of such organs to exercise direct and continuing control over administration, or upon the degree to which the values that animate administration are similar to those which dictate political choice. To the degree that control fails in the presence of incompatible administrative values, it is difficult to assume that the "republican spots" of democratic officials may remain untouched.

The impact of "management science" as a system of organization and integrated values upon the administration of contemporary democratic governments and upon democratic values is, then, clearly an important area of study for the political theorists of democracy.

4. Herbert Simon, *Administrative Behavior: A Study of Decision-Making Process in Administrative Organization* (New York: Free Press, 1957), p. 62.

And while the structure of modern administration has been shaped by many schools of thought, its greatest development has taken place under the shadow of modern technology, which has created new demands for expertise, for the extension of government services, and for the control of the social by-products of the industrial revolution. It has been the argument of previous chapters that central to the development of a synthesis of technological and administrative thought was the invention and diffusion of Scientific Management, a "forgotten revolution" which created the elements of a new "management science" apparently suited to the demands of administrative expansion. Given knowledge of the Scientific Management movement, it is possible to discuss the influence of the administrative values, which are its heritage, on the politics of democratic states in respect to the basic problems of administrative control, and the integration of administrative and political values that arise from the failure of logic and experience to sustain the traditional "administration-politics dichotomy."[5]

MODES OF ADMINISTRATIVE INFLUENCE AND THE TECHNIQUES OF POLITICAL CONTROL

The rise of formal bureaucratic administration is comparatively recent in the history of human organizational techniques, dating from Europe's "age of absolutism," when great kings consolidated power by substituting the work of hierarchies of servants of humble origin, directly dependent upon the monarch's power, for the services formerly rendered by contentious barons.[6] The separation of this form of administrative structure from the person of the monarch himself was the product of the rise of popular government, epitomized in the French Revolution and its aftermath, while the industrial revolution influenced the reshaping of both governmental and corporate administration along the depersonalized and increasingly structured and

5. Kaufman, pp. 1057-73.
6. Weber's discussion of the great bureaucracies of ancient times, the Chinese, Egyptian, Roman, and early Roman Catholic Church, points out that the compensation of officials in kind and the existence of a subsistence rather than a money economy meant they were not full bureaucracies in the modern sense. See Max Weber, "Bureaucracy" in H. Gerth and C. W. Mills, eds., *From Max Weber: Essays in Sociology* (New York: Oxford University Press, 1958), pp. 204-5.

specialized lines of the machine-model of bureaucracy now considered universal. When, before the turn of the twentieth century, the forces of civil service reform stressed the dichotomy between politics and administration, they were placing the new labels of democratic theory upon the ancient struggle between the king and his servants.[7]

Thus, in discussing the rise of administration as science and counterposing it to a more traditional "politics," identified as decision-making or as Will, Wilson and those who followed him were naming an important new phenomenon in the history of state organization. Traditional definitions of political organization had persisted from the time of Aristotle, who classified governments according to the number of those governing and whether they served their own interests or those of society as a whole. Recognizing that traditional theories of politics centered on the ways in which power is used to attain socially defined ends—the Will, either of the One or of the Many—Wilson and the progressive "political scientists" saw in the new techniques of administration a pattern different than that of traditional politics: power wielded without regard to persons, either the One or the Many, but rather to attain social ends whose usefulness and means of attainment could eventually be determined by science itself. For if all are rational, then cannot rational calculation and the administrative organization that embodies rationality serve the good of all better than the erratic processes of politics?

The transfer of the machine analogy to social organization, which was entailed by the new understanding of administration, had begun with early technology, but much of the speed with which it was carried forward in the first decade of the twentieth century must be attributed to the activities of the international Scientific Management movement, whose origins and influence have been the subject of the first part of this book. This new phenomenon, the belief in a "scientific" theory of organization that arose out of the industrial revolution, proved upon examination to be more than a theory of administration

7. The interrelationship of the growth of administration and the growth of state power is admirably documented in G. R. Elton, *The Tudor Revolution in Government* (Cambridge: Cambridge University Press, 1953); G. Aylmer, *The King's Servants: The Civil Service of Charles I* (New York: Columbia University Press, 1961); Emmaline Cohen, *The Growth of the British Civil Service, 1780-1939* (London: Frank Cass & Co., 1965); Ernest Barker, *The Development of Public Services in Western Europe* (London: Oxford University Press, 1944); and Hans Rosenburg.

subsidiary to politics. Rather, it was in its extended version a rival theory of politics seeking to displace those antique theories which traditionally described the uses of power. Akin to the divine right of kings, it proclaimed instead the divine right of the technocratic administrator, putting science in the place previously occupied by the deity and justifying the power of the ruling class by defining that power as the result of their position as the intermediary between man and the Eternal, the sole interpreter of Truth. It was a theory of politics that proclaimed the victory of the experts and defined "politics," or the contest for power, as obsolete.

Whether the ideology proposed by the scientific managers could actually succeed in realizing its aims is another question, of course, since even scientists fall out, and politics somehow resurrects itself even in the most frictionless arrangement of experts. Such politics, however, proceed without the benefit (or disadvantage, depending upon one's point of view) of the formal political channels arranged by tradition. There is no denying that the "rules" of covert office politics are different than the formal routines of democratic politics, whatever the unity of human nature that their existence proclaims. Two normative worlds, two modes of decision-making and the arrangement of human affairs, laid claim to the same space, and pointing out that each contains elements of the other could not minimize the basic conflict.

The barrier of nomenclature erected between the minor choices of governmental action (administrative choice) and the main policy choices of leadership, be it elective or authoritarian (political choice), was a thin partition indeed, insufficient even then to preserve the traditional forms of politics from the assaults of the new antipolitical theory of politics that was embodied in the structure of scientific "administration." Even in the nineteenth century it was apparent that "administration" had become the master of kings; how could it remain the servant of democrats? The inescapable conclusion of those who studied the machine model of specialized bureaucratic administration was that its great advantages made it a permanent social force, while its internal structure created powerful techniques for the propagation of its influence among the organizations exterior to it.[8]

The modes of such administrative influence are various; to begin with, an administrative organization constructed on a specific set of

8. Weber, "Bureaucracy."

inherent values which provides information for political decision-making may so bias its information outputs as to control the decision premises of political choice, and hence the choice itself.[9] The very existence of a multilevel hierarchy may introduce distortions in the information which it processes, as each additional level influences the accuracy of communications, both upward, in respect to the leadership, which then finds its decision-premises controlled by the structure of bureaucracy itself, and downward, as those who carry out orders find the commands of leadership subtly corrupted by the biases of the organization for which they work.[10]

In addition, the attitudes of bureaucratic personnel are shaped by their work environment. Weber points out that the balance of expertise in government is held by administrators rather than legislators, for the latter face frequent elections and are subject to more rapid turnover than bureaucrats, whose life tenure and specialization give them a greater command of information on specific topics, and therefore an innate advantage over politicians in maintaining control over policy.[11] Individuals in the employ of administrative systems spend eight of their waking hours every day internalizing bureaucratic values, creating the possibility that they may see them as appropriate ones to apply in activities outside of their official duties.[12]

All of these modes of influence tend to break down the ability of the political system to control bureaucracy, while at the same time they introduce the values and the vested interests of the state's own administrative "servant" into the political process itself. The recent upsurge in public service unionism, carried out as the extension of democratic principles to administration, increases this tendency toward "guildism," to use Emmette Redford's term, without changing the basic problem of bureaucratic control itself. And the essence of the problem is that first among the vested interests of administration is the advocacy of continued administrative growth, and so the bureaucracy

9. James D. Thompson, *Organizations in Action* (New York: McGraw-Hill, 1967), p. 133, cites Simon in relation to this point, which he develops at greater length.

10. Thompson, p. 124. See also "Tullock's Model of Hierarchical Distortion," in Anthony Downs, *Inside Bureaucracy* (Boston: Little, Brown & Co., 1967), p. 116.

11. Weber, "Bureaucracy."

12. The role of an administrative science in general socialization was a selling point of Scientific Management according to Taylor, who saw the system as a tutor of virtue for the masses.

swells in proportion to its influence, increasing still farther the social significance of the value premises upon which administrators act. How well the activities of administration correspond to the needs and values of society as a whole becomes, then, in a democracy, a question of how well the agents of popular politics control the bureaucracy itself.

The mechanisms by which a democratic politics may exercise control over its own administration are designed to combat the sources of administrative influence at their roots, but in doing so, they undermine the effectiveness of administrative action. To reduce the comparative gap in competence between administrators and outsiders, the "empire building" and information monopolies of managers, the classic technique is to reduce the tenure of civil servants in specific offices and geographical locales to a specific and brief period of time, while to increase the relative power of the legislator, office-holding can be made to be at the pleasure of the elected leadership. Election to office itself is an extension of this idea, while the ancient Chinese practice of regular bureaucratic transfer, and the Athenian practice of selection and rotation of officials by lot reflect the desire of every sort of political system to reduce the "insolence of office" and to keep administrative officers responsive to the leadership and to popular need.

These very mechanisms, however, are those that are the foundation of the infamous "spoils system" that modern American merit administration was designed to combat. Absence of expertise in the face of the need to administer expanding technologies, and the easy responsiveness of public servants, without absolute standards of performance, to the pressures of bribery and corruption discredited the principle of rotation in office as a means of protecting democratic government against the excesses of its own administrative officials.[13] Even the leaders of modern totalitarian states, with their superior ability to manipulate bureaucratic structures and a life-and-death

13. It has been shown that little in the way of formal structural differences existed between the patronage system of the Federalists and that of the Jacksonians. The comparative corruption of the spoils system that replaced the "gentleman's understanding" about competence was the result of the infusion of different political values. See Leonard White, *The Federalists: A Study in Administrative History, 1789-1801* (New York: Free Press, 1965) and *The Jacksonians: A Study in Administrative History, 1829-1861* (New York: Macmillan Co., 1954).

power over individuals, when faced by an intransigent bureaucratic class, found that excessive resort to rotation in office, backed by increasingly severe penalties for malfeasance, tended to paralyze state operations rather than to channel them in the required policy directions.[14]

Another obvious means of preventing the bureaucratic ethos from dominating policy choice through the need for expertise is to place representatives of the policy-making organs with veto power at every decision point in the bureaucratic system. Trotsky's military commissar system, in which "Red" commissars countersigned the orders of the "experts"—the military officers inherited from the old regime— is the most famous example. Aside from the cost of duplicating the hierarchy, the problems of this technique revolve about the growing community of interest between watched and watcher. Valid as a temporary measure, such a system loses effectiveness over time and becomes host to many interesting forms of corruption, as the "family circles" (conspiracies of the local factory director, bookkeeper, party and secret police chief to forge production data) of the 1930s illustrate.

A different approach to keeping bureaucratic interests subordinate to democratic politics in the policy process has involved attempts to transplant concepts of representation into the administrative system itself. Since the isolation of administration from politics has produced an elite group of experts that increasingly dominates democratic political processes, the argument runs, this body of experts should itself be made representative of the larger groups in society.[15] Yet, even when greater numbers of women and minorities are admitted to the higher levels of the career civil service, there is no guarantee that they will in fact behave as representatives of the social groups in which they originate, or simply as bureaucrats, for the formal mechanisms tying the representative to his constituency are lacking. Morally significant as such arguments are, they frequently do not indicate any

14. Krushchev's secret speech on the crimes of Stalin gives many examples of the failure of Stalin's apparatus of terror to enforce economic laws, end "corruption" of the bureaucracy, or command a superior military policy. Perhaps the most elaborate attempt to coordinate rotation in office with the need for technical expertise was Lenin's abortive plan in *The State and Revolution.*

15. See, for example, Harry Kranz, *The Participatory Bureaucracy: Women and Minorities in a More Representative Public Service* (Lexington, Mass.: D.C. Heath and Co., 1976).

very convincing mechanism whereby the authoritarian stance of bureaucratic administration may be controlled. Yet another variation on this plan, the admission of representatives of client groups to the decision-making process of the administrative body that serves them, runs into the question of cooptation as well as that of an extended guildism, where clients and bureaucrats protect their mutual interests against those of society in general as expressed by its parliamentary institutions.

One valuable approach to popular protection, if not always control, is that represented by the various grievance procedures and offices that have evolved to deal with administrative insensitivity and abuse. Some, such as the administrative courts of continental Europe, have evolved from older institutions, while other types of hearing panels are more recent in origin. The most well known foreign institution in this category is that of the ombudsman, whose independence derives from his status as a parliamentary, not an administrative, officer, and whose investigations of potential areas of administrative abuse of liberty help to strengthen basic principles of democratic government.

A more direct attack on the problem of increasing control without decreasing administrative competence involves the introduction of techniques that will reduce the levels of hierarchy within the administration, and hence its innate capacity to distort information, without shrinking the capacity of a system as a whole; this is a difficult task when levels of command multiply in relation to the extent of the bureaucracy. The most recent of such means involves the use of automatic data processing (ADP) to reduce reporting levels, and thus increase the speed and accuracy of the flow of administrative information. This, however, increases control over one aspect of bureaucratic operations while increasing the power and discretion of the class of ADP experts who design and maintain the new system.[16] A more traditional way of dealing with this problem is to introduce free-floating agents of popular control who hear complaints and are given special powers to skip administrative levels and cut "red tape." This is one of the principles behind the Scandinavian ombudsman system, the military inspector-general system, and the ability of congressmen in the United States to investigate the complaints of constituents. The

16. Herbert York, *Race to Oblivion* (New York: Clarion, 1970) discusses in eyewitness detail the transfer of power to technical elites as an outcome of the arms race.

problems that face such "tribunes of the people" are, on the one hand, cooptation by the bureaucracy, and, on the other, powerlessness vis à vis administrative organizations, should the latter be hostile, due to the very reasons that other elected officials find themselves at a disadvantage: the comparative expertise of administrative personnel and the extent and secrecy of the bureaucratic labyrinth.[17]

Yet another significant approach to the problem of control consists of the mechanisms of Scientific Management itself, as embodied in the internal and structural methods of control advocated by the public administration of the 1920s and 1930s. This school of thought, culminating in the 1937 Report of the President's Committee,[18] pointed out that as bureaucracy grows in size, its random extension and erratic lines of authority break down clear lines of responsibility, making it a "headless fourth branch" of government, beyond the control of the executive branch and of Congress. Internal reorganization, designed to centralize control, will increase its responsiveness and hence preserve democracy from the growth of what Lyndall Urwick called a "leviathan." His belief was that it was the wild and uncontrolled growth of bureaucracy that was the monster; he felt that the clean and efficient control of Scientific Management procedures would harness it for the sake of civilization.[19]

This reform of bureaucracy's internal control structure is based on

17. It has been pointed out that the success of the Swedish ombudsman rests on the strength of Swedish public opinion and the fact that Swedish public records are open for inspection. Donald Rowat, ed., *The Ombudsman: Citizen's Defender* (London: George Allen & Unwin, 1968).

18. See U.S., The President's Committee on Administrative Management.

19. Urwick, *Making of Scientific Management*, 1:162-64. There is a basic problem with Urwick's sardine imagery; horror films abound which derive from the principle that small and familiar animals (such as crabs, flies, lizards, and rabbits) become terrifying when enlarged, demonstrating a propensity to trample tall buildings and consume the population of entire cities. It appears that, according to this basic cultural sentiment, the introduction of reforms to cause the "leviathan" to revert to a beneficent but enlarged sardine would still leave us with an object of awe, and, essentially, horror. Something of the sort is expressed in Kranz's *Participatory Bureaucracy*, p. 15:

The bureaucracy *is* the predominant center of political power and authority today—not just a "fourth branch of government" but most of the pulp and outer covering as well. Elected executives, legislators, and judges cannot be effective without bureaucracy, but bureaucrats can initiate, adopt, interpret, enforce, and ignore laws without the other branches.

an increase in the division of labor with its concomitant reduction in discretion, increasing centralization buttressed by the introduction of new techniques of statistical control, and the reaffirmation of the idea of value-neutral, universally applicable management science through personnel training. Such techniques would indeed appear to increase control of the center over the distant bottom layers of the bureaucratic pyramid, but it cannot evade the ancient question: *quis custodiet ipsos custodes?* The mechanisms of control require masters skilled in their use, and the problem of the political versus the administrative is repeated in the relationship between the policymakers of representative democracy and the technicians of management.

THE VALUE STRUCTURE OF SCIENTIFIC MANAGEMENT

If much of the success of control mechanisms over administration depends not upon the precise structural conception of the mechanism itself but upon the compatibility of the basic values of the controlled and the controller, then the assessment of the relative similarity of such values becomes a useful way of discussing the effectiveness of democratic control. It has been argued earlier that much of the ideology of the technicians of management can be found to have originated in the complex of values advanced by the Scientific Management movement. And while it is obvious that powerful beliefs held in common by political and administrative actors preserve the coherent action of the American governmental system, the ways in which the doctrine advanced by Scientific Management differ from what might be considered the traditional beliefs of American democracy[20] are singularly instructive if the problem under consideration is that of the influences which administration may exert on political democracy in the United States. For implicit in the idea of a neutral administrative science there is, for many historical reasons, a series of doctrines about the nature of power in organizations that constitute the heritage of the machine age in American governance.[21] In the great debate over the proper relationship between administration and the

20. For the sake of comparison, the definitive statements of traditional American democratic organization will be those of the Constitution and the *Federalist Papers* of Hamilton, Jay, and Madison.

21. That these doctrines are already becoming dated is surely the case, and the implications of the newer "age of electronics," including the effects of cybernation—and most lately, electronic spying—have yet to be explored.

democratic state, it then becomes important—even essential—to re-examine the techniques of organization propagated by the Scientific Management movement and to disentangle the values that have been propagated with them. Looking over the history and ideas of Scientific Management as discussed in previous chapters, it is possible to summarize and to classify them in order of the particular to the general, deriving a list that looks like the following:

(a) The Scientific Management approach to organization

1. Efficiency in organization is advanced by the minute subdivision of tasks, which increases the speed of their performance and the replaceability of the individuals who perform them.

2. Efficiency in the microdivision of labor requires exact, standardized, and scientific job analysis replacing amateurism and the "rule of thumb."

3. Efficiency in the coordination of the microdivision of labor requires an exact and absolute control based on an impersonal, written rule system presided over by a specialized corps of technical experts. This system must replace personalized, coercive authority based on insufficient knowledge—the management equivalent of the "rule of thumb."

4. An efficient organization can be easily recognized because it incorporates the above characteristics to the greatest possible degree.

These statements constitute the core of Taylorism as a machine model of organization. Only organizations that look like machines can efficiently accomplish tasks and make individuals within the organization reliable by making them replaceable. Thus, the Taylorites, having determined to get a foothold in the reorganization of the U.S. Navy, inspected shipboard fire-control systems, recently reorganized on the British model after the disasters of the Spanish-American war. They declared the degree of routinization and standardization they found in the reformed system to be a perfect example of Scientific Management, proof of the inevitable triumph of rationalization and disproof of the accusations of their opponents that they were idiosyncratic and doctrinaire reformers. Effective organizations that were built on nonmachine models were, by this standard, obviously inefficient. It is not that in many cases their observations were not accurate, but that the Taylorites cheerfully assumed that their principles were universally applicable without exception, thus (potentially) stabilizing their social environment and buttressing their psyches.[22]

(b) The Scientific Management approach to government

1. "Democracy" means the satisfaction of the common man's material needs, not a "debating society" theory of government.

2. Elective democracy caters to the lower instincts of the masses at the expense of expertise.

3. "Authority" of the traditional governmental type is an ineffective, personalized, coercive attempt at control and must remain so until the introduction of scientific measures of performance.

4. From the above statements it may be concluded that that government which is more efficient at encouraging high productivity and arranging fair distribution of goods is best (as well as "most democratic").

5. State power is therefore properly exercised by a technical elite through a process of scientific planning of the production and distribution of goods for the benefit of the entire population.

While the Scientific Management concept of the role of governmental authority seems in many ways reactionary today, it is only fair to remember that it embodied many advanced ideas at the turn of the century. The elitism of technical expertise seemed more "democratic" than the old federalist idea of the elitism of property ownership, and the promise of "efficient" government fairer to the citizenry at large than the favoritism and graft of the spoils system.

The bad experience which the scientific managers had with congressional intervention after the Watertown Arsenal affair, and their natural tendency to measure organizations, including democratic assemblies, according to their own standards of efficiency led most naturally to a negative assessment of "democracy" as it appeared in 1915—influenced as it was by bossism and special interests. H. L. Gantt discussed most overtly the Scientific Management philosophy

22. See Chapters 2 and 3 above. Fire-control systems remain a perfect example of man-machine organizations on a mechanistic model, but other tasks demand other types of organization to attain similar effectiveness. For a portrait of an effective, idiosyncratic, crotchety organization of nonstandardized parts, see the description of the Manhattan Project in Nuel Pharr Davis's *Lawrence and Oppenheimer* (New York: Fawcett, 1968).

of government,[23] although it was also manifest in the city government reforms of Philadelphia carried out by Cooke and in many of the later governmental organizational methods devised by the scientific managers.

Taylor's concept of "military authority" owes little to a personal knowledge of military command, but represents an important attitude of the scientific managers concerning the ignorant, bullying, coercive aspects of traditional authority in both government and industry. The depersonalization of authority represented by the rules of Scientific Management was a considerable improvement over many of the methods and attitudes that prevailed at the time. Muckraking literature on the conditions of labor at the turn of the century leaves no doubt that the noiseless machinery of organization advocated by Scientific Management, however Kafkaesque it appears at present, was preferable to many other practices of the period.

Most unusual as it seems, the idea that "democracy" could be defined in terms of increased social productivity begins, at least in Scientific Management theory, with Taylor's plans to counter the growth of unionism and the American fears of socialism by increasing labor productivity and therefore the relative rewards of labor. The extension of this idea into national planning was not part of this first theoretical proposal, but was developed by Taylor's followers, especially Gantt, during the mobilization of World War I. Of course, even among the original exponents of Scientific Management, the definition of what constituted "fair distribution" varied from author to author. Taylor, as we recall, felt that the workers' share of the increase in productivity should amount to no more than a sixty percent increase in wages; more would result in drunkenness.

(c) Scientific Management's view of society

1. Social conflict is caused by an absolute lack of material goods rather than by the inequality of their division.

2. Social peace can be attained by raising the total amount of goods in society to the point where the poorest classes feel their consumption is adequate.

3. The upper and lower classes are characterized by laziness, ignorance, and the pursuit of frivolous pleasures; envy and malice prevent them from raising social output. Only the middle class is

23. See Alford.

sober and industrious; its freedom from envy and its constructive nature is demonstrated by its acquisition of scientific knowledge and its application of this knowledge to the increase in the absolute output of society.

4. Society attains efficiency to the extent that it swells the ranks of the virtuous middle class, and suppresses the characteristic vices of the upper and lower classes.

5. Social progress consists of the increase of efficiency in society, which produces peace and plenty. The worth of individual organizations in society is assessed by their contribution to this goal, that is, by their own internal efficiency.

Taylor's vision of two inimical classes, enviously quarreling over the shares of a meager industrial output both are too avaricious to increase, is the background for this theory of the redemptive role of a technically trained, professional middle class. Their position outside of the war between capital and labor, and their devotion to the pursuit of objective truth, as shown in their scientific training, both qualify them to be the natural arbitrators between labor and capital. Because their ranks are open to all men of talent, they are the only elite whose rule can be conceived of as "democratic"; they are the group best fitted to advance the interests of society as a whole. Taylor's vision ends in a middle-class utopia, where the places in the "planning room" that directs the factory, and eventually industrial society, are open to the ambitious men from the factory floor and the serious sons of the owners who are willing to drop their class allegiances and mannerisms. The advancement of society through higher levels of productivity, in his view, rests on the reconciliation of capital and labor on the grounds of neutral expertise.

(d) Scientific Management and the nature of man

1. Man in his natural state is lazy and pleasure-seeking.

2. Man achieves happiness through material consumption.

3. Because (1) and (2) are incompatible, man must overcome his nature, through discipline, to achieve happiness.

4. The visible reward of discipline is the production of goods for consumption. Man therefore achieves happiness through virtue, and virtue through discipline, while the degree of discipline may be measured by the efficiency of production.

5. Organization amplifies men's efforts either to produce, in which case it is virtuous, or to evade the discipline of production, in which case it is perverse ("organized soldiering").

6. "Science" is an objective series of rational laws not readily understood by everyone, which, properly applied, raises production.

7. Organizations should be controlled by men who understand science in order to attain efficient production (read: virtue).

In many ways, Scientific Management is a kind of secular Protestant ethic, substituting output, or efficiency, for the amassing of money as the visible sign of grace.[24] The higher and lower instincts of man, efficiency versus the immediate consumption of goods or time, are continually at war, and even science itself can be used to aid in the gratification of man's lower instincts rather than in his pursuit of virtue. Thus, Taylor berated himself and the engineering profession in general for taking pleasure in the design of technically interesting machines that are not efficient in terms of productivity or profits.

In summarizing the ideological aspects of Scientific Management, however loosely, it becomes apparent that, while the Taylorites claimed that their empirical observations about the nature of factory organization proved the validity of their view about mankind, in fact, the development of factory organizations represented the application of their original concepts of the nature of man.[25] The same technology of organizational observation and experiment, applied without the ideological preconceptions about human nature of the first Taylorites, was perfectly capable of recognizing the importance in manufacturing of informal organization, friendship, personality, and freedom to exercise personal feelings of craftsmanship. The Hawthorne experiments, conducted with the methodology of Scientific Management, discovered the greater efficiency of flexible work structures able to take advantage of informal organization,[26] while pioneer experiments at IBM showed that job enlargement, or the reduction of specialization,

24. For Taylor's religious background, see Chapter 1.
25. Chapters 2-3 indicate that the development of Scientific Management was based on the application of general ideas to specific tasks rather than out of empirical observation alone.
26. See Fritz J. Roethlisberger and William J. Dickson, *Management and the Worker* (Cambridge, Mass.: Harvard University Press, 1939).

increased the quality of output and thereby raised production efficiency.[27]

The array of effective organizational techniques which are unlike those prescribed by Taylorism indicates that neither the value judgments nor the organization of Scientific Management is irreversible. But neither are they easy to reverse, and their natural tendency has been not to regress over time but to propagate to deal with new technologies. Much of Scientific Management, for example, because of its precise and deterministic aspects, has combined well with automatic data processing, as the evolution of the Gantt chart, via cybernetics, into the PERT chart shows us.[28] Debate centers, therefore, not only on the possibility, but even the desirability of reversing the Scientific Management heritage in modern organizations. Occasionally, on reviewing contemporary literature dealing with the Scientific Management heritage, it is difficult to avoid the idea that industrial societies have invested in a rather costly electric can opener; although they are uncertain as to the wisdom of the purchase they are determined to get on and make the best of it. For every experiment that shakes values, there are more to show that things can be made tolerable as they are, perhaps the most direct contradiction to the reorganization of work, for example, coming from the new discipline of organizational psychopharmacology.[29] And, too, the misuse of the Hawthorne findings indicates how easily pre-existing values corrupt new insights into unpleasant, new forms of manipulation. And while many of these innovations would not have pleased the puritan conscience of the early Taylorites, who were firmly opposed to drink, drugs, and caffeine, these new developments clearly represent an attempt to protect the investments made in ongoing systems by buttressing and even extending their logic of administrative con-

27. Drucker, *Practice of Management*. For commentary on microspecialization's contribution to work alienation and job enrichment solutions, see: B. Garson, "To Hell with Work," *Harper's Magazine* (June 1972); W. Serrin, "The Assembly Line," *Atlantic Monthly* (October 1971); and W. Serrin, "The Job Blahs: Who Wants to Work?" *Newsweek* (26 March 1973); R. N. Ford, "Job Enrichment Lessons from AT&T," *Harvard Business Review* (January 1973); D. Jenkins, "Democracy in the Factory: A Report on the Movement to Abolish the Organization Chart," *Atlantic Monthly* (April 1973).

28. See Moder and Phillips, pp. 6-9.

29. Stephen P. Robbins, "Organizational Psychopharmacology: Drugs, Behavior, and the Work Environment," *Proceedings of the Midwest Academy of Management* (Kent, Ohio, April 1974), pp. 143-61.

trol. The choices that were made, then, decades ago, to incorporate specific types of Scientific Management organization into the executive branch also represent an investment in a specific set of interlocking organizational values and cultural attitudes which, depending upon their compatibility with those of society at large and with its elected officialdom, either aid or hinder the efforts of the political system to exercise control over its own administrative organs.

THE PERSISTENCE OF ADMINISTRATIVE VALUES

Not all administration is Scientific Management. But much of modern American business and public administration is, for various historical reasons, the heir to the Scientific Management movement. And those organizations which were shaped by Scientific Management represent enclaves of ideology which cannot but affect the kinds of policy choice and even the policy goals of those who must rely on them for information or for the execution of work. No system of organizational control can force subordinate organizations to work in opposition to their own internal ideological biases.[30] But the control systems designed for mass organizations operate effectively when there is a basic agreement on fundamentals.[31] The problem of democratic government is that it is a mixed organizational system designed to deal with a variety of tasks ranging from the technical to the inspirational, and that where its technical-administrative tasks have been appropriately taken over by the management ideologues who are masters of specialized technical organization, the remainder of its nontechnical functions and the democratic control mechanisms that are related to them are inadequate to contain the pressures for authoritarian control that emanate from its successful, specialized technical organizations.

The goal of Scientific Management ideology is the perfection of social efficiency through the elimination of politics. And if that ancient pursuit of "The Good" which is presumed to be the occupation of governments consisted exclusively of the provision and

30. Arendt points out that, while the German bureaucracy carried out in detail the "final solution," the Danish bureaucracy successfully evaded this duty through opposition, and the Bulgarians failed to accomplish it due to the hopeless corruption of their administration. It appears that, in the last analysis, bureaucratic control is a thing of the mind, not of physical organization.

31. See n. 17 on the ombudsman.

enjoyment of great numbers of manufactured goods, then there is little question that the expansion of the Scientific Management model to include the operations of the state would be the appropriate occupation of legislator and citizen alike. But because "The Good" remains ill-defined, the wisdom of such a single course is dubious, and the elimination of politics improbable. The question of the optimal relationship between management technology and the administration of democratic states then remains to be answered. Though the restructuring of democratic organization itself is a possible if not a desirable answer,[32] the most probable area for the resolution of these incompatible value systems is in the development of organizational techniques appropriate to the management of technology, which preserve the efficiency of operations at the same time that they make possible the restructuring of administration and its authoritarian biases from within.

The essential contradiction is the result of the inadequacy of traditional politics, especially democratic politics, to handle the task of making the technical decisions required by the management of modern technologies, while at the same time "administration" of the type that results from such management is inadequate to handle the expression of those authentic and ineradicable political differences that must inevitably arise from even the most "managed" technical society. The natural differences between men do not disappear in industrial society any more than in any other society, but reassert themselves in new form; the elimination of "politics" through the expansion of administration simply means the elimination of the formal channels for handling and resolving political differences that are not amenable to technical solutions. The expansion of management technologies does not eliminate the sources of difference, but, if anything, entrenches them more firmly by increasing specialization and the consequent reinforcement of special interests, viewpoints, and needs. In this sense, the bureaucratization of political choice does not simplify matters, but returns government to a more primitive state, consisting of the unregulated and unstable structure of secret power

32. Sincere complaints about the lack of efficiency of the constitutional system of checks and balances and the procedural guarantees of the Bill of Rights were once commonly heard among the scientific and technical personnel of the Department of Defense. They simply could not understand why Congress had to vote on expenditures for equipment that they had scientifically determined to be necessary.

plays carried out behind a monolithic facade, the state of affairs described by Kremlinologists as "cryptopolitics"[33] and by the Enlightenment philosophers as Oriental despotism.[34] It is not a despotism of princes, however, but of experts.

The great anarchist Bakunin, whose violent dislike of every form of authority gave him an instinctive insight into the forces that give rise to authority, long ago predicted that the effects of the increasing social dependence on technology would be to advance the cause of new elites, and he denounced the coming rule of "savants and pedants."[35] But the rise of absolutist management technologies suited to state administration could not be delayed by such latter-day organizational Luddites. On the one hand, the conditions that gave rise to the new management ideology of efficiency and control—rising materials and labor costs, pressure to expand the educated middle class, and an incipient conflict over the correct division of rising industrial output between employer and employee—did not diminish. Rather, they have continued to be very much in evidence, despite the displeasure of moralists, traditionalists, anarcho-syndicalists and others who held the new authority system in low repute. On the other hand, were these basic conditions to reverse themselves tomorrow, the natural lag time involved in changing organizational ideologies of any kind would indicate that the problems engendered by the conflict of management and democratic ideologies would not vanish without the prolonged effort involved in restructuring basic modes of action.[36]

Were it possible to uncover overwhelming evidence that the structure of Scientific Management must be dismantled immediately, it is difficult to imagine that such an effort would not require many decades, if one could judge by the rate at which Scientific Management itself spread. Even when its particular aspects were well-rooted in contemporary culture, its spread required nothing less than an exacting, well-planned, long-range campaign, carried out with crusading zeal by uncountable organizational entrepreneurs. And as yet, no

33. See T. Rigby, "Crypto-Politics," in Frederick J. Fleron, ed., *Communist Studies and the Social Sciences* (Chicago: Rand, McNally & Co., 1969).

34. See Montesquieu.

35. Mikhail Bakunin, "Statism and Anarchism," *The Political Philosophy of Bakunin: Scientific Anarchism*, ed. and trans. G. Maximoff (New York: Free Press, 1953), p. 82.

36. See Rolf E. Rogers, *The Political Process in Modern Organization* (New York: Exposition Press, 1971), on the ideological-religious system of organizations.

such overwhelming evidence has been unearthed. Scientific Management has, in truth, a very mixed record. It is at one time both the foundation of modern administration, and the old-fashioned way of business debunked by each new management theory; it has stressed "narrow-minded" materialism and monetary incentives, and yet is the source of much of modern high consumption; it has put down craft skills while it opened new avenues of professionalization; designed to quash unionization, many of its principles have been used as union demands and even to organize the unions themselves. It has found an uneasy accommodation with many different political systems, whose common denominator is dependence on, or the desire for, extensive and advanced industrial establishments. And perhaps most important, at a time when diminishing resources and rising costs had begun to put pressure for greater efficiency on American industry, it developed mechanisms for uncovering and systematizing improved production techniques, and at the same time engineered the delicate class compromise on which the imposition of these efficiency techniques on a mass basis rested.

The progress of Scientific Management was not unalloyed triumph. It ran into roadblocks: labor opposition in all the nations examined in this study and, in England, an alternative philosophy to the distribution of power and provision of worker welfare that made the wide-scale application of a Scientific Management solution to these questions unattractive. Another roadblock was met when the declining worker autonomy and unidimensional motivation system on which Scientific Management's productivity increases depended seemed to be undermined by rising general prosperity, and the spread of antiauthoritarian and antimaterialist philosophies; this was, however, partially countered by the recent economic downswing and inflation that have made all jobs scarcer, and restored some of the luster of the money motivator. And, too, Scientific Management had no answers for those who claimed that its progressive systematization of industry and management would speed up the pooling of a class of discarded unemployables exterior to the workplace, not eliminating, but only shifting the arena of class conflict. Recent fears of resource scarcity have even cast doubt on the permanence of the Scientific Management solution to class conflict, for a lessening of the rising tide of consumer goods (particularly large cars and the gas to run them) may, in the eyes of some critics, resurrect class differences and do much to undermine the passivity of labor.

The checkered history of evolving Taylorism does not detract from the brilliance with which it originally unified common elements of American machine culture into a class compromise that postponed the potential industrial conflict of the turn of the century. The compromise had costs, however, among them the erosion of valued, traditional political institutions. And because it did not eliminate class conflict forever, in shifting it to new grounds, it made the preservation of the political means of peacefully resolving social change and distribution issues, in particular the working democratic institutions of American government, all the more essential. Yet it is clear that the heritage of Scientific Management in business, government, and education not only tends to promote the idea that democracy and efficiency are mutually exclusive, but it has left an additional legacy in the form of a problem-solving approach that says potential conflict can and must be handled by the intervention of managerial elites. The rediscovery of the resource shortages, productivity, and conflict problems that originally spurred the development and adaptation of Scientific Management might very well revive the pressures to "engineer" another solution. Knowing the history of the international Scientific Management movement, it is difficult to judge how imminently and with what emotions we should expect the next industrial prophet.

Bibliography

BOOKS

Adoratskii, V. V., Molotov, V. M., Savel'ev, M. A., Sorin, V. G., eds. *Leninskii sbornik*, vol. 22. Moscow: Partiinoe Izdatel'stvo, 1933.

Aitken, A. G. H. *Taylorism at the Watertown Arsenal: Scientific Management in Action, 1908-1915.* Cambridge, Mass.: Harvard University Press, 1960.

Alford, L. P. *Henry Lawrence Gantt: Leader in Industry.* New York: Harper & Bros., 1932.

Alger, Horatio. *Phil, The Fiddler.* Chicago: M. S. Donahue, n.d.

Arendt, Hannah. *Eichmann in Jerusalem: A Report on the Banality of Evil.* New York: Viking Press, 1963.

Argyris, C. *Integrating the Individual and the Organization.* New York: John Wiley, 1964.

Arkright, Frank. *The A B C of Technocracy.* New York: Harper & Bros., 1933.

Armytage, W. H. G. *The Rise of the Technocrats: A Social History.* London: Routledge & Kegan Paul, 1965.

Arnhold, Karl. *Arbeitsdienstpflicht.* Düsseldorf: Verlag: Gesellschaft für Artbeitspadagogik, 1932.

————. *Betriebs- und Arbeitsführung.* Leipzig: Bibliographisches Institut A.G., 1936.

————. *Der Deutsche Betrieb: Ausgaben und Ziele nationalsozialistischer Betriebsführung.* Leipzig: Bibliographisches Institut A.G., 1939.

Aylmer, G. *The King's Servants: The Civil Service of Charles I.* New York: Columbia University Press, 1961.

Babbage, Charles. *On the Economy of Machinery and Manufactures.* 2nd ed., enl. London: Charles Knight, 1832.

————. *The Exposition of 1851; or, Views of the Industry, Science, and Government of England.* London: John Murray, 1851.

Babcock, George D. *The Taylor System in Franklin Management.* New York: Engineering Magazine Co., 1917.

Bakunin, Mikhail. *The Political Philosophy of Bakunin: Scientific Anarchism.* Edited and translated by G. Maximoff. New York: Free Press, 1953.

Barghoorn, F. *The Soviet Image of the United States: A Study in Distortion*. New York: Harcourt, Brace & Co., 1950.

Barker, Ernest. *The Development of Public Services in Western Europe*. London: Oxford University Press, 1944.

Beer, Max. *A History of British Socialism*. 2 vols. 1st ed., 1919. London: George Allen & Unwin, 1940.

Bell, Daniel. *The End of Ideology*. New York: Collier Books, 1962.

Belyaev, N. *Genri Ford*. Moscow: Zhurnal'no Gazetnoe Ob'edinenie, 1935.

Bendix, Reinhard. *Word and Authority in Industry: Ideologies of Management in the Course of Industrialization*. New York: Harper & Row, 1963.

Berle, Adolf A., and Means, G.C. *The Modern Corporation and Private Property*. New York: Macmillan Co., 1933.

Berriman, Algernon Edward, et al. *Industrial Administration: A Series of Lectures*. Manchester: Manchester University Press, 1920.

Blau, P. and Meyer, M. *Bureaucracy in Modern Society*. New York: Random House, 1971.

Blauner, R. *Alienation and Freedom*. Chicago: University of Chicago Press, 1964.

Bowen, Ralph Henry. *German Theories of the Corporative State; with Special Reference to the Period 1870-1919*. New York: McGraw-Hill, 1947.

Brady, Robert A. *Business as a System of Power*. New York: Columbia University Press, 1943.

_____. *Crisis in Britain: Plans and Achievements of the Labor Government*. Berkeley and Los Angeles: University of California Press, 1950.

_____. *Organization, Automation, and Society: The Scientific Revolution in Industry*. Berkeley and Los Angeles: University of California Press, 1963.

_____. *The Rationalization Movement in German Industry: A Study in the Evolution of Economic Planning*. Berkeley and Los Angeles: University of California Press, 1933.

_____. *The Spirit and Structure of German Fascism*. New York: Viking Press, 1937.

Braverman, Harry. *Labor and Monopoly Capital: The Degradation of Work in the Twentieth Century*. New York: Monthly Review Press, 1974.

Bricard, Georges. *L'Organisation scientifique du travail*. Paris: Librairie Armand Colin, 1927.

Bruck, W.R. *Social and Economic History of Germany from William II to Hitler*. Cardiff: Oxford University Press, 1938.

Brzezinski, A., and Huntington, S. *Political Power USA/USSR*. New York: Viking Press, 1964.

Bulletin of the International Management Institute, no. 5. Geneva, 1927.

Bulletin of the International Management Society, vols. 1-2. 1927-28. (Mimeographed.)

Burnham, James. *The Managerial Revolution*. New York: John Day Co., 1941.

Bury, J.B. *The Idea of Progress*. New York: Macmillan Co., 1932.

Callahan, Raymond E. *Education and the Cult of Efficiency*. Chicago: University of Chicago Press, 1966.

Cardwell, D.S.L. *The Organisation of Science in England*. London: William Heinemann, 1957.

Chakhotin, Sergei S. *Organizatsiia: Printsipy i metody v proizvodstve, torgovle, administratsii i politike*, Berlin: Izd-vo "Opyt," 1923.

Chandler, Alfred D., Jr. *The Visible Hand: The Managerial Revolution in American Business*. Cambridge, Mass.: Harvard University Press, Belknap Press, 1977.

Chase, S., and Tugwell, R., eds. *Soviet Russia in the Second Decade: A Joint Survey by the Technical Staff of the First American Trade Union Delegation*. New York: John Day Co., 1928.

Chase, Stuart, *Technocracy: An Interpretation*. New York: John Day Pamphlets, no. 19, 1933.

Child, John. *British Management Thought: A Critical Analysis*. London: George Allen & Unwin, 1969.

Clark, Wallace. *The Gantt Chart: A Working Tool of Management*. New York: Pitman Publishing Co., 1925.

_____. *Grafika Ganta*. Translated by Walter Polakov. Moscow: n.p., 1926, 1931.

Cohen, Emmaline. *The Growth of the British Civil Service, 1780-1939*. London: Frank Cass & Co., 1965.

Cole, M. *Robert Owen of New Lanark*. London: Batchworth Press, 1953.

Cooke, Morris. *Academic and Industrial Efficiency*. New York: Carnegie Foundation for the Advancement of Teaching, Bulletin no. 5, 1910.

_____. *Our Cities Awake: Notes on Municipal Activities and Administration*. New York: Doubleday & Co., 1918.

Cooke-Taylor, R.W. *The Modern Factory System*. London: Kegan Paul, 1891.

Copley, Frank B. *Frederick W. Taylor: Father of Scientific Management*. 2 vols. New York: Harper & Co., 1923.

Crozier, Michel. *The Bureaucratic Phenomenon*. Chicago: University of Chicago Press, 1964.

Dakin, D. *Turgot and the Ancien Regime in France*. New York: Octagon Books, 1965.

David, Henry. *The History of the Haymarket Affair: A Study in the American Social-Revolutionary and Labor Movements*. New York: Russell and Russell, 1936.

Davis, Nuel Pharr. *Lawrence and Oppenheimer*. New York: Fawcett, 1968.

Deutscher, I. *The Prophet Armed: Trotsky, 1879-1921.* New York: Oxford University Press, 1954.

————. *Russia in Transition.* New York: Grove Press, 1960.

————. *Russia, What Next?* Oxford: Oxford University Press, 1953.

Devinat, Paul. *Scientific Management in Europe.* Geneva: International Labor Office, 1927.

Djilas, Milovan. *The New Class.* New York: Praeger, 1968.

Dobb, Maurice. *Soviet Economic Development Since 1917.* New York: International Publishers, 1948.

Dorfman, Joseph. *Thorstein Veblen and His America.* New York: Viking Press, 1934.

Downs, Anthony. *Inside Bureaucracy.* Boston: Little, Brown & Co., 1967.

Drucker, Peter. *The End of Economic Man: A Study of the New Totalitarianism.* New York: John Day Co., 1939.

————. *The Practice of Management.* New York: Harper & Row, 1954.

Dubreuil, H. *Standards: Le Travail américaine vu par un ouvrier français.* Brussels: Bernard Grasset, 1946.

Dunham, A.L. *The Industrial Revolution in France, 1815-1848.* New York: Exposition Press, 1955.

Durkheim, Emile. *Socialism and Saint-Simon.* Yellow Springs, Ohio: Antioch Press, 1958.

Earle, E. *Makers of Modern Strategy: Military Thought from Machiavelli to Hitler.* Princeton: Princeton University Press, 1941.

Ellul, Jacques. *The Technological Society.* New York: Vintage Books, 1964.

Elsner, H. *The Technocrats: Prophets of Automation.* Syracuse, N.Y.: Syracuse University Press, 1967.

Elton, G.R. *The Tudor Revolution in Government.* Cambridge: Cambridge University Press, 1953.

Emmerich, Herbert. *Federal Organization and Administrative Management.* Birmingham: University of Alabama Press, 1971.

Fabian Society. *Fabian Essays.* London: George Allen & Unwin, 1889.

Farnham, Dwight T. *America versus Europe in Industry: A Comparison of Industrial Policies and Methods of Management.* New York: Ronald Press, 1921.

Fayol, Henri. *General and Industrial Management.* London: Sir Isaac Pitman & Sons, 1949.

Feiwel, George R. *The Soviet Quest for Efficiency: Issues, Controversies, and Reforms.* New York: Praeger, 1967.

Feldman, Gerald D. *Army, Industry, and Labor in Germany, 1914-1918.* Princeton, N.J.: Princeton University Press, 1966.

Feuchtwanger, E.J. *Prussia: Myth and Reality: The Role of Prussia in German History.* London: Oswald Wolff, 1970.

Florence, P.S. *The Logic of Industrial Organization.* London: Kegan Paul, Trench, Trubner & Co., 1933.

Florinsky, M. *Russia: A History and an Interpretation.* 2 vols. New York: Macmillan Co., 1947.

Follett, Mary Parker. *Dynamic Administration; The Collected Papers of Mary Parker Follett.* New York: Harper, 1942.

Ford, Henry. *Der internationale Jude: Ein Weltproblem.* Leipzig: Hammer-Verlag, 1922.

_____. *My Life and Work.* Garden City, N.Y.: Doubleday, Page, and Co., 1923.

_____. *My Philosophy of Business.* New York: Howard McCann, 1929.

_____. *Today and Tomorrow.* Garden City, N.Y.: Doubleday, Page, & Co., 1926.

Francis, Peter. *I Worked in a Soviet Factory.* London: Jarrold's Publishers, 1939.

Frederick, J.G., ed. *For and Against Technocracy.* New York: Business Bourse, 1933.

Frenz, Gustav. *Kritik des Taylor-Systems.* Berlin: Verlag von Julius Springer, 1920.

Friedman, Georges. *Industrial Society; The Emergence of the Human Problems of Automation.* Glencoe, Ill.: Free Press, 1955.

Galbraith, J.K. *The New Industrial State.* New York: Signet Books, 1968.

Galerie, Jean Planus, Paul, et al. *Le Planning: Theorie et Practique.* Vol. 1. Paris: Editions OCIA, 1950.

Garraty, John A., ed. *Labor and Capital in the Gilded Age: Testimony Taken by the Senate Committee upon the Relations Between Labor and Capital, 1883.* Boston: Little, Brown & Co., 1968.

Geck, L.H. *Soziale Betriebsführung.* Munich: C.H. Bech'sche Verlagsbuchhandlung, 1938.

George, Claude S., Jr. *The History of Management Thought.* Englewood Cliffs, N.J.: Prentice-Hall, 1968.

Gerth, H., and Mills, C.W. eds. *From Max Weber: Essays in Sociology.* New York: Oxford University Press, 1958.

Giedion, Siegfried. *Mechanization Takes Command: A Contribution to Anonymous History.* New York: W.W. Norton & Co., 1969.

Gilbreth, Frank B., Jr., and Carey, Ernestine Gilbreth. *Cheaper by the Dozen.* New York: T.Y. Crowell Co., 1948.

Gilbreth, Frank B. *Applied Motion Study.* New York: Sturgis and Walton, 1917.

_____. *Bricklaying System.* Chicago: M.C. Clark, 1909.

_____. *Primer of Scientific Management.* With an introduction by Louis D. Brandeis. New York: D. Van Nostrand Co., 1912.

Gilbreth, Frank B., and Gilbreth, Lillian M. *Fatigue Study: The Elimination of Humanity's Greatest Unnecessary Waste.* New York: Sturgis and Walton, 1916.

Gilbreth, Lillian Moller. *The Quest of the One Best Way; A Sketch of the Life of Frank Bunker Gilbreth.* [n.p., 1925] University of California at Berkeley, General Library.

Goebel, Otto. *Taylorismus in der Verwaltung.* Hanover: Helwingsche Verlagsbuchhandlung, 1925.

Goldman, Emma. *Living My Life.* 2 vols. New York: Dover, 1970.

————. *My Disillusionment in Russia.* New York: Thomas Y. Crowell Co., 1970.

Goodsell, Charles T. *Administration of a Revolution: Executive Reform in Puerto Rico under Governor Tugwell, 1941-1946.* Cambridge, Mass.: Harvard University Press, 1965.

Gould, Jay M. *The Technical Elite.* New York: A.M. Kelley, 1966.

Gramsci, Antonio. *Selections from the Prison Notebooks of Antonio Gramsci.* New York: International Publishers, 1978.

Granick, David. *The European Executive.* London: Weidenfield & Nicholson, 1962.

Greer, Germaine. *The Female Eunuch.* New York: McGraw-Hill, 1970.

Gulick, Luther. *Administrative Reflections from World War II.* Birmingham: University of Alabama Press, 1948.

Gulick, Luther, and Urwick, Lyndall, eds. *Papers in the Science of Administration.* New York: Columbia University Press, 1937.

Habbakuk, H. J. *American and British Technology in the 19th Century; The Search for Labor Saving Inventions.* Cambridge: Cambridge University Press, 1962.

Haber, Samuel. *Efficiency and Uplift: Scientific Management in the Progressive Era, 1890-1920.* Chicago: University of Chicago Press, 1964.

Hackett, J. *Economic Planning in France.* London: George Allen & Unwin, 1963.

Haines, A. *German Influence upon English Education and Science, 1880-1866.* New London: Connecticut College Press, 1957.

Hartmann, Heinz. *Authority and Organization in German Management.* Princeton: Princeton University Press, 1959.

Hicks, John D. *The Populist Revolt: A History of the Farmers' Alliance and the People's Party.* Minneapolis: University of Minnesota Press, 1931.

Hitch, Charles. *Decision-Making for Defense.* Berkeley and Los Angeles: University of California Press, 1966.

Hitler, Adolf. *My New Order.* New York: Reynal and Hitchcock, 1941.

Hofstadter, Richard. *The Age of Reform.* New York: Vintage Books, 1960.

Holzer, R. von. *Systematische Fabriks-Rationalisierung.* Munich: D. von Oldenbourg, 1928.

Hoogenboom, Arl Arthur, and Hoogenboom, Olive, eds. *The Gilded Age.* Englewood Cliffs, N.J.: Prentice-Hall, 1967.

Hoxie, R.F. *Scientific Management and Labor.* New York: D. Appleton Co., 1921.

Illich, T. *Deschooling Society.* New York: Harper & Row, 1971.

Kakar, Sudhir. *Frederick Taylor: A Study in Personality and Innovation.* Cambridge, Mass.: MIT Press, 1970.

Karger, Delmar W., and Bayha, Franklin H. *Engineered Work Measurement: The Principles, Techniques, and Data of Methods-Time Measurement, Modern Time and Motion Study, and Related Applications Engineering Data.* New York: The Industrial Press, 1966.

Karl, Barry Dean. *Executive Reorganization and Reform in the New Deal: The Genesis of Administrative Management, 1900-1939.* Cambridge, Mass.: Harvard University Press, 1963.

Kerr, Clark, Dunlop, John T., Harbison, F.H., Meyers, C.A. *Industrialism and Industrial Man.* Cambridge, Mass.: Harvard University Press, 1960.

Kessler, Count Harry. *Walther Rathenau: His Life and Work.* New York: Harcourt, Brace & Co., 1930.

Klein, B.H. *Germany's Economic Preparations for War.* Cambridge, Mass.: Harvard University Press, 1959.

Klyce, Scudder. *Universe.* Winchester, Mass.: Privately published, 1921.

Knight, Charles. *Knowledge Is Power: A View of the Productive Forces of Society and the Results of Labor, Capital, and Skill.* London: John Murray, 1855.

Kranz, Harry. *The Participatory Bureaucracy: Women and Minorities in a More Representative Public Service.* Lexington, Mass.: D.C. Heath and Co., 1976.

Kravchenko, Victor. *I Chose Freedom.* New York: Charles Scribner's Sons, 1952.

Kuczynski, J. *Germany: Economic and Labour Conditions Under Fascism.* New York: International Publishers, 1945.

Laslett, P. *The World We Have Lost.* New York: Charles Scribner's Sons, 1965.

Lehmann, M.R. *Rationalisierung und Sozialpolitik.* Nuremberg: Verlag der Hochschulbuchhandlung Krische & Co., 1930.

Lenin, V.I. *Polnie sobranie sochinenii,* vols. 28 and 36. Moscow: Gosudarstvennoe Izdatel'stvo Politicheskoi Literatury, 1962.

_____. *Selected Works.* New York: International Publishers, 1971.

_____. *Selected Works,* vol. 7. London: Lawrence & Wishard, 1937.

_____. *The State and Revolution*. New York: International Publishers, 1954.

Leonard, Jonathan. *The Tragedy of Henry Ford*. New York: G. P. Putnam's Sons, 1932.

Levasseur, E. *Histoire des classes ouvrières et de l'industrie en France de 1789 à 1870*, vol. 1, 2nd ed. Paris: Arthur Rousseau, 1901.

Lewin, L. C., ed. *Report from Iron Mountain on the Possibility and Desirability of Peace*. New York: Dial Press, 1967.

Lyden, Fremont J., and Miller, Ernest G., eds. *Planning Programming, Budgeting*. Chicago: Markham Press, 1972.

Maier, Charles. *Recasting Bourgeois Europe: Stabilization in France, Germany and Italy in the Decade after World War I*. Princeton, N.J.: Princeton University Press, 1975.

Manuel, Frank E. *The New World of Henri Saint-Simon*. Cambridge, Mass.: Harvard University Press, 1956.

_____. *The Prophets of Paris*. New York: Harper Torchbooks, 1962.

Marx, Leo. *The Machine in the Garden: Technology and the Pastoral Ideal in America*. New York: Oxford University Press, 1956.

Maynard, H. B., ed. *Industrial Engineering Handbook*. New York: McGraw-Hill, 1956.

Meijer, J. M., ed. *The Trotsky Papers, 1917-1922*. The Hague: Mouton & Co., 1964.

Mayo, Elton. *The Human Problems of an Industrial Civilization*. New York: Macmillan Co., 1933.

_____. *The Political Problem of an Industrial Civilization*. Cambridge, Mass.: Harvard University Press, 1947.

_____. *The Social Problems of an Industrial Civilization*. Boston: Graduate School of Business Administration, Harvard University, 1945.

Merewitz and Sosnick. *The Budget's New Clothes*. Chicago: Markham Press, 1971.

Merritt, R. H. *Engineering in American Society, 1850-1875*. Lexington: University of Kentucky Press, 1969.

Meyer, Donald. *The Positive Thinkers: A Study of the American Quest for Health, Wealth, and Personal Power from Mary Baker Eddy to Norman Vincent Peale*. Garden City, N.Y.: Doubleday & Co., 1965.

Meynaud, J. *Technocracy*. 1st ed., Paris, 1964. New York: Free Press, 1969.

Michelet, J. *History of the French Revolution*. Chicago: University of Chicago Press, 1967.

Moder, Joseph J., and Phillips, Cecil R. *Project Management with CPM and PERT*. New York: Van Nostrand Reinhold Company, 1970.

Moellendorff, Wichard von. *Deutsche Gemeinwirtschaft*. Berlin: Verlag von Karl Siegismund, 1916.

Montesquieu, Charles de. *The Spirit of the Laws*. New York: Hafner, 1958.

McGivering, I. C., Matthews, D. G. J., and Scott, W. H. *Management in Great*

Britain: A General Characterization. Liverpool: Liverpool University Press, 1960.

Nagler, Bernard, ed. *Patent Pending.* Los Angeles: Price, Stern, Sloan, 1968.

Nelson, Daniel. *Managers and Workers: Origins of the New Factory System in the United States, 1880-1920.* Madison: University of Wisconsin Press, 1975.

Nevins, Allan. *Ford: The Times, the Man, the Company.* New York: Charles Scribner's Sons, 1954.

Noble, David F. *America by Design: Science, Technology, and the Rise of Corporate Capitalism.* New York: Alfred A. Knopf, 1977.

Pasvolsky, L. *The Economics of Communism.* New York: Macmillan Co., 1931.

Pamphlets on Technocracy (Binder's title). New York: Technocracy, Inc., n.d.

Pease, E. R. *The History of the Fabian Society.* London: Frank Cass & Co., 1963.

Person, H. S., ed. *Scientific Management in American Industry.* New York: Harper Bros., 1929.

Pickens, Donald K. *Eugenics and the Progressives.* Nashville, Tenn.: Vanderbilt University Press, 1968.

Polakov, Walter. *Man and His Affairs from the Engineering Point of View.* Baltimore: Williams & Wilkins Co., 1925.

_____. *The Power Age: Its Quest and Challenge.* New York: Corvici, Friede, 1933.

Pouget, Emile. *L'Organisation du surmenage.* Paris: Librairie des Sciences Politiques et Sociales, 1914.

Prescott, Samuel Cate. *When M.I.T. Was "Boston Tech," 1861-1916.* Cambridge, Mass.: Technology Press, 1954.

Price, M. Philips. *My Reminiscences of the Russian Revolution.* London: George Allen & Unwin, 1921.

Priouret, Roger. *La France et le management.* Paris: Denoël, 1968.

Rabchinskii, I. *O sisteme Teilora.* Moscow: Gos. Tech. Izd., 1921.

Rathe, Alex W., and Gryna, Frank M. *Applying Industrial Engineering to Management Problems.* American Management Association, 1969.

Rathenau, Walther. *In Days to Come.* London: G. Allen and Unwin, 1921.

_____. *The New Political Economy.* N.p., 1918.

_____. *The New Society.* New York: Harcourt, Brace, 1921.

Reichskuratorium für Wirtschaftlichkeit E. V., Berlin: Selbstverlag des RKW E. V., 1926.

Reinmann, Günther, *Das deutsche "Wirtschaftswunder,"* Berlin: Vereinigung Internationaler Verlagsanstalten, 1927.

Richman, Barry M. *Soviet Management: With Significant American Comparisons.* Englewood Cliffs, N.J.: Prentice-Hall, 1965.

Riesman, David, and Jencks, Christopher. *The Academic Revolution.* New York: Doubleday & Co., 1968.

Roethlisberger, Fritz J., and Dickson, William J. *Management and the Worker.* Cambridge, Mass.: Harvard University Press, 1939.

Roll, Erich. *An Early Experiment in Industrial Organization: Being a History of the Firm of Boulton & Watt, 1775-1805.* London: Frank Cass & Co., 1931, reprint 1968.

Rosenberg, Hans. *Bureaucracy, Aristocracy, and Autocracy: The Prussian Experience, 1660-1815.* Boston: Beacon Press, 1966.

Rourke, Francis. *The Managerial Revolution in Higher Education.* Baltimore: Johns Hopkins Press, 1966.

Rowat, Donald., ed. *The Ombudsman: Citizen's Defender.* London: George Allen & Unwin, 1968.

Saint-Simon, H. *Henri Comte de Saint-Simon, Selected Writings.* Oxford: Basil Blackwell, 1952.

_____. *The New Christianity.* London: B.D. Cousins, 1834.

_____. *Social Organization, the Science of Man, and Other Writings.* New York: Harper & Row, 1964.

Saint-Simon, Louis, duc de. *Versailles, the Court, and Louis XIV.* Selected and translated by Lucy Norton. New York: Harper & Row, 1958.

Scheele, Godfrey. *The Weimar Republic: Overture to the Third Reich.* London: Faber and Faber, 1946.

Schlesinger, Arthur. *The Crisis of the Old Order.* Boston: Houghton Mifflin Co., 1957.

Servan-Schreiver, J.J. *The American Challenge.* New York: Avon Library, 1969. First Engl. ed., Atheneum House, 1968.

Seubert, Rudolf. *Aus der Praxis des Taylor-Systems; mit eingehender Beschreibung seiner Anwendung bei der Tabor Manufacturing Company in Philadelphia.* Berlin: Verlag von Julius Springer, 1920.

Shields, B.F. *The Evolution of Industrial Organization.* London: Sir Isaac Pitman & Sons, 1930.

Simon, Herbert. *Administrative Behavior: A Study of Decision-Making Process in Administrative Organization.* New York: Free Press, 1957.

Simpson, Kemper. *Big Business, Efficiency, and Fascism: An Appraisal of the Efficiency of Large Corporations and of their Threat to Democracy.* New York: Harper and Bros., 1941.

Smiles, Samuel. *Lives of the Engineers: George and Robert Stevenson.* Vol. 5. *The Locomotive.* London: John Murray, 1904.

Smith, Adam. *An Inquiry into the Nature and Causes of the Wealth of Nations.* New York: Modern Library, 1965.

Smith, Andrew. *I Was a Soviet Worker.* New York: E.P. Dutton, 1936.

Smith, Henry Nash, ed. *Labor and Capital in the Gilded Age: Testimony*

Taken by the Senate Committee upon the Relations between Labor and Capital, 1883. Boston: Little, Brown & Co., 1968.

Spargo, John. *The Bitter Cry of the Children.* Facsimile reprint of 1906 edition. Chicago: Quadrangle Books, 1968.

Speer, Albert. *Inside the Third Reich.* New York: Macmillan Co., 1970.

Spriegel, William R. *The Writings of the Gilbreths.* Homewood, Ill.: R. D. Irwin, 1953.

Starling, Grover. *Managing the Public Sector.* Homewood, Ill.: The Dorsey Press, 1977.

Stephens, L. *Life and Writings of Turgot.* London: Longmans, Green & Co., 1895.

Sternsher, B. *Rexford Tugwell and the New Deal.* New Brunswick, N.J.: Rutgers University Press, 1964.

Stolper, Gustav, et al. *The German Economy, 1870 to the Present.* 1st ed., 1911. New York: W.W. Norton & Co., 1967.

Taylor, Frederick W. *The Principles of Scientific Management.* 1st ed., 1911. New York: W.W. Norton & Co., 1967.

_____. *Shop Management.* New York: Harper Bros., 1919.

_____. *Two Papers on Scientific Management.* London: Routledge & Kegan Paul, 1919.

Thompson, C.B., ed. *Scientific Management.* Cambridge, Mass.: Harvard University Press, 1914.

Thompson, James D. *Organizations in Action.* New York: McGraw-Hill, 1967.

Thompson, Victor. *Modern Organizations.* New York: Alfred A. Knopf, 1961.

Tikhomirov, L. *Russia, Political and Social,* vol. 2. London: Swann Sonnenschein & Co., 1892.

Tocqueville, Alexis de. *The Old Regime and the French Revolution.* New York: Vintage Books, 1964.

Trotsky, Leon. *Lenin.* New York: Minton, Balch & Co., 1925.

_____. *My Life.* New York: Charles Scribner's Sons, 1930.

Tugwell, Rexford. *The Emerging Constitution.* New York: Harper's Magazine Press, 1974.

_____. *The Industrial Discipline and the Governmental Arts.* New York: Columbia University Press, 1933.

Unwin, George. *Industrial Organization in the Sixteenth and Seventeenth Centuries.* 1st ed., 1904. London: Frank Cass & Co., 1963.

Urwick, Lyndall. *The Golden Book of Management.* London: Newman, Neame, 1956.

_____. *The Making of Scientific Management.* 3 vols. London: Management Publications Trust, 1949.

_____. *The Meaning of Rationalization.* London: Nisbet & Co., 1929.

U.S. Congress, Joint Committee on Atomic Energy. *Hearings on the Loss of the Thresher.* Washington, D.C.: Government Printing Office, 1967.

U.S. Congress, Senate. Committee on Education and Labor. *Report of the Committee of the Senate upon the Relations between Labor and Capital, and Testimony Taken by the Committee.* 5 vols. Washington, D.C.: Government Printing Office, 1885.

U.S. Congress, Senate. Committee on Education and Labor. *Systems of Shop Management.* Report no. 1930, 17 July. Washington, D.C.: Government Printing Office, 1912.

U.S. Congress, House. *State of Labor in Europe: 1878.* Washington, D.C.: Government Printing Office, 1879.

U.S. Commission on the Organization of the Executive Branch of the Government. *The Hoover Commission Report on the Organization of the Executive Branch.* New York: McGraw-Hill, 1949.

U.S. The President's Committee on Administrative Management. *Administrative Management in the Government of the United States.* Washington, D.C.: Government Printing Office, January 1937.

U.S. Congress, House. Presidential Commission on Economy and Efficiency. *Message of the President of the United States on Economy and Efficiency in the Public Service.* 458. Washington, D.C.: Government Printing Office, 1912.

U.S. Congress, House. Presidential Commission on Economy and Efficiency. *The Need for a National Budget.* 854. Washington, D.C.: Government Printing Office, 1912.

Vauban, S. *Essay for a General Tax: Or, a Project for a Royal Tithe, Submitted to the House of Commons.* 2nd ed. London: John Matthews, 1710.

_____. *Projet d'une dîme royale.* Edited by E.F. Coörnaert. Paris: Librairie Felix Alcan, 1933.

Veblen, Thorstein. *The Engineers and the Price System.* New York: Viking Press, 1921.

_____. *The Instinct of Workmanship and the State of the Industrial Arts.* New York: Macmillan Co., 1914.

_____. *The Place of Science in Modern Civilization.* New York: Viking Press, 1919.

_____. *The Theory of the Business Enterprise.* New York: Charles Scribner's Sons, 1920.

Venturi, Franco. *The Roots of Revolution.* New York: Alfred A. Knopf, 1960.

Vignes, M. *Histoire des doctrines sur l'impôt en France.* Paris: V. Gérard et E. Brière, 1909.

Waldo, Dwight. *The Administrative State.* New York: Ronald Press, 1948.

Webb, Sidney. *The Works Manager Today.* London: Longmans, Green & Co., 1917.

Weill, Georges. *L'École Saint-Simoniene: Son histoire, son influence jusqu'à nos jours.* Paris: Ancienne Librairie Germer Baillière et Cie., 1896.

Wells, H. G. *Washington and the Riddle of Peace.* New York: Macmillan Co., 1922.

White, Leonard. *The Federalists: A Study in Administrative History, 1789-1801.* New York: Free Press, 1965.

————. *The Jacksonians: A Study in Administrative History, 1829-1861.* New York: Macmillan Co., 1954.

Whyte, William H. *The Organization Man.* New York: Doubleday & Co., 1957.

Wildavsky, Aaron. *The Politics of the Budgetary Process.* Boston: Little, Brown & Co., 1967.

Wilson, Edmund. *To the Finland Station.* Garden City, N.Y.: Doubleday & Co., 1940.

Winter, Gustav. *Der falsche Messias Henry Ford.* Leipzig: Verlag "Freie Meinung," 1924.

Winter, Gustav. *Der Taylorismus: Handbuch der wissenschaftlichen Betriebs-und Arbeitsweise für die Arbeitenden aller Klassen, Stände, und Berufe.* Leipzig: Verlag von S. Hirzel, 1920.

————. *Das Taylorsystem und wie man einführt in Deutschland.* Leipzig: Verlag Carl Findeisen, 1919.

Witte, I. M. *F. W. Taylor, Der Vater wirtschaftlicher Betriebsführung.* Stuttgart: C. E. Peoschel Verlag, 1928.

Wolfe, Bertram. *Three Who Made a Revolution.* New York: Dial Press, 1948.

Woolston, N. Y. *The Structure of the Nazi Economy.* New York: Russell and Russell, 1941.

Wyllie, Irvin. *The Self-Made Man in America: The Myth of Rags to Riches.* New York: Free Press, 1954.

York, Herbert. *Race to Oblivion.* New York: Clarion, 1970.

Yost, Edna. *Frank and Lillian Gilbreth: Partners for Life.* New Brunswick, N.J.: Rutgers University Press, 1948.

Zaleski, Eugene. *Planning for Economic Growth in the Soviet Union, 1918-1932.* Chapel Hill: University of North Carolina Press, 1971.

ARTICLES, SPEECHES, MONOGRAPHS
AND UNPUBLISHED MATERIAL

Anonymous. "Living on the Ragged Edge." *Harper's Magazine,* December 1925.

Beard, Charles A. "The Myth of Rugged American Individualism." *Harper's Magazine,* December 1931.

Carnegie, Andrew. "Business." Chicago: Washington Institute, undated pamphlet.

Fabian Tract no. 108. "Twentieth Century Politics: A Policy of National Efficiency." London: Fabian Society, 1901.

Ford, R.N. "Job Enrichment Lessons from AT&T." *Harvard Business Review,* January 1973.

Garson, B. "To Hell with Work." *Harper's Magazine,* June 1972.

Gerould, K.F. "The Plight of the Genteel." *Harper's Magazine,* February 1926.

Gutter, M.D. "The American Technocratic Movement." M.A. thesis, University of California, 1967.

Hutchinson, Lincoln. "American Engineers in Russia, 1928-1932." Unpublished manuscript survey in Hoover Library, Stanford University.

"Ivan Works in the Factory Now, and Needs a Clock." *Business Week,* 21 September 1929.

Jenkins, D. "Democracy in the Factory: A Report on the Movement to Abolish the Organization Chart." *Atlantic Monthly,* April 1973.

Kaufman, Herbert. "Emerging Conflicts in the Doctrines of Public Administration." *American Political Science Review,* December 1956.

Kennan, G. "The Sources of Soviet Conduct." *Foreign Affairs* 25 (1947).

Landau, Martin. "Redundancy, Rationality, and the Problem of Duplication and Overlap." *Public Administration Review,* July/August 1969.

Maier, Charles. "Between Taylorism and Technocracy: European Ideologies and the Vision of Industrial Productivity in the 1920s," *Journal of Contemporary History,* January 1970.

Manning, Florence M. "Carl G. Barth, 1860-1939: A Sketch," *Norwegian-American Studies and Records,* vol. 13. Northfield, Minn.: Norwegian-American Historical Association, 1943.

Moellendorff, Wichard von. "Die Neue Wirtschaft" in *Auf der Schwelle der neuen Zeit,* Berlin: Verlag Dr. Wedekind & Co., 1919.

"An On-the-Record Interview with DDR&E's Fubini." *Armed Forces Management,* July 1965.

Polakov, Walter. "How Efficient Are the Russians?" *Harper's Magazine,* December 1931.

Rigby, T. "Crypto-Politics," in Fleron, ed. *Communist Studies and the Social Sciences.* Chicago: Rand, McNally & Co., 1969.

Rothschild, E. "GM in More Trouble." *New York Review of Books,* 23 March 1972.

"Russia Places Contract for $182 Million Plant." *Business Week,* 26 March 1930.

Sanford, Donald George. "Walther Rathenau: Critic and Prophet of Imperial Germany." Ph.D. diss., University of Michigan, 1971.

Serrin, W. "The Assembly Line." *Atlantic Monthly,* October 1971.

Taylor, Frederick W. "Governmental Efficiency." *Bulletin of the Taylor Society,* December 1916.

Thayer, Frederick. "The President's Management 'Reforms': Theory X Triumphant," *Public Administration Review,* vol. 38 July/August, 1978 #4, pp. 309-314.

Thompson, Victor. "Toward a New Public Administration: The Minnowbrook Perspective." Book review. *The American Political Science Review,* June 1972.

Trotsky, Leon. "Khozyaistvennoe striotel'stvo Sovetskoi Respubliki." *Sochinenii,* vol. 15. Moscow: Gos. Izd., 1927.

_____. "Osnovye zadachi i trudnosti khozyaistvennogo stroitel'stva." *Sochinenii,* vol. 15, 6 January 1920. Moscow: Gos. Izd., 1927.

_____. *Trud, distsiplina, poriadok spasut Sotsialisticheskuiu Sovietskuiu Respubliku.* Monograph. Moscow: Izd. "Kommunist," 1918.

Wildavsky, Aaron. "The Political Economy of Efficiency; Cost Benefit Analysis, Systems, and Program Budgeting." *Public Administration Review,* December 1966.

Wilson, Woodrow. "Democracy and Efficiency." *Atlantic Monthly,* March 1901.

Wilson, Woodrow. "The Study of Administration," *Political Science Quarterly,* 2 (June, 1887), 197-222; reprinted 50 (December, 1941), 481-506.

Wrege, Charles D., and Perroni, Amedeo G., "Taylor's Pig Tale: A Historical Analysis of Frederick W. Taylor's Pig Iron Experiments," *Academy of Management Journal* 17, no. 1: 6-27.

Zeitlein, L. "A Little Larceny Can Do a Lot for Employee Morale." *Psychology Today,* June 1971.

Index

Designer: Wendy Calmenson
Compositor: In-House Composition
Printer: Thomson-Shore
Binder: Thomson-Shore
Text: Compset Times Roman
Display: VIP Americana
Paper: 50 lb. P & S offset vellum B32